THE ROWDY MITCHUM SAGA AS IT'S NEVER BEEN TOLD BEFORE

For the first time in print, complete with 356 photographs, the truth behind the legend of Robert Mitchum, one of the most romantic and cantankerous personalities of our time. Told by the only man who lived it with him, his brother and chronicler John Mitchum.

Robert Mitchum: Movie star . . . family man . . . producer, writer and poet . . . fighter and drinker . . . the powerhouse personality with a powerhouse punch who helped to make Hollywood as wild and woolly as the Old West . . . Here is the controversial and complex inner man, his joys and pains, his follies and foibles.

John Mitchum: A talented character actor in his own right, who has appeared in 800 TV shows and 80 feature films . . . the only man to write a record album for John Wayne . . . singer and musician . . . barroom brawler . . . raconteur and storyteller supreme . . . he has remained a constant companion and observer of the rugged Mitchum saga since it began.

The Mitchum brothers grew up on a small farm in Delaware, they rode the freights across America in the Depression, and each pursued an independent career in films and TV. Their bond of brotherhood provides Hollywood with one of its most fascinating stories. Meet the Mitchum family members, character actors, stunt men, con artists, hoodlums, teenage terrors, sluggers and boxers and Hollywood hangers-on as the Mitchum brothers embark on the most colorful careers in the history of movies and television.

THE ADVENTURES OF ROBERT AND JOHN MITCHUM

D1614808

Attention: Schools and Corporations

THEM ORNERY MITCHUM BOYS by John Mitchum is available at quantity discounts with bulk purchase for educational, business or sales promotional ("premium") use. For information contact Erica or John Stanley in care of Creatures at Large Press, P.O. Box 687, Pacifica CA 94044 or call (415) 355-READ.

Attention: Individual Readers

You can purchase other copies of this book, including a deluxe hardcover version numbered and signed by John and Robert Mitchum, by writing to Creatures at Large Press and including $13.50 for each trade paperback edition required, or $41.50 for each hardcover desired. The deluxe version has been limited to only 200 copies and comes individually numbered with slipcase with the title engraved on the outside.

California residents must include an extra 78 cents for the trade edition, $2.60 for the hardcover. Enclose check or money order (no cash, please) to Creatures at Large Press, P.O. Box 687, Pacifica CA 94044. You can also receive our up-to-date catalogues, by writing to this address, that list information about other publications offered by Creatures at Large Press, including editions in the popular Creature Features Movie Guide series.

THEM ORNERY MITCHUM BOYS

(The Adventures of Robert and John Mitchum)

By John Mitchum

Told With 356 Photographs

Edited and Designed by John Stanley

Cover Design by Kenn Davis

Creatures at Large Press
P.O. Box 687
Pacifica CA 94044

THEM ORNERY MITCHUM BOYS.

First Printing ©1989 by John Mitchum.

All Rights reserved. This book, or parts thereof, cannot be reproduced in any form without permission. Published in the United States of America by Creatures at Large Press, P.O. Box 687, Pacifica CA 94044.

Designed and Edited by John Stanley.
Cover Design by Kenn Davis.

"Introduction" ©1989 by Mick Martin.
"Silent Night" ©1989 by Robert Mitchum.
"All the Pretty Horses" ©1989 by John Mitchum.
"Beautiful, Beautiful Huntsville" ©1989 by John Mitchum.
"Chicago—My Home Town" ©1989 by John Mitchum.
"Why Are You Marching, Son?" ©1989 by John Mitchum.
"To Jones" ©1989 by Robert Mitchum.
"To Jones" ©1989 by Robert Mitchum.
"PostMitchum-Script" ©1989 by Bonnie Mitchum.

Library of Congress Catalogue No. 88-92904

Library of Congress Cataloging-in-Publication Data:

Mitchum, John, 1919-
Them ornery Mitchum boys.

Includes index.
1. Mitchum, Robert, 1917- 2. Mitchum, John, 1919-
3. Actors—United States—Biography. 4. Entertainers—
United States—Biography. I. Title.
PN2285.M5 1989 791.43'028'0924 [B] 88-35221
ISBN 0-940064-06-5 (pbk.)
ISBN 0-940064-07-3 (deluxe)

International Standard Book Numbering Agency Information:

ISBN: 0-940064-06-5 (Trade Paperback Edition)
ISBN: 0-940064-07-3 (Signed Deluxe Hardcover Edition)

A DEDICATION

TO MY WIFE BONNIE—*without whose personal devotion and professional effort this book would never have been finished.*

TO MY BROTHER ROBERT—*whose life and talents have been a veritable lighthouse of caring and dedication.*

TO OUR MOTHER ANN—*whose ninety-four years on this earth have never been marred by unkindness or greed.*

TO OUR STEPFATHER MAJOR HUGH MORRIS—*whose gentility belied a core of steel courage and honor.*

TO JOHN STANLEY AND HIS WIFE ERICA—*whose courage in editing and publishing this book is only matched by their enthusiasm.*

TO MICK MARTIN—*who brought John Stanley and me together and who has been a stalwart friend through two years of elation and despair.*

A THANK YOU

During the writing and production of this book, several people contributed above and beyond in giving their time and services so that the concept behind "Them Ornery Mitchum Boys" could come to full fruition.

Thanks goes to Dan Faris and Steve Imura of the San Francisco Cinema Shop, 604 Geary Street, for opening up their vast collection of photographs. It was Dan who found stills from my very first film, "The Prairie," perhaps the only set in existence.

Another hearty round of applause for Malcolm Willits and his staff at the Collectors Bookstore, 1708 N. Vine Street in Hollywood, for also allowing us to dig through the photo archives. Malcolm has the patience of Job.

We bow humbly to Pat Broeski, a superb movie-world writer for the Los Angeles Times, for research assistance that would otherwise have left gaping holes in this book.

And we thank Jim Rose of Rose Publishing, Newark, California, for setting the type for this book and paginating its pages with such loving concern.

A SPECIAL THANKS

To sister Julie and various children and cousins who loaned their precious family photographs for this book.

Thanks be to God.

John Mitchum

Definition:

Ornery: Disposed to be contrary or stubborn; hard to manage.

TABLE OF CONTENTS

To Jack — Sept. 6 1936

Ten years ago, when you were seven, I wrote in my own little book this little character sketch:

Jack —
the miracle of dawn on the mountain top — the agelessness of the Sequoias — light wind over wheat fields — rain on a parched tongue — Lily of the Valley — 23d Psalm.

Today, when you are seventeen, I find that you have not changed, except in stature and intensity -
For always, whatever the environment, the circumstance - or the inducement, you will be you, and neither veneer nor buffing can eliminate the you — Mother

A Son's Reward

This letter was written to John Mitchum by his mother, Ann, on the occasion of his 17th birthday. It reads: "*To Jack—Ten years ago, when you were seven, I wrote in my own little book this little character sketch: 'Jack—The miracle of dawn on the mountain top—the agelessness of the Sequoias—light wind over wheat fields—rain on a parched tongue—Lily of the Valley—23rd Psalm.' Today, when you are seventeen, I find that you have not changed, except in stature and intensity. For always, whatever the environment, the circumstances—you will be* you, *and neither veneer nor buffing can eliminate the* you. *Mother, Sept. 6, 1936.*"

INTRODUCTION

By Mick Martin

JOHN MITCHUM is a man of many and diverse talents, but his greatest gift just may be his ability as a storyteller. His tales of Hollywood's heroes and villains—both on and offscreen—have that rare insight that could only come from someone inside the dream factory.

As a movie buff, it has been a dream come true for me to listen as John has told his ribald, raucous and revealing tales of the movie world, and it always seemed to me that his stories should be collected in a book so other film fans could revel in them.

"Them Ornery Mitchum Boys" is the result of long hours of labor by John, his lovely (and talented) actress-wife Bonnie, and the intrepid publisher-author John Stanley, whose three editions of "The Creature Features Movie Guide" attest to his perfectionism, dedication and unerring good taste. Thanks to them, we now have a Hollywood book to beat all Hollywood books.

This is not another lightweight, self-aggrandizing autobiography in which a movie personality glosses over the rough spots to paint a rosy picture of

Photos by John Stanley

an idyllic (and unbelievable) life in the movies. "Them Ornery Mitchum Boys" presents John and his superstar brother Robert with warts as well as warmth and wit.

Into their lives walked a host of the famous, the infamous and the unforgettable. They are all in these pages; vibrant characters from real life who beat the hell out of any fictional substitutes. John has known many of the greats and the not-so-greats of the silver screen, and his reminiscences bring readers closer than ever before to behind-the-scenes moviemaking.

I feel very fortunate to be considered a friend by John and Bonnie. It's not just the chance to hear his stories or the joy of seeing them together on stage in Nevada City, Ca., although these are definite delights. It is their down-to-earth honesty and genuine warmth that makes one so very grateful to know them.

The way John came into my life is typical of his style. I was at my desk one day when the phone rang. A voice said, "This is John Mitchum." He

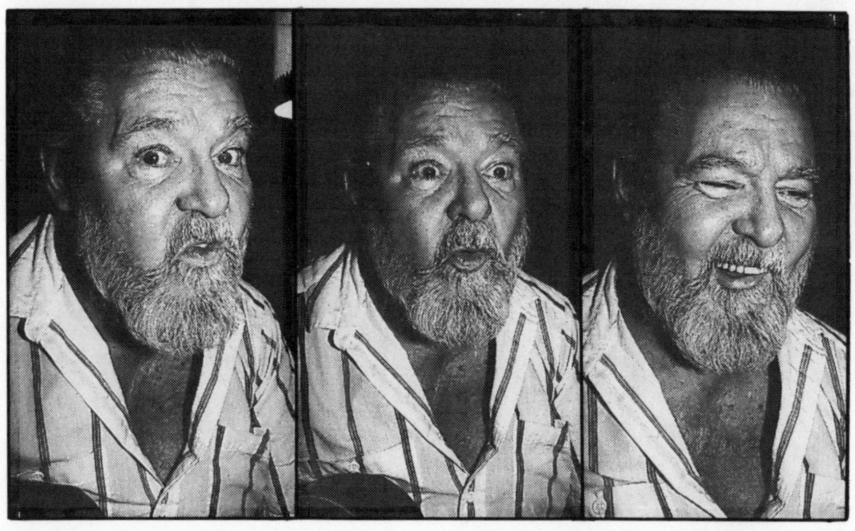

wanted to thank me for singling out his performance as Dirty Harry's partner, Frank di Georgio, in my review of "The Enforcer." I stifled the urge to say, "Yeah, who is this really?"

Not once in the ten years I had been writing for *The Sacramento Union* as its film critic had a movie actor called to thank me for a mention in a review. But it turned out that this was indeed the marvelous character actor who had played off Clint Eastwood so well in "Dirty Harry," "Magnum Force" and, most memorably, "The Enforcer." Mitchum's solid, pivotal supporting performance in the latter had moved me to sing his praises as an under-appreciated character actor.

Typically, John was more pleased to be singled out as a character actor than because of his performance. He preferred to take my comments as a tribute to other supporting players in the movies with whom he worked and whom he had admired.

"I never had—even remotely—the desire to be a big star," John told me later. "Neither, by the way, did Bob. He just didn't want to work at Lockheed

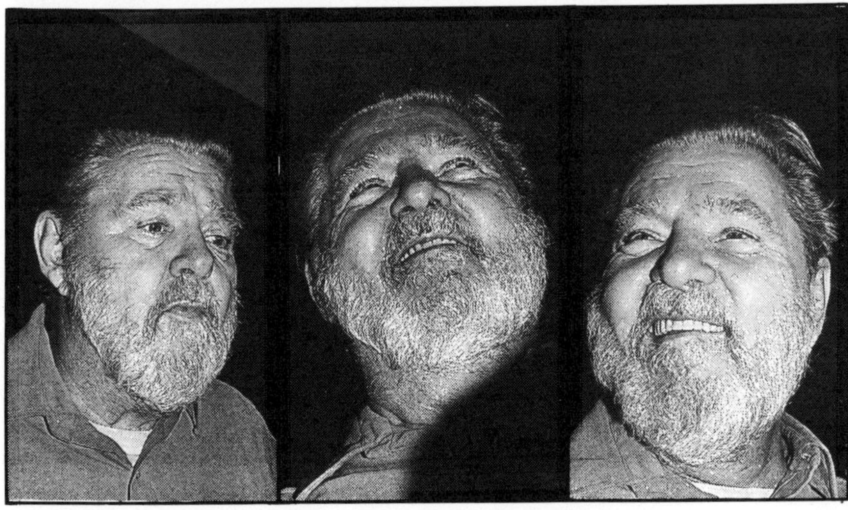

all his life. Me, I'm proud of being a character actor."

In the Golden Age days of Hollywood, it was often the supporting players—character actors all—who supplied the most memorable moments. Who can think of "The Maltese Falcon" without remembering the superbly sinister performances by Peter Lorre and Sydney Greenstreet? What would "Dracula" have been without Dwight Frye's Renfield? And Walter Brennan immeasurably lifted "To Have and Have Not" by simply asking people, "Ever been stung by a dead bee?"

The character actor has become an increasingly rare breed over the years. This makes the true practitioners of the art all the more special and their screen moments even more precious.

"Cool Hand Luke" would hardly have been as memorable without John's dear friend, Strother Martin, intoning, "What we have here is failure to communicate." Similarly, who can forget John's reply of "You're a sweet man, Harry" to one of Dirty Harry's typically caustic remarks in his first

scene as di Georgio in Don Siegel's classic original or the excuse of "Too much linguini" when he can't follow Harry over the fence into Kezar Stadium to confront the film's serial killer? Such are the golden moments of character acting that movie buffs dearly love.

John has brought such moments to many films, including "Chisum" with John Wayne, "The Outlaw Josey Wales" with Eastwood and "El Dorado" with Wayne and the man he calls "Brother Robert." Other films included "Knock on Any Door" with Humphrey Bogart, "Submarine Command" and "Stalag 17" with William Holden, "Bandolero!" with James Stewart and Dean Martin and, with Robert, "The Lusty Men," "One Minute to Zero" and "The Way West." He worked with Charles Bronson in "Telefon" and "Breakheart Pass." His first teaming with Eastwood came in "Paint Your Wagon," in which John played the man who sold his wife (Jean Seberg) to Eastwood and Lee Marvin. He was the jailer in "High Plains Drifter," too.

Even more prolifically, John has appeared in hundreds of television shows, and had recurring roles on "F Troop" (as Hoffenmueller) and "Riverboat" (as Pickalong). For the '50s anthology series, "Fireside Theater," he played "everything you can think of" on the twice-weekly show. He also turned up on "Gunsmoke," "Maverick," "Perry Mason," "Dragnet," "The Untouchables," "Bewitched," "Batman," "The Waltons," "The Twilight Zone" (twice), "Lassie" and "Little House on the Prairie."

But John is more than just an actor. You might even call him a Renaissance man.

Singer, songwriter, screenwriter, raconteur and all-around performer, John has worn a number of creative hats over the years. He wrote the album "America, Why I Love Her" for John Wayne and recorded another LP "Our Land—Our Heritage" with his dear friend Dan Blocker (Hoss of "Bonanza"). He has a number of scripts in various stages of production including the chilling "Ezekiel 7," which Robert Mitchum has agreed to star in. His love of American history has culminated in a script for a proposed miniseries which tells the story of this country through its music.

But of all his talents, those who know him most appreciate his ability as a storyteller. His gritty, funny and amazing stories of Hollywood and the rough-and-ready Mitchum boys are priceless, and now you can share in the joy of hearing about the real Hollywood in the words of someone who lived it.

Want to hear something remarkable? Read on.

By day Mick Martin is the film critic for the Sacramento Union, but by night he pursues a greater love, music, as a blues harmonica player. Mick Martin and the Blues Rockers is a group now legendary in Northern California, and so is Mick's literary contribution to film, "Video Movie Guide," which enjoyed its fourth edition from Ballantine Books in the closing months of 1988. Mick, who writes and edits the mass-market paperback series with Marsha Porter, also considers himself a devoted family man and lives with his wife and daughter in North Highlands, a community outside Sacramento. As if that's not enough, Mick spearheaded "Best on Video," a videocassette series that came out in 1988 on a national basis, and he harbors a deep-rooted desire to write for the movies.

SHOWDOWN

ON A CRISP morning in October, 1952, while I was walking down the main street of Colorado Springs, Colorado, a belligerent young cowboy stopped me.

He eyed me balefully for some moments and grumbled, "They tell me you're Robert Mitchum's brother."

He glared, waiting for my answer.

Finally I said, "Yes, I am."

"You're a liar!" he snorted.

And stalked away.

BOOK ONE

GROWING PAINS

BOOK ONE

BYE-BYE, SHIRLEY MacLAINE, BYE-BYE

LOOKING BACK through time reminds me of watching a pebble being thrown in a pond, and seeing the concentric rings reaching ever farther into the once-still waters. I lay much of my brother Robert's phenomenal success in the motion picture business to a sea of people touching his life like that pebble ripples the waters. The voices, the attitudes, the subtleties of his myriad of friends have created an ever-expanding mind and, from that expansion, he can reach down and select whatever suits the moment. Most of those people would fit into a potpourri of *Reader's Digest* "most unforgettable characters."

Well, cowboy, it was in the summer of '62 when I met one of the best of them, Shirley MacLaine, who had just made "Two for the Seesaw" with Brother Bob. George Fargo, known to one and all as Grey Cloud, had worked in many of Bob's pictures and was hailed by him as "the ultimate extra." George had made a prediction to Bob: "I'm tellin' you, Goose! The dame's gonna make you look like a blank wall!" Bob had furiously dismissed the comment.

Grey Cloud had been so dubbed by Bob because his head and shoulders were continuously shrouded in marijuana smoke. This may have been the reason that Robert chose to ignore Fargo's judgment.

Bob proceeded with the picture, trying to throw Shirley off the track by courting her with flowers, sweet talk and romantic murmurings. This had two effects:

Shirley did a fantastic job. And she became passionately interested in Brother Robert.

Now she was staunchly implanted at my front door and I was aghast. She stood in front of me barefoot, sheathed in a very expensive cocktail dress. She grasped her high heels, her purse and an envelope in her right hand and a half-gallon of vodka in a carrier sling looped over her left shoulder.

"May I come in?" She didn't say it, she purred it.

"Of course." I was still looking at her shoeless toes.

"Read this!" she snapped, handing me the envelope.

I read the epistle.

Dear Shirley,

As I walked in the evening on the Pacific's shore, the winds brought faraway smells of places long forgotten. The roar of the surf brought back sounds of long ago, sweeping over me like a miasma. Loneliness!

I walk in loneliness, Shirley. I cannot bear to ask that you share that loneliness. I must walk to its beat alone! Please understand.

Ever, Robert.

Robert Mitchum worked twice with Shirley MacLaine: In 1962 in "Two for the Seesaw," he played a Wyoming doctor, Jerry Ryan, who has a fiery affair with a New York dance instructor—art imitating life. They worked the following year in "What a Way to Go," with Mitchum's millionaire character, Rod Anderson, dying a violent death—a plot development that Shirley might have imagined in her private fantasies a time or two.

The light dawned.

I looked up to see her staring at me. "What does this mean?" She was demanding the ultimate truth.

I took a long breath. Bob was on the TV screen at that moment, dressing down Charley McGraw for some miscreant deed in that Korean War epic, "One Minute to Zero." I wondered why she didn't just ask him. "It's a kiss-off, Shirley. I've seen the same letter a half-dozen times before."

"That son of a bitch!" she roared, hurling her unshod high heels at the hapless TV set. Fortunately, she took poor aim or she might have interferred with Bob winning the Korean War.

I told her that I was just heading out the door to go to a party that was being held just up the street.

"Can I go?"

"Only if you bring the vodka."

In better spirits now, she agreed. Together we reached the home of the host, Russ McMenamin, a big, rawboned man famous in the Los Angeles Fire Department for rushing into the worst of blazes with his traditional battle cries of "Hi-de-ho" and "La-dee-dah" endearing him to his fellow firefighters.

When Russ opened his front door, his eyes flared wide. "Why, you're Shirley MacLaine!" The large stein of beer in his hand inadvertently drained into her lovely cleavage.

Shirley, in stained dress and bare feet, had a great time that night.

In the morning, the review came out: "Shirley MacLaine was dynamite in 'Two for the Seesaw.' Mitchum was a blank wall."

A TIME TO DIE, THE GIFT OF LIVING

BOB AND I had the same mother and father, Ann Harriet Gunderson Mitchum and James Thomas Mitchum. Be aware that all that I have to write about my father comes second-hand. I had barely been conceived when his life was cruelly taken in a tragic railyard accident. Recently discharged from the U.S. Army as a private, my father James was working in the navy yard in Charleston, South Carolina, when he was caught between the couplings of two boxcars. An engineer received the wrong signal and backed up the train instead of going forward. Father lived just forty-five minutes. My mother cradled him in her arms as he died.

Mother continued to live in Lane, South Carolina, my father's home town, which still doesn't break any population records. The town was part of the Old South, stylized and courteous. My mother tells of a gentleman who passed her every morning with a polite nod and a soft "Good morning." When a suitable length of time had passed after my father's death, he stopped at her gate and gently proposed to her. "I think it proper now, Mrs. Mitchum, to ask if you would care to step along through life with me in double harness." Mother, who apparently did not think of herself as livestock, politely declined, returning soon after to Connecticut.

My life on this good earth officially started in Bridgeport, Connecticut, on September 6, 1919, just seven months after my father's death. I was two months premature, probably due to Mother's grief. Robert had preceded me to Bridgeport by two years and a month, his natal day being August 6, 1917. Our sister, Annette, was born three years earlier, on July 23, 1914.

Bridgeport was a bustling manufacturing city, rampant with mills that turned out heavy industry products. Its busy harbor with access to the open sea made it a source of wonder to eager young minds. We lived close to the American Chain Company and the Remington Arms Factory.

I was not quite six when I encountered the joys of sex for the first time. Two sisters, Constance and Doris, friends of my sister Annette, took me into the bedroom Bob and I shared and stripped me naked. They began

James Thomas Mitchum: The Father Of Them Ornery Mitchum Boys

Annette boxes with our father, circa 1916, in the backyard of our home in Bridgeport, Conn.

Marriage portrait: Ann Harriet Gunderson Mitchum and James Thomas Mitchum, 1913. Mom was 20, dad was 22.

playing with my dinky and it became most interested in the proceedings. All the while Brother Robert, who had been locked out of the room by the sisters, was carving a hole through the door with a razor blade. Just as he cut enough of the door panel away to allow him a peek in, the sisters, tiring of their game, covered me up again. It was such a traumatic happening that I have spent all the years since trying to get even.

I also remember an incident from my sixth year when Mother asked Bob to mail a letter and I pleaded to go along. "Hold onto Jack's hand!" ordered Mother, worried about Stratford Avenue. Even in 1924 cars were a deadly menace. Carried away by the excitement of being with my big brother on a mission, I tore loose from his grasp and dashed into the street. One of the juggernauts of the day knocked me down. As I valiantly attempted to rise, a second car ran me down anew.

Well now, consternation reigned on Stratford Avenue. I was dragged off the pavement by onlookers and rushed to the corner drugstore. While I was being doctored, Brother Robert ran pell-mell across the boulevard and down Logan Street to our home.

He burst into the kitchen, blurting out the dreadful news to Mother. "Jack's been run over by two cars!" He saw the horrified look on her face and added, "But he ain't dead yet!"

A star was born in Bridgeport Memorial Hospital. I had suffered a concussion (I still carry the steel plate in the back of my head), a broken jaw, a broken shoulder blade and arm. My jaw, wired in place, made me a celebrity in that institution. While racing around the corridors in my wheelchair, I entertained the staff and my fellow inmates by singing "It ain't gonna rain no more, no more, it ain't gonna rain no more. How in the heck can I wash my neck if it ain't gonna rain no more?" Through the tightly wired jaw it sounded rather odd. The hospital help—including my own personal nurse Gladys King—loved me.

❄❄❄

Forty years later, Gladys and I met again in the austere courtyard of Saint Mark's Episcopal Church in Van Nuys, California. Her memories of our hospital stay together as vivid as my own, she told me that she and her husband had been missionaries with the Saint Luke's Missionary Group in China for twenty years. "Just before World War II," she said, "we were sent to Manila in the Philippines by the Japanese and interned at the Los Baños Internment Center. We survived the ordeals until February 23, 1945, when we were scheduled for execution. We had literally resigned ourselves to our fate. Early that morning, the sky filled with paratroopers from the 11th Airborne. They defeated the Japanese guards in a violent fight and we were saved."

❄ ❄ ❄

Our uncle by marriage, Wilfred Jean Tetreault, was another unforgettable character. Uncle Bill was a French-Canadian born in Pawtuckett, Rhode Island. Later, he moved to Bridgeport to find work. He met my father James there and the two became inseparable. Bill was a professional wrestler—he and my father plainly loved to fight. The two had a standing boast that they could whip any three men in town—a boast they made good on many an occasion. My father's death left Bill inconsolable. He made a vow on my father's grave: "Jim's kids'll never go hungry as long as I'm alive!" He never forgot that oath.

Our maternal grandfather, Gustave Olaf Gunderson, was a Norwegian sea captain. He was a huge man, nearly two hundred sixty pounds, very little of it having a sense of humor. We lived in his home in Bridgeport, but he also owned an eighty-acre farm in fertile Delaware as an investment. In 1925, he sent Uncle Bill and his wife (our Aunt Gertrude) to the farm with our grandmother, Petrine. Bob and I didn't know it then but fate, coupled with our infinite capacity for trouble, ordained that we too would soon become Delawarians.

In rapid succession, we managed to pile such woes on our poor mother as to cause her despair. In the fall of '25, for some obscure reason, I built a fire in a shallow pit in the empty lot behind our house. In my own mind I was on safari in darkest Africa. In reality, I was much too close to the ice cream factory.

Piled in the service yard of that factory were hundreds of tinder-dry wooden crates. When a vagrant wind carried a live coal from my "camp fire," the factory became a memory in a remarkably short time, and the charred area swarmed with firemen and a few men in blue uniforms.

One impressive cop collared me, holding me at arms' length. "Do you know who did this?" he barked.

I looked at him placidly. "Uh huh." I stopped there—unconvincingly.

He didn't stop—he shook me violently. "Who? Who, by God?"

"My brother!" The idea had suddenly intrigued me.

"How do you know he did it?" He eyed me coldly, cocking his head.

Bridgeport, 1916: Dad goes for a ride with Aunt Gertrude Tetreault steering.

Portrait of Robert, Annette (Julie) and yours truly in the spring of 1920, taken inside our family's two-story home in Bridgeport. Annette must have been around five. Dressing youngsters up as sailors was considered very fashionable in those times.

"He always does stuff like that!"

Fortunately Bob had an airtight alibi. He had been with a group of his peers on the other end of town. Nothing could shake their story. Fortunately for me, the bluecoats never thought of questioning me again.

After Mother stopped reeling from that shock, she was informed that during a mock reenactment of a World War I battle, Ernie Frye had become a real casualty, his left eye shot out with a BB gun. No one knew who wounded our favorite neighborhood friend; I know I didn't commit the act. Our mother and Ernie's were the dearest of friends and remained so forever. Ernie also remained forever as a reminder that air rifles, in the hands of young sharpshooters, are no longer toys.

The tremors from the shooting had barely subsided when Bob came close to shaking hands with the Grim Reaper while we were down at the docks in November. For some insane reason, we went fishing off a dock with our friend, Hymie Gensler, all of us bundled up in woolen shirts, sweaters and winter coats. We caught no fish, but while traversing a beam between two pilings, Bob fell into the icy water and was shocked numb almost immediately. Had not a Portuguese fisherman been working aboard a boat moored nearby, Bob would have gone under. The good Samaritan speared Bob's clothing with a pike pole, hauling him from the frigid water. In an instant, Bob was iced over, but still managed, with difficulty, to move slowly down the dock.

Hymie Gensler's face appeared from behind a piling. He cleared his throat and, with the solemnity of a turtle, asked in his accented English, "Bobbie, did you get vet?"

An inner explosion deep inside that heap of ice galvanized into action. For a few moments, Hymie ran for his life. That burst of energy probably saved Bob's life, for he managed to walk home despite his intense cold. Pleurisy set in then, and continues to plague Bob to this day.

The next summer lent no respite to our dear mother. Bob also fell before the onslaught of a motor car but luckily was only grazed. However, a passing

DOUGLAS (STU)

1	2	3
MACDONALD	BRADY	MARTIN

3
DOUGLAS (ST) DOUGLAS (G)

4	5	6
REEKIE	HUNTER	MUDIE

7	
ROBERTSON	CAMPBELL

SUBS, DOUGLAS (P), DUFFY (D), THOMSON
8 9 10
CUNNINGHAM, BELL, LEE
11
DRYSDALE, COSGROVE. McINTYRE.

1
LAMONT

2 NEWLANDS

4 JAMIESON

3 DUFFY

5 MACDONALD

6 HARROWER

7 ANDERSON

8 WALL

10 DUFFY

11 CHRISTIE

9 COWAN

SUBS – BYERS(K), PATTERSON, ANCELL.

CUNNINGHAM, ANDERSON, MACDONALD

doctor diagnosed a severe concussion. Our mother, called to the scene, looked down at Bob and asked, "Son, are you alright?"

"Yeah, mom, I'm okay."

"The boy has a severe concussion!" the doctor snapped.

Mother looked at him quizzically. "Why do you say that?"

"Look at his eyes!" cried the doctor. "Look at his eyes!"

"Oh." Mother laughed quietly. "His eyes." Then she added, "They always look like that."

That sleepy-eyed look Bob lends to the screen is not part of the act.

❄❄❄

Our next saga lay in an aura of mysticism, adventure and dreams of exotic places. Accompanied by a bright young Irish lad, Davy Fitzgerald, Bob and I attempted to pirate away a small yacht tied up to a marina not far from home. Bob became self-appointed Captain—all-powerful, all-seeing. Davy Fitzgerald was assigned second mate, wise to the ways of the sea. At six years of age, I was relegated to deckhand's work as ship's carpenter.

Davy had an English pit bull, one of those alligator-jawed monsters whose eyes turn red when it is annoyed. The dog, whose eyes were always at least pink, was constantly on the prowl. Before we boarded our prize, Davy tied his companion to the cleat that held the bowline in place against the dock. There the dog sat, stiffly alert for any sign of trouble.

Bob pored over the nautical maps that were to take us to the South Seas. (They were harbor charts but we didn't know that.) Davy busily inspected the anchor and chain, the wheel, the lines. I as carpenter tested her seaworthiness by boring a hole in her bottom. Panic welled over me when water began gushing into her hold. I called for the Captain to come below. She was settling with a foot of water in her by the time "Ol' Cap" hove into view. One look convinced him to abandon ship. By the time we came topside, she had a very noticeable list to the stern. Only a stout hawser kept her from going to the bottom.

As we fled dockside, the owner came screaming down on us, hatchet in hand. Davy's dog, its eyes no longer pink but red, leaped nobly into the fray and the owner, just as berserk, made a lunge at the dog. Only the rope's stoutness kept the man from great bodily harm; the snapping jaws of the terrier missed his throat by mere inches.

He stopped out of range, glaring somberly at the raging beast. "Goddamn!

Grandma Petrine Gunderson and Granddad Gustave Olaf Gunderson in a 1898 portrait; at far right is our mother, Ann Harriet Gunderson Mitchum. I'm impressed at how pretty she looked in those days.

Ann Gunderson Mitchum, John Newman Mitchum, Annette, Robert Charles Durman Mitchum, circa 1921. Wasn't I a pretty little kid?

He tried to kill me!"

Mother was a beautiful woman. That and that alone saved us. When the boat owner met her, he visibly melted, assuring her the damage was slight.

"Why," he said, glancing fondly at me, "the little tyke didn't know what he was doin'. The hole he bored in her can be patched up clean as a whistle." He not only dropped any idea of charges against us, he wound up painting the house for Mother.

"Needs touching up," he told her.

❄❄❄

Mother married newspaper reporter Bill Clancy in 1923, falling into the trap of feeling we needed a father. Clancy was an alcoholic who turned maniacal whenever he drank. One of my earliest remembrances was coming home with Bob to a dark and empty house, its windows broken out, its doors shattered. Neighbors talked in subdued whispers of Clancy's attempt to kill Mother, who had fled for her life. Only the intervention of the local Italian butcher had saved her. She had darted into his store and Clancy, close behind, ran smack into the flat side of a meat cleaver. It had rendered him *hors de combat.* The police took over and we never saw our new stepfather again.

Nearly half a century passed before it came to me in a flash what a tortured man Bill Clancy must have been. He had written a poem that had wedged itself deeply in my mind, and I realize now that Clancy had the heart of a poet, trapped in the false armor of the "tough guy" image the Irish were forced to wear in their new world. He wasn't tough—he was terrified. I wonder how many hundreds of thousands of men there are who would rather paint a beautiful picture than fight, or sing a sweet song than snarl, but cannot. The times have trapped them in a squirrel cage of mixed feelings, and there is no escape.

Captain Gustave Olaf Gunderson in his merchant service uniform; beneath that external image of stern authority and monstrous hulk of a man lived a piquant sense of humor and beat a warm heart.

JIMMY, THE EASY MARK

By Bill Clancy

Say Cull, do you know Jimmy Casey?
The guy we used to kid?
It'll slip you a fit alright, alright
When I tell you what he did.

For Jimmy was awful easy
Just like a kitten! Tame!
We called him the fall guy!
The lemon! And Jimmy deserved the name.

Well, the gang was all together
In Battery Park one day,
And to have some fun with Jimmy,
We'd go up to him and say,

"Say, Jim, what are you gonna be
When you grow up to be a man?"
And Jimmy would always answer,
"I'll be a priest, if I can!"

And then we'd give him the "ha-ha"
And tell him to smoke again!
For priests ain't never dead ones!
Priests are regular men!

We were goin' on with our kiddin'
And havin' a barrel of fun,
When we heard the blast of a whistle
And we saw all the people run.

We left our kiddin' in Battery Park
And followed that awful sound.
When we saw widow McCarty's house on fire
We were rooted to the ground.

From out of a window—way on top—
Amid the smoke and the haze,
The widow McCarty's blue-eyed kid
Was leanin' out to our gaze.

We could hear her callin' "Mama"
And wringin' her hands and hair.
When from out of the crowd a figure shot
And made for McCarty's stair.

Up through that fiery furnace,
Up through the smoke and the flame,
Up to that golden-haired prisoner
The unknown hero came.

We saw her snatched from that hellish hole
And soon the sound of feet
Came down that fiery furnace
With its precious load to the street.

A ragged coat turned 'round her head
Had shielded the kid from harm.
She was brought to the sidewalk safe and sound
And placed in her mother's arms.

But the guy who did the "hero" trick,
He lay there, stiff and stark.
We picked him up and looked in his face.
It was Jimmy, the "easy mark."

The terror of a shattered home, a broken life, and my being run over twice was too much for Bob. He ran off, only to be found in the capital city of Hartford, forty miles away. He was all of seven, already developing a penchant for "running off." For a long time, I felt this was a weakness of character. When I finally perceived that he wasn't running away from anything, but rather was running toward something, I awoke to that strange quality he possesses that has set him apart from most of us. He simply released himself from emotional bondage, setting out to find the world and its truths. He's still doing it.

Major Hugh Cunningham Morris

***

Unknown to us, a new man entered our mother's life. He was an Englishman of "good family" and a thoroughly professional military man. We wouldn't become aware of his qualities for years because we were too naive to relate innate gentility to steel courage.

Major Hugh Cunningham Morris of Landsend, England, was a newsman on the well-established *Bridgeport Post*, where Mother worked as a linotype operator. The two fell in love, but it was a well-guarded secret. Although the Major crept more and more into our lives, he was so self-effacing that we were scarcely aware of his presence. Brother Robert wrote poetry that mysteriously was printed—as was my first effort at story writing—in the *Post*. Bob's poetry showed infinite promise while my story, a dramatic tale about a prankster who puts a tack on a chair at a party, left much to a newsppaer reader's imagination.

The Mitchum Gang circa 1921: Annette and Bob are standing, I'm imprisoned in the carriage somewhere near our Bridgeport home. Shortly after this was taken I stopped sucking my thumb and might have inspired Bob, in later years, to create our game "Suck-a-Thumb Poo-Poo."

(The victim who sat on a tack was a cop. My run-in with the bluecoats during the factory fire must have scarred me for life. I am still apprehensive when a squad car hoves into view.)

That summer, mother sent me to Aunt Jennie's house in Killingly, Connecticut. Jennie lived on a rocky farm with her husband, John, and they were an incongruous pair. Jennie outweighed John by a huge margin, dominating her domain with an iron hand. All I can remember of that ill-fated trip was Uncle John teaching me how to hoe corn. I stood weeping inconsolably in the field: "I don't want to make 'ring around the corn,' I wanna go home to mama."

Go home to mama I did, only to be shipped posthaste to a new home in Delaware. There Bob and I entered a strange and alien world.

RISE AND SHINE!

WOODSIDE, Delaware, was rural indeed in 1926. Uncle Bill dubbed the place where he lived the Woodside Farm. His rallying cry at six o'clock every morning was, "Rise and shine on the Woodside Farm." Hard to accomplish when there were three adults and five children sharing a single outhouse, a hand-pump for washing and coal-oil lamps to light the way.

Rural Delaware depended on horse power for farming and transportation.

Ours was supplied by two horses whose names won no prize for imagination; one was Jim, the other was Harry. They pulled plows, harrows, wagons or buggies, doing exceedingly well. Bob and I, newly departed from an area alive with excitement, were suddenly dropped into an existence where a train whistle late at night became a haunting, vaguely exciting experience. Delaware taught me much. I learned that the smells of newly plowed fields, acres of apple blossoms and new-mown hay have a solid reality that never leaves you. Delaware also taught me about bigotry and red-necked perverseness.

Bob enrolled in Felton High School, a misnomer if ever there was one. It went from the first through twelfth grades. I enrolled in a kindergarten class in the tiny town of Canterbury. One day I was sent home in disgrace because I couldn't tell time and was incarcerated at the Canterbury grade school for an entire semester. During this time Bob and I began to create—not on purpose, mind you—the legend of "them ornery Mitchum boys."

Bob and a friend, Manuel Barque, visited me at lunch one day. A small but determined group of young ruffians, spearheaded by a local tough named Mutt Wyatt, attacked my brother. Manuel studiously avoided the fracas to "keep from getting my clothes torn." Bob was getting the worst of it (there were four of them attacking him) so I jumped into the fray only to have Wyatt get me in a headlock. I promptly bit him in the armpit. He screamed but I kept chewing until he was a hospital case. In the meantime, Brother Robert, with the aid of a paper punch, put several deep holes in the head of his nearest adversary. That ruffian, too, went to the hospital.

The Legend was born. We didn't consciously try to keep it alive but somehow it just grew and grew and grew.

In a short time, I was transferred to Felton School, to which a journey was an adventure in itself. First we walked close to a third of a mile up a dirt road to the main highway, then we boarded the school bus that sped to Felton, some five miles away. "Sped" is another misnomer, for the vehicle picked up farm children all along the way.

On the first day, my innate desire to please, to be a part of the group, got me into deep water. A redhaired young girl continually traversed the length of the bus, chatting amiably with all who knew her. I didn't know she was Annie Fitzgerald, the driver's daughter and the apple of his eye.

The young miscreant I sat next to kept nudging me. In a hoarse whisper, he urged me to "GOOZANEE." I didn't understand until, with explicit movement of wrist and extended forefinger, he conveyed what "GOOZANEE" meant. Entering into what I thought was to be hilarious fun, I goosed Annie on her next pass.

I didn't know what hit me! The girl was built like a fullback. The roar of laughter from the entire ensemble made me keenly aware that I had been set up. After a terrible dressing-down by the father/bus driver, I resolved to learn Delawarian and Delaware. My jaw ached for two days.

Bob and I had to fight constantly. Each time we got off the bus a crowd of enthusiastic rowdies shouted, "Here come them city dudes!"

It got to be routine but it also got me into some bad habits. The country boys fought with no style or grace. Their swings, although prodigious, were not exactly championship style. I emulated them, becoming quite a rowdy myself. I didn't notice that Brother Robert's style was completely different. His two years of experience over my newfound windmill attack gave him the extra edge to always come out the winner. In time I would also learn. But not in Delaware.

Life on the farm had its primitive side. All heating came from wood-burning stoves, but the farm also encompassed forty acres of woodland. One lovely summer day, Uncle Bill assigned Bob and me to collect firewood. He then went about his chores, confident that we would bring back enough to stoke the fires for the evening meal, with enough left over for breakfast. Little did he reckon with his nephew Robert's penchant for big things.

We pushed deeper into the woods than Uncle Bill intended. Suddenly Bob stopped. In front of us was the loftiest pine in the woods. Towering, majestic, clean-limbed—but not for long. After much energetic hacking and sawing on our part, the monarch trembled slightly and, after more flailing of axes, began to groan. Bob surveyed it with the expertise only an hour in the woods can bring, declaring, "When she starts to go, it'll go that-a-way." Oddly enough, he was right. The tall pine went down with a thunderous roar, both of us out of harm's way.

According to Grandmother, Uncle Bill, who was resting in a chair on the front porch, went three feet in the air at the sound of the crash. Choking down sobs, he leaped from the porch and darted into the woods.

We saw him, sobbing uncontrollably, burst into the clearing as if fired from a circus cannon. We were quickly informed that this was the tree he had made a deal to sell to the telephone company. We had chopped away what, under the circumstances, would have been a sizable profit to the Woodside Farm.

That same tree figured in another crisis in the life of Uncle Bill. By now, he was used to discovering his tools left out in the rain, or finding the gate

A portrait of Robert and me, taken in Bridgeport in 1925, around the time I burned down an ice cream factory. I must have been very precocious.

left open and his milk cows grazing through the truck garden. He had, at that point in time, three kids of his own. Louise was the oldest, Patricia next in line, and Gilbert the youngest. Gilbert, or "Sonny" as he was called, was just a toddler, not adding as much to the havoc around the farm as those "ornery Mitchum boys." However, Uncle Bill would whale the tar out of all three for the slightest infraction, while Bob and I never had as much as a spanking. In some odd way that was due to Bill's oath on our father's grave. We were sacrosanct.

'FINDERS KEEPERS —LOSERS WEEPERS'

ONE MORNING Bill's patience came nigh to breaking. I awoke early, thrilled to see a white horse standing in the farm yard. I shook Bob awake, cautioning him to be quiet. He gazed in silent awe, then uttered the magic words that made the horse ours: "Finders keepers—losers weepers!" We dressed and crept down the stairs to collar our prize. Bob approached the horse warily, grabbing at the broken rope that hung from its neck.

"We'll put him in the tool shed," he whispered. "After breakfast, we'll figure out what to do with him."

Breakfast was torture. I could scarcely contain myself. Our own horse! My eyes surely beamed with excitement.

Bill was uncomfortably aware that Bob and I had a secret. He suddenly put down the Aunt Jemima Pancake Syrup, leveling his stern gaze at me. "Alright, by Jeez! What's up with youse?"

"Nothin', Uncle Bill! Nothin'!" I gulped out the words. I shot a look at Bob as his face clouded into storm warnings. That fact was not lost on our uncle.

"By Jeez! Out with it! Now!"

The drama was too much for me. Much as a spillway releases flood waters, I blurted out the truth. "We got a horse!"

Bill's head slewed from me to Bob. He knew where the guiding genius behind any plan lay. "Where," he asked heavily, "is this horse?"

Bob stared bleakly at him, then at me. "In the tool shed." He brightened considerably. "But Jack found him!"

Without another word, Bill got up from the table and motioned for us to follow him. Grandmother, Aunt Gertrude, Bob, Louise, Patricia, Sonny and I followed in tow.

Dramatically, Bill wrenched the door open, as if half-expecting a snorting, prancing stallion to appear. For a long moment, he just stood in the doorway, then he gave a low, moaning sigh. "Well, I'll be God-damned!" He turned sadly to Grandmother and Gertrude. "He's dead!"

Earlier that morning, we learned later, the old horse had wandered into an orchard loaded with green apples and eaten himself to the verge of death, which had arrived during our breakfast. In the mounting heat, he was so bloated we couldn't drag him through the doorway. Bill hand-sawed out a section of the shed, hooked up old Jim and Harry to a towline, and dragged the poor dead creature into the woods. He pulled it as far as the ex-telephone-pole tree and undid the towline. Still without a word, he led the work horses back to the barn and unhitched them. About then, a white-haired old Negro came into the yard. He surveyed Bill. "Suh," he asked slowly, "has you seen a old white hoss what has busted loose?"

The Gang of Woodside Farm

Uncle Bill Tetreault steadies me, Louise, Pat and Gilbert while Harry the Horse carries the burden of innocent youth on Woodside Farm. Below, Jim the Horse bears a similar burden as Bob shows off his horsemanship while I keep both feet firmly on the ground.

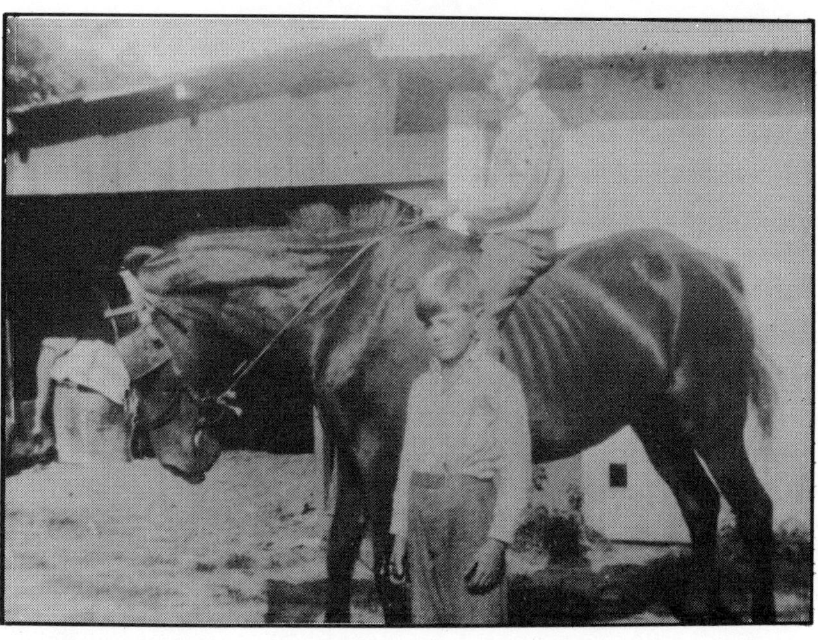

Bill heaved a deep sigh. Bob and I were tense with fear. This man owned the horse and the horse was dead. What would happen to us? "Finders keepers—losers weepers" indeed!

"Your horse is dead," admitted Bill. "The boys found him and put him up, but he'd eaten somethin' that killed him. He was bloated somethin' awful."

The old man began crying softly. "Broke his tether and got into my apple orchard. Had that horse seventeen year." He turned to go, then paused to look back. "Don' know what I'm gwine to do now."

He walked slowly out of the yard, turning east on the dirt road. We never saw him again.

Bob cut several strips from the side of the dead animal to make himself some horsehide belts and put them on the woodshed roof to dry in the hot sun. That was a mistake. A horde of buzzards swooped down on the roof, fought and crapped all over the strips, and eventually flew off with the now putrid remnants of the old white horse. We had to clean up the smelly mess.

Bill ordered us to get some firewood again. Although weeks had passed since the horse incident, Bill hadn't forgotten about his tree. "Don't take no saws out there," he warned, "just axes. Cut branches off that tree youse ruined for me."

We went to the tree but there was no way that a human being could work there. We ran back to the farmhouse, barely able to keep from throwing up a three-hour-old breakfast.

"Why ain't youse got the wood?" Bill roared.

"Uncle Bill," Bob roared back, "nobody can work around that tree! Nobody!"

"By Jeez! We'll see about that." Bill grabbed Bob's axe out of his hands and strode angrily into the forest with the two of us at a respectful distance behind. When he reached the tree, he took a half dozen savage whacks at it, then started retching violently. He staggered toward us and, after he had reached the relative safety of cleaner air, he stared at us with tears streaming down his face, tears forced by the nauseating stench of a month-dead old white horse.

"By Jeez," he gasped, "for once youse is tellin' the truth!"

❄ ❄ ❄

Christmas on the farm was a magic time. Snow was usually on the ground and transformed the murky forest into an enchanted place. Holly berries glistened brightly against the dark green leaves, and the snow mantle that encased the whole panorama breathed the spirit of the time. Thanksgiving, just past, still held kitchen memories of smells that brought a deep glow of inner satisfaction. The refrain of "Over the river and through the woods to grandmother's house we go" brought sharply into focus the real meaning of the word Thanksgiving.

But Christmas! The family, en masse, would go into the woods to select the tree, and there were hundreds. The one we kids chose would always be too big for the house. Finally, a lesser one would be picked, chopped down and toted inside. Its decoration was also a family affair and, although there would be flareups as to job responsibilities, we always approached Christmas Eve with an awe that transformed us into docile little angels.

Afoot in the deep, dark recesses of Brother Bob's heart, however, was new mischief, even relating to the Savior. He once wrote an obligato to "Silent Night" (which one of my dearest friends, Father Thomas W. Vaughan, the "jazz priest," would love to record).

Silent Night

Silent night
(so deep and quiet)
Holy night,
(you oughta try it baby)
All is calm!
(with you around me)
All is bright!
(so glad you found me!)
Round yon Virgin
(purest Alma Mater)
Mother and Child.
(you're an alligator!)
Holy Infant
(blow the breezes through me!)
So tender and mild.
(shoot the Jesus to me!)
Sleep in Heavenly Peace.
(sleep—oh, won't you rock-a-bye, my pretty Dixie Baby!)
Sleep in Heavenly Peace.
(I'm livin' in a great big way!—Jada!)

One never knows what thoughts lurk behind those hooded eyes.

❄ ❄ ❄

One Christmas morning, we waited impatiently for the "Rise and shine on the Woodside Farm!" When it came, we rushed down the stairs to Wonderland. There, beneath the tree, was an Elgin bicycle, in those days America's favorite two-wheeler. Every kid wanted one. Officially it was Bob's but with the admonition that I be allowed to use it—sparingly. After wobbling down the driveway and crashing into the mailbox, I was denied that privilege. From then on, it was ride double or walk. Bob was a cheerful, strong pedaler and our horizons expanded tremendously.

❄ ❄ ❄

Bob, always an avid, serious fisherman, enjoyed his first taste of fly casting as a result of that bicycle. He pedaled to McGuinness' Mill Pond early one morning and hooked and landed a big mullet. He pedaled furiously home, brandishing his catch to the world. Since then, he's fished in many remote areas of America, always with great success.

❄ ❄ ❄

Years later, when he was an established movie star, Bob and Joe Haworth (a fellow actor and a trusted friend who house-sits for Bob and his wife Dorothy when they are away) were angling in a remote spot on the Snake River in Idaho, a primitive area that boasts some of the world's best stream fishing. With their limit in the creel, they clambered back up the bank to their car, where a huge ranch-type fellow stood, gazing at the license plate. "See you're from California." He said it to no one in particular.

"Yes," Bob answered. "We are."

"Where do you live in California?" Looking straight at Robert, he gave no sign of recognition.

"In a place called Mandeville Canyon. It's out in West Los Angeles."

"That anywhere near Burbank? I got a brother lives in Burbank."

Bob thought for a long moment. "Oh," he said, "I suppose it might be fifteen, sixteen miles from Burbank."

The rancher brightened. "Then you got to know Harry. He's bigger'n me. 'Bout six-five—240 maybe. Lives right in Burbank."

Bob shook his head. "No," he said slowly, "I've never met Harry."

The rancher bridled. "You're not very friendly out there in California, are you? Harry ain't hard to spot, I can tell you."

Bob sought to mollify the gentleman. "Well, you see, sir, there's a mountain range between Burbank and where I live. Mandeville Canyon runs off the west side of that range. Burbank's way off to the east . . . "

The rancher calmed down. Mountains and canyons he was familiar with. "Oh, well, if there's a range 'tween you, I can see that." He looked at Bob again. "Where did you say that was?"

Bob gestured with his hands. "Here," he pointed, "is the ocean. Here," now he paused dramatically, "is the Will Rogers Ranch."

The rancher reached up and took off his old straw hat, staring solemnly at Bob and Joe. "Ain't that too bad 'bout ol' Will?"

Bob wanted to fall over laughing. Will Rogers had been gone for thirty years. But the rancher was friendly now—and he was awfully big.

❄❄❄

Barney Jenkins and his wife, Maggie, lived three-quarters of a mile from us on the dirt road going east. Barney was the dirtiest man I had . . . no, I shall say have . . . ever seen. If there ever lived a man you could grow potatoes on, Barney was that man. His wife wasn't much better but Barney bested her by being just plain dirty in every other respect.

An enterprising farmer, Barney utilized dozens of little patches of ground that his farmer-neighbors thought too small to bother with. He planted the out-of-the-way plots in strawberries, then hired us kids to pick them for the standard two cents a basket. In all fairness, he always paid promptly.

One morning, quite early, we were bent over the still-moist strawberry plants in a tiny, V-shaped patch. As the bright sun just reached its peak, the stillness was shattered by an enraged Barney Jenkins, who pointed a grimy forefinger at his poor, careworn wife. His language was formidable; none of us ever forgot it. "That," roared Barney, in response to a statement poor Maggie had mistakenly uttered, "is a God-damned, sister-pimpin,'

As I looked in 1926 in my official Felton School class picture.

father-suckin,' brother-fuckin,' dog-dickin' *black lie!*"

He surveyed the thoroughly crestfallen Maggie, then added triumphantly, "Son of a bitch!"

Red-faced, we hunched over the berries while Barney, flushed with victory, roared out in song, "Oh, the bulldog on the bank, the bullfrog in the pool! R-a-a-m-m your mammy!" Then he quietly returned to his work.

DREAMS OF DIAMONDS

THE MAJOR visited the farm with Mother the following summer, most anxious to see us. Neither Bob nor I was aware they were married. I suspect they were curious to see if we still had our moving parts intact, but I am sure of one thing: The Major viewed first-hand the miracle of his oldest stepson's mind at full throttle.

Bob read in a magazine that diamonds are found primarily in blue clay deposits in Africa. Not long afterward, Uncle Bill asked him to clean out the cows' stalls. When Bob's shovel hit the clay floor, it was a cobalt blue. Immediately, he snared me as the shoveler. I dug a pit so deep that had an errant cow wandered into it, a derrick would have been needed to get her out. While I plied the shovel, Bob sat dreamy-eyed on the edge of the stall, outlining what he would do with his riches.

In the midst of Bob's reveries, the Major strode into the barn accompanied by Uncle Bill.

"Blue clay? Blue clay!" Uncle Bill roared as he shook his head in stark disbelief as Bob explained our endeavor. "It's piss what's done that! Cow piss! On yellow clay! Delaware's full of yellow clay and there ain't been one God-damned diamond found in the whole state. Now you fill that hole up. *NOW!* Jack, you go inside and clean yourself up." Breathing heavily, he stormed out of the barn.

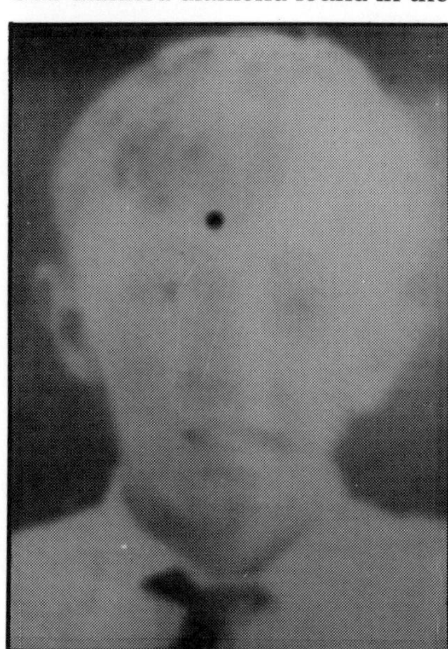

As Brother Bob looked in his 1926 Felton School class snapshot.

The Major explained how the uric acid in the urine caused the clay's yellow pigment to turn to such a beautiful blue. Bob began stoically filling up the yawning pit. His immediate dreams of dynasty might have been shattered, but there were other grandiose dreams lurking in that nimble mind.

Our sister Annette (later to rename herself Julie) visited the farm to introduce us to her future sailor-husband, Ernest Longaker. By coincidence, Brother Bob had just killed a blacksnake and hung it on the outhouse door. The screams of Annette—who had decided to visit that august dwelling—brought the whole tribe running to her aid and the wrath of the U.S. Navy down on Robert.

To us, Ernie seemed to represent the entire might of the Navy. He sternly rebuked Robert and, for once, Bob had little to say.

Brother Bob surely had his ornery side. He would get me down on the ground, pin me on my back and drool in my face. Gentle John would finally get loose and chase him all over the farm. Because I had a corn-knife in my hand, he felt it ill-advised to stop. He just plain outran me.

The Major continued to surprise us. He had brought with him an English saddle, an object of ridicule from the local gentry. How could any man sit on a horse with *that* saddle?

The Major was a great horseman. Not only had he been properly trained to ride to the hounds, but he was a professional bareback rider, billed as St. Elmo the Great in an Australian circus. He was a deep well and, as the years rolled past, Bob and I found him to be a tremendous man.

He owned a beautiful collie named Bosun. (Again, neither Bob nor I knew then that the Major had Captain's papers for any tonnage, any waters.) Bosun was a handsome animal but, as a city dog, he had one fatal flaw.

During the summer months, the local farmers would often go fox hunting. They were a motley group, not the red-coated, black-capped riders on sleek horses that the Major knew. One young farm lad rode a red mule, by far the best jumper of the lot.

Bosun loved the hunt but preferred to run not behind the fox but beside him. Once the Major saw Bosun match the animal stride for stride, swearing later that Bosun seemed to be urging the fox onward. Irate farmers muttered that some day they'd "get that damned dawg." One day someone did: Bosun was killed by a car. Bob and I have always suspected that the driver did it deliberately.

Major Hugh Morris in the North Africa desert in 1916, fighting in a campaign against the Bedouins. In later years he regaled me with a tale of war: During a charge a cannon shot decapitated his beast's head and he was pinned beneath the fallen camel carcass and forced to watch "the brave lads rout the enemy from sand dune positions" while he lay helpless, unable to participate.

Before Mother and the Major returned to Bridgeport, the Major gave Bob the English saddle. At least that's what I recall. Cousin Gilbert is insistent that the saddle and bridle were stolen from the farm by Robert and me. Somehow, that fits the image of "them ornery Mitchum boys" better than my memory. Whatever the case, that saddle "gift" was the catalytic agent that sparked a near-tragedy.

GUNFIRE AT CLEARWATER CREEK

UNCLE BILL was death on guns. He refused to have one on the farm. Bob wanted one desperately and when a young friend envied "that slick saddle," a trade was quickly negotiated. Bob was now the proud owner of a beautifully balanced, single-shot, bolt-action Winchester. I shot that rifle many times, and to this day I've never fired one that was more accurate. Bob concealed the weapon in a clump of bushes in the cow pasture until he could figure out a more fitting hiding place.

Delaware is full of clearwater streams stuffed with pike, catfish and bass, and one of the ways we put the Winchester to use was shooting into the water. A rifle bullet hitting close to a fish stuns it by concussion; it will float to the surface. The deadly accurate Winchester netted us plenty of game. It was more than just a sport because we'd then fry the fish for dinner.

Two of our hunting companions were Benny and Solly Markowitz, a rarity in rural Delaware in that they were Jewish. But to us they were simply friends—mother had kept us totally free of any prejudices in our formative years. The subject of anti-Semitism just never came up because in her world it simply didn't exist.

Benny, the older brother, was a short but powerfully built youngster with incredibly heavy eyebrows. He was the more assured of the two, while Solly had a gentleness that set him apart from Benny.

They shared an old Benjamin rifle that often misfired. At each misfire, the cartridge would have to be ejected, turned around to an unmarked spot on the primer and tried again. It often took three or four attempts before the rifle would fire.

Bob was on one bank of a small stream while Benny and Solly were on the opposite bank. Benny wanted to shoot a large noisy crow and asked to swap rifles with Bob, who leaned across the water and handed him our Winchester, butt first. Benny tossed the old Benjamin at Bob. When Bob grabbed at the rifle in mid-air, it went off. The sharp crack was followed by an eerie silence. The bullet had struck Solly in the buttocks, exiting the front of his stomach.

"Hey fellows, I'm hit . . . " Solly said it so softly no one believed him.

"Ah, c'mon," Benny scorned. "You ain't hit!"

"No, I'm hit." Solly pulled up his shirt front. Blood welled from beneath.

I was shocked by the nightmarish sight. My helplessness quickly dissolved into tears. Ten-year-old Bob swiftly moved into action.

Bob and Benny clumsily carried Solly some distance to a farmhouse. Benny looked over his shoulder to see me picking up the two rifles. "Don't forget the fish!" he snapped, ever the practical one.

Solly was hospitalized and his life was saved. By some miracle, the bullet had emerged without hitting a bone or an artery.

That settled our hash in the community. Bob's total innocence never washed away the conviction of most local farmers that we were prejudiced and fundamentally evil. I was lumped into the hopper indiscriminately. We were dubbed as "them ornery Mitchum boys" and the name stuck.

Bob became more introverted than ever, while I became disinterested in guns.

(Recently, Bob and I discussed his feelings about the shooting. "I was horrified," he told me. "I thought in those days that if you were shot, you died." Bob was adamant as to his role in the event. "It wasn't my fault. I was more concerned about how to get help for him.")

❄❄❄

About a half-mile away from our place lay the Hamilton farm. Ralph Hamilton was a gruff man, not given to a sense of humor. It didn't add to a pleasant afternoon when the Hamiltons came home from a trip to Dover to find that "them Mitchum boys" had been visiting their sons, Wheezer and Jim. Little did they take into account that we were just visiting. According to Mr. Hamilton, neither Wheezer nor Jim could have ever constructed the dastardly plan that demolished the family buggy.

The four of us thought it would be hilarious when Wheezer suggested hitching their milk cow to the buggy. The major error Jim and Wheezer made was in putting the frightened animal into the shafts facing the wrong way. When they hooked the cow to the traces, all hell broke loose. I swear, I never dreamed that a cow could buck so hard and high. In a matter of moments, the Hamilton's buggy was kindling.

When we saw the Hamilton's Model-T turn from the highway to their dirt road, Bob and I split for home. From past experiences, we knew that protestations would be to no avail, and we legged it across a wheat field as fast as we could go. Bob was considerably ahead of me until a big blacksnake suddenly appeared in front of my feet. The monster looked to be a hundred feet long.

I passed Bob in a burst of panic.

Just then, we heard a great roaring and babbling of voices from the Hamilton's farmyard. We were banned forever from that place. Once again, we were innocent. (Well, almost.)

❄❄❄

But we had many idyllic moments, too. The eastern shore teemed with soft-shelled crab and Jones Beach was our favorite haunt. Armed with a couple dozen rotting fishheads tied to a clothesline, Bob and I would pedal there to go crabbing.

The crumbling dock area jutted out over a deep backwater area that ran into Delaware Bay. We would catch a sackful of crabs within a few hours, pedal back to the farm and partake in a succulent feast.

On one occasion, I started to pull up my line, but couldn't. I tugged with all my might. A huge sea turtle—easily weighing two hundred pounds—had grabbed onto the bait and kept holding it until I jerked it to the surface. The creature blinked at me for several moments, released the bait, then casually disappeared beneath the murky waters.

Bob was at the other end of the dock and saw nothing. I had pulled up a sea monster and there was no way in the world that I could prove it.

WATERMELON COMMANDOES

TOWARD THE MAIN highway lived a Negro farmer named Mack Chase, the gentlest, kindest man I'd ever met. He always had a soft "Good maunin'" for anyone he saw and his smile exuded warmth. Despite all of these admirable traits, Brother Bob had another dastardly strategy in mind.

The plan was to raid the large watermelon patch adjacent to Mack's cornfield.

Bob took Pat, Louise, Sonny and me into his confidence. "The way I figure it," he mused, "is that if we all walk backwards into the cornfield, ol' Mack won't be able to figure out who got one of his melons. All the tracks'll be comin' *out* of the cornfield. How can he figure out *who* went in?" It was irrefutable logic. Dutifully, we all trekked toward the main road, then turned and started walking backward up the long rows between the corn stalks. A hot summer sun and a long dry spell had made the dirt clods as hard as rocks. Each gingerly placed step made our bare feet more raw until we came to what Bob ascertained would be the "right spot."

Hunkering down and peering through the stalks, Bob spied the largest melon in the patch, about eight feet from the last row of corn. Of course, I was given the honor of plucking it. "Jack," Bob commanded, "you go get that one!"

Artfully, I rolled into the patch, crawled on the scratchy ground like a commando on a battlefield, and finally managed to wrestle the rattlesnake melon back into the shade of the cornfield. With great nonchalance, Bob unsheathed his knife, slashing open our prize. It was as green as a fresh shamrock. Our disappointment changed to fear, then to downright humiliation when we heard ol' Mack say, "Chilluns," as he looked sorrowly at his wasted melon, "why didn't you ask ol' Mack foh a watermelon? He'd a-picked you a ripe one."

Walking backwards indeed. Ol' Mack hadn't been fooled for a minute.

❄❄❄

In the summer of 1927, golf courses were a rarity in Delaware. My mother's brother, Charles Gunderson, came down to the farm to visit his mother, Petrine; he brought with him golf shoes, an awesome pair of heavy, steel-spiked monsters that could have passed for Chinese gunboats.

He was disgruntled to learn there was no driving range for miles around. He put the shoes in his sister Gertrude's clothes closet. When he packed to return to his berth aboard a freighter docked in New York, he left them behind.

Aunt Gertrude, frustrated that the spiked brogans dominated her closet, ordered Uncle Bill to "do something." Some inherent gene of French frugality kept him from throwing the shoes out, but one lovely day in late August, the right moment came for their logical disposal.

Bill spied shoeless Barney Jenkins sauntering down the dirt road that passed the farmhouse, dressed in straw hat, flannel shirt and bib overalls. Bill ran into the farmhouse, returning to the front porch in time to see Barney come abreast of the lane that led into our yard. "Barney!" Bill hailed the ambling dirt-pile loudly. "Come up here a minute, will youse?"

Barney, a naturally suspicious man, eyed Bill for a long moment, then turned into the lane. "I paid your younguns already."

Uncle Charles O. Gunderson, circa 1929, when he was an engineer on a freighter. As a youth he dreamed of becoming a song-and-dance man, but his father thought that was a damn foolish notion and dissuaded him. Too bad. At right is Grandma Petrine Gunderson, whose sagacious advice would guide me in my personal decisions into my adult years.

"I know, I know. This has nothing to do with that." Bill smiled at Barney. "I've got a present for youse."

Barney's eyes looked furtively at Bill. No one had ever given him a gift. "What kind of present?"

"Golf shoes. Real nice golf shoes." Bill held out the items as though they were emeralds—they were a mustard yellow that brought a bilious sickness to mind. Barney seemed fascinated by the evil-looking spikes that graced the soles. He slipped them on his grimy feet and, thanking Bill profusely, strode majestically down the dirt road.

Every Sunday, until the cold became too severe, Barney would stroll casually down the road to the highway. Every thirty feet or so he would stop and turn to survey his tell-tale tracks. He would shake his head in appreciation of his marvelous gift.

By God, Barney Jenkins had left his mark on the world.

❄❄❄

I didn't see Uncle Charlie again until years later when I came back from the war in 1946. He came once again to visit his mother. I was living in California and I had bought a war-surplus, five-man life raft, a marvelous recreational vehicle. I'd paddle out past the kelp beds, anchor it and fish for whatever would bite. I'd sip cold beer and read while waiting for a strike.

Uncle Charlie, now a gruff and war-experienced first officer on a freighter, asked me what I was going to do with "that little thing" as I lashed the raft to the top of my car. I explained my routine to him, expecting a pleasant day, and he decided he wanted to tag along. Once we were snugly anchored off the kelp beds, he rolled up his pants legs and took off his shirt, exposing his milk-white skin. I feared the worst.

"Uncle Charlie." My tone was tentative.

"What?"

"You'd better put your shirt back on and roll down your pants legs."

He exploded with Viking fury. "I've been to sea all my life. Longer than you've been born. Don't tell me what to do!"

You can always tell a Norwegian but you can't tell 'em much. I let it drop, studiously paying attention to my fishing.

The bridge of a big freighter rides about forty feet above the sea's surface. My little raft rode almost at sea level. The sun, reflecting off the water, began tanning that milk-white skin.

The next day, Charlie paid the toll for his arrogance. Grandmother applied lotion to his back and shoulders as he sat in agony, looking quite pathetic, his boiled feet and shins dunked in a tub of cool water. His arrogance, however, remained much in evidence.

"Look at me," he cried in anger. "I'm boiled like a damned lobster!"

I asked if he recalled that on several occasions the day before I had suggested he cover himself up against the sun.

"Yes," he admitted, "you told me I should cover up." Then he straightened up, pointed an accusing finger at me and roared, "But you didn't insist!"

❄❄❄

By 1927 our days on Woodside Farm were rapidly coming to a close, although we were not aware of it. Uncle Bill planted a rather large vineyard of Concord grapes and we waited in great anticipation for the first harvest. The strong vines grew rapidly.

Games were a great part of our life on the farm. As usual, Brother Robert was the great innovator, invariably spicing up our play. Hide-and-seek was a favorite, the haymow a special place for concealment. There, in the waning light of day, the hider had the distinct advantage: While the seeker probed around in the dimly lit mow, the hider could dash down the ladder and touch base ahead of the seeker. Until Bob put his nimble mind to work again.

One late afternoon, Pat, Louise, Gilbert and I were hiding when Bob poked his head up into the haymow. We could see him as he eyed all of the dark recesses. He widened his eyes and placed a forefinger alongside his temple. "Suck a thumb-poo-poo!" he yelled musically.

Suck a thumb poo-poo? Who ever heard of such an innovation in a hide-and-seek game? We roared with

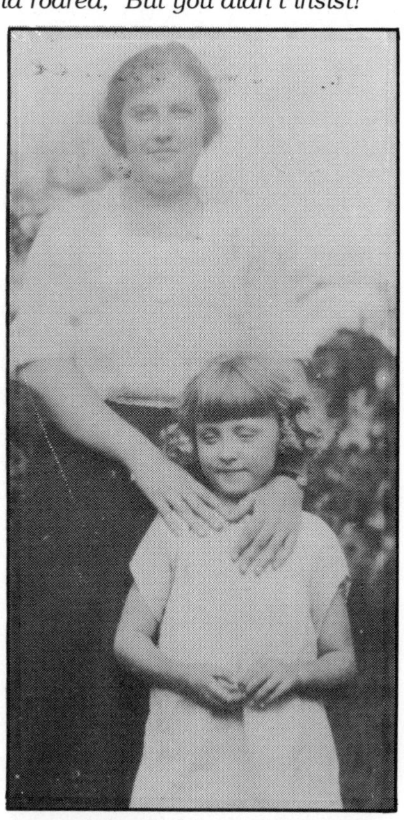

Around the time I was born mom sent sister Julie, then around six years old, to Putnam, Conn., to live with Aunt Eleanor Gunderson, Charlie's wife.

laughter. Bob raced down the ladder to tag us all.

The contest was on. Each of us would come up with outlandish pronouncements. Gilbert would intone, "Oh, the pitiful howling of the hound, the pitiful howling of the hound, the pitiful, pitiful, pitiful, pitiful, pitiful howling of the hound!"

Louise would grab a magazine and clutch it to her heart with "Freckles, remove that ugly mask!"

We all tried, but none of us could top "Suck a thumb poo-poo."

RUNAWAYS

IN THE FALL of '27, Robert again decided to ramble. This time he included Manuel Barque and me in his plans. We were going to "run off" to escape the oppressions put upon us by school officials and the "big folks." "Big folks" included anyone over twenty-one.

At the farm we had three "big folks"—Bill, Gertrude and Grandmother. They were kind to us to the extreme, but we didn't think of it that way. We hadn't ever been exposed to the real world.

Bob had just been expelled for shooting a paper clip with alarming accuracy at the private parts of our favorite teacher, Miss Robbins. She was a vivacious, red-headed Virginia miss, and I was in love with her. She taught our class to sing "Welcome, sweet springtime, we greet thee with song." She put a song in my heart until I learned that she was having an affair with the principal. I didn't exactly know what an affair was but it broke my heart anyway. It was another good reason for me to run away.

Avoiding the highway, we walked the railroad tracks for some twenty-five miles. Night found us on the outskirts of Bridgeville, where we holed up in corn shocks that stood like Indian teepees. Cold settled down in deathly silence, broken only by field mice scurrying for corn kernels and the whoop of horned owls searching for the field mice. Dogs bayed in the distance. The mournful sound of a train whistle echoed and re-echoed across the windswept fields.

A new sound was now heard: Manuel Barque's sobbing. Soon my wailing was added, then the intrepid Robert's. The crying trio wended its way across the frozen field to an isolated farmhouse, dark and foreboding. Bob knocked on the back door. Soon, a kerosene lamp shone through the window panes that overlooked the back porch.

"Land sakes alive, Hiram!" A woman's voice called out to someone in the interior of the home. "It's three younguns."

The farmer and his wife brought us into the kitchen and surveyed us with disbelief.

"We run off!" Bob's pronouncement brought a clucking sound from the woman and a more practical one from the man. "Martha, fix them some hot cocoa while I call the sheriff."

We were so cold, hungry and homesick, even the word "sheriff" didn't bring a twinge from any of us.

Manuel's father picked us up at the sheriff's station about four in the morning. We drove the twenty-five miles in total silence.

When we arrived at the farmhouse, Uncle Bill greeted us with tears streaming down his gaunt cheeks.

"I swore on your father's grave that youse would never go hungry, never be without a roof over your head and that youse would get an education. He stopped to blow his nose loudly. "I've dug wells, painted houses, plowed fields, worked wheat fields—anythin' to keep all of youse under one roof. And how do youse repay me? You run away!"

He started crying all over again.

Aunt Gertrude quietly ordered us to our rooms. Much relieved, we crept up the stairs to bed.

Later, Grandmother came into the darkened bedroom, carrying a tiny peach tree twig. She stood looking down at us, tears webbing from her eyes. "I suppose I have to punish you," she said. She tentatively flicked the twig at us a few times, then fled the room, sobbing uncontrollably.

Now, over a half-century later, that "flogging" looms in our minds as the worst we've ever taken. "This hurts me more than it does you" was never more clearly defined than in our sainted Grandmother's valiant attempt to "punish" us.

❄ ❄ ❄

Although our religious training was never highly organized, we were dealt subtle doses in such a manner that, to this day, God is a very real entity to me. He is not a long-bearded fellow who sits in Heaven and pronounces judgments on us like a local magistrate dealing out traffic fines. God is an eternal stream of truth that in its purity remains ever constant.

We all know that driving a car at eighty miles an hour in a fifteen-mile-an-hour zone can only result in disaster. Ignoring truths that have existed from the beginning of time has the same dismal result. God is love. If we all really acted on that premise, crime and war wouldn't exist.

Mankind pays lip service to the basic creed but, in reality, avoids its application like the plague.

Grandmother had given some land to the small Negro community so they might build a church. When the building was finished, it was picture-perfect, nestled in a clearing in the woods and facing the road that Barney Jenkins often trod. It also faced out on our family's grape vineyard.

The first harvest of the Concords was an excitement to us all. Bob, Sonny, Louise, Pat and I drifted along the long rows searching for any grapes that looked even remotely ripe. We made ourselves sick by gorging pounds of them into our stomachs.

One Monday morning, we became bedeviled with a "fun" idea.

Lilly Mae, a slender, graying and gracious lady of about fifty, was cleaning her church after the Sunday meeting. Now wouldn't it be fun, we decided, to throw dirt clods into the area she'd already cleaned? Then we'd dart into the cool hiding places among the green vines. We did just that, feeling vaguely alarmed when the front door of the church slowly closed.

The feeling intensified the next day. Lilly Mae, dressed in her Sunday best, headed straight down the dirt road toward our farmhouse. She looked terribly dignified in her finery, adding a touch of elegance to her carriage with a parasol shading her soft brown face from the sun.

She was going to "tell"! What is more paralyzing to young minds than that dreaded word—"tell"?

Straight to Grandmother Gunderson she went. Soon that soft, Norwegian-tinted voice drifted to our ears. "Children . . . "—how we dreaded that sound—". . . Come into the parlor. I want to talk to you all." The voice was soft, but the steel rod in it glinted through.

A more contrite group of waifs never existed. We slunk into the parlor, heads bowed and eyes studiously examining the floor. Grandmother, all ninety pounds of her, eyed us sternly. "Lilly Mae has something she wants to say to you. I think you'd better listen." We looked at each other dumbly. Lilly Mae surveyed us sadly. No anger, no hostility, just a deep sadness.

"Children," she said in her gentle Southern accent, "when you threw dirt into the church, you weren't harming me. You were desecrating God's house. I know it's just a little country church, not a big cathedral or temple, but God is there just the same. He is everywhere and He is Love. So when you do things that are mean and small in His eyes, you hurt Him, not me. All I ask of you is to think about it.

"Do you really want to be mean and small?"

Personally, I'd rather have taken a beating. I could have crawled into a rat hole. When I sneaked a look at my fellow conspirators, I knew that they felt the same.

Grandmother spoke up. "Lilly Mae has invited us up to her house for lemonade and cookies. Get yourselves cleaned up." She turned to Lilly Mae. "We'll be there in half an hour."

After Lilly Mae left, the scrub brush whined. Soon, spanking clean, we were ready for our visit, which proved to be an eye-opener. From its exterior appearance, the house of Lilly Mae was a shack: the porch sagged, the wood was unpainted, and it had an air of abject poverty. The interior, however, was spotless and nicely furnished. And Lilly Mae was a charming hostess. The lemonade was cool and fresh, the cookies delicious. The lesson was driven home without fanfare or bombast.

I can attest to the fact that Grandmother and Lilly Mae made it nigh unto impossible for me to be swayed by color, creed or outward appearances. To this day, Bob and I are more impressed by what a person actually does than by what he says, what he actually lives by and up to, than what he professes. Aesop was right: "Fine feathers do not make fine birds."

'DID YOUSE? OR DIDN'T YOUSE'

THE DELAWARE WINTER of '28 came in fiercely, isolating the Woodside Farm in a sea of white. Uncle Bill hitched up Harry to a makeshift sled in an effort to get us to the main highway to meet the school bus. In vain, the animal plunged and reared through the deep drifts. The futility was only enhanced when we learned later that the school had been closed.

We dug snow tunnels to the barn and outhouse where Bob and I whiled away many an hour, leafing through the Sears & Roebuck catalogue. Most youngsters centered on the bikes, guns, boats and fishing rods . . . I freely admit that I enthusiastically pored over all the young female models in their slips and bras.

Brother Bob had already been expelled once from school—a fact that weighed heavily against him in a bizarre incident that marked the end of his formal education.

The Felton High School's girls' basketball team faced Smyrna High in a crucial game. During the playoff, young Francis Butler crept into the Felton girls' locker room and proceeded to commit a heinous act with a shower cap belonging to one of the players, Rita Sabidra. After Felton won the game, the joyous athletes swarmed into the locker area, screaming and dancing with delight. Rita picked up her shower cap and threw it triumphantly at the ceiling. Her triumph rapidly metamorphised into confusion, humiliation, then rage. That rage roared from the gymnasium all the way to the principal's office.

The principal was a dapper little Frenchman, Dr. Petrie, who wore a morning coat and striped trousers as his badge of office. He confronted Robert, along with Francis Butler and Manuel Barque, with the awful crime that had been perpetrated on Rita Sabidra.

Robert laughed aloud.

When he stopped laughing, he realized with a creeping horror that he had laughed alone. Within sixty seconds, he was court-martialed, found guilty and banished forever from Felton High School.

Bob decided to hoof the five miles from Felton to the Woodside Farm. As he walked along the concrete DuPont Highway in deep reverie, he didn't hear the *pack-ah-pack-ah-pack* of Uncle Bill's Model-T Ford as it crept up beside him. Bob looked up, startled as the Ford pulled over.

"By Jeez!" roared Bill. "Why ain't youse in school?"

Bob cast his eyes to the concrete. "I've been expelled, Uncle Bill."

Bill looked at him blankly. "Expelled? Why?"

"They say . . . " Bob's voice trailed off.

"They say what?" The "what" was a command performance—and Bob knew it.

"They said I shit in a hat!"

Willie's mouth gaped like a beached fish for several beats. When his voice finally returned, it was bleak and cold. "Did youse shit in a hat?"

Bob stood his ground. "No, Uncle Bill, I didn't."

Bill ordered him into the car, made a U-turn, and they went *pack-ah-pack-ah-pack* back toward the school.

I had been blissfully unaware of the expulsion until I heard Bill's voice careening through the school like a tornado. It was a lovely spring day and the windows were all wide open. A balmy breeze wafted through the rooms, carrying Bill's pronouncement to Dr. Petrie, the school board, the students and, presumably, to the entire state of Delaware: "Bob didn't shit in *no* hat!"

The little Frenchman was totally unaffected by Bill's rampage. He looked steadily at our uncle for a long moment then said, "Mr. Tetreault, there is no need for this display of emotion. The expelling of Robert stands."

Uncle Bill stopped short. Had he heard correctly? Everyone in Delaware always called him "Tater-ho" or "Ted-row." Here was a man who pronounced Tetreault as it should be pronounced. Te-tro, . . . yes, Tetro!

He eyed Dr. Petrie suspiciously. "How do youse know my name?"

"I am French, Mr. Tetreault." He looked at Bill with a sigh of disappointment. "As you are."

The football coach offered to throw Bill out. When Bill countered with an offer to tie the coach into a pretzel, Dr. Petrie stepped in with an counteroffer to call the Sheriff. Bob then put forth an iron-clad resolution that he and Bill leave, an offer accepted ruefully by the coach and with gratitude by Dr. Petrie.

Robert was no longer a member of Felton High School.

❄ ❄ ❄

An odd statistic in the penal codes of America is that only two states among all fifty—Maryland and Delaware—allowed public flogging as a method of punishment lasting into modern times. Maryland erased the whipping post from their books in 1953, but it is still a possibility to be legally flogged in Delaware. The most prevalent victims were wife-beaters.

I witnessed such a flogging in Dover in 1928. At nine years of age, it was a traumatic experience. The sight of the man—around twenty- five, with a shock of blond hair—being bound to a post, stripped of his shirt and cat-o'-nine-tailed before a mob of spectators appalled me.

Our whole avuncular family was there as part of a rare travel treat. Eleven-year-old Bob said that the people watching acted as if they were on a holiday before the first lash was laid on the man's milk-white back. Nine times the leaded lash bit into flesh and, with each whistling stroke, the crowd became more silent.

By the time his back was a bloody horror, there was no sound other than that of the flail against torn skin. The crowd dispersed.

My last remembrance before Uncle Willie hauled me off was seeing the unconscious man being released and slumping down onto the dusty ground. The sight and sounds rose up to haunt me at odd times for many months to come.

THE PASSING OF BIG DADDY

IT WILL BE forever remembered in American history that 1929 was "The Year of the Crash," when the stock market crumbled. It was a catastrophic time for us on the farm, too.

So was the previous year, when "Big Daddy" Gunderson died. Somehow, his passing seemed to signal the end of Woodside Farm. He had bought it, and now he was gone.

This strange and enigmatic man, while in his twenties, captained a Norwegian fishing trawler in some of the harshest water in the world. His ship sank in a raging storm and he, with four others, rode out the storm in a lifeboat. The boat drifted in the North Sea for nearly a month. When it was finally sighted, Gus Gunderson was alone. The others, he said, had perished. A board of inquiry was puzzled that our grandfather-to-be was hale and hearty, had suffered no appreciable weight loss, and was in good spirits. The ugly thought of cannibalism surfaced, but there were no witnesses and Captain Gustav Olaf Gunderson was exonerated by the board.

His strength was prodigious. On Woodside Farm, he once crept beneath a loaded haywagon carrying three workers and almost turned it over, laughing uproariously at the cries of the startled farmers. He got his neighbor Enoch Rash drunk one evening and carried the besotted farmer a quarter of a mile to his farmhouse, dumping him unceremoniously on the porch in front of his termagant wife. "Here's your husband," he roared. "He's drunk!"

When he returned to his own farm, he stood alone in the yard and sang "Santa Lucia" in a voice as perfectly true and clear as the late, great opera star Jussi Bjorling. To this day, I have never heard it sung so sweetly.

The musical genes ran through the family as Grandfather's three sisters were singing stars in their own right in Norwegian opera; their inherent abilities have come down the generations to Brother Bob and Sister Annette/Julie and to me.

Old Gus died in 1928, eaten alive by stomach cancer. Yet none of us ever heard a whimper out of him. He only came close to breaking down on that day he called us all into the kitchen and told us of his condition. "I'm going into the hospital," he confided, "and I'm not coming out." With his eyes glistening with held-back tears, he told us all that he loved us. It was the first and last time I ever heard him say it. When he left, a great silence fell over us. Big Daddy would be no more.

In 1929 Uncle Bill brought a bumper crop of Concord grapes to the marketplace only to find that he faced a six-cent loss on each hamper harvested. Already mortgaged to the extreme, the farm sank under this new salvo of economic disaster. Once again, Bob and I found ourselves adrift in the backwash of the times.

Our sister, Annette, was then living in Philadelphia with her sailor husband, Ernie Longaker. We were shipped unceremoniously to "The City of Brotherly Love."

At a railroad station in Wyoming, Delaware, in the early half of 1929, Bob and I posed with our half-sister Carol Morris, Major Hugh Cunningham Morris and our mother Ann. In my white shirt and pants I assumed my usual arrogant stance, showing the world just how tough I could be in those youthful, rebellious days. Bob chose merely to look sleepy-eyed, a condition he carried over into his professional pursuits and which he continues to affect to this very day.

THIS IS BROTHERLY LOVE?

ANNETTE, a petite, small-boned, graceful girl, was already a professional dancer. She had banded with five other girls to form the Yankee Doodles dance team. Their closing number was a routine embracing the tune "Six Yankee Doodles from Connecticut." It was unmemorable except that I remember it. They toured the Deep South for a time, breaking up when Annette married. Show biz was in her blood, and soon she would make the transition to the Big Apple. But for now she and Ernie lived close to 26th and Aspen, at that time a ghetto-like locale that causes those who know it to cluck sympathetically for anyone who has ever been dumped there. All I remember of the area is the nearby aquarium and the fascinating sight of all those strange fish.

Also deeply lodged in my brain is the memory of a graphic lesson I learned from a young man who must have studied the great Benny Leonard, then the world's champion lightweight boxer. This kid had all of his moves.

At a party I met a very pretty girl. With the brashness of youth, I announced to all within earshot that she was *my* girl.

A quiet, slender young guy informed me that she was *his* girl. I took umbrage, challenging him to combat. In Delaware, I had learned to swing with the best of them. When one of my great roundhouse punches landed, the tide always turned in my favor.

Outside, in the chill autumn of Philadelphia, those roundhouses never landed. The young Philadelphian beat a steady tattoo on the face, head and chin of one John Mitchum. I became a battered, beaten shell of my former self. When I arrived back at Annette's apartment, Bob looked at me in utter horror. He sneered, "Did you hit him?"

"No," I snapped defensively. "I didn't!"

Bob roared, "Why not, for Chrissake?"

My answer, etched forever into the family's history, caused Bob to shake his head in disbelief. "He jumps away!"

Bob decided it was time I really learned how to box. For a fortnight, he pummeled me about the head and shoulders, then pronounced I was ready. He escorted me to an encounter with that nameless devil, informing him I was now ready for a rematch. In much the same manner that present-day ring warriors stare at each other and mouth defiant threats, I glared at my opponent haughtily. "I'll bet, by God, you cain't do that again!"

He surveyed me coolly, gliding to meet me.

And he did it again.

Robert upheld the family honor by whacking my tormentor to the ground, whereupon he bounced his head on the pavement a few times to drive the lesson home that all Mitchums weren't suckers for a left. I literally sneaked home. It's a terrible blow to one's ego to be beaten twice. It's even worse to find that your brother can dispose of your conqueror so easily.

❄ ❄ ❄

I was roped into joining a neighborhood gang whose chief reason for existence was to promote fights with other gangs. My group would tie milk bottles to the ends of broomsticks, lay in wait in dark alleys, then bash unsuspecting rivals over their heads. I was in three "gang fights" but never dared get close enough to use my own makeshift mace. As a matter of fact, I left Philadelphia in the summer of 1930 with a record of three gang fights, two fistfights and the almost-Guinness- Book-of-Records' achievement of never having hit *anyone.*

MANHATTAN MELODIES —AND MURDERS

WHEN LIZA MINNELLI or Frank Sinatra belts out "New York, New York," the message rings loud and clear. *New York is it.* The constant motion, the oceans of people, the roar of traffic and the all- night action of downtown Manhattan have a distinct, fascinating flavor all their own. So did 56th Street and Ninth Avenue to the waif I was when I arrived there at the ripe old age of ten.

Mother and the Major had moved to Manhattan from Bridgeport earlier in 1930, and had sent for Bob and me to join them. My first experience there was hardly one that could be construed as glamorous. Mom sent me out to mail a letter on the first evening I arrived.

"Go out of the apartment, turn left, go to the corner and mail the letter. Turn around, and come straight home!" Well, I mailed the letter alright, but paused to gaze in awe at the enormous skyline of nighttime Manhattan. It was then that a man approached me with a proposition.

"Hey, kid, do you need a job?"

Nineteen thirty? The Depression? No money? Of course I needed a job.

He explained that a friend lived in a nearby apartment and needed a kid to deliver hand bills. The pay was a dollar a day.

He rang the buzzer at his "friend's" apartment for a long while, then said he'd show me a trick with a dime. He pretended to "lose the dime" in my clothing and suddenly I was aware that I was being manhandled rather personally.

All the lifting of peach and apple cases on the farm, all the wild swinging of Delaware and the power-punching learned in Philadelphia surged to the surface. I caught the pervert squarely in the solar plexus. He gasped and fell to the dark floor of the tenement as I fled to the street and I found my way safely home. To this day, Mother has never heard the "trick with a dime" story, and Brother Robert gently reminds me of my initial naivete whenever I become impatient with the younger generation.

My next New York encounter came on the day I enrolled in P.S. 59. My rural Delaware accent was in full flower and, as I stood chatting in line, I was fetched a fearful blow to the head. Dazed and not a little chagrined, I turned to face a lithe young Negro boy with fists flailing. His explanation was disarmingly simple. "You stepped on my toe!"

After my head stopped ringing, I decided that I'd best acquire a New York accent. (Bob and I could always imitate accents easily.)

I had been in school only a few weeks when I met a charming young lad about my age, who invited me to spend the night with him and his uncle, who was in his thirties. The lad had one very odd eye; it was almost opaque, and didn't seem to function properly. When I met the uncle I was taken by his Canadian accent. He was a delightful man and took a keen interest in me. I was flattered.

After my fourth overnight stay, they revealed why they had brought me into their fold: The uncle was a jewel thief who had trained his nephew in the art of breaking and entering. The boy was already an expert in determining the authenticity and quality of gems by their cut and appearance.

"Would you," the uncle inquired, "like to become a member of our rather elite profession?"

At that time I was very agile and quite strong. As I was only eleven, I was also quite slender. Because I was the perfect size to slip easily through transoms, they felt I would be a real asset to the family business.

I wasn't shocked by the proposal, nor was I really interested. I told them I'd most certainly consider it and let them know in a few days. We had a nice dinner, beautifully prepared by the uncle, and retired for the night.

In the morning, I left early to get home and prepare for school. When I stepped out of the apartment, I was horrified to see a man's body stuffed in a trash can in front of the apartment. I noticed two additional details: Piano wire wrapped tightly around his neck, and a knife protruding from his back.That afternoon, I told my friend that I would pass on his uncle's proposition. I didn't tell him why.

I guess it had something to do with the neighborhood.

* * *

Our sister Annette was now dancing in a Broadway show and was a friend of Leonard Barr, one of America's great vaudevillian performers, an eccentric dancer par excellence. (He's also Dean Martin's uncle, but that's not part of this story.)

We were still living on 56th Street and, to say the least, the apartment was crowded. Bob and I slept on a wide cot just outside the kitchen door. One morning, about three o'clock, we awoke to see a cadaverous man seated in the kitchen. He wildly moved two fingers of his right hand around the table top and didn't stop when our mother asked if he'd like some coffee.

"No, thanks," he rasped. The fingers kept drumming.

"Tea?" Mother inquired patiently.

"No! No tea." The fingers drummed on.

"Water?" she asked meekly.

He stopped drumming instantly. "What? And get my stomach all wet?"

Bob fell out of bed laughing so we both got up to meet Leonard Barr.

Annette asked him what all the drumming was about. He explained he was rehearsing a new dance routine. He described it as a nervous man crossing Broadway during lunch hour. It became part of his repertoire.

* * *

At one time the apartment had been part of a suite. A plain wooden door separated the area where Bob and I slept from what was now another apartment where two New York University students lived.

One night, when Bob and I were alone, we heard laughter and merriment next door. Bob peeked through the large keyhole, then recommended I take a turn. The two young men and their girl friends were stark-ass naked. Bob and I fought for the rights to that precious keyhole when I saw it fill up with flesh. One young miss' lovely rump was pressed firmly against the door, directly in line with the keyhole. Robert simply couldn't resist his impulses. He dashed into the kitchen, quickly returning with a fistful of uncooked sphaghetti. When he stroked the young lady's bottom with a long strand, she howled like a banshee. Consternation reigned.

❄ ❄ ❄

We moved from the relatively luxurious surroundings on 56th Street to a superb example of Early Ghetto on 98th Street, near Central Park West. In those lean days, Brother Robert was the wolf-pack leader, constantly on the alert to danger, adventure, or something to eat. Now and then he'd lope alongside me, directing me to any of the three. A prime example was his association with a Puerto Rican lad whose nickname, to absolutely no one's surprise, was "Shrimp."

"Da Shrimp" stood some 4-foot-11, weighed a cool ninety-nine pounds, and was the most dapper dresser I ever knew. Here we were in the wallowing doldrums of the Great Depression, and there was Shrimp, every thread impeccably correct. His shoes were elegant, his wrist watch magnificent. And his apartment . . .

I have never seen such an accumulation of "things" outside of the American Museum of History. Guns, swords, busts, typewriters, daggers, paintings—a treasure trove of goods. All of them, I would discover, stolen. "Da Shrimp" headed a mob of thieves with a logical, efficient modus operandi. He would read the society pages, learn that Mr. and Mrs. So-and-So were leaving on vacation, and beeline to their residence.

After checking to make sure they were really gone, he'd send in the boys to clean out the place.

On one of his expeditions, he saw a beautiful grand piano in a Riverside Drive apartment.

By coincidence, he had just read a request for such a piano in the want ads of *The New York Times,* placed by a prospective buyer in New Jersey. When Shrimp called, the buyer was eager to purchase a Steinway for the modest fee that Shrimp proposed.

Shrimp rented a truck, printed *PIANO MOVERS* on the sides and went to the apartment with his cronies, Frankie, Dean, George and Freddy, now outfitted in white coveralls with *ACE PIANO MOVERS* lettered on their backs. They brought the piano to the street and were about to heave it into the truck when a policeman strolled around the corner and eyed them amiably. Shrimp asked the friendly cop if he would help them lift the piano, since his considerable bulk would make it easier. The smiling face agreed and soon the piano was on its way to New Jersey.

Shrimp netted a cool $2,500. That, in 1931, was a tremendous amount of money.

❄ ❄ ❄

New York is many things to many people. To me it was a wonderland of sounds, sights and smells that linger in the corners of my mind to this day. I would hurry to the Museum of Natural History as though drawn by a magnet, spending hours drinking in the exhibits. One in particular was of a family of mountain lions gracing a cave that overlooked the Grand Canyon of the Arizonas.

Today, with the advent of television, the impact of such a spectacular sight might well be lost on modern youth, but it started a fire inside me that has yet to burn out.

Those exhibits made me want to see those great vistas, to cross those mighty mountains, to become an active part of a world that only existed then in the confines of that magnificent museum.

Bob and I would prowl through that great edifice, absorbing African villages, South Seas isles, Eskimo habitats and American Indian camps until we were awash with a desire to see them for ourselves. We would cross Central Park to the east side, spending hours at the Museum of Fine Arts "oohing and aahing" over the collection of pistols, swords, vases, urns, armor and jewels that held untold tales of the past. We secretly vowed that someday, somehow, we would see faraway places and be an active part of a much bigger world than we knew.

At night, during the summer months, we would go to the Mall in Central Park with hundreds of others to hear Edmond Franklin Goldman's band, a must for us in those days. He featured a trumpet player, nothing short of miraculous, who kept us enthralled throughout the evenings.

One evening, as Bob, Shrimp and I left the park to return to our respective apartments, we passed two creatures of the netherworld. One took a long, limpid look at me and lisped, "Cute!"

"Her" partner studied me casually then, turning away indifferently, intoned, "Long on neck but short on brow."

Robert, again as a brake to my ego, would often look me over, then repeat that infamous put-down: "Long on neck but short on brow."

❄ ❄ ❄

It might appear that I was a brawler, even at the tender age of eleven. I refute the inference on the grounds that Fate always seemed to force me to use my fists. For example, one bright summer morning, I was sitting on the front steps of Shrimp's apartment when a young boy and his girl passed by. The girl had a classically beautiful derriere. I would defy anyone other than a blind man not to have stared at it. The boy friend, Hermie Goldstein, promptly whacked me in the chin for daring to look. I leaped up from the stoop and the fight was on. Before long I had Hermie leaning helplessly against an iron railing. Suddenly, I became aware that the immediate neighborhood was awfully quiet.

I looked behind me and stopped beating on my antagonist.

Hermie belonged to a mob bossed by an arrogant bully, Bernie Sweeney—nineteen, stocky and physically tough. His gang numbered close to twenty ruffians, who now stood nearby, clutching pieces of pipe, bottles and assorted clubs. Like a pack of hungry wolves, they were waiting patiently for me to finish off their wounded member before closing in.

It was late morning and I wondered where all the cops were who inevitably showed up whenever we didn't need them. Bernie smiled smugly as his gang slowly closed in for the kill. Suddenly, all hell broke loose.

Shrimp seemed to appear from nowhere, walking straight up to Bernie Sweeney and jamming an automatic pistol into his solar plexus. His finger pressed against the trigger; his arm shook with a rage that boded ill for the Irishman.

"Jock," the Shrimp hissed, "is my fren'! Nobody touches Jock! You got your bums, Bernie. But I got Frenchy, Dean, George and Freddie. An' we don' carry sticks an' stones, Bernie." Here he pressed harder against the terrified Sweeney's stomach. "We carry guns, Bernie. Guns! So—Jock—don'—get—hurt, Bernie! You got dat?"

Sweeney was transformed into a lump of uncongealed pudding. He gulped for air, never taking his eyes off the deadly piece that was a hair's breadth from blowing him away. "Yeah, Shrimp! Yeah! Nobody touches him!" Sweeney was scarcely audible but his whole group nodded in mute agreement. It was best they did. That afternoon, Shrimp's mob made a quiet appearance on the street. Their message was crystal clear.

❄ ❄ ❄

One morning I awakened to bright sunshine, brimming with plans for a busy day: The Empire State Building, the Hudson River, Central Park, the Museum of Natural History. I leaped out of bed and reached for my pants. No pants. *No pants?*

My sailor brother-in-law, Ernie Longaker, Annette's husband, had given me a pair of the old-style button-front Navy blues, which had grown very dear to me. Besides, they were the only pants I had. They were definitely not on the chair over which I had draped them the night before.

Brother Robert offered a solution. "You know how careless you are," he said casually. "You thought you were tossing them on the chair but you threw them out the window."

I looked out the window but, four stories down, I could see no trace of my beloved sailor pants. On the following day, as I walked disconsolately down 98th Street in my new but totally uncharismatic pants, I spied my tell-tale buttoned-down trousers. They now graced Joey Chicori, a "Sly Stallone" of his day who cut quite a swath in the female population of 98th. I approached him like a destroyer bearing down on a cruiser. "Hey, Joey. Where d'ja get my pants?" I was brimming with indignation.

"Dese ain't your pants. De're my pants. Your brudder sol' 'em to me." He showed righteous indignation.

"Sold 'em to you?" I was aghast. "For how much?"

Joey reared back and stared at me. "Fifty cents. Dat's how much."

Possession is nine-tenths of the law. Especially when someone is as big as Joey Chicori.

❄ ❄ ❄

A fixture on 98th Street was a long-jawed, lean Colombian nicknamed Nick. No one knew his last name and nobody ever bothered to find it out. He smoked marijuana so adroitly that whenever he saw a patrolman coming, he would invert the reefer, placing it inside his mouth until the cop went by. Few knew how Nick earned a living, but Bob got a broad hint after he had a falling out with Joey Chicori and was approached by Nick one late afternoon with a horrifying proposition.

"I like you, kid." Nick was matter-of-fact about it. "You're a good friend of da Shrimp, so I like you. Now you got trouble wid Chicori. For a buck I get rid of him. For anyone else, a fin. For you, a buck."

The Colombian suggested that he would hide in the darkened basement which Chicori called home, then slip a knife between his ribs when he came down the steps. For a buck. Bob gently turned down the offer. Nick's style wasn't for him.

The janitor of Shrimp's apartment building was his uncle, Charlie Costello, who brewed up man-made anisette in his basement. On many a soft summer night, we'd sit up on the rooftop, sipping anisette and passing around a pair of powerful binoculars that Shrimp's gang had purloined from a Riverside Drive apartment.

Towering up from 90th Street were some early high-rise apartments, whose occupants were unaware that their every nocturnal movement was being ogled by a pack of youths who could make out the birthmarks on a girl's rump with those glasses. We saw old men chasing pretty young girls around their rooms, young men creating fanciful modes and methods of sensual activity, even some sessions of he-ing and he-ing, along with some she-ing and she-ing. It was quite an education for an eleven-year-old.

❄❄❄

In 1930 Annette met a fascinating New York cab driver. He was a legitimate heir to the Orloff dynasty, a family of White Russians almost completely decimated in the 1917 Bolshevik revolution. The Orloff Diamond was famed as one of the magnificent gems of the world. And now Sergei Orloff, an heir to that tradition, drove a hack in Manhattan.

He picked Annette up on a routine call. She was charmed by him, as we all were—he was the living embodiment of what Russian aristocracy was all about. His struggle with the English language was a delight to hear.

One morning, he stopped by the apartment for coffee, perplexed by an incident the previous night. "A man got in my cab and kept calling me his Bodeyay. You are my Bodeyay. Okay, Bodeyay?'" He turned to my mother. "What is this Bodeyay'?"

Bob sprang to the rescue, explaining the term "buddy" to the confused Russian, who broke out into a warm smile. He had a new friend in America.

As our first Christmas in New York approached I was again caught up in the Christmas spirit. Even though the Great Depression lay like a miasma of pain over the land, the sound of sleigh bells excited me as much as ever. Grandmother Gunderson had promised to send us a grand package of goodies from the farm: A turkey, yams, a smoked ham and fresh country butter. We waited with marked impatience for the treasure to arrive. Christmas Eve came. No package. The larder was bare except for a jar of mustard and a bag of shelled walnuts Brother Robert had filched from a restaurant.

Mother would choose a half-walnut as though it were caviar, dip the morsel into the mustard and savor it. "My, how delicious." She smilingly enticed us all to try some. I confess that walnuts and mustard beat the hell out of nothing.

On Christmas Day the package arrived. We had a house choked to the gunnels with people and among them was Sergei Orloff. When dinner was served, we all gave thanks in our individual ways and Sergei cut into the butter. The inside of that cube was the most bilious-looking green I have ever seen. Sergei's face paled. Perhaps he thought that the Russian Secret Police was trying to poison him. Mother, as usual, came to the rescue. She examined the cube, finding a piece of copper wire in its depths. She deduced that the butter churn had been scrubbed with a wire brush. The rest of the butter was fine. The joys of Christmas filled the air again.

HANGING OUT AT THE STABLES WITH WAXY GORDON AND THE BOYS

BROTHER ROBERT has always had an ability to ferret out the most unusual characters. I am convinced that this ability, coupled with a phenomenal memory, molded him into a superb actor. He is a fantastic mime. I am sure that his facile ease with foreign languages stems from being able to catch every pronouncement perfectly and to trap it somewhere in his mind forever.

I look back at our youth and remember the Markowitz boys, Charlie Costello, Nick the Colombian, Joey Chicori, Shrimp Cruzado, Sergei Orloff, Leonard Barr and hundreds of others. I have but to mention a name and that person springs to life through Bob's reenactment, complete with gestures and dialects.

Predictably, in *that* neighborhood, the scales weighed heavily in favor of Robert finding gentlemen who walked on the seamy side. The crowd that hung around "Waxy" Gordon's Riding Stable confirmed that supposition.

Waxy was a mobster of repute. Ill, of course. His riding stable most certainly was a front for a more lucrative business and the men who regularly drove up to the stables were a hard-eyed lot.

I never had anything to do with them, although I came close to getting killed by a lesser hoodlum, Joe Mazzula, who hung around the fringes of the more formidable mugs to bask in their dubious light. Mazzula had an arrest record at the 101st Precinct that more than matched the station's numbers.

According to Brother Bob, Joe was once arrested while driving through Central Park in a Rolls Royce. The police knew that Mazzula, unless he had just finished rolling a drunken sailor on Riverside Drive, couldn't afford subway fare.

"How come youse guys figured it wasn't my car?" Joe asked.

He was wearing a ratty black-knit skullcap, dirty leather jacket and faded denims.

The cops looked at each other and couldn't help laughing.

Have you ever been caught staring at somebody and couldn't avert your eyes? One day Mazzula, high on something, saw me doing just that. The staring contest was on.

He became intensely agitated and screamed "Stop starin' at me, kid!"

I was all of eleven, as foolish as I was brash. "I can look at you if I want," was my snappy retort.

Mazzula's voice became a fierce whisper. "I said, don't stare at me!" His hand crawled inside his leather jacket and closed on the butt of a .38 revolver. He was drawing it out when "Sully" Sullivan, a bear of a man, locked his powerful arms around Mazzula in a smothering hold.

"Run, kid, run!" shouted Sully.

I stood my ground. "I ain't gonna run from nobody."

"He's just a kid, Joe," Sully growled to Mazzula.

"Tell him don't stare! Don't stare!" Mazzula screamed the words. I broke and ran for home. That voice rang with madness; I can hear it to this day.

That night, Brother Robert and I had a quiet chat. Sully, who liked Bob very much, had told him about his "brazen" brother. Bob's advice: "Stay away from Waxy Gordon's Stables. Sully won't protect you from me!" I stayed away.

❄❄❄

Bob was thirteen when an event cemented forever his love for theater. A friend of Annette's was a dancer at the glamorous (to us) Minsky Burlesque Theatre, a landmark on 52nd Street. Bob evinced a desire to see the show but his tender age was a drawback to gaining entrance. The lady friend devised a plan. She took Bob to the theater with her in a taxi and, upon being deposited close to the stage door, enclosed the enraptured Robert in the folds of her ample fur coat and smuggled him past stagedoor security.

Recently Bob told me, "She had absolutely nothing on under the coat. I found myself engulfed in a sea of fragrant, whirling flesh. I lost my heart to the theater forever."

A natural ability to absorb and duplicate sights, sounds and feelings. . . a host of characters from which to draw . . . and an intimate taste of the raw earthiness that is so often a part of being "in the business" . . . all these things produced a star.

Times were hard. It's no myth that college professors sold apples on the streets. I saw a lot of them but seldom had the nickel for a purchase. Thus, I was ecstatically happy when a local market hired me as a delivery boy. Orders would be called in from steady customers who lived in the elegant high-rise apartments that lined Central Park West. I would tote the groceries up to the building, ring the corresponding apartment bell on the dumbwaiter, and wait for the apparatus to reach the basement floor. I'd put the groceries in the compartment and haul it up by a pulley arrangement to the customer's floor. For this, I received a magnificent fifty cents a day. I was delighted—until Brother Robert stepped in.

"What kind of job is that?" he demanded. "Now, if you really want to make it worth your while, let me help you." He took an empty coffee can, pasted a piece of white paper to it and artistically labeled it *TIP BOX.* He instructed me to display it prominently on my next delivery.

I walked toward the looming apartment building with a sense of impending disaster. Fearfully, I raised the dumbwaiter to the eleventh floor. There was an ominous silence, then a torrent of invective flooded the shaft, burning me with humiliation and embarrassment. I was fired when I stepped through the front door of the grocery store.

By 1932, the Great Depression had taken an even grimmer hold on America. The Mitchum boys were not unscathed. Annette's husband was being transferred to the Navy base in Long Beach, California. The cost of living in New York was becoming insurmountable. A change for us was inevitable.

YOU CAN TAKE THE BOY OUT OF THE COUNTRY BUT . . .

WE MOVED BACK to Delaware. The sights and sounds of New York—the subway trains, the Hudson River, Central Park and New Year's Eve in Times Square—faded into memories. We now lived in a makeshift apartment in the "metropolis" of Rising Sun, known to the local gentry as Five Points (it boasted five hundred hardy souls). Orchard country surrounded us, abounding in apples and peaches.

We stayed with Grandmother, the Tetreaults and their four children (Louise, Pat and Gilbert now had a baby sister, Gloria) in an apartment that had been divided into a duplex on the ground floor of a church of a fundamentalist conviction. I am eternally grateful to the Christian spirit that flowed from its minister, for our first winter there was abysmal.

Since we were at the mercy of the elements, firewood was a precious commodity. All on my own, I came to the conclusion that it was better to be warm and slightly immoral than dead and holy. I would crawl into the church's basement, gather a load of the church's beautiful firewood, put it on the porch, then transfer it to the roaring wood stove that kept us alive.

Bob and I assuming our personas as "Them Ornery Mitchum Boys" on Woodside Farm in 1929. Behind me, his tail jutting to the right, is our hound dog Sport.

Quite early one morning, I was in the basement loading up when I saw a pair of boots planted in front of the basement window. I crawled hurriedly through the window only to see the preacher heading toward me. My heart stopped for a beat until he nodded solemnly at me and said "Good morning," walking on out of sight. In my many sojourns into the basement, I had left a trail of bark on the porch that a blind man could have followed.

That gracious man knew of our need and never mentioned it once in the year we lived there.

Delaware hadn't changed much in the two years we had been gone. In my experiences in Philadelphia and New York I had learned to "jump away." The local youths in Rising Sun challenged Robert but once, then they all wanted to "put on the gloves" with me. In quick succession, I bested all takers, including Eddie Graham. That seemed a great accomplishment at the time. Eddie starred in baseball, basketball and football, but he couldn't box worth a damn.

I would meet Eddie one last time in 1951, while I was in Colorado Springs making "One Minute to Zero" with Brother Bob. During World War II Eddie had served directly under Lorne Norstad at Supreme Headquarters Allied Expeditionary Forces Headquarters and had been called back to service when the Korean War broke out.

He was one of the top experts in the field of nerve gasses, and the Army Air Force refused to let him go. Bob had contacted him and—to put me on—asked him to impersonate the great middleweight boxer Rocky Graziano on the picture's location.

I had a grand reunion that day, for the man standing beside an Army tank—dressed in a garish sports coat and open shirt and sporting dark glasses— was Eddie, and not the bruising fighter I had expected to meet. Bob and I visited his home and were impressed by the importance of his position with the Air Force. That importance weighed heavily on Eddie—too heavily. It was a sad blow to hear just a few short years later that the stress of his position had caused his heart to fail. He was a casualty of war as certainly as if he had been killed in combat.

Charley Maloney was another of my childhood chums in Rising Sun. He was wildly enthusiastic about everything he did but always fell just short of attaining his goal. I boxed Charley often. He alway lost, but each time he came back with unrivaled enthusiasm to try again. Once, in a football game against Newark, Delaware, he got bounced to the ground so severely that he received a mild concussion.

It was in October and the playing field was as hard as concrete. Charley jumped up, grabbed his fallen helmet and ran ninety-six yards to a spurious touchdown—the wrong way!

Like Eddie Graham, Charley Maloney led a life that inevitably took him to a strange fate. During World War II he was a Tech 5 in the 16th Cavalry of the Tenth Army Divison, Battalion 129. He was assisting an officer into a command car in Luxemburg when a sniper's bullet cut him down. After the war, he was brought home to lie in Barrett's Chapel Cemetery near Frederica, Delaware.

THAT ALL-ENCOMPASSING WORD

THE HUB OF RISING SUN was Faulkner's Store, where a customer could buy anything from sewing needles to shotgun shells. And you could hear all the local gossip for free. It was on the porch of the store that I first heard the all-encompassing word, "poontang."

The word flowed in and out of conversations so continually I dared to show my ignorance to the small knot of townsfolk clustered around the storefront by asking what it meant.

"What's poontang?" the oldster repeated in amazement. "If the Lord made anything better'n poontang, He kept it for hisself!"

Years later, at the base of towering Pikes Peak in Colorado Springs, Bob was interviewed by a girl student writing for her high school paper. "How do you like Colorado? It's not like New York, is it?" She went on in her inquisition by asking if he spent much time hunting and fishing.

"I fish for relaxation," Bob replied.

"You don't hunt?" Her tone carried a veiled belligerence. (After all, everyone is supposed to hunt in Colorado.)

Bob surveyed her coolly. "My brother and I spent our stripling years hunting the elusive poontang."

"What's a poontang?" She sat with pencil at the ready.

"A furry little creature—small, if you're lucky—that hides in crevasses, rocks and rills throughout the land." Bob eyed her blandly.

She wrote furiously, then looked up at him. "Did you get any?" She didn't crack a smile.

Bob heaved a heavy sigh. "Practically decimated the breed."

She scribbled rapidly. "Were they good eating?"

Robert rolled his eyes heavenward. "'Mighty lak a rose'!"

That too went into the hopper.

Five hundred papers were printed before her shocked journalism teacher ordered the presses to halt. The studio bought all the copies at $2,500—$5.00 apiece.

❄ ❄ ❄

My awareness of the difference between boys and girls was enhanced by some of the pithy remarks of rural Delawarians. For instance, on seeing a woman bending *low* over her garden patch, one of my young compatriots chortled—no doubt in imitation of his elders—"Bend over, baby, I'll drive y'home!"

When a high school star pitcher told his girl friend "I can give you twelve inches," she roared with raucous laughter; he added lamely, "Well, I'm gonna do it four times."

And when Eddie Graham would miss the ball in warmup practice, he'd holler "Balls! Ever see 'em on your grandmother?" That didn't make sense but we thought it was hilarious. There were a lot more unprintables floating around, but having the seamier sides of the difference between boys and girls so graphically pointed out to me at that early age did nothing to dilute my feelings of respect and adulation of womankind. I love 'em.

❄ ❄ ❄

One of the openers to an evening of eye-popping discussions at Faulkner's came under the heading of "Who's puttin' out?" The answer followed a set pattern. "Maude's puttin' out," someone would proffer. "Hell," another someone would growl, "everybody knows Maude's puttin' out."

Invariably one person would throw out a tentative feeler. "Hear tell Clara's puttin' out." Ol' Ed Faulkner would turn on the scoundrel scornfully. "She ain't puttin' out to nobody but Turk." Since Turk was 6-foot-3 and a superb athlete, no sane person would carry that discussion any further.

A large mill pond was just a mile down the road. All during the hot summer months, it was a hub of activity. Bob and I would borrow a skiff and fish on the pond at dawn's first light. It teemed with pike and bass.

Ol' Man Voshel owned the pond and the gristmill and he gave wholeheartedly to the community. He even built a float with a diving board on it. A strange ritual developed because of that float.

In early summer, it was crowded with youngsters who appeared asleep or dulled by the morning sun . . . until Maude Schwartz yelled from shore, "Anybody wanna come to the cabin?" Instantly, the float was abandoned. Bodies arced into the water and eager, knowledgeable youths hastened forthwith to a deserted shack in the woods lining the northeastern shore.

Fifteen-year-old Maude, as a ritualistic event, took on five boys per session. Five—no more, no less. That is, until the preacher's son decided to join in the fun. Bill Whedbee was much younger than the other four boys who swam in such great haste to "meet" Maude, so it came to pass that ol' Maude turned him down, breaking her string of quintet humping.

His "dick" was too little, she complained. Besides, it had turned blue from the cold water.

FUGITIVE FROM A CHAIN GANG

IN THE SUMMER of 1932, Bob disappeared on one of his journeys, riding into Georgia on a freight that carried a large number of hobos. In the boxcar, a young boy of about twelve stood at the open doorway and aimed outward, but the erratic bouncing flung his urine onto a nearby outstretched leg. The enraged bo threatened to punch the youth out but was stayed when a soft, Georgian voice drawled from the sidelines, "Leave the boy alone."

The bo turned and, in a decidedly New England accent, ordered the Georgian to get up and fight. The Southerner, a tall redhead, climbed to his feet. However, when he unfolded his lanky frame, he had a wicked looking stick-blade in his hand.

The Yankee gasped, "Why, you've got a knife!"

"Do you expect me to fight with my hands? Like a kid?"

The Yankee retreated in silence to the far end of the car, the incident closed. Even at fourteen, Bob was wryly amused that the tough guy backed down so quickly at the sight of cold steel.

Bob was picked up on a vagrancy charge one Friday night in Savannah, Georgia, and held in the city jail until the following Monday, when he was brought before the judge. The administrator of justice eyed him balefully, then absent-mindedly shuffled some papers on his desk. Bob was numbed by what he heard.

"You're guilty of robbing a shoe store. I hereby sentence you to five years in the State Penitentiary."

"Your Honor!" Bob's voice rose in terror. "When did this robbery take place?"

The judge became angry at what he judged to be insolence. "You know very well it happened on Saturday night."

"Your Honor, sir," Bob went on, "if you'll check your records, you'll find that I've been in your jail since Friday."

The judge's mouth fell open and his eyes showed his embarrassment. Unfortunately, some people in the court laughed aloud. The judge lightened the sentence—but not much to the ears of one as young as Bob: "Ninety days on the Brown's County Farm." He banged his gavel in wounded pride. Robert became a member of the infamous Georgia Chain Gang at the age of fourteen—for vagrancy.

Day after day, he and the other unfortunates on the gang shuffled along the highways, cutting weeds and underbrush that threatened to engulf the concrete or macadam. "The Man" kept a steely eye on them, cradling a high-powered rifle. One morning, Robert decided to run for it. The guard got off a few shots as Bob disappeared into the heavy undergrowth that presaged a huge swamp ahead.

Bob swam, crawled and sometimes walked his way to freedom in South Carolina, which borders the swamp on its northern rim. He collapsed from exhaustion in a weed patch where he was found by two young girls. They brought him to their home, fed him and cleaned his clothes. When he regained his strength, he started the long journey home to Delaware.

The chain used each night to shackle him to his bunk had eroded a large hole in Bob's left ankle. The scum and debris of the swamp nested in that sore and by the time Bob got back to Delaware, blood poisoning had set in.

The local doctors urged Mother to give them permission to amputate his terribly swollen leg.

She refused, instigating a regimen of treatment by taking dark, heavy swamp leaves from the nearby bogs, boiling them, and placing them over Bob's gaping ankle wound.

The natural drawing of the leaves sucked out great masses of infection and, within days, the swelling decreased dramatically. In two weeks' time, the amazed doctors pronounced him completely cured.

Voshel's millpond stirred Brother Bob into an enterprise that kept him busy for most of the summer of '33.

For therapy, he began constructing a dugout canoe. With infinite patience he chopped, he chipped, he scraped, he burned and whittled his way into the bowels of a huge log.

During his periods of labor, I fell deeply in love with Thelma Lister, a slender wisp of a girl. Much too shy to tell her of my devotion, I worshipped her from afar. I'd sit on the sand at Bower's Beach, peer at her from a safe distance of over a hundred yards and dream of being bold enough to go up to her and pledge my troth. That day never came.

Meanwhile, back at the log, Brother Robert had hacked it into some semblance of a Mexican dugout canoe. It didn't look at all like the graceful proas of the Polynesians. As a matter of fact, it looked a bit ungainly.

When spring came and the ice thawed from Voshel's, Bob dragged the canoe down to the icy waters and pushed it in. It promptly sank like a stone. Later, someone explained to him that green oak wood is not conducive to making a watertight canoe. I suspect a tear slid from Bob's eyes when he saw his labors glide silently to the murky bottom of the lake.

MURDER AT REHOBETH BEACH

ONE OF THE LAST things that we did in Delaware was to go with a church group to Rehobeth Beach. It was an idyllic time of year. The weather was balmy, the ocean a bright blue with soft white caps caressing each wave.

It was early evening and, as I walked toward a miniature golf course for a round of play, I noticed a young couple walking hand in hand along the edge of the brightly lit course. I saw, but did not heed, a young man who walked steadily toward the cooing pair.

Suddenly the young man became starkly real as he lifted a gun and pumped three shots into his rival's body. The youth, moments before so blissfully in love, now already dead, walked automatically for a few more steps, then slid in what seemed slow motion onto the sidewalk.

For some moments there was silence, then a terrified screaming rent the air. The young killer simply stood motionlessly in front of his hysterical former lover until the police took him away.

❄ ❄ ❄

Our counselors planned to erase the picture of the murder from our minds on the last night we were in Rehobeth by taking us on a "hoo-dang" hunt. There are no "hoo-dangs" but we didn't know that. Two dozen of us beat sticks, shone our flashlights and hollered "Hoo-dang, hoo-dang" for two hours without catching a glimpse of those singularly elusive birds. Those of us who strayed farther afield caught more than one sight of a whiskey runner; we stumbled on a boat being unloaded right there on the beach. Recognizing us as kids, the contraband pirates shouted at us, firing several shots into the air. In short order, we were legging it pell-mell toward the distant lights of the boardwalk.

Charlie Grace was the catcher for the Caesar Rodney baseball team and, quite honestly, the slowest man afoot on the squad. We were all amazed to see Charlie sprint by us as though we were anchored.

When we reached the safety of the boardwalk, Bill Whedbee asked,

"What's the matter, Charlie, were you scared?" Charlie's lip pouted petulantly and his answer lies forever engraved in our memories. "Ain't a fellow got a right to run if he wants to?" He snarled it out, but he never did admit he was scared.

During this period, I had been attending school at Caesar Rodney High School in Delaware. (Caesar Rodney was one of the signers of the Declaration of Independence and had ridden his horse from Dover to Philadelphia in record time in order to be at that famous conclave.)

There, I had met a beautiful young lady, Dorothy Spence, and my heart was hers. I made the mistake of introducing her to Brother Robert. He insisted that I skate with him from Rising Sun to Camden that he might "spark" her. I would sit moodily aside as he murmured sweet nothings into her attentive ears. Abruptly at nine o'clock, he would order me to saddle up and skate back to Five Points. I hid my thoughts of this scurrilous rapscallion, this arrogant big brother, this pallid womanizer.

Dorothy and Robert have been married since 1940.

Oh, by the way, in Cherokee the word for "love" is "poontang."

❄ ❄ ❄

Brother Robert had a lot of experiences behind him by 1934. He had "run off" as a child in Connecticut and had just recently returned from his ill-fated trip to Georgia. My only try at "runnin' off" was our escape attempt with Manuel Barque that ended 25 miles away from the Woodside Farm.

Now Bob proposed that he and I—along with Carroll Davis, a young man he had met while serving in a Civilian Conservation Camp—leave Delaware and head for California. Our first stop was to be Ensley, Alabama, for that was Carroll's birthplace. Bob was sixteen, I was fourteen on this most adventurous trek of our lives.

As usual, Bob had a plan. With Mother's blessing, we prepared to wend our way to the Golden State. I was touched by my mother's parting gifts to me—a pair of clean socks and a new handkerchief. It doesn't seem like much today, but at the time it represented about all the money she had.

Our beloved grandmother Petrine with our mother Ann, in a photo taken around 1941 in the backyard of the house we rented then at 954 Palm Avenue in Hollywood. The chickenhouse in the back had been converted into modest lodging for any family member with no place to spend the night. Mom and I often played canasta in those days, and sister Julie would cajole me with "How can you win? She cheats!" To which my mother would reply, "Of course I do. How else could I win?"

BOOK TWO

WESTWARD YEN

BOOK TWO

WHICH WAY IS WEST?

THE THREE of us hitchhiked back to New York City where Brother Robert promptly brought us to the great Grand Central Market on the lower west side of Manhattan. Hundreds of trucks were gathered there, vehicles of every description from all over the country.

Bob approached a ten-tonner loaded with cabbages that bore a Florida license. "Could we hitch a ride with you when you head back down South?" he asked.

"Where you-all headin'?" the driver asked.

"Alabama," said Bob.

"Soon's we're unloaded, get aboard."

I loaded up on the sights, sounds and smells of the marketplace while the cabbages were unloaded. Then, with my meager pack on my back, I clambered into the stake-bodied truck with Bob and Carroll Davis. Soon, we were on our way through the Hudson Tunnel to a thrilling new world.

Seeing the landmarks of Washington D.C. for the first time is still etched

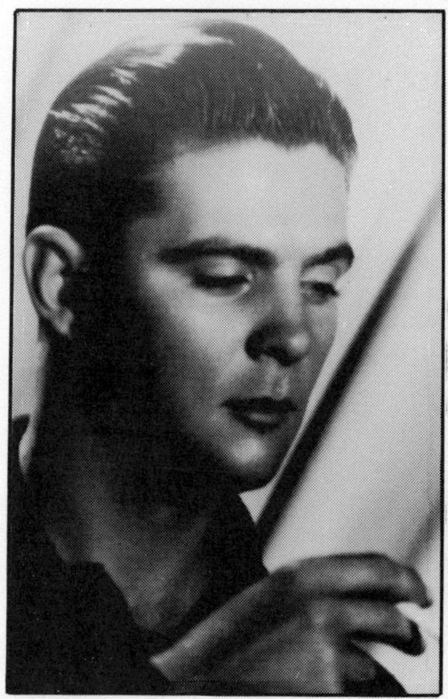

I was taking on a new image in the 1930s . . . handsome, suave, debonair, sophisticated . . . the yachting cap was on loan from a friend.

in my mind. The Washington Monument and the Capitol itself brought a sense of awe that I have never shaken. The truck moved steadily through the city maze, heading into Virginia. We noticed every now and then that an empty whiskey bottle was dispatched from the cab and the truck would accelerate appreciably, but I really didn't care much.

Roaring through the North Carolina mountains was heady stuff. My first sight of palmettos in South Carolina brought me an even greater excitement. I felt a great pang of sorrow when the truck flew by a road junction that led to Lane, the little town where my father had been born, but which to this day I have never seen.

❄ ❄ ❄

The speedy trip ended safely, in spite of our growing trepidation over those hurled bottles, on the outskirts of Jacksonville, Florida. Now the journey to Ensley began. Our rides were slow in coming and it took a while to reach the small city of Dothan. Once again, Brother Robert's acumen and experience came to the fore.

Ravenously hungry and a little short of "the ready," we were forced to knock on doors. Bob headed resolutely for the nicest residential area. "Why," he reasoned, "should we hit up poor people who can barely manage for themselves?" His reasoning proved more than correct. It brought not just a meal but exposed me for the first time to elegance.

Bob rapped on the back gate of a mansion he had intuitively chosen. A charming, urbane Black man appeared. "What is it you gentlemen want?" the servant asked.

"The three of us've come a long way today, sir. We're hungry. Could you help us?" Bob was gravely dignified.

"How fortunate for you." The servant beamed at us. "The master of the house and his lady were just now called away to Birmingham on urgent business. I had just finished preparing lunch for them when I found they had to leave immediately." He disappeared into the house, reappearing in a short while bearing a large silver serving dish whose center displayed a beautifully baked fish with parsley decorations, slices of lemon and paprika. He returned a second time with another tray regally bearing new potatoes, fresh peas, warm French bread and a set of serving plates, complete with silver cutlery. As we sat on the curb, three young waifs in soiled, tattered clothing with no money, we marvelled at the service; not only did we have magnificently prepared foods on the finest of tableware . . . the servant brought us goblets of white wine.

Many years later, I saw "O. Henry's Full House," a 20th Century-Fox quartet of vignettes based on short stories by O. Henry. "The Cop and the Anthem" featured Charles Laughton as an impoverished gentleman who, on Christmas Eve, sweeps into an elegant restaurant and orders roast duck. His dinner clothes have long passed their day of splendor and his white gloves are full of holes, but because he wears an air of disdainful arrogance, he is accorded a full dinner. When the check is presented, he flicks an ash from his newly lit Cuban cigar, looks balefully at the waiter and rasps, "No money."

We left Dothan blissfully content. What a thrill to find that such gentle, kind people lived in the world.

We arrived in Ensley early the next afternoon to discover that Carroll Davis' sister was a marvelous cook. We gorged ourselves on bacon, eggs and hominy grits—oh, Lord, the South shall rise again. Carroll's brother-in-law was some character: He had worked in the steel mills at Birmingham without paying his gas bill for two years. He revealed to us an elaborate underground schematic of pipes and valves he had improvised that tapped into the main line before it reached the local meters.

At the age of fourteen, I couldn't understand why he had spent so much time and energy to thwart the gas company out of what, even then, was a small amount of money. "Beat 'em! By God, I beat 'em!" he exclaimed. (Vaguely, I became aware of the strange phenomenon that mankind feels it has to "beat" somebody at something. It's a recurrent theme. I've seen it since in thousands of guises.)

Bob and I spent two idyllic days in restful Ensley, then decided to hitchhike to California. As the vaunted bard of the Scottish Highlands, Bobby Burns, once wrote, "The best laid plans of mice and men oft gang agley." They sure as hell do!

ADVENTURES WITH THE WARRIOR RIVER MOUNTAIN MEN

AFTER A FULL SOUTHERN BREAKFAST, we bade farewell to Carroll and his family and put out our thumbs toward what we fervently hoped was California. A 1929 Buick sedan carrying three men stopped and the passenger in front beckoned us to get in. The driver, a burly young man in his early twenties, was a little drunk. His passenger introduced himself as Frank, allowing that it was his car but that he was letting Joe drive because *he* was too drunk to be in the car without "somethin' to hold onto." Half of the back seat was taken up by Billy Bob and his guitar. Billy Bob, a lean, slight man with a black beard, stopped playing the instrument long enough to thrust out his hand to us.

We introduced ourselves and then Joe, tippling from a bottle, turned and asked us where we were heading.

"California," Bob quaked his answer.

"Ah don' know where'n hell that is, but we're goin' to the Warrior River."

Billy Bob launched into a parody on the verse of that great old tune, "When You Wore a Tulip." The lyrics he sang were a far cry from those sung in music halls throughout the country. They were, however, pungent enough to be remembered.

"I met her in a whorehouse in an old Kentucky town.
She didn't wear no gown.
Her drawers were hangin' down.
I loved her in that whorehouse in an old Kentucky town.
And in her belly, I throbbed a ten-pound boy!"

Bob and I looked at each other, wondering if we'd ever get to California. We joined in the singing of the legitimate words of the chorus with Bob taking the tenor to my melody. The three were impressed and we felt that our singing was our salvation. As long as we harmonized, they were jovial. "If You Knew Susie" kept them engrossed enough that Joe drove off a dirt road and crashed through a lady's clothesline. With the mountain woman's drawers and other unmentionables flapping from the hood ornament, he veered back to the road. The lady's screaming could be heard for some time, then the sound of the old Buick's engine reigned.

That is, until Frank yelled out, "By God, she's here! This is where she is!" Joe stopped the car on a promontory overlooking a great valley. The three piled out and began furiously digging into the dirt. Frank roared out, "Got 'er, by God! I got 'er!"

"'Er" was a gallon of white lightning. Joe, Frank and Billy Bob passed it around to each other, then Joe suddenly remembered his manners. Affably he handed the jug to Brother Robert. "Have a drink." Bob took a swallow of the stuff without blinking an eye. Now it was my turn. Joe watched me expectantly.

"I do not drink." My holier-than-thou reply triggered a reaction that drastically changed the tenor of the morning. Joe breathed heavily as he thrust the jug at me again.

"You have a drink," he ordered, "or we'll throw you off the God-damned mountain!" I took a long look at the three Warrior River mountain men and decided that I'd better take a sip. It tasted pretty good and, as a matter of fact, I'd lied just a little bit about my temperance.

On the Delaware farm, Grandmother had stocked up a cache of homemade wines. My favorite was wild cherry. I'd sneak down to its hiding place in the cellar, fill up a pint jar with it, and sit on the front porch reading *Young Wild West* and sucking on the wine jar. When Uncle Bill finally decided to throw away the big chair I always sat in, a dozen jars clattered to the porch floor. Grandmother's eyes popped wide. "So! That's what happened to all my wild cherry wine!"

Now, on the way down the mountain, Frank explained that we were all going to a cabin camp to "raise a little hell." Shortly after our arrival, the owner of the camp took offense to the hillbilly style of intrusion and stormed off, loudly proclaiming that he was going to fetch his shotgun and, "By God, run you boys out!"

Frank yelled after him, "By God, I got my German Luger an' ain't no sonbitch gonna run me offa nowheres!" He took his pistol from under the front seat and stalked off into the darkness. It wasn't long before we heard the *boom* of the shotgun, followed by the *blam-blam-blam* of the Luger. The white lightning had begun to take effect on me and I remember that it all seemed like a nightmare. Bob and I felt like captives in an alien world. When Frank returned unscathed, we wondered whether he had killed the cabin camp owner, but were too afraid to ask.

The next destination of the three rowdies was a school dance being held in the river area. By now, the five of us were roaring drunk and I have the dream-like memory of climbing into a tall tree and the school children screaming in terror while Frank emptied his Luger at me. Bob yelled at me, "Get outta that tree. He thinks you're a possum!" I got out. Fast.

Our last stop was Joe's house, a greying, rickety shanty right out of "Lil Abner." The front porch was decorated with a half-dozen young girls bedecked in dresses made from Gold Medal flour sacks. I remember distinctly that each curvaceous ass was covered by that golden logo. As we stopped on the porch, Joe's grandmother, toothless and smoking a corn cob pipe, tittered a greeting at us. "Hee, hee, hee. You boys has had a little too much tea, ain't ye?" She proceeded to the outdoor well and pulled up a bucket of water. Frank started in on the guitar and we sang until I fell off the porch.

I awoke at the crack of dawn to find fifteen huge razorback hogs rooting around Bob and me on the ground. I cautiously tugged on Bob's sleeve.

With great apprehension, he stared at the grunting beasts. "We'd better get out of here," he whispered. "While we still can!"

We sneaked out of the yard and walked toward Birmingham for most of an hour. Finally, an old Black man, driving a team of mules and hauling a load of firewood, gave us a ride. When we told him of our odyssey with the hillbillies, he told us we had been in the clutches of some of the rowdiest folks in the neighborhood and had done well to slip away before they woke up. "They don't like Yankees," he elaborated. "Not one little bit."

We were very grateful to him and vowed to catch the first freight west. A long train was moving slowly out of the yards, so we climbed aboard with no trouble. A brakeman struck up a conversation with us, finding out from Robert that our father had been a railroader. It stood us in good stead—he told us where to get off the train so we wouldn't get arrested in the yard at New Orleans.

There's a long, slow approach to that beautiful city across Lake Pontchartrain. The train moved casually across the water on an interminably long trestle, and I couldn't believe I was being allowed the privilege of crossing the America that until now I had only read about.

Reality struck home, however, once we arrived in the industrial section of New Orleans on the East Bank of the Mississippi River. A huge policeman sauntered over to us, obvious transients that we were, and eyed us coldly. "Y'all comin' into N'awlins or gettin' out?"

"Gettin' out" was Bob's prompt reply.

The big cop made an indifferent gesture to the west. "There's the rivah!" he drawled. Without a suggestion as to how to traverse the mighty water, he turned away, his eyes blazing with the implied threat that we'd better get across mighty quick.

Bob went up the loading ramp that brought cars aboard a ferry boat getting ready to cross the river and almost immediately got us a ride with a benign young salesman.

I have crossed the Mississippi many times since, often at 36,000 feet, but have never felt that same first thrill Bob and I shared on that ferry ride. There is a sadness to modern travel that wondrous, scenic places are forsaken for excessive speed. There is an advantage in leisurely travel that allows one to see and enjoy so much passing beauty.

When we arrived in Gretna, just across from New Orleans, I lay down on a loading platform and fell asleep. I dreamed that Brother Robert was giving me a savage jousting so I woke up in an evil mood, ready for battle—until I became aware that a burly railroad detective was blistering my sneakered feet with a bastinado, while Robert urged me to be serene. Hard to come by serenity when your feet are being cudgeled.

On the train that took us out of Gretna (with my feet still burning), we met a young man named "Chi Chi" McNulty who, in the parlance of the times, was as "queer as a three-dollar bill." Robert admired Chi Chi's penchant for organization. When the train broke up in Lake Charles, Chi Chi organized a loosely knit fraternity of hobos into an efficient horde of scavengers, even designating one bindlestiff to procure salt and pepper. Robert, being one of the more astute members of the fraternity, was ordered to fetch coffee, which was costly and hard to come by. Chi Chi assigned himself to dogrob some stew meat.

"You," he pointed to me, "get carrots." From what his scavengers brought him, he cooked up a delicious "jungle" stew.

Chi Chi was something else. He was self-proclaimed "royalty," grandly announcing that he was "The Queen of Pershing Square." The Square is a one-block park in downtown Los Angeles, long regarded as a trysting place for gays, winos and pigeons. There should be a plaque there for Chi Chi McNulty—he's one hell of an organizer.

The next morning in Lake Charles was uneventful until the train we planned to take started moving slowly out of the yard. Bob ambled over and climbed aboard as I stopped by the water tower to get a drink. I turned the hose on, took on enough water to sate a camel, then stood up to see a .38 revolver and a .45 automatic inches away from my temples. One was in the grasp of a railroad detective, the other in the shaking hand of the town constable. With a decidedly Cajun accent, the constable ordered me to stand still. "Don' move!" he shouted. I stayed put.

The train was picking up speed so Bob began yelling at me. "C'mon, they won't shoot!"

The two cannons were horribly close. I stared at my now rapidly disappearing brother. "See ya," I whispered. I was promptly marched out of the yard and out of town.

REMEMBERING THE ALAMO

LATER THAT NIGHT, I crept into the train station and, for the first time, rode the "blinds." At either end of a passenger train are steel stirrups used by trainmen to climb up to inspect the top of the train. By putting one foot in the lead car's stirrup and the other into the following car's stirrup, a "bo" was assured of a fast, dangerous, dirty ride, since in those days coal was the major fuel in service. In such a manner I rode to Orange, Texas.

From there I randomly caught the first train that looked like it was leaving. It left alright, but took me in a direction that led not to California. When it came to a stop in Little Rock, Arkansas, I was one disconsolate bum. A huge engine was chanting softly in the station; its passenger cars looked inviting. I approached the cab and hailed the engineer. "You going near California?"

That kind man grinned down at me. "Yep. Goin' to Dallas."

The ride to Dallas was a swift one, the train arriving at six in the morning. Our mother had promised to send us a letter in care of Dallas so I waited on the Post Office steps until the General Delivery window opened. I picked up a most welcome epistle: Not only had she sent a cheery note but a ten dollar bill. I went to the nearest restaurant and ate enough for two. After all, Bob wasn't there—by his own choosing.

Dallas held a fascination for me. In the dozens of Western novels I had read, its name cropped up constantly. I wanted to stick around but two policemen in a squad car politely, and firmly, suggested that since California was a long way off, I'd better get started. I was back in the freight yards before my enormous breakfast had settled, eyeing a long freight slowly moving southward. I climbed into the nearest car, finding out instantly why I was its sole occupant. It was a cattle car, empty but for the numerous calling cards its previous occupants had left strewn in unsymmetrical patterns about the wooden floor.

I rode to San Antonio amid those bovine mementos. Arriving at the Alamo, I looked for a spot where I might bathe before I went sightseeing. A gas station attendant pointed me to a hose behind his garage where I washed myself off. But the stench clung tenaciously to me for quite a while. The desert heat between San Antonio and El Paso helped. I flaked a lot.

There's an awful lot of Texas and by the time I arrived in El Paso I had drunk in scenes that brought *Young Wild West* back in flaming color. The rugged beauty of the vast desert expanses had engulfed me with an undying sense of awe and humility.

One night, the train slowed and moved into a siding so that a passenger train overtaking us could pass. I lay on the catwalk atop the car, watching the stars in the heavens grow brighter and brighter until it seemed that one could reach up and pluck one from the sky for his very own. Now and again a comet hurtled earthward to burn away into nothingness. Carried by the soft desert breezes, the howls of coyotes drifted across the desert floor.

Now a new sound permeated my consciousness as the freight train engineer, a half-mile away in his cab, blew his whistle in a signal to the approaching passenger train. The whistle wailed into the night; the mournful call echoed and re-echoed to be lost finally in silence. Then, very faintly at first, the answering echo came, reminiscent of the "Indian Love Call" theme. Far in the distance, the passenger train's headlights appeared. Suddenly, it was on us.

Clickity-clack, clickity-clack, clickity-clack, clickity-clack. The sound was hypnotic, keeping me spellbound as I could see passengers eating their dinners as the dining car sped past. Feelings swept over me—not envy, not jealousy, not anger—only a sense of sorrow, knowing that I would never be a part of a whole family. I thought of my long-dead feather, whom I had never seen. I missed Bob and I wondered where he might be wandering at that moment. When the freight started up again I wondered what lay ahead.

❄ ❄ ❄

El Paso still holds an excitement that I first felt in 1934. My initial moments there were memorable. I jumped off the freight train, running to a line outhouse that loomed from a small knoll at the edge of the yards. As I closed on it fast with a sense of desperation, I spied an ominous message painted on its faded door:

BEWARE! EL PINCHO!

A "bo" on the train had told me that Texas "crabs" could jump six feet. And I believed him. No matter. Nature was calling, and "El Pincho" frolicked on this day. "Crabs" are hard to get rid of in one's britches, especially when bath water for one's itchy skin is hard to come by. Hard to forget a welcome wagon like that one.

I spent the last of the ten dollars in El Paso. Broke but satiated, I hopped another freight and continued to rattle through New Mexico. During the night the train roared through Las Cruces, Deming and Lordsburg, stopping in Winslow, Arizona, where it broke up.

True to my propensity for making the wrong decision, I jumped on the first train to leave the yard. It took me on a long, circuitous route that brought me down to Douglas, smack on the Mexican border. It added a couple of hundred miles to my journey but gave me an insight into the Mexican character.

I was hungry enough by then to eat a bear and, in my desperate condition, found the courage to try to bum a meal. The likeliest spot seemed a Mexican restaurant near the yards. I went to the back door with great trepidation. In my halting Spanish, I asked the Mexican who opened the door if I could have something to eat. He bade me enter his restaurant, where he fed me as though I were a paying guest.

That man's innate gentility and charm flooded back into my conscious mind much later in my life when John Wayne asked me to write the lyrics for a record album we worked on together, "America, Why I Love Her."

In his own inimitable style Wayne said, "Mitch, could you write something especially for the Latinos? After all, I married three of 'em!" So I wrote "Mis Raices Estan Aqui," *which Wayne loved. And all because that unknown restaurateur was kind to me on a hot and airless day in Douglas, Arizona.*

❄ ❄ ❄

The trip from Douglas to Los Angeles was uneventful. We pulled into the yards at dusk. There were about 40 of us "bos" who were immediately rounded up by the police and escorted to a lovely bastille known as Lincoln Heights. We were paraded in front of a night court judge who solemnly pronounced that we were accused of "avoiding railroad fare." He gazed down at us with total indifference. "Are you guilty or not guilty? Guilty!" he roared, banging down his gavel and sentencing us to three days in his "hotel."

There were no juvenile halls in those days. Miscreants of all shapes, sizes and colors were thrown into "the tank," a huge, barred room lined with tiers of bunks. For my three-day stint, we received scant attention, but I did enjoy the chance to shower with hot water.

I was released early on the third morning and started hitchhiking down Alameda Boulevard toward Long Beach when a Japanese farmer picked me up. I'd never seen an Oriental before and I gawked at him as though he were from outer space.

When I reached the apartment house where our sister Annette lived (she was "Julie" now), I found Brother Robert in the bathtub. He was covered with lather and on my entrance, he splashed the soapsuds away from his eyes. He stared at me for a long moment.

I had been abandoned in Louisiana, had lost my way to Arkansas, had been shunted down to the Mexican border in Arizona and had been jailed for three days in Los Angeles.

That laconic fart looked up at me blandly and asked, "What kept you?"

SUN, SURF AND GIRLS, GIRLS, GIRLS

A DISASTROUS EARTHQUAKE had rocked Long Beach and its environs only a few months before we arrived in California. The aftershocks were still strong enough and often enough to make a lad, brought up on more stable ground, mighty nervous. There is little else in the world that can give you a more complete feeling of total helplessness than a sharp jolt, a deep growling from the earth's bowels and a wild ride in a chair or couch, then a chance to sit and wait trembling for the next tremor. I had been officially introduced to California.

❄ ❄ ❄

Our sister Julie lived just five blocks from the ocean and Bob and I became instantaneous beach bums. At that time, Long Beach did not have the huge breakwater it has now; quite often, the waves would be enormous. We became adept body surfers as well as astute girl- watchers—the beach was a magnet to every pretty little thing in the city. These were halcyon days of surfing, volleyball . . . and girls.

During those golden times, true to form, Bob made friends with a man who most certainly qualifies as one of the most unforgettable men in our young lives. His name was Elmer Ellsworth Jones, originally from Wilkes-Barre, Pennsylvania. "Jonesy," his brother Johnny and another recalcitrant named Ross left the East Coast for the West Coast driving an old Maxwell. They progressed by siphoning gas from other cars for the entire trek across country. It was Jonesy's plan; he had recently been released from a reform school after perpetrating a highway robbery at the age of fourteen. He was the "king of the hill" at the reform school, a fact that gains in stature when you realize he never weighed more than 170 pounds. Jonesy could hit like a sledgehammer with either hand. And quite often did.

Jonesy boxed with me on the beach every day. I took secret pride in the fact he told Bob that I never showed "quit," even when he poured some fearful shots into my middle.

In 1951 I worked with Robert Ryan in John Wayne's "Flying Leathernecks." Ryan and I boxed together at the Hollywood YMCA and I was delighted when Bob told me that Ryan had come to him burbling about my ability. "I couldn't lay a glove on him!" Ryan said, shaking his head. I felt doubly elated when I found that Ryan held the Ivy League Championship while at college for three years.

❄❄❄

Those sessions with Jonesy taught me a lot but inadvertently set me up for a reputation that stuck for a long time.

I started school again at Long Beach Polytechnic High School in September, 1934, enrolling in the eleventh grade. A young lady invited me to a Halloween party and I accepted, delighted to be part of the school's social

In 1939 I was 165 pounds and ready for all comers; this was taken on Palm Avenue in West Hollywood after a workout at the Hollywood YMCA Gym.

set. The only costume I could come up with was a white sailor suit I borrowed from my brother-in-law. Such clothing in Long Beach at that time was about as original as a bank clerk wearing a suit, shirt and tie. To complicate matters, our party's hostess decided it would be great fun to crash another girl's party.

We were greeted at this other girl's door with a sullen animosity that boded ill for someone. We soon left, but loitered in front of the house, laughing and talking, when the door suddenly burst open. The young lady's stepfather bounded down the front steps to the sidewalk. Without warning, he punched a member of our group, knocking him to the ground.

"What in the world'd you do that for?" I asked. His response was to charge straight at me, mouthing obscenities and screaming that I'd get the same treatment. I caught him with a left hook. He fell into me, clasping his arms around my neck, even though he was out cold. My punch broke his nose severely and my white sailor suit became a gory mess. The image of the stepfather draped on me, blood pouring from his head, impressed the others tremendously. At school they spoke of me in hushed, revered tones. I was just fifteen years old and my first California victim was a 37-year-old member of the Long Beach Fire Department.

My reputation quickly grew out of all proportion.

***

My enrollment at Poly High was guided by the gods, for fate gave me three teachers who were to shape much of my life. My science teacher was Theodore Reddick, a man who physically resembled Knute Rockne and who could mentally compete with Einstein's equals. He taught me to let my native curiosity grow and expand, until I became interested in everything.

Those were Depression days still and Reddick—to whet the curiosity of our young minds—invested in diving equipment from his own pocket, so that his students might study the sea floor firsthand. He created a club for the study of reptiles, and we became members of the Junior Herpetological Society of America. Several of our members went on to become noted scientists in the field. Reddick took us, at his own expense, on field trips all over the Southwest, teaching us how to trap and care for reptiles.

My first encounter with a rattlesnake occurred on a weekend in the desert area near Riverside. In the morning, we fanned out to search for specimens. Our snake sticks consisted of shafts of golf clubs whose heads had been broken off and replaced with steel hooks and prongs welded in place. I went about diligently prying up rocks that (I would have staked my life on this) could never conceal a rattlesnake. While everyone else moved off, I dug away at a flat rock, certain I would come up empty-handed. The rock started to slide down the hillside and I leaped back. *Bzzz bzzz* oh shit! I had uncovered a six-foot, red-rock rattler. And he wasn't a bit pleased about it. At the sound of his buzzing, most of the members ran back and were excited.

"A beauty!" "What a terrific specimen!" "What luck!"

Luck? It was now my responsibility to pin down the damned thing and bag it. It was a big snake, not only in length but in circumference. Despite my fears, I managed to pin it down and hold its head in the prescribed manner. Eager fellow herpetologists held open a burlap sack while I carefully threaded the writhing body into the bag. I thrust the head away from me, but someone failed to close the sack fast enough and Red-Rover was looking me straight in the eye. We finally secured the bag and I took secret pride in the fact I hadn't fainted dead away.

❄❄❄

Reddick, again almost single-handedly, arranged for the Long Beach high schools to participate in competitive rowing. The 1932 Olympics had been held in Long Beach and two eight-oared shells had been left behind by the Japanese team. Reddick saw to it that the shells became the property of the school system.

As a result, an already intense rivalry between Poly and the cross-town school, Woodrow Wilson, flared up anew. The grueling discipline that it takes to compete in such racing taught me that teamwork is essential to crewing.

Reddick took all the recalcitrants of the school and taught them to pull together, to work as they had never worked before. We became fast enough to take to the water against UCLA. We didn't beat them but we accounted well for ourselves.

Reddick took me aside one day and gave me a lecture that sank home. "You have God-given ability, but you have a tendency to take everything for granted. You loaf through life. Sooner or later, the turtles will pass you by unless you hone your efforts."

John J. Frisch taught journalism at Poly High with such marked professionalism that he instilled a genuine interest for writing in each of us, and he opened his home to us every weekend. He had a fabulous record collection and great artists were ours to hear: Tito Schipa, Beniamino Gigli, Enrico Caruso, Lawrence Tibbett, John McCormack, Lily Pons and Kirsten Flagstad.

Frisch's library was massive. We read while listening to the music, holding lively discussions among ourselves until the late hours. Frisch was always available to answer our questions.

Mary Shouse was the third instructor who helped shape my life. She headed the music department and permeated the staff with her penchant for perfection. Through her I became involved in studying not only voice, but choral directing, solfeggio and composition.

Our senior class performances ended in 1936 with an operetta, "Sweethearts," in which I sang the role of Petrus Von Tromp. I went into

I'm on the far left in the Prussian outfit in this cast shot of "Sweethearts." Next to me are Paul Plattenburger and Joe Frye (both high school drama stars who never pursued acting careers). At far right is Walter Windsor, who went on to become the very wealthy owner of several radio and television stations.

the cavernous bowels of the famed Western Costume Company (next to Paramount Pictures on Melrose Avenue) to be fitted in a smartly designed uniform for my role as an Austrian nobleman in military attire. I felt I was taking a giant stride into a life that held excitement, glamour and promise. I was in "show business." To be fitted in a costume in halls and dressing rooms where Spencer Tracy, Clark Gable, Errol Flynn and Lionel Barrymore had trod awakened my imagination to glorious heights. I have been in that place dozens of times since but that 16-year-old boy had a thrill that has never been duplicated. Mary Shouse enshrined herself in my heart.

* * *

Brother Robert added to his collection of friends another one of the misfits that he drew like a magnet draws iron filings: Frederick Crawford Fast from Toledo, Ohio. Because he was gay, his father—a wealthy auto parts manufacturer—had disowned him. Freddie survived because his doting mother sent him remittance monies.

On my graduation day from Long Beach Polytechnic High School in 1936, I felt a triumphant sense of succeeding, for the moment of triumph had been preceded by many traumatic moments in which I feared I would never graduate.

Freddie, who at various times had lived in Paris, London and Rome, receiving a good education in the process, carried himself at all times like a cultured gentleman. It came as a real surprise when he asked if he could accompany me on a trip I planned in the summer of 1935. I wanted to go back to Delaware to see my grandmother and my schedule would be at the whim of the freight trains. I explained to Freddie that riding freights was a vastly different mode of travel than the passenger train to which he was accustomed. He remained undaunted.

His reason for going was dramatic: His father had disowned him and had adopted a "straight" son. Freddie wanted to go back to Toledo as a derelict so his father might see to what depths of despair he had been driven. I shook my head at this but agreed to let him come along.

IN A LONELY PLACE, ON A LONELY TRAIN

EVERYTHING WENT smoothly on the trip into Tucumcari, New Mexico. The train moved gracefully along a hilly landscape carpeted with lush green grass. We saw a great herd of wild horses galloping toward the peak of a range, breathtaking in their sleekness.

Then reality crept in. Seated on the catwalk atop our boxcar was a florid, middle-aged gay with a red bandanna around his neck. Surrounding him—like a group of sub-tenders around a mother ship—were five young boys who obviously adored him. He looked at me with bland superiority. "What's the next town?" He lisped his words.

"Tucumcari," I answered.

"Ooh," he tittered, "off we're going to shuffle—shuffle off to Tu-cum-ca-wee!" His entourage giggled, but their laughter was shortlived.

Town police and railroad detectives swarmed all over the yards when the train came to a stop. A manifest train carrying cigarettes had been hijacked early that morning and woe be unto any "bo" entering that town. During the Depression, thieves would board a train and force the engineer to stop the engine. They would then break open the sealed cars and transfer the booty onto a waiting truck driven by accomplices. To stop these thefts, the trains often carried armed guards whose orders were "Shoot to kill!"

As we were ushered out of the yards unceremoniously, we realized that the head railroad detective was a vicious bastard whose gun carried a number of notches. Undaunted by the odds stacked against him, Freddie Fast marched resolutely back into the yards to seek that somber man. "Christ, Freddie!" I gaped at him in astonishment. "He'll kill you!"

Freddie pulled his wallet from his jacket, fishing out a card which he imperiously handed to me. It looked official, bearing the name of the president of the railroad. "A friend of the family's," he blithely stated. "When that nasty man sees this, he'll change his tune."

"What in the hell are you two doing back in the yards?" the dick screamed.

"My good fellow," Freddie beamed at him, profferring the card. "I am a friend of the president of this railroad and I can assure you he would understand my situation."

I could see the explosion coming. It swirled around in the man's brain like a tornado, then it roared from his mouth in a babbling torrent of words.

"You fucking bum! You insane bastard! You—you—SHIT! *GET OUT OF*

MY SIGHT BEFORE I KILL YOU! BOTH!" He added that one word so I propelled the still jabbering Mr. Fast to the safety of the streets. The irony was that he did know the president of the railroad. But according to the logic of the detective, if you look like a bum, act like a bum, smell like a bum—you must be a bum.

❄ ❄ ❄

Later that night we crept back into the yards and boarded a train that was already under way. Catching a freight on the fly can be a dangerous business but it was either that or remain stranded in Tucumcari. We knew there were guards riding the train but, at a point some twenty miles or more out of town, I got so cramped that I had to move off the ladder or fall. When I placed my foot down, I accidentally kicked the coupling rod.

Shuddering at what I had done, I watched in horror as the train separated. The moon grew bigger and bigger in the now rapidly widening space I had created, then the automatic air hit as emergency cords were yanked. Both sections of the train rolled to a stop and "bos" flew off that train like fleas off a dog. The guards yelled and snapped their flashlights all over the place. Freddie and I leaped off the train and hid in the cacti. We didn't stop to consider that the place was crawling with rattlesnakes.

The train was hooked up to the car I had uncoupled and chugged and steamed back to life. Neither of us attempted to reboard it.

We had abandoned the train in our hurried exodus just a few hundred feet from a siding that ran past a storage shed containing ties, signal lamps and track-repair equipment. We slept on the floor, heaping piles of burlap atop our tired bodies to enjoy a modicum of comfort.

About six in the morning, the door burst open. We jerked awake to see a huge Black man staring at us. It turned out he had been riding just behind the water tender when I cut the train. The guards caught him and threw him off some ten miles farther into the desert; he walked for hours along the tracks. Big rattlers lay next to the rails absorbing their heat; he threw warning gravel ahead of him for the entire length of his forced hike.

"If I find the mother-fucker who cut that train, I'm gonna cut his throat!" Fate saved me for as he glared down at us, we heard—and ran to—a big freight that slowed almost to a crawl at the crest of a big hill. Soon we were on our way again—back to Tucumcari.

Obviously, we were not going to catch any trains out of that town for some time. Remembering the techniques of Brother Robert, I walked the streets until I spied a car with a Kansas plate. Freddie and I staked it out until the driver appeared. He was an affable young man, readily agreeing to give us a lift to Topeka.

Freddie sat in style in the passenger's seat while I crept into the back. The floor and the seat were piled high with whiskey—our benefactor was a bootlegger. He and Freddie chatted cheerily while I, from my cramped quarters, observed my surroundings closely. It didn't escape my sharp eyes that there were several bullet holes in the car.

❄ ❄ ❄

We took back roads for most of the trip. Prohibition was in full swing and "revenooers" were on the prowl. When the Kansan dropped us off in Topeka, I murmured thanks—along with a silent prayer.

We arrived in Toledo, Ohio, late at night in a driving rainstorm. Freddie's mother came down to pick us up and we drove to their home in silence. The rainstorm didn't hold a candle to the storm brewing inside the house. Freddie's father was furious. He raged like a madman, then made the mistake of picking on me.

"How dare you," he roared at his disowned son, "dirty my home with this filthy guttersnipe." Freddie fled upstairs.

"Mr. Fast"—something in my voice quieted him down—"your son asked me to let him tag along so he could come back to reconcile your differences. I'm on my way to Delaware to visit my grandmother. I have no money, so I'm forced to travel the way that I do. Tell Freddie I sincerely hope you can both be better friends." I reached down to get my pack.

Just then Freddie reentered the room with a razor in his hand and tears rolling out of his eyes. "You foul bastard!" he shrieked at his father. His mother and I blocked Freddie but he kept waving the razor. With some difficulty I disarmed him. He told his father that I was a real friend, and that I didn't deserve this treatment.

Calm suddenly prevailed. His father gruffly apologized to me. I still wanted to leave but Freddie's mother begged me to stay. I remained for two days and, in that time, the two parents found I could be articulate, entertaining, mildy talented—and that I definitely liked girls.

Freddie and his father did find a common ground of respect, and I felt free to go on my way.

DEATH ON BOXCAR CURVE

IT WASN'T nearly as much fun visiting Delaware as I had thought it would be. California's sea and mountains and girls had dwarfed my interest in the Blue Hen state. My sense of loneliness was heightened when I found I had picked a westbound freight that took water "on the fly." The fireman would let down a big metal scoop that fitted a trough filled with water. At 50 miles per hour the scoop took up an awful lot of water and the train didn't have to stop for long stretches.

It started to rain.

In the misty twilight I could see families sitting down to dinner as we thundered past their houses. Sometime during the night, in Kane, Pennsylvania, we stopped to add a few more cars.

A man climbed into the box car I was occupying. Dawn came up and I could see him staring at me in a way that made me uncomfortable. He drank wine from a bottle in a paper bag.

Finally he stood up and lurched toward me. He was unshaven, dirty, and he had decayed teeth. As he got closer, I detected the smell of rotting leaves.

He grinned his rotten teeth at me. "I'm gonna fuck you, kid." He pawed at me, moaning softly. "C'mon kid, it's gonna be fun."

I hit him with a perfect left hook to the jaw. As he staggered back toward the open door, I followed with a straight right to his face. He fell out of the fast-moving train. I saw him land headfirst on a huge rock. As his body receded from my view, I saw that it wasn't moving. I was certain he was dead.

The trip home was a long, long, lonely one.

RATTLESNAKES—AND TWO-LEGGED SIDEWINDERS

DURING THE SUMMER I spent with grandmother, Brother Robert again joined a Civilian Conservation Corps camp, a Rooseveltian method of providing young people with productive work. Bob wound up in a forest area near Chico, in Northern California, where he was bullied by Simon Parra, a truculent chap whom Bob finally agreed to give his time. I asked Bob if he knocked out Parra, a man who outweighed him by thirty pounds or more. His answer was in keeping with his penchant for understatement. "I scratched him up a little."

* * *

Late in the summer, I brought home several rattlesnakes. Among them was a sidewinder a little over a foot long with a head about the size of the first joint of my index finger. I came home to see it coiled up in the palm of Bob's hand. "Don't move!" I warned him. "When I tell you, drop your hand from under him as fast as you can and pull it backwards!"

He did as I told him and the surprised rattler landed on the floor. I hooked it and put it back in its cage. "Jesus Christ!" I was shaking. "Why in God's name did you do that?"

Because of the rattler's diminutive size, Bob honestly thought it wasn't dangerous. When I explained that drop for drop its poison was many times stronger than that of a red-rock or a black Pacific, he became quite humble.

"The sidewinder was fascinated by your pulse," I told him. "It wouldn't've been too long before he would've struck you and you'd've been in deep trouble." Bob never toyed around with my snakes again.

A few nights later, I took a crowded bus, packing a freshly caught red-rock into a heavy grocery bag with the intention of showing off my new prize at a snake-club meeting. A snake will lie quietly inside such a bag, only striking if pressed by a living creature. Well, a living creature on the crowded bus started pressing me where I stood. He was about forty, big and beefy. I said, "Sir, would you please not push? I'm having a hard time keeping the bag from being crushed."

He stared at me contemptuously. "Don't give me any lip, kid. I'll push you any time I want."

"Well, alright," I sighed, "but my snake isn't going to like it."

In seconds I had a clearance of three feet in all directions.

"A snake! He's got a snake!" Pandemonium. The driver stopped the bus. "Have you got a snake?"

"Yes, sir," I replied calmly. "I have, but he won't hit anyone unless they press against the sack."

The rear door opened. "Out!"

I've often thought I should have let the big bastard keep pushing against the sack.

* * *

Before the onslaught of civilization, Laguna Canyon was a primeval place where intrepid young herpetologists found rattlesnakes aplenty. But snakes weren't the only things I discovered in the wilds.

This underwater scene was painted for me on my 17th birthday by my stepfather, Major Hugh Cunningham Morris, a gentle, talented and warm man. Once, in the South Seas, he was bitten on the heel of his foot by a deadly sea snake. Despite the venom-induced swelling, he pulled through. He was an astonishing man and to me this painting denoted the fathomless depths of his character.

On one foray I found myself at the bottom of the canyon alone with a fourteen-year-old girl, Alice Smith. I was almost seventeen and by now thought myself quite worldly.

She looked at me for a long moment, then bluntly asked, "Have you ever done it?"

"Done what?"

"You know what I mean. Have you ever done it?"

With an air of bravado I confessed to six "doings."

"I've done it forty times!"

I was about to ask her if she wanted to make it forty-one when my friend, Dick Hunton, hove into view.

Years later, at Camp Gordon Johnson in the Florida Panhandle, I was reading a sports magazine someone had left on my bunk. There was a photograph of Alice Smith, who had blossomed into a professional wrestler. I could see that she could take any man she wanted.

❄ ❄ ❄

Elmer Jones baffled me. Even remotely he was not a handsome man, but his rough charm had women flocking around him. He rented a little house behind the Long Beach Post Office; one girl would be going out the back door while another one was coming through the front.

Jonesy neither gave nor took any quarter, whether with women or in a fight. He cut a swath through the town like a thresher shark in a school of herring. You had to take him on *his* terms. Naturally, he created a few enemies. One of these was a merchant sailor whose name was also Jones. Paul Jones was 6-foot-3, weighed in at 215 pounds, and hated Jonesy.

In those years, downtown Long Beach was dominated by a strand called The Pike. It included an amusement park, curio shops, numerous bars and several dance halls. One of the latter was the Rose Marie, but don't let the soft name relax your guard. It was a tough joint.

One night Jonesy picked up a girl there whose reputation didn't exactly make her a candidate for "woman of the year." That gave big Paul the opportunity he was seeking. He sat amidst his cronies, sneering at Jonesy. "Well, Elmer," he drawled, "apparently you don't care what kind of pig you take on."

Jonesy got up and walked to Paul's table, calling him several selective nasty names and ending up with the Arthurian statement, "When a broad is out with me, she's a lady."

Paul stared insolently up at Jonesy. "Well, you've done everything but spit in my face."

Jonesy glared down at him. "That," he said with all the warmth of a swaying cobra, "can be arranged." Huck, hurack, tu. It was arranged.

Big Paul turned to his entourage. "Do you guys wanna see me go?"

"Yeah, yeah, Paul. We wanna see you go." His half-dozen cronies couldn't have been more prophetic.

The two Jones boys fought at the end of The Pike in a vacant lot. Big Paul was good, but not good enough. He thudded some frightful body shots into Jonesy; Elmer returned in kind to Paul's jaw with a vengeance. Finally, he felled Paul with a savage left hook. The fight wasn't quite over. Members of Paul's group insisted that the two shake hands.

"I never shook hands with a prick I beat in my life," said Jonesy. Paul's cronies finally talked him intu it. He went over to shake the now stirring warrior's hand. Big Paul pushed his hand away. Jonesy, newly enraged, lifted the reeling man up and thundered a right hand, uppercut fashion, under his chin, knocking him senseless into the bed of a truck. Without another word, Jonesy stalked away.

Though triumphant, Jonesy bled internally for several days. Big Paul's

Elmer Ellsworth Jones (E.J.) and Bob in Hollywood in the early 1940s. Elmer kept a cellar apartment on the Strand in Long Beach which he dubbed "The Palace of Purity," for the very reason that purity had nothing to do with it. In those days they called themselves "The Two Goniffs."

THE BATTLING MITCHUMS

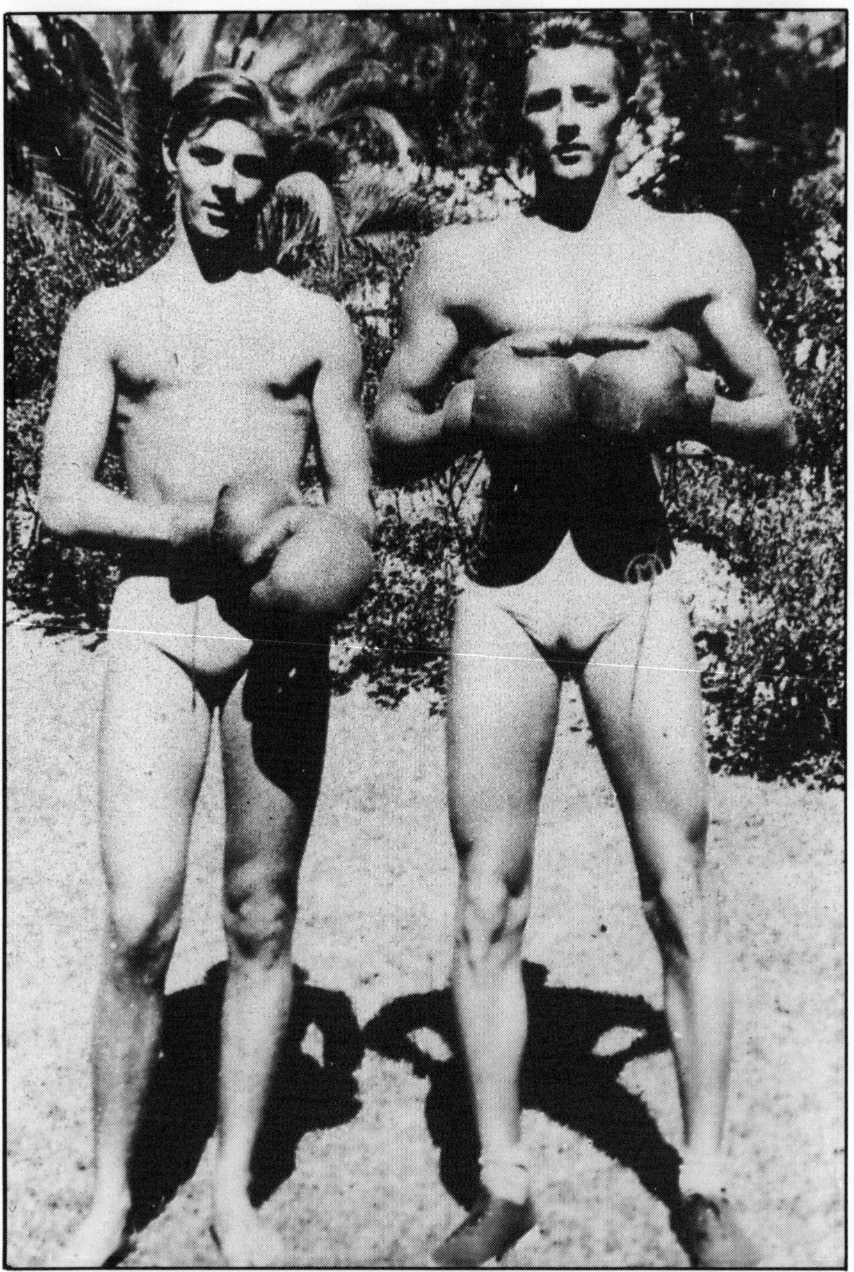

In 1937 Bob and I were invited to a Hollywood mogul's weekend party and staged a boxing exhibition for a group of studio kings. In those days Bob whipped me consistently, and it wasn't until after the War that we evened up and I considered myself on a boxing par with him.

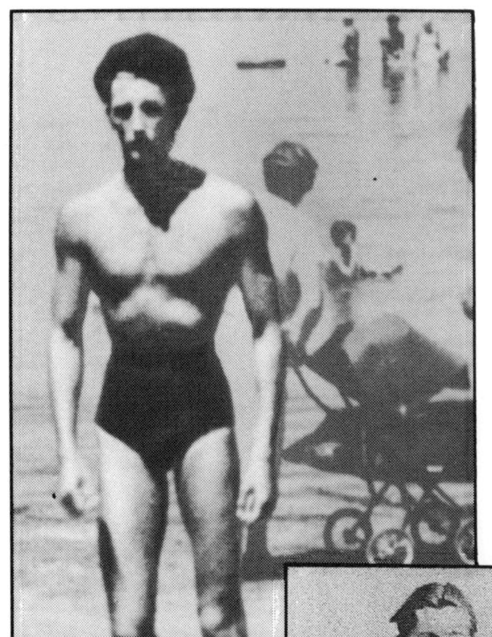

Tall, dark and handsome: A common sight on the long beach at Long Beach in 1938, when Bob was just 18 and a constant distraction to most of the girls bathing nearby, especially statuesque blonds. I can't say that I wasn't making more than a few female acquaintances of my own in those warm, balmy days when our world still seemed far from the threat of war. We practically lived on the beach.

Another day at the beach: Bob's on the left, I'm on the right. Between us is Bill Gibbon, who went on to become a high-ranking executive in the National Cash Register Service. Bill's father, a friend of Major Morris, liked to tell how he captured a one- legged Boer during the Boer War and was forced to carry him six miles to friendly lines.

fists had done a lot of damage, but not where it showed.

❄❄❄

Our sister, Julie, coaxed and wheedled until Bob agreed to sit in on a casting session at the Long Beach Players Guild. He was reticent about going because he had no formal training in theater. He didn't realize that his hoboing, his ordeal on the chain gang, his host of unusual friends and his indomitable will had given him an education on which he could draw as an actor. He was a natural, but then he had Shrimp Cruzado, Charlie Costello, Joey Chicori, Sully Sullivan, Chi Chi McNulty, a Georgia judge, Freddie Fast and the awesome Elmer Ellsworth Jones as mentors.

He first trod the boards in August, 1937, as a last minute write-in on the playbill in the comedy "Rebound." One reviewer wrote: "Outstanding also were Veronica Rourke and Robert Mitchum. Mr. Mitchum's performance as the sophisticated John Cole was climaxed by his fine emotional scene with Sara."

Brother Bob never looked back.

He rapidly became the male star at the Guild. His reputation flourished.

In April, 1938, his "Stage Door" portrayal was immortalized: "Robert Mitchum is aptly cast as the egotistical playwright."

His July, 1938, depiction in "The Petrified Forest" electrified audiences. A reviewer noted: "Bob Mitchum, as the notorious Duke Mantee, with his assistant gangsters . . . holds at bay a miscellaneous assortment of persons who have stopped at the stand for food, and the fear and suspense of the situation bring out the dominant traits of each."

Various newspaper people said of Bob's March, 1939, acting in "Ghost Train": "Robert Mitchum upheld the high standards of Guild players with his portrayal of the asinine Englishman who is found to be a Scotland Yard sleuth . . . Heading the cast of favorites are Bob Mitchum . . . " Also, "Robert

Three of Bob's co-stars at the Long Beach Players Guild: Barbara Britton (I knew her in school as Barbara Brantingham, a sweet, gentle and lovely girl); Galen Drake (a leading man soon dwarfed by Bob); and Laraine Day, in those days a strict Mormon. I never could understand her marriage to Leo Durocher, the foul-mouthed baseball coach.

Mitchum, in the role of an English boor, was outstanding."

In January, 1940, the comedy "Dear Octopus" prompted a critic to write: "Robert Mitchum has become so steady in character parts that as the grandfather he loses many scenes through his naturalness . . ." and ". . . the long cast is well chosen and particularly well trained. It included Robert Mitchum . . ."

The playhouse's director was a remarkable man named Elias Day, a genius of theater. Under his tutelage, Frank Goss, Laraine Day (nee Laraine Johnson), Barbara Britton (nee Barbara Brantingham), Galen Drake, Fred Stuthman, Hugh Beaumont (future star of "Leave It to Beaver") Iola Josephson and others to follow made a successful inroad into Hollywood's entertainment fields. Robert stood tall among them.

❄ ❄ ❄

I became an unofficial "guest" to this group and they tolerated me well enough. One night our little clique left a rehearsal and went to our favorite hamburger joint. Afterward, in the Mitchum family car—a 1933 Studebaker sedan which we affectionately called "The Green Hornet"—we started to disperse our party to their separate homes. Don Russell walked Nancy Kelley to her door and just as he came back, a Long Beach police car roared around the corner, throwing a red light on us. Sister Julie, Brother Robert, Don Russell, Dick Hunton and I were ordered to get into the squad car.

When we had the temerity to ask "Why?", we were told there had been several robberies in the neighborhood. Don had finished his first semester at law school so he asked, "Am I under arrest?" (If he was, the City would be in line for a lawsuit for false arrest.) The cop didn't answer but simply ordered Don into the car. Once again he asked, "Am I under arrest?"

The cop threw a right hand that knocked Don out as cold as an iceberg, and his body was dumped into the back of the patrol car.

The rest of us quietly obeyed orders.

They never did book us, but we were put in separate cells. Following Julie's lead, we all did our own "thing." Julie sang torch songs, Robert recited Shakespeare, Dick Hunton sang "Myself When Young" from the "Rubaiyat of Omar Khayyam," while I roared out "On the Road to Mandalay." All of this had a chorus of constant moaning from Don Russell and his aching head.

We were released at four in the morning. The teeth-gritting station personnel couldn't stand us any longer. Dick sidled up to the desk sergeant. "This isn't going to be in the papers, is it?"

The sergeant eyed him balefully. "Of course not. Why do you ask?"

Dick drew himself up haughtily to his full six-one. "I sing with the Sunny Side Mausoleum Quartet," he whispered sepulchrally. "I'm the bass."

❄ ❄ ❄

I scattered my forces and, true to my vacillating nature, changed goals continually. I had aspirations to become an opera star, a writer, a sea captain and the heavyweight champion of the world. To that end, I studied voice, boxed, and went to sea. I also wrote for the school paper and for the annual. I penned long-forgotten short stories, then put pen and paper aside.

MY INTRODUCTION TO DECADENCE

IN THE SPRING of 1940 I walked up Palm Avenue to Sunset Boulevard. Just as I reached the Club Bali, the owner Izzy Orthwaite stopped me. "Hey, John, you wanna earn ten bucks?"

I eyed him speculatively. "What do you want me to do?"

He introduced me to Edgar Montillion Woolley, better known as Monty Woolley, the Yale professor turned actor. Monty was loaded down with six heavy suitcases and was moving into the Chateau Marmont on Sunset Boulevard. All I had to do to earn the ten spot was carry those heavy bags up to his fourth floor apartment. At the time I was making 35 cents an hour at a name plate company, earning $10 every 28½ hours.

Woolley had newly arrived in California to play the arrogant Sheridan Whiteside in a film being shot at Warners, "The Man Who Came to Dinner." I was impressed by his stentorian approach to life, but was more than taken aback when he offered me $100—to urinate and defecate on his chest.

I already had my ten, so I left his apartment in a speechless state of nausea. I had fought for my life against a pervert in a Pennsylvania box car, so I certainly didn't need the likes of Woolley.

I related the incident to Robert and he gleefully put the decadence to song. To the old English air of "Come to the Fair," he wrote these lyrics:

There was an old man who came out to the West
Singing "Heigh ho, shit on my chest!"
I pulled down my trousers, unbuttoned my vest
With a heigh ho, I shit on his chest.

The Beard: Edgar Montillion (Monty) Woolley in 1945, the year he starred in "Molly ane Me."

Whenever Bob and I spotted Woolley on the boulevard, strolling jauntily along, we would assume a Napoleonic stance with our hands in our shirts, and with Robert on the tenor and me on the baritone, we would belt out the cute little ditty.

In high dudgeon Woolley would wheel in the opposite direction and stride purposefully toward an escape route, his nose high in the air.

I asked Robert the "why" of it all.

"Hard to imagine," he replied. "He went at it even before it was stylish."

Jonesy met a strange fellow that summer who became an adopted member of our group simply because he was wealthy enough to afford martinis which he made for us by the pitcherful. Alfred Loudon was a very intelligent, knowledgeable gentleman from Virginia who was a buyer for one of the most prestigious furniture stores in New York. Although he was a trifle on the gay side, we got along amicably.

Since money was always hard to come by in the '30s, I accepted when Alfred asked if I would drive him all over Southern California for ten dollars a day. I drove him to lovely Lake Arrowhead, stylish Laguna Beach, elegant San Diego and other points of interest. Alfred decided he wanted to see a bit of Baja Mexico.

We went into the "longest bar in the world" in Tijuana, an establishment that, at that time, probably was. It was seven in the morning and we were the only patrons. Since neither of us spoke Spanish, Alfred pointed to a bottle of White Horse Scotch on a shelf behind the bar. The bartender broke the seal, poured us both a measure, added soda and eyed us passively. We had two more drinks, then Alfred put what seemed to be enough money to cover the tab on the bar and we started to leave.

All hell broke loose. The bartender informed us, in a torrent of Spanish and with *mucho* gesturing, that we had bought the bottle. Since I didn't have any cash, I waited for Alfred to pay. He adamantly refused. In a brief time, rifle-brandishing police herded us into a decrepit paddy wagon. We were unceremoniously locked into a dungeon of the medieval jail, remaining alone and stonily silent until about eleven o'clock.

Clink! Clank! Clunk! Clang! We could hear the jailor opening the doors that led to our cell. He stood impassively before us. "You buy de bottle?"

Alfred's face contorted with anger. "I did not order the bottle. I ordered *drinks* from the bottle. I will never buy the bottle!"

Clang! Clunk! Clank! Clink! The morose jailer retraced his steps. Alfred and I sat in stoic silence until about one o'clock.

Clink! Clank! Clunk! Clang! The jailor returned, bringing us some debris that he indicated was edible. I passed.

"I demand to see our consul," said Alfred. "I am an American. I have a right to speak to the consulate. I— "

The jailor interrupted. "You buy de bottle?"

"Never!"

Clang! Clunk! Clank! Clink! The morose one disappeared again.

At eleven that night, in quiet tones, I assured Alfred that if he didn't "buy de bottle," I would break his face. Loudon, a man of occasional perception, grudgingly handed me a ten-dollar bill. "*You* buy de bottle!"

The bottle, which had cost us fifteen hours of our precious freedom in that miserable hole, cost $2.50.

❄ ❄ ❄

In the fall of 1937, I enrolled at Long Beach Junior College. I was voted hands down to box for the honor of the freshman class. My opponent had fought six fights at the Long Beach Arena and I suspect that certain members of my group were aching to see me get whipped.

His name, "Killer" Hill, was designed to throw fear into an opponent, much as modern-day fighters try to stare down each other just before the bell. In the first round I hit him so hard his legs crossed; he fell down like a whirling dervish. Fortunately for me, he broke his ankle in the fall and that ended the fight. Unfortunately, my reputation took another giant step forward.

My best friend Dick Hunton, shown here during his seafaring days. Dick became a counselor at Indiana State Reform Prison for 25 years. When I saw him recently he was lean and hard as ever, albeit a little more nervous having spent all those years around hardened prisoners.

ALL I ASK FOR IS A TALL SHIP

DURING THAT SUMMER my stepfather secured for me a deckhand's job on *The Invader*, a 136-foot, two-masted schooner commanded by Captain Gurnhardt, a German who lived up to everyone's stereotyped conception of a Teutonic sea captain. I bought a set of sailor pants, deck shoes, a salty blue shirt and a white sailor hat, imagining myself standing proudly in the bow yelling, "Whales, dead ahead!"

The yacht, which served as the camera boat during the filming of the Spencer Tracy classic "Captains Courageous," had a Swedish steel hull, two giant Corliss engines and, under full sail, cruised at eighteen knots. The master stateroom was luxuriously designed with accoutrements to please a king.

Under full sail, we were tacking to leave the harbor on my maiden voyage when I heard Captain Gurnhardt screaming at me. "Look out, you God-damned fool!" I looked up just in time to see the main mast boom heading straight for my head. I ducked, feeling the "swoosh" of its passing centimeters over my crown.

I looked blankly to port, seeing my white hat spin into the sea. Daydreams of faraway ports and dark-skinned natives in proas vanished as my 220-pound commander delivered a profane sermon on sailing in English, German and roaring anger.

It was a good lesson: After that I never took the sea or anything on it for granted. It held me in good stead, for I was to sail on a three-masted schooner, *The San Wan;* a 206-foot power boat, *The Memory;* and on the very ship seen in "Captains Courageous," *The Mariner*, a 106-foot Gloucester schooner whose seaworthiness was tested by mountainous waves and howling winds during a full-blown hurricane off Cabo San Lucas.

My captain on the last three ships was Arthur Kollberg, a Swede who had sailed since he was nine. A fine man and a superb sailor, he greatly affected my life.

I greatly affected *his* life for a fleeting moment when I talked him into hiring Elmer Jones, my Long Beach fighting friend. I told the Captain that Jonesy was a fast learner and that I would help him whenever possible. In the one day I had to train him in seamanship, I forgot to tell him a very important thing that came back to haunt me.

We moved out of the Fellows and Stewart Yacht Basin and entered the main ships' channel at San Pedro to fuel up. As we neared the fuel dock, Kollberg cut the engines from the bridge and ordered Jonesy to throw out the bowline. I had placed the heaving line—long and slender, with a lead weight attached to it—on top of the bowline, but neglected to explain to Jonesy that it was the *heaving* line he was to throw onto the fuel dock. I was horrified to see him staggering around on the bow with a huge coil of heavy *hawser* in his arms.

A lumber schooner, loaded to the gunnels, was bearing down on us. Jonesy, thoroughly frantic by now, tried to hurl the hawser toward the wildly gesticulating man on the dock whose job it was to haul the heaving line—and then the hawser—to a cleat. The hawser fell into the channel and Kollberg used all of his skills to avoid colliding with the huge freighter bearing down on us. I hauled the hawser in as Kollberg backed away from the schooner until he was safe and could once again approach the dock. This time I handled the operation and it went smoothly. Kollberg banished Jonesy to the bowels of the ship and the engine room. I endured a dressing down from both parties that took the paint off the stanchions I was leaning on.

* * *

A luxury yacht, *The Memory* was owned by Henri Bellous, a White Russian who wore a black beret and an air of mystery. He spoke of arming the ship with five-inch guns and machine guns, and of "bearding the lions" in their lair. He offered Kollberg a large sum of money to take her down to the South Seas, but the captain didn't jump at the chance. Later I asked him why he had refused.

"She's not seavorthy," he said in his Swedish accent. He paused for a long moment. "I'm going to see yust how she might handle in a heavy sea."

A week later we went to Catalina Island. It was a beautiful day; the sky was azure, the sea a cobalt blue. I could tell by the gleam in Kollberg's eyes that he was up to something.

The Catalina Channel can be very rough when the wind kicks up in the late afternoon. On the way back to the mainland, we were into some very choppy swells when Kollberg suddenly veered the ship broadside. The results were amazing. *The Memory* yawed wildly, and down below dishes, glassware, furniture and people were tossed about violently.

In a few seconds Kollberg brought her back on course. He looked at me solemnly. "Those were about four-foot troughs. Vere Bellous vants to go, they get to be forty-foot deep. She'd never make it!"

I found out later that someone did take *The Memory* toward the South

Pacific. And Kollberg's prediction came true.
She was lost at sea with all hands.

❄❄❄

Brother Bob hoboed back to Delaware to see Dorothy. The little girl he had wooed on her father's front porch in Camden had grown into a beautiful young woman.

Her innate gentility and charm swept Brother Robert off his feet.

He stopped off in Toledo to visit Freddie Fast, picking up $25 by winning a smoker fight with a local middleweight. Hoboing 2,000 miles to earn 25 bucks! None of us had any inkling how serious those two were about each other, but Bob and Dorothy were already betrothed. He had to work out

By 1939 I was wearing my own sailor's cap. In this snapshot I was standing next to the keel of The Memory while it was in drydock for a paint job.

some scheme to earn a living and he was hard at that, too.

Bob was steadily amassing a great many credits. One of these was a Christmas play that he wrote; it showed that he was a many-dimensional artist.

Meanwhile, Captain Kollberg asked if I wanted to take a trip with him aboard *The Mariner.* I jumped at the chance. He was taking *The Mariner* to Mazatlan, Mexico, with the owner, wealthy Pasadena socialite Morrie Morrison. Among the charter party were the famous Byrd brothers, cousins of polar explorer Admiral Richard Evelyn Byrd. The elder of the two brothers was famous as "Dry Hole" Byrd, a Texan who sank dozens of wells without hitting anything but dust. Then he hit a field so vast he consequently became a multimillionaire.

Also on board was William Barbee, the president of the Western Division of the Coca-Cola Bottling Company. His traveling companion was a sultry brunette, lovely to look at and, I surmised, delightful to hold. She took a shine to Morrison; although it became a sticky wicket at their level, it didn't filter down to the crew.

We had a good following breeze all the way down the coast. One morning I came up on deck and drank in the total beauty of a clear sky, gorgeous water and white sails catching a steady wind. Abruptly, hundreds of porpoises raced beside us, cutting in and out from under our bowsprit in what must have been a joyous time for them. Just as suddenly, the school disappeared and the sea was again a thing of calm beauty.

One night I was at the wheel, immersed in my own thoughts that there exists a Power so real, so eternal, so strangely beautiful that any man privileged to feel and to acknowledge it must be blessed. The stars shone so brightly they seemed to beckon me symbolically to rise to their heights. The soft wind, pressing steadily against fore and main sails, whispered to me to absorb all that was around me. A silver moon lit up a path that seemed to spread forever ahead of us.

Captain Kollberg wordlessly paced the deck from bow to stern. He looked at the compass and was satisfied. Then he turned to me and said, "I feel a peace in my soul ven I'm on the sea that I can never feel on the shore."

I've thought of this many times since. Life came from the warm shallows of a long-forgotten sea. It was born and nurtured there, surviving millions of years of torment and culminating in man. Scarce wonder that his source of peace was the sea.

Captain Kollberg prowled forward, stared dead ahead, then came back. "Bring her two degrees to starboard," he said. I complied after acknowledging the order, but asked to know why.

"See that?" He pointed at something that had a different color than the sea around it. "That's kelp. This far offshore, it had to've broken free from rocks. Kelp doesn't grow free-floating."

Within ten minutes, we passed an uncharted mass of rock looming from the ocean. I silently thanked God the Captain had been on deck. The rock was scarcely forty feet off our port bow.

EL GITANO, THE PISTOLERO OF MAZATLAN

THE COOK ON The *Mariner* was Johnny Flaatken, a young German who had lived for five years in Mexico. He was one hell of a chef, and quite a character to boot. After we tied up in Mazatlan, the Captain gave us both the afternoon off.

At that time, Mazatlan was a sleepy little fishing village. Its streets were narrow, lined with hawking vendors who sold fresh clams and oysters laced with lemon. Automobiles roared around corners with horns honking to warn recalcitrant pedestrians that the car had come to stay. The crowded stalls displayed colorful sombreros and beautiful serapes as we made our way through the streets.

We arrived at a beer tavern ridiculously named Club Hollywood. We sat down, ordered two beers and were mildly amused when three men entered through the swinging doors. The leader wore an outfit reminiscent of Hopalong Cassidy's. He wore two guns while his henchmen each carried a single gun in a worn holster.

For a time, I didn't take them seriously. Then their two-gun leader pointed at me, calling me a *puto, cabroncita,* and sundry other names sullying my manhood. (Even in a strange language, one usually understands an insult.) I walked directly to his table where he and his cronies were guzzling cerveza. They scowled up at me.

"So you think I'm a *puto*?" I said to "Hoppy." "Get up! We'll see about that."

He got up with both revolvers drawn and cocked—and aimed directly at my eyes. "*Si*," he whispered.

I prayed inwardly, "If he's any kind of a man, he won't shoot me in the back." So I turned, very slowly, and stalked out of the Club Hollywood with Johnny, never to return.

My mama did not raise a fool. Cocky? Yep. Arrogant? You bet. But not stupid.

Through Mexican friends, Bob found out several years later that I had accosted the head pistolero for the Governor of Sinaloa. He could have shot

Captain Arthur Kollberg standing on the boat deck of The Memory, while it was docked in San Pedro Harbor. On that day he was fed up with his wife and her infidelities and he proposed to me that we steal a nearby schooner, the Gypsy Girl, and sail her to the South Pacific and foresake civilization forever. I was tempted but decided against it. I never saw Kollberg again.

me like a dog and gotten away with it without a murmur. Bob also learned that the pistolero was "El Gitano," the gypsy, and that he had assassinated the Governor. He became a folk hero to his people and lived to a ripe old age.

❄ ❄ ❄

A Mexican crew caulked the decks of *The Mariner* while I was staring into El Gitano's barrels. Our charter party had had enough of marlin fishing, so the passengers flew back to the States, leaving the crew and Tommy, a polo-playing friend of Morrison's, to return the ship to Fellows & Stuart Yacht Basin in Wilmington. As we set out uneventfully, I noticed that William Barbee had purchased a case of authentic Napoleon Brandy and a Mexican outrigger canoe. The brandy was stowed below decks and the canoe was lashed to the rigging. We would soon set sail.

BANSHEE OF THE SEA

AT SIX O'CLOCK the next morning, I sleepily poked my head out from the foc'sle hatch to see a leaden sky. I nearly jumped out of my skin when my body vibrated to what I thought was a deafening cannon shot. The startling noise was our main sail disintegrating—we had no radio, hence we had no warning—as a hurricane came howling down on us like a banshee. In seconds, the foresail followed; both were split as cleanly as with a knife.

The winds exceeded 130 miles per hour. We lost our lifeboat, we lost our motor launch, we lost everything not battened down. Then we ran out of fuel. Realizing that if *The Mariner* took on water we would capsize, we lowered the split main sail . . . but a third of the way down, a "fist" formed in the line and wouldn't go through the block.

Captain Kollberg ordered me to the wheel. "Keep her steady as you can into the vind," he barked as he went aloft.

The ship rose, carrying tons of green water on her bow. Kollberg held on for life as the ship shuddered and shook like a maniacal beast. When she dipped into the waves, he scrambled up the rigging until she reached the peak. Then he held on again until she made another dip. Finally, about sixty feet above the deck, the captain reached the fateful block. He tied himself to the rigging and worked the fist loose with a marlin spike. At the age of 60 he fought the equivalent of two fifteen-rounders.

With the sail down we rode out the storm. When it became obvious we were no longer in immediate peril, Captain Kollberg came to me at the helm. "Yakkee," he said, unable to pronounce "Jack," "if ve don't get help soon, ve're in terrible trouble!"

My "why?" was silent. My eyes said enough.

"If ve don't get help soon, ve'll be in the 'trades.'"

I knew what that meant: The trade winds blow almost continually from 30° North and 30° South latitudes toward the Equator. Anything drifting in those winds would be pushed thousands of miles across the South Pacific. We'd drift at their mercy with no food, no water, no nothing.

❄ ❄ ❄

A miracle happened the next morning. Just the tip of a stubby mast showed above the crest of a wave, then a Mexican fishing boat hove into full view. Her crew didn't need much explanation as to our plight. We had no steerage and no sail.

It took some time to transfer a barrel of oil to *The Mariner*. The seas were still extremely high but the job was finally accomplished. Gratitude is not a big enough word to describe our feelings toward the Mexicans and the good Lord above. When the engine of *The Mariner* kicked over, it was hard to suppress a tear.

We were running straight into the seas and our fuel was burning up rapidly. Kollberg pulled into a large cove, delighted to see a sleek motor-sailor lying to. Her captain sold us another barrel of oil and again we headed north. The seas were still angry so Captain Kollberg anchored for the night in a cove at San Cedros Island. I stood watch that night, listening apprehensively to the sound of the anchor grating against the rocky bottom.

In order to stay awake, I baited a fishing pole with a slab of bacon and threw it over the side. Within minutes, something took the bait and I hauled in a three-foot tiger shark that thrashed around and snapped at everything in sight. I hit it with an oar, which the sea monster proceeded to bite in half. I whacked it with assorted objects close at hand and finally drove a boat hook into its gills, returning it to its ocean home. In the moonlight, I saw it swim away as if nothing had happened.

At daylight, we started out again for California with me at the wheel while everyone else slept. The ocean fascinated me. It was smooth but the swells were amazingly long. They seemed to reach forever and, in their great size, looked too large to exist. Later, when we were nearer to the Mexican mainland, I could see them crashing against the cliffs.

Just a few miles away from San Cedros, I looked astern and thought I saw an explosion on the island. There were other "explosions," each closer to the boat. Something was breaking the serene surface of the blue Pacific. It was bearing down on *The Mariner* at a tremendous speed. I rang down for the captain.

"Vat is it now?" He was disgruntled from lack of sleep. I answered by pointing astern. When he saw our pursuer, he rang down to stop the engine. After he did so, we felt a tremendous bump that shook the whole boat.

The crew scrambled on deck while the captain explained: "It's a sperm vale. Some ship probably killed its mate and he's looking for the killer."

The bumping ceased but we were now frozen with fear. With a great swooshing sound, the whale appeared on our port side. He measured longer in the water than *The Mariner*; his starboard eye was as big as a pie plate. Whenever anyone moved, that vengeful eye followed the movement.

Morrie Morrison's friend Tommy went below, came up with a .306 hunting rifle and cocked it. From deep somewhere in his baggy pants, Captain Kollberg pulled out a Colt .45, pointed it at Tommy and told him to put the rifle down. When he demurred, the captain told him he'd shoot him instantly if he didn't. Tommy put down the rifle.

"You'd only anger him by shooting him vith that pop-gun," explained Kollberg. "He'd fluke us to bits and these waters are filled with tiger sharks. No vun vants to go that vay."

Tommy silently carried the "pop-gun" below just as the whale sounded. His flukes glided under the water and he didn't appear again.

We ran out of fuel one more time, in a fog so thick one couldn't see the bow from midship. Captain Kollberg rigged up a jury sail to steer away from the distant sound of heavy surf pounding against unseen cliffs. Morning came as we crept along in a very slight breeze, suddenly bursting into brilliant sunlight. The line of demarcation between fog and sun-swept ocean was as clean as if cut with a knife.

The breakwater of Ensenada Harbor lay off our starboard bow about two miles. Captain Kollberg asked for two volunteers to row the dugout canoe into the harbor. (It had survived the hurricane, having been lashed securely to the rigging.) I wanted to go but was vetoed by the captain. The first mate and another sailor lowered the craft into the water and paddled furiously toward the entrance to the harbor.

In about an hour, they came back aboard a fishing boat with the canoe in tow. We bought an ample supply of oil, making the rest of the trip without incident. I was grateful. I'd had enough excitement for awhile.

LITTLE GUSTS BEFORE WINDS OF WAR

I COULDN'T relate to school. The age-old system of reward and punishment was unreal to me. "If you don't turn your homework in on time, I'll give you a lower grade" seemed hardly important.

I had outbluffed guns pointed at my eyes, survived a hurricane, been threatened by a monstrous whale and observed life and death from a very close perch.

So—I joined the Long Beach Players Guild, becoming actively involved in theater, appearing in several plays in lesser roles than Brother Robert.

My real interest lay in music so I followed my music professor's advice and sang in his choir at the stately First Presbyterian Church of Long Beach, a place with high, stained-glass windows and a magnificent altar. My professor, Raymond Mormon, was a meticulous craftsman—not a showman, not flamboyant, just quietly good. Through him, I learned much that held me in good stead. *(In the years ahead, I too became a choral director, working for the Bureau of Music in the city of Los Angeles for over ten years.)*

Brother Robert dominated the stage at the Players Guild. He began to attract important people in the business, one of them an agent who came to see him on the advice of Larry Johns, the then-current director. The agent, Paul Wilkins, went backstage and told Bob he wanted to handle him.

Bob's answer was indicative of his native guardedness. "How do you mean that?"

Paul laughed. "I'm an agent and I'm convinced that you have a great future ahead of you. That's how I mean it."

They formed a lifetime friendship. Robert's career in the motion picture business was ready to be launched.

❄ ❄ ❄

We met a wonderful couple through our theater affiliations, Juanez and Lee Suydam. Although neither was in show business, Juanez actively procured talent for shows donated to the local veteran's hospital, and I sang in many of those shows. It was now well into 1939 and Lee invited me to go camping and trout fishing in a remote part of the High Sierra.

We found Three Pines Lakes, which started at an elevation of 9,000 feet and climbed to 9,500 feet, teeming with California golden trout. It was an idyllic time.

. . . Until a young couple struggled up the trail to our camp, carrying their dog in a newspaper. The poor creature was dying of distemper. Lee told them he thought their pet wouldn't make it. It was when they again picked up the sick animal, cradling it in their arms, that the newpaper's headlines blazed into view:

HITLER INVADES POLAND!

Our sister Annette was already quite a looker in the late 1930s, as this glamour pose clearly reveals. During World War II she became a night club chanteuse working in L.A. at the Villa Riviera. One night a G.I. called her Julie instead of Annette and—remembering that a numerologist had once told her that she should assume the name Julie—she began billing herself as Julie, dropping the Annette forever after. The soldier proposed to her before he shipped out, and then was killed at sea before reaching the battle zone.

BOOK THREE

OF SOLDIERS, OF ACTORS

BOOK THREE

THE NIGHT BOB SAVED THE LIFE OF AN ASTROLOGIST

THE FRIARS' RESTAURANT, the place for youths during the '30s, was close to the Players Guild and only a block from the ocean. We would congregate there, comb our hair like Adolf Hitler, then hold the comb against our upper lip and mock the rantings of Der Fuhrer.

I can remember when the German heavyweight Max Schmeling wrested the world title from Joe Louis, the "Brown Bomber," in a gruelling bout. Hitler was crowing to the world that Schmeling's victory proved the supremacy of the Aryan race. Louis had his rematch with Schmeling and destroyed the German in less than two minutes. Now Hitler's boasts were ashes—the young Alabama Black had demolished Hitler's hero. We all thought this would teach old Adolf he'd better not mess around with Americans. All that it really did was put Schmeling into a German paratrooper's uniform. After the war he was to live out his life in obscurity.

Reports, all bad, flooded in from Europe. Stuka dive bombers destroying Poland (1939). German armor pulverizing country after country (1940). Our world of smug complacency was rapidly coming to a close.

❄ ❄ ❄

We lived on Wisconsin Avenue in Long Beach in the last days of 1939. Bob and I were as brown as Tahitians from the summer sun. As usual, we were going to the beach early one morning when I stepped onto the front porch and saw a young couple soliciting their God to the elderly lady living next door. The pair was laden down with pamphlets to persuade anyone who might listen that ninety-eight percent of the world preferred the wrong church. I rushed back inside to warn Bob of our impending visitation.

When the solicitors stepped into our house they drew back: Seated crosslegged on the floor were two turbaned, swarthy Arabs in white, flowing robes.

They started their canned speech nervously, then put a record on their little portable player. The disc intoned the endless virtues of their God. Anxiously, they eyed us.

Bob looked at me, heaving a great sigh. "Christians?" he asked wearily.

"Christians," I answered gravely.

Bob leaped to his feet, pulling a great carving knife from the folds of his robe as he roared, "Infidel dogs!"

The couple fled from the house, leaving the little record player behind. We enjoyed it for a long time.

Soon after, we moved to West Hollywood on Palm Avenue. The war was a grim reality now, for it was increasingly obvious that America would be dragged into it. Our aircraft plants were humming so loudly the atmosphere became permeated with war.

Bob met the renowned astrologer, Carroll Righter, and became his employee. Righter was crossing the country on a lecture tour and hired Bob to write his material. Bob also did the driving during the extensive, exhausting tour. One night he ran off the road into the murky waters of a Louisiana bayou. After fighting his way to the surface, Bob saved Carroll's life by diving back into the submerged car and dragging the astrologer to the surface.

Famed astrologist Carroll Righter, whose life Bob saved when their car crashed and plunged into a Louisiana swamp.

Bob left the tour in Florida with $2,300 in his poke and headed for Delaware. He left the Sunshine State in 90-degree weather only to arrive in the Blue Hen state in four feet of snow.

Dorothy Spence was astutely aware that the frozen wreck she saw standing in front of her couldn't make it through life without her. It was in the early spring of 1940 that Dorothy became Mrs. Robert Mitchum in the simplest of marriage ceremonies by a Methodist minister.

The setting was a plain farmhouse with no family or friends to wish them well. They came back to California to a dark and forbidding world.

THE LITTLE WHEEL RUN BY FATE

AT THE END of 1939 Germany seemed invincible, Italy strutted pompously on the outer fringes of the conflict, and Japan quietly appraised her chances of ruling the entire Orient.

While we sang "Don't Sit Under the Apple Tree," Pearl Harbor was waiting to be destroyed.

Poland fell to the legions of Hitler and a strange aura of dread spread over the world.

The speed of the conquest caused people to stop and stare into the dark void that seemed the future.

The ancient enemies of Germany looked the other way as the Stuka dive bombers laid their deadly eggs into the chimneys of Polish homes and factories.

Brother Robert began writing material for Sister Julie's nightclub act. He also helped write and compose music for a fund-raising effort for Jewish war refugees, produced by Orson Welles and performed at the Hollywood Bowl.

Bob wrote a special routine for Benny Rubin, a talented stand-up comedian. It was a poignant, beautifully done piece about the rape of Europe. Rubin unabashedly cried tears when he recited it.

Brother Bob has a heart as big as the world, but don't cross him.

The New Mrs. Robert Mitchum . . .

Dorothy Spence, the girl whom I had had a secret crush on, as she prepares to become a Mitchum on a very eventful day in Delaware in 1940. The inset reveals the beauty that had attracted me . . .

. . . And the New Mrs. John Mitchum

Actress Gloria Grahame introduced me to her sister Joy (above) and I fell in love, an emotional response that I came to regret when her mother moved in with us and became critical of everything I did. Joy was too much like her mother for our happiness to last for very long.

One night Elmer Jones, George Azud and I stepped into a pleasant bar on Hollywood Boulevard with Bob to have a drink. When the waiter came back with the drinks and our change, four male strangers slid into our booth. Jonesy had paid for the drinks with a twenty-dollar bill and there were eighteen singles in change on the table.

One of the intruders swept up the money, sneering. Brother Robert spoke to him quietly—cloaking a fierce desire to deck the idiot—suggesting he put the money back on the table. The guy informed Bob that he and his buddies had just been released from jail for robbery, suggesting they were tougher than nails.

"You," he pointed a finger at Bob, "are the son of a preacher."

"You," he looked at Azud, "are the son of a college dean."

"You," he leaned toward Jonesy, "are the son of a bank clerk."

At this point, I wondered who I was the son of.

"You," he sniffed disdainfully at me, "are the son of a choir director."

Bob sighed and looked coolly at the jerk. "My father," he said, "was a soldier in the army during World War I. He was part Scotch-Irish, part Blackfoot Indian. He was killed in 1919, crushed between the couplings of two freight cars. Me? I just recently escaped from a Georgia chain gang."

Benny Rubin in a 1943 photo.

He pointed to George Azud. "George is a China Marine. He is in mufti at the moment but is very much in the Corps. Killing any or all of you wouldn't bother him a bit."

They looked at George and saw that he was, indeed, a stoically cold man. He didn't smile or snarl. He just sat there with that Marine stiffness that reminded me of a pit bull eyeing the neighborhood cat.

"Jonesy," Bob went on, "was recently paroled from Cherry Hill Penitentiary in Pennsylvania. Incidentally, he was the boss of the yard." Jonesy made the eager, whining sounds a terrier makes when he spots a rat.

"And now," Bob grinned expansively, "this is my baby brother who can whip all four of you." (I could feel myself grinning—I *loved* to fight.) Bob smiled again. "Do you still want to keep the money?"

The tough guy pushed back the bills. The four of them slid wordlessly out of the booth, slinking out to track easier prey in the environs of Hollywood.

I moved back into the family fold when our stepfather, the old Major, and Mother moved from Long Beach to 954 Palm Avenue in West Hollywood early in 1940.

That address became a central point for many Hollywood characters because Sister Julie and Brother Robert had a penchant for attracting unique personalities of the era. Among them was John Banner, a director for little theater productions in West Hollywood Theatre Group. Brother Robert and I worked in a dreadful play—the title is deservedly unremembered—involving Nazi spies, Mata Hari-type ladies and aircraft workers. I played a policeman who arrested the surviving villains after Bob's wife in the melodrama poisoned the head man. Banner went on to play a number of unheralded roles as an evil German in the horde of Nazi pictures that

Among the films in which John Banner (of Austrian descent) played pre-"Hogan's Heroes" Germans (usually conquest-happy Nazis) were "The Moon Is Down," "Tonight We Raid Calais," "Once Upon a Honeymoon," "The Fallen Sparrow," "To the Victor," and "Operation Eichmann." I remember John as a melancholy, sad man. In spite of his cherubic, almost comedic countenance, I don't think he was ever really happy.

flooded the cinemas.

It was ironic that Banner escaped Germany and certain death only to portray his persecutors in such American films as "Operation Eichmann" and "Hitler." His greatest triumph came as the bumbling Feldwebel Schultz in TV's long-running "Hogan's Heroes." He had planned to retire to Austria in 1973 and live in a chalet but died suddenly of a massive heart attack. His lampoonish Schultz portrayal lives on in syndicated glory.

Bob had gone to Florida with Carroll Righter and returned from Delaware a married man. He and Dorothy moved into the Palm Avenue house. Grandmother Petrine, Sister Carol and myself were already ensconced there, as were Sister Julie and her son Tony (Julie had already divorced her sailor husband on grounds of total incompatibility.) Adding the Major and Mother, that totalled nine people. As America's factories geared up for war, it was obvious we would eventually be involved. I went to work for the K&B Name Plate Company, filling orders for thousands of plates to be used in warplanes. Each plate had to be acid-etched; the job was tiring and messy. For my valiant efforts to save

That's me playing Herman Goering opposite Richard Basehart's Fuhrer on the set of "Hitler." Both of us are wondering how in hell we're going to maintain our respective careers once the film is released and seen by the public.

the world for democracy, I earned the magnificent sum of 35 cents an hour. If Hermann Goering had any idea how many instrument panels that one little plant was churning out, he would have given second thoughts to bragging about the invincibility of his Luftwaffe.

In 1961, Richard Basehart portrayed Der Fuhrer in a terrible picture, "Hitler." I played the part of the rotund Goering. The only highlight I added to that inept film was a routine that George Fargo (a professional extra) and a group of studio stormtroopers portrayed—off-camera. We goosestepped across the set's cobblestone streets singing to "Col. Bogey's March" music:

"Hitler — he only had vun ball!
Goering — he had two — ja, small!
Himmler — vas very sim'lar,
While Goebbels — had no balls at all!"

We didn't improve the movie or director Stuart Heisler's peace of mind, but we had fun spoofing the swastika.

❄ ❄ ❄

Bob worked diligently in two worlds. He tried for some time to earn enough money to support Dorothy by writing and entertaining. It wasn't enough and he, too, joined the war effort, working nights at Lockheed in order to do plays in the early evenings and go on auditions during the days.

One of the plays Bob was cast in opened in a theater in downtown Los Angeles. It was not memorable (neither of us can remember its title) being a little theater rendition akin to "Tobacco Road." Cast opposite Bob was a brilliant young actress who was soon to make a name for herself in the movie world, Gloria Grahame.

Robert, solidly entrenched on the graveyard shift, suffered from insomnia. Small wonder: With Julie practicing on the piano, seven-year-old Tony being a typically noisy child, Carol singing and dancing about the house and the Major harrumphing, Brother Robert was rapidly losing his equilibrium.

"Why don't you quit that factory job and start to act seriously?" Mother put the question to Robert, who was at a loss for an answer. "You can do at least as well, if not a lot better, than most of the idiots I've seen. Try it."

As 1940 drew to a close, Robert gratefully left Lockheed and contacted Paul Wilkins, the talent agent. He and Dorothy moved to a house just a few doors away from us.

Bob took a parttime job as a salesman at a shoe store and Dorothy worked parttime as an insurance company secretary. Between them, they eked enough to pay the rent: $27 a month.

Bob had one suit, a blue pin-stripe, so paper thin in the seat that he patched it with black adhesive tape so his shorts wouldn't show through. He wore that suit to interviews, carefully sliding into a chair so the tape would remain in place.

Getting picture work turned out to be tougher than Bob ever imagined. In order to keep active in theater, he did as much stage work as possible. On the night of May 8, 1941, Bob was performing in Gorky's "The Lower Depths" when director Michael Stanislavsky gave him permission to leave the theater.

Bob borrowed a car and drove Dorothy to a hospital to have their first child, James, named after our father.

THE GRIEF OF JOY

GLORIA GRAHAME had introduced me to her sister, Joy, whom I dated steadily. Nine years my senior, Joy impressed me with her steadiness and her air of aristocratic assurance. She was attractive in a distinctly different way than Gloria. Joy's driving strength, the pressures of the war, my brother's being married, all my friends being married . . . before I knew it, Joy and I were on our way to Arizona to tie the knot.

I recall vividly one fact: Despite our warm relationship, marriage wasn't what I wanted. At 21, I felt too immature for such a serious step. I remember a desperation falling over me when the actual ceremony began. It wasn't long before I realized her assurance was actually a dominance that held sway in every aspect of her—and my—being. She was *right* in everything. No one else's viewpoint mattered.

President Roosevelt had, in March of 1941, worked out the famous Lend-Lease agreement with England's Prime Minister, Winston Churchill, and now America was supplying Britain with ships previously consigned to mothballs. Our war effort went into full gear.

In the spring, I went to San Diego to work at Ryan Aircraft, learning the sheet metal business, then I returned to Hollywood. Joy and I rented an apartment on Cahuenga Boulevard and settled down to married life—and Bob's old nemesis, Lockheed.

While I was dating her sister Joy, Gloria Grahame (left) was still a young innocent, only just beginning to find her stride as an actress on the stage in some productions with Brother Bob. Gloria's mother Jean asked me if I would teach Gloria how to make love—how to kiss "and all that business." I turned down the proposition cold, knowing that Joy would always be watching me out of the corner of her eye. Still, now that I think about the generous offer, I must have been out of my mind at the time.

Joy was bountifully pregnant with what would prove to be our daughter, Victoria. I was trying to grow up, to be a husband, son, son-in-law and father-to-be, and aircraft worker.

Bob still strove valiantly to get a toehold in the picture business, while being a husband and new father.

And the Japanese steamed toward Pearl Harbor.

AND THE BIG WHEEL RUN BY THE GRACE OF GOD

IN 1938, while I crewed aboard *The Memory*, owner Henry Bellous spent prophetic hours educating me about the inner workings of the power struggle that he felt would soon engulf the world. This, coupled with stories about my stepfather the Major, a secret agent for the British government while stationed in Austria, gave me a growing awareness of the intrigue and treachery that laid the groundwork for war. A memento of that intrigue was the staghorn dagger the Major had kept as a souvenir from his clandestine days in Vienna. It still bore the bloodstains of a fellow agent who had been eliminated by Hitler's espionage agents. My stepfather had removed the knife from the corpse, never bothering to wipe it clean.

Now, on the morning of December 7, 1941, as our battleships lay smouldering in ruins at Pearl Harbor, a feeling of deep sadness swept over me. I somehow sensed that a terrible toll of death and destruction would roll over the world before it was finished.

The fat was in the fire. In a matter of hours, my country became officially at war with the Axis. Now we were certain that Hitler was not a joke, that Mussolini was a vicious despot, and that Tojo was as ruthless a war leader as any in the infamous annals of history.

When I reported to work the next day, I was astonished by the attitudes of some fellow workers. My group leader became the voice for many. Long on macho, he fell short on acumen. "We'll have those damned Japs whipped in six weeks," he crowed.

"No we won't," I countered, forgetting for a moment that the truth often hurts. "It's going to be a long, long war. The Japanese are battle-trained, well-armed, fiercely dedicated to their Emperor Hirohito. Hell, they're among the most tenacious fighters in the world."

A hostility grew as the group leader and his friends eyed me coldly. "What are you?" he snarled. "A Goddamned Communist?"

I was under suspicion for months. Whenever a ship was sunk, or a bastion was lost, or an aircraft was downed, I was the target for baleful eyes. I began to suspect myself.

One night at 12:30 a.m. I left the plant, happily surprised to find Brother Robert waiting for me. He suggested we find our way to Tiny Naylor's, a landmark restaurant on the corner of La Brea and Sunset for over 40 years—despite the fact Robert nearly wrecked it that night.

We seated ourselves at the counter and the waiter sauntered up, flipping menus at us. His insolent air made Bob look quizzically at me. I returned the look to Bob. The counterman feigned a yawn. "Make up your minds yet?"

We gave him our orders. He strolled away for a good two minutes, then oozed back. "We ain't got it," he announced.

I looked at him while Bob stared straight ahead. "What have you got?" I asked.

He shoved the menus closer to us. "You can read, can't you?"

I was hard-pressed to be polite but I managed. "We asked you for something on the menu and you informed us that you 'ain't got it!' Perhaps it'd be simpler if you would tell us what you *do* have."

Imperiously, he reached down, whipping the menus from under our noses. "I don't have to serve your kind."

Bob picked up his water glass, hurling it at the waiter and missing him by inches, then carefully aimed my water glass at the cowering wretch and let fly. The cringing counterman ducked, but the plate glass window behind him didn't. It exploded into a thousand shards and sounded like a Japanese dive bomber attack.

The cook and the dishwasher ran for their miserable lives as Bob and I ran to his car. We roared out of the west end of the parking lot just as Hollywood's finest leaped from their squad cars to rush into the beleaguered restaurant. In seconds, we were winding down side streets, returning to Palm Avenue to have a sandwich with Mother.

We never did go back to Tiny Naylor's.

❄ ❄ ❄

On December 18, 1941, my daughter Victoria was born. I was working very long hours, sometimes as much as two full shifts a day. Bob was having a tough time of it too, for his first picture was yet to come.

On February 23, 1942, a Japanese submarine surfaced off the coast of Santa Barbara, pumping thirteen rounds of 5½-inch shells into an oil installation at Ellwood. While that was happening, I was staring at my dinner with a growing feeling of despair. I had to be at work at four but I knew that something was painfully wrong. I gave in to my feelings and went to see Doctor Alfred Huenergardt, a friend of the family's. He immediately put me into the old Alvarado Street Hospital and relieved me of an appendix that was about to rupture—or maybe it *did* rupture, I don't remember.

I was so sick I didn't know that on the eve of the 24th, the Navy received a warning from Washington of an impending attack from Japanese aircraft. At midnight, radar picked up a blip some 120 miles west of Los Angeles. At 2:27 on the morning of the 25th, it appeared to be only three miles away. At 3:06, a balloon-like object was sighted over Santa Monica and anti-aircraft batteries hurled some 1,400 three-inch shells into what proved to be an empty sky.

I lay there, unable to move, sick as a wounded dog, watching the tracers arc into the sky. "Christ," I thought, "the first attack on our soil and I'm flat on my back." It was a helpless feeling.

❄ ❄ ❄

In the spring of 1942, Joy's mother was broke so Joy insisted Mother Hallward and 16-year-old daughter Gloria Grahame move into the duplex Joy and I were renting. My feelings in the matter weren't consulted . . . as usual.

I was working two consecutive shifts. My job was to cut layers of aluminum sheets on a screeching router, while oily smoke whirled about my face and the metal constantly nicked my fingers. One morning I wearily came home around 7:30 a.m., only to be accosted by Mrs. Hallward: "Do your hands always have to be so grimy?"

Between my mother-in-law and Joy, I was made to feel inferior, no matter how hard I tried to please. My manners were never socially acceptable; my mode of dress was always disdainfully corrected. I was "ungentlemanly" and my friends were unwelcome, being from the "wrong" strata of society.

Sometimes—when my sense of humor bubbled to the top—it reminded me of watching a Gilbert and Sullivan musical: The natural ingenue, Gloria, doing her American teenage things; the supercilious Mrs. Hallward and her rabidly Anglophile daughter, Joy, going through their affectations of the speech and manners of British aristocracy. Granted, Mrs. Hallward *was* English, though not of the aristocracy—but Joy was born and raised in Pasadena, California.

William Boyd built a career portraying Hopalong Cassidy in a series of Westerns that became successful all over again when they were sold to TV in 1949. Boyd lived to be 75, dying in 1972 from Parkinson's disease and congestive heart failure.

Mrs. Hallward was a stage mother of the worst sort. She pushed Gloria into deplorable situations. One of these involved Gloria with a wealthy young man-about-town who took her to a Hollywood party and—together with a long-famous star of stage and screen—sexually abused her, leaving her pregnant and infected with gonorrhea.

Desperately, Joy came to me seeking help for Gloria. I alleviated the problem by sending the panic-stricken child to Dr. Huenergardt, who discreetly took care of both problems.

I couldn't believe my ears when the foppish man-about-town—an heir to two fortunes—called Gloria for another date. She begged me for advice so I gave it to her. "Tell him to come over."

He drove up in a Cadillac convertible, dressed in yachting clothes, and acting most effete. I told Gloria to wait in her bedroom while I answered the doorbell.

"Terrible war," he offered, taking a seat. "I might be called soon." He smiled at me. "Coast Guard, you know."

I looked at him somberly. "I know what happened to Gloria a few weeks back."

He stopped dead in his tracks. "What about it?" He was insolent—in *my* house.

I became deadly cold. "First, I

One can discern Bob's special screen charisma, even in his first released film with Boyd in 1943, "Hoppy Serves a Writ." But his range, as Hollywood was soon to realize, far exceeded his ability to play the heavy and ride a horse.

don't want you to ever take her out again."

He bristled, then got downright hostile. "What do you expect to do about it?" He stood up.

"Well, now," I told him, "if you bother her again, I'll knock you flat on your ass."

The damned fool informed me he had taken up boxing in college. He warned me that he had been tops in his class. I surveyed him critically.

Gloria came down the hall just in time to see the wretch catch a straight right hand full in the face. The blow knocked him across the kitchen floor, and he fell on his ass just under the wall phone. The instrument fell down by his side, dangling there as he moaned pitifully. "My nose!" he cried. "You broke my nose! Call Dr. Huenergardt!"

I picked up the phone and did so, delighted that the fop coincidentally had the same physician. "Doctor, this is John Mitchum. I'm sending you another customer."

MY BROTHER THE MOVIE ACTOR

EARLY in 1942, Brother Robert was finally signed by a producer, Harry Sherman, to do his first picture and went on location to Lone Pine, near Death Valley National Park, to film "Border Patrol," a United Artists release in William Boyd's Hopalong Cassidy series.

"Border Patrol," which also featured Duncan Renaldo and George Reeves, wasn't released until April, 1943, one month after the opening of his second picture with Boyd, "Hoppy Serves a Writ." Bob was finally getting a chance to show his stuff on a horse in these action-oriented, low- budget United

The Cowboy Days

Before graduating to A productions after World War II, Bob appeared in seven Hopalong Cassidy programmers: "Border Patrol," "Hoppy Serves a Writ," "The Leather Burners," "Colt Comrades," "Bar 20," "False Colors" and "Riders of the Deadline." Bob also had leading roles in four non-series Westerns: "Lone Star Trail" opposite Johnny Mack Brown, "Beyond the Last Frontier" with Eddie Dew, "Nevada" with Anne Jeffreys and "West of the Pecos" with Barbara Hale.

Artists Westerns.

Bob had been told to wait on the corner of Cahuenga and Hollywood Boulevard for the stretch limo to take him to the Lone Pine location. Veteran actor Pierce Lyden was also waiting to be picked up on the same corner.

(Years later, remembering that meeting and first picture together, Bob penned his autograph on a photo dedicated to Pierce as the man "who witnessed my deflowering." Lyden and I worked on many Westerns and TV series in later years and remain in close contact. He's authored four profusely illustrated books about movie badmen. Bob and I are well represented.)

Some dozen years later, I sat in Bill Boyd's office and heard this from Hoppy himself. "I was watching your brother from behind a wagon when he went up to the horse he was assigned to ride. The pony still had his winter range hair on him and had already thrown the cowboy Bob was replacing. The poor 'poke, an actor named Charlie Murphy, had been killed in the fall. We all wondered whether Bob was man enough for the job.

"Well, he mounted that pony and got thrown pretty hard. He climbed on again and hit the dirt again.

"Then he walked up to that horse, grabbed him by the bridle and told him off. 'You son of a bitch!' he whispered. 'I need this job, so it's you or me!'"

Hoppy looked at me solemnly. "Then Bob hauled back and whipped that pony a right hand that made it roll its eyes backward. Bob climbed on him for the third time. Rode him well for the rest of the picture."

Hoppy stopped talking to look out the window at the Western set down on

That's old-time cowboy sidekick Andy Clyde shoving a six-shooter into Bob's back while William Boyd looks on in the 1943 Hopalong Cassidy actioner "Colt Comrades." Bob may have made disparaging remarks about these roles but they were sure paying the bills.

Always on the lookout for a shapely ankle, J. Carrol Naish was caught signing his autograph for "pretty showgirl" Ruth Rathborn at the Cafe Zanzibar in New York. This 1945 shot was used by Wide World Photos for a series about "Big Name Hunters." No doubt Miss Rathborn was "big game" to Naish.

the company street. "Look at that," he cried. He pointed to a "cowboy" parading down the steet, walking with happy abandon. Hoppy gritted his teeth. "That's what casting sends you nowadays. Wouldn't make a pimple on a real cowboy's ass!"

❄ ❄ ❄

Bob did an incredible amount of acting in 1943. He worked in fifteen films, a tribute to his acting ability and his stamina. Among these were "Mine-sweeper," "The Leather Burners," "Colt Comrades," "Riders of the Deadline," "The Lone Star Trail," "Beyond the Last Frontier," "Corvette K-225," "Follow the Band" and "Bar 20." And a propaganda war picture from Universal called "We've Never Been Licked," which depicted how Richard Quine (an actor who later became a film director) overcame a Japanese spy ring operating in America and prevented it from stealing a secret formula.

For years, that film was run at College Station in Texas. The "Aggies" treasured it because it was their campus, Texas Agricultural and Mechanical College, that was used for the main location. They ran that print until it was completely worn out.

The last picture Bob filmed that year was another war epic, "Gung Ho!", depicting the 1942 attack on Makin Island by Carlson's Raiders. It was one rousing combat film starring Randolph Scott as Evans S. Carlson, and it featured Noah Beery Jr. and J. Carrol Naish as fighting Marines.

Bob told me that Naish's wife Gladys, having a penchant for strong drink, once backed her brand-new Cadillac from her driveway straight into an oncoming ambulance. The slightly damaged vehicle of mercy now had a new mission, and straightaway took Mrs. Naish to the hospital. J. Carrol showed up later in a black suit with appropriate shirt and tie, carrying a black "doctor's" bag. After ascertaining that his wife was alright, he made his "rounds" at the hospital by checking all the attractive females' vital signs. He started on the top floor and, when he finally scurried out to his car, had examined—titillated—a number of patients not necessarily in dire circumstances.

Richard Bartlett, a very good motion picture director, invited me to dinner at his home one evening along with the Naishes. Also invited were Rusty Richards—at one time the top tenor with the Sons of the Pioneers—and his wife Amy. Mrs. Naish was quite taken by Rusty and his singing, and gushed on about it at some length.

J. Carrol listened to the gushing, then glared at her. "Shut your mouth!" he snarled, adding through gritted teeth, "Gladys, sweet darling!" This went on until he led her out the door. The last I heard was, "Get in the Goddamned car! Gladys, sweet darling!"

* * *

The night "Gung Ho!" was previewed in Hollywood, Bob and J. Carrol stopped by to pick me up. They had four Marine Raiders with them who had fought on Guadalcanal. A strange feeling crawled over me during the screening. Here were Marines who had actually faced the enemy and I was watching a movie depicting their sacrifices. It came as a surprise to me to find that those gyrenes who had been close to the dreadful reality of war were in awe of film people as much as the film people were in awe of the Marines. I began to look at movie crews in a different light.

* * *

By 1944 the war was swinging our way. The newsreel theaters that sprang up on Hollywood Boulevard were doing a landslide business. It was reassuring to see news and documentary-type films showing that the enemy was losing. American and British naval power had been amply restored and great advances were being made against the Japanese in the Pacific by the middle of that year.

Bob did five movies in '44. In "Thirty Seconds Over Tokyo," he was barely noticed as part of the daring Jimmy Doolittle raid of 1942. But in RKO's production of Zane Grey's story, "Nevada," co-starring Anne Jeffreys and Guinn "Big Boy" Williams, Bob's portrayal of a cowboy named Nevada, his first starring role, earned picture makers' attention. From then on his roles began to take on greater significance.

"Girl Rush" (1944) was a musical-comedy Western designed for the lowbrow, now-forgotten comedy team of Alan Carney and Wally Brown. Bob, playing Jimmy Smith, dressed in drag to get the goods on the outlaws. With him in this scene is Paul Hurst. It was not one of Bob's more memorable films of the 1940s.

BAD MEDICINE

MY DRAFT NOTICE arrived and I was caught on the horns of a dilemma. Joy was pregnant with our second child but something was fearfully wrong with her. She was wasting away to nothing and her doctor, a society man recommended by her mother, seemed to be too busy to take care of her. Instead he sent an assistant, who would stop by the house to give her shots for "water retention." That was all the attention she got. Finally, unable to stand Joy being ignored in this way, I went to the doctor's stylish office on Hollywood Boulevard. I was dressed in my work clothes and must have looked out of place with the women patients dressed in expensive clothes and wearing even more expensive jewelry.

The nurse eyed me coldly. "What is it that you want?" Her tone wasn't friendly at all.

"I have to talk with the doctor about my wife, Joy Mitchum." I looked at her evenly. "I think that she's dying."

The nurse got defensive as hell. "Well, now," she replied, "we seem to have an expert on our hands."

It was my turn. "No, but I have seen people die before and that's what I'm afraid I'm seeing now."

The doctor had entered the room without my having seen him. "Are you a physician, Mr. Mitchum?" His tone was unctuous, irritating.

"No, you know that I'm not."

"Well," he went on condescendingly, "since you aren't, why don't you let me make the decision as to her condition?"

I'd had it with him by then. "Because, doctor, you just send up your assistant. You haven't seen her for a month."

He let me know then that his aide was a fine young man, that I was out of line and should—under armed guard if necessary—leave his office.

"Fine," I said coldly, "but if she dies, so do you."

"Are you threatening me? I'll have you jailed for that!"

I told him he could do that but, sooner or later, I'd get out and he would have to answer to me. It was then that he became gratuitously condescending. "Perhaps we should call in a specialist!"

"Perhaps you should." The hackles on my neck felt stiff. Oh, how I ached to hit that supercilious bastard.

He brought in Dr. Buell Sprague, a magnificent doctor who found that Joy was carrying—along with our child—a cancerous tumor that was as large as a cantaloupe. He saved her life, but the baby never made it.

I have yet to hear an "I'm sorry" from Joy's obstetrician. Since he's long-gone, I suppose I'll have to wait until I get to Valhalla.

* * *

Joy's English father, long-divorced and happily remarried, now lived in Swampscott, Massachusetts. Mr. Hallward invited Joy to stay with him while I was in the Army, so we decided we'd move there before I was called. On the very day we were scheduled to leave, I was unexpectedly called down to the old Pacific Electric Building for my army physical. The train was scheduled to depart at five that afternoon. (Reservations in those times were hard to come by.) I was at the induction center at eight that morning, with plans to meet my family at Union Station at 4:30. At three o'clock, I was still not processed. At four, I informed a bellicose sergeant that I had to leave in half an hour.

"You're in the Army now, by God!" he roared.

"No I'm not. I haven't been sworn in yet and that's that."

The officer in charge was more understanding, advising me that when I got to Massachusetts, I had to report to the nearest induction center. I did just that. Three months later, I was a raw recruit at Fort Devens, Mass.

During those three months, I lived in the town of Swampscott, a delightful place set in a lush farming community amid gently rolling hills and orchards. Across the street from Mr. Hallward's house was a small field in which an old gentleman hoed corn, usually from six in the morning until noon, stopping only to have a sandwich and cold water to wash it down. After watching him for several days, I walked over to him.

"Sir," I asked, "excuse me, but how old are you?" I couldn't help but be in awe of his stamina.

He looked at me with the most piercing blue eyes I'd ever seen. "Ninety-three."

"You must have seen an awful lot of changes around here."

"See that house down there?" He pointed at a farmhouse to the north. "Italians live there. Folks around here look down on Italians. They used to look down on the Irish. Now, they're our leading politicians." With that parting shot, he picked up his hoe and went back to the corn.

(It wasn't many years later that the Catholic John F. Kennedy became 36th President of the United States. Yes, old man—an awful lot of changes.)

WHICH WAY IS THE ENEMY?

BECAUSE OF MY SEAFARING background, I was assigned to the 361st Harbor Craft Company, the most bizarre outfit any army, anywhere, at any time, has ever created.

Our captain, a former Boston toy manufacturer, assumed command of the 361st presumably because he once owned a racing sloop—none of us enlisted men could discern any other reason. He was a big, florid man—indecisive, weak and quite petty.

To top it off, his name was Clapp. Nathaniel D. Clapp.

We shared an instant mutual repulsion: He wanted to lead and couldn't; I didn't want to follow and had to.

The 361st was assembled in a temporary post, Camp Gordon Johnson, in the panhandle of Florida. The camp sat on sand that constantly shifted as the winds blew. The primary duties of the raw recruits were to undergo the humilities of basic infantry training, to sweep sand and to sweep sand.

Our boats were based at Carabell, a port town within walking distance from our barracks. The 361st had a potpourri of vessels ranging from launches to freight service boats measuring 136 feet in length. We also had seagoing tugs—I was eventually assigned to one of those. Beyond the efficiency of our drill sergeants and the sleekness of our vessels, all sanity ended in the 361st.

Among our enlisted personnel were three men with bad-conduct discharges from the Navy who had been given a choice: the 361st or Leavenworth Prison. One of these men piously changed his spots, volunteering to be the

Chaplain's assistant. It didn't take long to figure out that the communion wine was the pivotal reason for his religious resurgence.

We also had three Italians. Not Italians from Brooklyn, Chicago or Detroit; these were literally off the boat from Italy. They were seamen from an Italian merchant ship that had been docked in New Orleans when Pearl Harbor was bombed. The captain, under sealed orders, promptly had his crew jettison vital machinery into the Mississippi River. The crew was jailed for "obstructing a navigable river." Some of these men were released when they agreed to work as farm laborers, then in short supply. Two years later, three of these men found themselves drafted into the U.S. Army—and the 361st.

During basic training, one of the Italians, Private Gambrioski, took umbrage against his lot in life. A man with buck teeth, a large nose and a cap that was much too small for his head, Gambrioski, in short order drill, would join the drill instructor in perfect cadence in what became a ritual. The D.I., a veteran of Guadalcanal, would start his sing-song cadence, "Hup-toop-threep-foh." Gambrioski could be heard overriding him. "I wanta go to the Red-ah-Cross!" The D.I. would yell back in perfect rhythm, "Shut your mouth, Gambrioski." This went on for days, with neither gentleman missing a beat. *(Much later I heard that Gambrioski and his cohorts were returned to their sunny homeland, but only after Italy surrendered.)*

❄ ❄ ❄

A soldier named Eddie Gazo played a central part in my running feud with the good Captain Clapp. Eddie looked like Rocky Graziano and had the same general build and attitude. He laughed a lot and, because of his devil-may-care attitude, we became fast friends.

A wounded veteran of the North African campaign, Eddie purchased an old Packard with his overseas money. I celebrated the finish of my basic training by riding in the luxury of the Packard with him to Tallahassee, a city brimming with beautiful young ladies who attended university there. Later that night, two soldiers asked if they could ride back to camp with us. Eddie agreed to take them along. While we sailed through the urban area of Tallahassee, the younger of the men had to unencumber himself of a load of beer and asked Eddie to stop. The youthful warrior proceeded to wet down the left rear wheel of the car parked in front of us. Just then, two soldiers and two girls came around the corner.

One of the soldiers, a sergeant, hit the young man a thunderous blow to the head. The poor kid, his member still in hand, fell like a rock to the pavement. "What'd you do that for?" I was so genuinely shocked I couldn't help blurting out my objection.

"Oh, you want some too!" The macho sergeant charged directly into my left hook. I landed several more shots on his visage before he was rendered *hors de combat.* By that time, MPs had arrived to escort us all to the Provost Marshal.

That worthy sat back, surveying the situation. "What did you hit him with?" he asked.

"With my hands."

"Don't you ever say 'Sir'?" he inquired.

"With my hands, *sir.*"

When it came to light that the kid's cheekbone had been fractured by the sergeant, the Provost Marshal ordered the MPs to deliver me back to my camp without penalty. It was there that it hit the fan.

"You're the first one to bring disgrace to the 361st!" Captain Clapp screamed. The fact that a 361st tugboat had recently erred in judgment and torn a nine-foot hole in the bow of a 10,000-ton ammunition ship in New York harbor was dwarfed by my own personal collision with the sergeant. However, I was put on restriction for two weeks and saw a lot of action washing dishes.

When I was "sprung," I treated myself to a trip to Wakullah Springs, a lovely resort area just a few miles west of Tallahassee. The springs are over 260 feet deep and so clear that, in a glass-bottom boat, you can espy heads from tails on a penny.

I purchased a darned good quart of whiskey, Coon Age, and tied it under the float that the hotel had moored in the Springs. I dived now and then into the cool water to retrieve it and take a sip. Early one morning I was quite alone out there. Except for Ol' Sam. I came up from my dive clutching my Coon Age to face a 14-foot alligator. I must have resembled the road-runner as I literally churned my way to the bank.

The old Black caretaker stood leaning on a rake, watching me as I thrashed my way ashore. "That's ol' Sam," he chuckled. "Been 'round here for years. He ain't never hurt nobody."

It took me several moments of deep concentration, but I decided to swim back to the float. I retrieved my fallen Coon Age and retired to my room to soothe my nerves.

THE OLD FIGHT GAME

FROM SOMEWHERE in the dark recesses of the Army came my orders, shipping me to radio school at Camp Crowder, Missouri. They arrived at a most propitious time. When I detrained at Crowder, it was late in the day and I was greeted by the first snowfall of the season. The lot of us sat on our duffel bags for over an hour before we were assigned to a barracks.

My army life took on a different hue. The captain in charge of "A" Company was a former "pro" football player and a confirmed jock. One cold morning after we all fell out, he told us we had been invited to join the Golden Gloves tournaments that were just now opening up to the services.

"I want volunteers for each weight division." He stared at us malevolently. Not a volunteer in sight.

"Alright then," he went on, "we'll go on 25-mile marches every day until I get my squad." My hand popped up. I would much rather fight than walk. A sufficient number of other hands joined in.

Our new orders were to go to school and train. All other duties were taken over by the non-boxers.

My first bout was with Jim Claitor: 6-foot-3, an even 200 pounds, and the heavyweight champion of Fort Monmouth, New Jersey. Apparently that was supposed to scare me to death for, on the night of the fight, his second came into my dressing room immediately after the camp doctor finished checking me out.

"You ever fight before?" He eyed me belligerently.

"No," I lied.

"Well, then," he went on, "you'd better forfeit the fight."

Outside the dressing room, I could hear the yells of the spectators. My bout was next.

"Too late for that," I answered.

"Well, then," he sighed, "he'll cut you to ribbons." And the second left.

The doctor turned to me and held up his stethoscope. "You can lie to him," he said, "but you can't lie to this. Do you know what your opponent's heartbeat registered? One hundred and twenty."

"What was mine?" I really wanted to know.

"Sixty-seven. You're really worried, aren't you?" Then he became serious. "They're betting ten to one against you."

My face fell. "I wish I had some money." As usual, I was flat broke.

"I've put a hundred on you," the doc beamed. "You get ten per cent."

Radiantly, I entered the ring. My second was Ivan Menard, an Arkansas lad. The crowd was yelling. "Ten to one on the tall guy," was the most prominent call.

"You got any money?" I asked Ivan.

"I've got ten," he answered apprehensively.

"Put it down," I ordered. He hesitated. "*Put it down!*" He took the nearest offer and I felt better.

The ring announcer quieted the crowd. "In the heavyweight bout of the evening, we have, fighting out of the white corner, from Baton Rouge, Louisiana, weighing in at one hundred and ninety-nine pounds, the heavyweight champion of Fort Monmouth, New Jersey—Jim Claitor!" The roar of the crowd was deafening. The announcer silenced them again. "In the black corner, from Hollywood, Cal—" All hell broke loose.

Brother Bob proved he was of star quality in 1945 in "The Story of G.I. Joe," an adaptation of the World War II writings of war correspondent Ernie Pyle (played by Burgess Meredith). Bob's role as the doomed Lieutenant Walker brought him his one and only Oscar nomination (as Best Supporting Actor). "G.I. Joe" is still one of Bob's personal favorites.

"Hoooollywood!" "Hiya, sweetie!" "Get her!" "Ooh la la!" "Hollywooood!" My weight and name were lost to the crowd. I sat in my corner, laughing aloud. I *knew* he was mine.

In the first round, Claitor jabbed me once on the forehead then once over the heart. My grandmother had hit me harder. At the round's end, I clinched with him on the ropes, whispering into his ear, "Wait 'til I hit *you!*"

He roared across the ring at the bell and was actually into my corner when I caught him with a right, flush on the chin. He keeled over like a tall tree freshly axed and rolled out of the ring and onto the arena floor. The fight was over thirty seconds into the second round.

The camp paper came out heralding the "Hollywood blockbuster." I sent Brother Robert a copy. In the accompanying letter, I gave him and Elmer Jones all the credit for my victory. "After learning what real belters are like," I penned, "Mr. Claitor seemed like a dancing master."

I had two more bouts at Crowder and wound up as the camp champion.

❄ ❄ ❄

On Christmas Eve, 1944, our company was given the privilege of staying in camp for fire duty. Our sergeant, after watching the captain depart, ordered us to stand by, then added, "If you do, you're crazy." Later that night, in Joplin, the captain winked at me when I danced by him with a young lady in my arms. He wasn't too pleased to learn later that our own orderly room had burned to the ground that same night.

Orders came again, returning me once more to Camp Gordon Johnson. And to Captain Nathaniel D. Clapp.

❄ ❄ ❄

In the spring of 1945, a movie starring Robert Mitchum, "The Story of G.I. Joe," came to the Post Theater. I felt a brotherly pride while waiting in line to see the film. Several soldiers in front of me were talking about "movie soldiers." The group consensus was that actors were all "queers," not "man enough" to be in the services.

The same GIs were silent when the picture ended. Its overwhelming pathos had caught them in its web. This was the film, directed by William Wellman, that would set Bob on the direct path to stardom. He portrayed an infantry captain (based on a real soldier Ernie Pyle had written about during the Italian campaign) who was loved by his men because he cared about each of them. One scene depicts him writing letters to the loved ones of those killed in action. The despair in Bob's performance was heartbreaking. And when Bob's body was brought down the mountain tied to the back of a pack mule, it was so poignantly depicted that there wasn't a dry eye in the theater.

Another fine peformance in that film was given by Burgess Meredith as Pyle, the famous World War II combat correspondent who was destined to die that same spring during the battle of Ie, a tiny island four miles off the coast of Okinawa.

Before filming began, director Wellman had been impressed by the test Bob did of the letter-writing scene—so impressed that he always regretted afterward that he hadn't filmed it. "He was fantastic!"

By early 1945, Bob was also in the service, stationed at Fort MacArthur, California, as a medical assistant.

I can testify to his authenticity as a medical examiner for I was approached years later by a man in Las Vegas who told me that he had met my brother once. "Oh?" I said, "where did you meet him?"

"Fort MacArthur," the gentleman crowed. "I mooned him pretty good."

❄❄❄

Life at Camp Crowder was fast-moving and exciting. Now I was back in Camp Gordon Johnson and the old country tune, "Life Gets Tedious, Don't It?", took on real meaning.

Eddie Gazo was still in the camp, and once again we teamed up to make a big mistake, heading for our favorite watering hole, Tallahassee.

In a crowded beer joint at the edge of town, we were invited to join one of my lieutenants, Charles Thibaud, at his booth. Seated across from him was a P-51 fighter pilot with a pretty young lady. The girl and Gazo had an instant rapport. The first indication of the pilot's resentment of Gazo's attentions to her was his vicious shattering of a beer bottle and the waving of the jagged glass at Gazo. The second indication was his loud cursing of the girl and Eddie. Only Thibaud's intervention prevented a nasty situation. Eddie and the girl headed for the car.

When I reached the car, the pilot was still harassing the girl and Eddie. I asked him if I could get in the car so he stepped back—and began cursing me. As I started to enter the car, Eddie shouted, "Look out!"

I turned in time to see the officer raise his right arm over his head, an open pen knife in his hand. Instinctively I threw a left hook which caught him squarely on the chin. He went down like a sinking Japanese cruiser.

Because it was an officer I had just belted, I was incarcerated at the Dale Mabry Field stockade. Since the P-51 pilot was automatically characterized as a gentleman, he was out on his own cognizance. I stayed in.

❄❄❄

On my first Sunday in that not-so-charming place, I heard the Black prisoners singing Gospel. They were separated from the Whites at that time; they had the second floor of the barracks, we had the first floor. I went up to listen to the rousing, primeval beat of the music and to hear the rich, deep voices.

When the song ended, a Black prisoner stopped in front of his "congregation." He surveyed them for a long moment. "I'm here to tell you the story of the mustard seed. The mustard seed, so small you cain't see it with the naked eye. But that seed fall into the crack in a mountain. The warm rain come. The sun come. And the mustard seed—it growed, and it growed, and it growed. Until it split that mother-mountain!"

He became even more the preacher. "Now—if you have the seed of the love of the Lord in your heart, like the mustard seed in the mountain, it may be so small you don't know it's there. But! If you love the Lord long enough, deep enough, hard enough, that love will grow, and grow, and grow until you can do anything!" He stopped to stare at his fellow prisoners, then added, "But get outta here!"

One Black asked me what I had done to be incarcerated. When I explained that I had whacked an officer, he clucked sympathetically. "Man, you in *real* trouble!"

I asked him what his crime was and he matter-of-factly answered, "Rape and murder."

STOCKADE DAYS

IN TWO WEEKS my trial came to a head at Dale Mabry Field and the pilot was the one in the dock. It was a most impressive affair. A general was flanked by two majors, then came two captains and finally two lieutenants. The court stenographer was a pretty young civilian girl.

The P-51 pilot glared at me from the dock. I was glad I wasn't in front of his gunsights.

The general called me before him. I saluted smartly while he looked down at his notes. "This report states that the accused cursed you violently before the altercation took place. What did he call you?"

I cleared my throat. "Sir, I'd rather not repeat his words, as there is a young lady present."

Now it was the general's turn to glare. "The Court *orders* you to repeat those words."

I looked at the girl, poised and ready with her pencil. "He called me a sonofabitch, a cocksucker, a mother-fuc—"

"*That's enough!*" roared the general.

The girl's face was beet-red as she transcribed the direct quotation.

The fighter pilot was fined $500 and shipped to North Africa. I went dutifully back to Camp Gordon Johnson. What a relief it was to learn that Captain Clapp and the 361st had been transferred to Hawaii.

❄ ❄ ❄

While I languished in the Dale Mabry stockade, our cousin Gilbert, a combat rifleman with the 35th Infantry in Europe, was fighting in France.

It never had occurred to either Bob or me that Gilbert would be the only Woodside Farm boy to see actual combat. He was little "Sonny" to us.

I last remembered Gilbert when he inherited a woolen sweater that had first been Bob's, then mine. Careless washings, a snowflake or two and occasional rains had shrunk it drastically; we nicknamed it the "hard" sweater. Gil wore it to a church social one cold winter's night, simply because he didn't have anything else. It snowed while the children waited for the church bus and Sonny told them that it wasn't cold. "Look at you all in your big coats. What are you gonna do when it really gets cold?"

Inside the church, the snow on the sweater melted and the wool contracted so much that his arms turned purple. The sweater sleeves had to be cut away.

Years later, for his 40th birthday in North Hollywood, I kept a sweater in my freezer for three days, delivering it to Sonny in its solid condition. "Dear God," he chortled. "My hard sweater!"

Gilbert landed on Omaha Beach on 11 June 1944, five days after the initial D-Day landing, fought at St. Lo and St. Jeanne d'Day for 33 consecutive days without so much as taking his boots off. Much later, he related to me a happening that put the war in microcosm, on a near-human basis.

"We were given a chance at R&R," he told me, "after we took and held St. Lo. We were heading for the beach area south of us and had to cross a river to reach the next small village close to the water. One company had crossed the bridge and another was strung out on it while my company was coming up in the rear. It was almost dark when suddenly a string of German fighters swooped down over us, dropping flares. God have mercy! The town was hit hard by the fighter-bombers that followed them in and the boys on the bridge took an awful beating. We scattered in the fields so we didn't get hurt much. It took us all that night and most of the next day to get that town put back together. In the afternoon, a jeep pulled into the center of town and a two-star general got out so we all started to salute him.

"'At ease, men.' he ordered. 'I know you took a beating last night, but we're in for more. The Krauts have made a breakthrough. We're surrounded.'

"He went into an immediate conference with our captain and soon, I was given my orders. I had an anti-tank gun and a squad that was down to eight men at the time and the captain, having given me my coordinates, told me to place my gun in an advantageous position.

"Well," Gilbert went on, "I took my truck and the anti-tank gun out into the French countryside. It was beautiful. Gradually, you became aware that it was deserted. However, there were plenty of livestock around so we decided to stop by a farmhouse, catch some chickens and have a good ol' country-fried chicken dinner. We caught the chickens alright. Then an L-C5 flew over us, waggled its wings and dropped a note by parachute.

"I sent my corporal out to get the note and when I read it, I shouted for my men to get away from the gun. Thank God they did for just as I read 'Enemy tanks approaching through northwest woods,' one of their 88s blew our gun and truck all to hell!

"We ran into the farmhouse and John, I'll be frank to tell you, only fear saved our lives. We ran out into the farmyard and dug deep foxholes in it. A good thing we did."

Gil told me that all that night the Germans bombarded that farmhouse with mortars until it was reduced to kindling wood. Strangely enough, the Germans were completely gone in the morning. Apparently, they had bigger fish to fry.

About ten o'clock, a soldier from their outfit reached them to inform them that in half an hour one of their lieutenants would pick them up at a bridge over a culvert. Gilbert ordered his squad to fall in and they marched to the rendezvous site. Suddenly, they heard a heavy rumbling. Gil told his men to lie in the ditch as though they were dead. Soon, through his fingers, he spied two German half-tracks, loaded with infantrymen, heading toward them. His heart almost stopped when the two vehicles halted on the bridge.

"Those Germans were arguing like crazy among themselves," Gilbert remembered. "They'd point in all directions and the word they used most was 'nein!' It was point and 'nein,' point and 'nein.' Then one soldier barked out an order and the half-tracks moved on.

"Hell, John!" Gilbert told me. "They were just as lost as we were."

❄ ❄ ❄

Bob was honorably discharged from the Army, and rightfully so. Not only did he have his wife and two children to support (Christopher had been born), but the financial load of helping our grandmother, our mother and our stepfather was on his shoulders. Our sister had recently divorced so she and her son, Tony, also needed assistance. We also have another sister, Carol, who then, at the age of eleven, was hardly self-supporting. Bob took care of them all for some time.

❄ ❄ ❄

Our old friend, Elmer Jones, had "beaten" the Army by joining the Merchant Marines. In no way was this due to a lack of courage—he volunteered consistently for combat-zone duties. His version of outfoxing the services lay in reference to his getting well-paid while in ports that were wide open to enemy bombardments or riding sea-lanes well-prowled by U-boats.

"No nineteen bucks a month for me," he snarled. Little did I know when I'd landed him the job on *The Memory* that he'd follow that nautical bent to all the corners of the globe.

HAWAII CALLING

MY ORDERS TO REJOIN my outfit came within two weeks' time and I found myself aboard a train bound for Vancouver, Washington. Lieutenant Thibeaud was in charge of those of us in the 361st who, for various reasons, hadn't traveled with the main contingent. We remained at Vancouver Barracks for ten days, then were trucked to Portland, Oregon, and loaded on a troopship bound for Oahu.

With boxing matches held each afternoon on the afterdeck, I was soon roped into fighting. The athletic director on board was Rudy Rudolph, a boxer who asked for volunteers. Again, there were no hands raised, so he asked me to stage an exhibition to get the troops involved. I agreed. Very shortly a lively set of bouts was under way.

I refereed a number of fights and one afternoon paid heed to a burly bastard shouting, "I wanna fight!" I looked the crowd over and announced on the mike: "Men, there's a heavyweight here who wants a bout. Do I have any volunteers?"

"No, no!" The Brute shouted for the entire Pacific to hear. "I wanna fight *you*!"

There was little I could do but agree, and the clash of titans was scheduled for the next day. At four that morning I was awakened by Lieutenant Thibaud and our warrant officer, who had been the Philippine's lightweight champion for a number of years. Thibaud, himself a good fighter, and the ex-champ led me into the latrine to coach me on how to beat The Brute. They drank bourbon and ate oranges during their strategy talks.

Fight time: My opponent was 5-foot-11, weighed about 240 pounds and looked like "two-ton" Tony Galento. Thank God there were only three two-minute rounds facing me. For five minutes and fifty-nine seconds, I jabbed, parried, blocked, hooked and danced my way to a victory. In the last second of the third round, he swung a desperation left hook, catching me on the right thigh. It all but broke my leg.

"Wow! You sure taught him a boxing lesson" . . . "Mitch, you're some boxer!" I was surrounded by dozens of well-wishers and admirers. Little did they know that if The Brute had caught me in the rib cage, they would have had to bury me at sea. As it was, I hobbled around the ship for three days.

Thibaud rewarded me with $50. I wondered how much he and the warrant officer had laid down on me. They could have lost it all had the Galento-type raised his sights a little. Imagine, John Mitchum a soprano.

Our troopship rounded Diamond Head with the sun rising high in the sky. Honolulu spread out before us with the Aloha Tower beckoning us to land. It was a heady sight.

As soon as I rejoined my outfit, my feud with the good Captain Clapp roared into another lap. It didn't help when I got into a beef with a soldier named Lenhardt. The main body of the 361st still had no knowledge of my ring experience, so all eyes were on me when I came down to the dock area and was challenged by Lenhardt to "put the gloves on." He regularly beat up on his fellow servicemen in "friendly" bouts, taking sadistic satisfaction in hurting people who had little or no boxing skills.

He tossed me a set of gloves, smiling. "We'll just take it easy." I had heard that line many times before.

"Sure," I grinned. "We'll take it easy."

With our gloves laced on, we faced each other. He threw a sneak right; I stepped inside it and struck him square on the chin. He went down on his ass and, for some moments, just stared at me.

"Get up." I must have sounded a little cold. I didn't like him, and I guess it showed.

"No. No," he whined. "You're a ringer!"

"Yes, I am, Lenhardt. But aren't you?"

He wouldn't get up. I suddenly became aware that the 180 men in our outfit were watching in silence.

I saw Lenhardt's face the next day and couldn't believe it. He had been savagely beaten by a skinny private named Thompson. Later I heard that Lenhardt had been on the deck of his tug and ordered Thompson to come from the dock to wash his coffee cup. Thompson, having suffered much under Lenhardt's rule, told him to wash the cup himself. Lenhardt, feeling he needed to prove his manhood, started to climb up to the dock. As his head cleared the dock floor, it was met by Thompson's G.I. boot. Lenhardt clung to the dock for dear life. To fall between the tug and the pilings could mean death by crushing. Thompson kicked him again and beat Lenhardt to a point where other soldiers mercifully pulled him away.

The company lauded Thompson. The captain laced into—me.

Clapp ordered me to "paint the latrines." On bleak Sand Island, our crappers were a series of forty old-fashioned "one-holers" in a drab building.

"What color, sir?" I asked in spritely fashion.

He became apoplectic. "I don't care what color! Paint the latrines!"

"Yes, sir." I saluted smartly and headed for the door.

"One more thing, Private Mitchum."

I spun around. "Yes, sir." (God, was I military.)

He glared as he said, "Just paint half the toilets!"

"Yes, sir." I snapped a salute.

"Dismissed!"

I painted the ceiling white, the walls a light blue and half of each seat red. Later a jeep roared up and the captain roared out. "You! . . . you! . . . you!" he sputtered. "The men can't sit down! You painted half the toilets!"

"Yes sir," I said cheerily. "I thought it a strange order when you gave it to me." He missed apoplexy by a hair.

* * *

One of our sergeants, "Moe" Mulvaney, was a big, beefy Irishman from Pennsylvania. He was assigned to a freight service boat ferrying supplies into the inland waters of Malaysia, and one day he bounded down the gangplank laughing uproariously. "I came around from the wheelhouse and heard our captain yellin', 'Cha-bang! I gotcha! Cha-bang! I gotcha!'" Moe laughed at his attentive audience. "I looked in his room and he's got his .45

out. He whirls and points at his wife's picture. 'Cha-bang! I gotcha!' He whirls again and points at his kid's picture. 'Cha-bang! I gotcha!' He sees me lookin' and I *know* he's practicing against the crew. I guess he's got a few memories of what a prick he's been to most of us."

Our master sergeant, Rex Sines, was a topnotch machinist. Slender, energetic and endowed with a great sense of humor, Sines was galvanized into action by Mulvaney's story. Whittling out three perfect replicas of .45s, he kept one, gave Sergeant Smith one and turned over the third to me. We swaggered down the docks with the phony pistols in our belts and, like the gunfighters of old, chased each other.

"Cha-bang! I gotcha!"

"Cha-bang! I gotcha!"

One day, a communique appeared on our bulletin board:

There will be no more cha-banging on the docks.

Captain Clapp
361st Harbor Craft Company

SAVED FROM THE DEEP SIX

BY ACCIDENT I ran into an old friend, Natividad Vacio, a singer and entertainer whom I had first met in 1939. "Natti" was part of a group of voluntary singers who met once a week in a church in Honolulu to keep their "hands" in choral music. Now that the war was over, servicemen were being badly beaten by gangs of young Hawaiians long resentful of G.I.s, sailors and Marines for claiming their women. General Blount looked desperately for any means to give American troops a better image.

Actor-singer Natividad Vacio, whom I have known since 1939, remains one of my best friends.

Out of this crisis came the American G.I. Chorus. Working quietly behind the scenes, Blount's liaison officer cut orders to make the chorus an official unit.

My orders were delivered to me in a unique way, even for the Army. I was waiting on the dock at three in the morning for a shore boat to pick me up and transport me to a freight service boat (my new assignment) when a jeep roared up. Its passenger was a radioman I had gone to school with at Camp Crowder. Elatedly he told me that he was my replacement, and gave me my new orders. I had been assigned to the G.I. Chorus.

A few weeks later, the freight service boat carrying that radioman went to the bottom in a typhoon off the island of Okinawa. There were no survivors.

During the early days of World War

II my stepfather (the old Major) had tried to join the war effort—not only to be in the thick of things, but also to help out the family's strained finances. He wrote Winston Churchill a letter begging that he be allowed back into the service. "Winnie" turned him down, for the Major's massive wounds were a matter of record. He applied to the U.S. services and they too turned him down.

Finally, he lied about his age, dropping some ten years off the truth, and signed aboard an ammunitions carrier bearing a Libyan flag. He made two trips to the South Pacific, sailing back as a first officer. Considering that at 62 years of age he had signed on as a deckhand, his promotions were phenomenal . . . unless you realized that he carried captain's papers for any tonnage, any waters.

Using his latest success as leverage, the Major applied for and received a commission in the U.S. Army as first officer on a refrigerator barge. On his first trip, his captain died mysteriously and, by wireless, he was given command. Docking in Honolulu, he ordered his crew to load enough good Hawaiian earth to cultivate a vegetable garden on the ship's bow. He was especially proud of his tomatoes and enjoyed fresh salads throughout the cruise.

The Major took part in the Philippines invasion, his only scrape with danger occurring when Japanese fighters strafed his decks.

"Blasted my bloomin' tomatoes! Bloody well destroyed them!" he told me later.

Then the Major headed for Okinawa, his hold fully laden with supplies. A typhoon—the same one that destroyed the freight service boat I had almost been assigned to—drove his vessel high onto a coral reef. Ironically the coral, penetrating her bottom, held her tight and fast. The Major tied a line about his waist and dove into the raging seas to rescue six sailors who otherwise would have perished.

Captain Clapp called me into his office a few months later, perplexed and annoyed. I had been ordered to appear at the Post Headquarters but he had no inkling why. Neither had I—until I saw the Major. He was in full captain's uniform and had wrangled a week's pass for me out of the Post Commander. President Truman had awarded the Major a citation for bravery for saving those six seamen. At that time, Dad was 65 years old.

We had a wonderful week. He would sit with me in a crowded bar and, at the right moment, sob, "My son, my son. I thought I'd never see you again."

Some serviceman would take the bait. "This your son?" he'd ask.

"Yes. My ship was lost in the typhoon at Okinawa. There were moments when I felt I'd never see him again."

We always got the same result. "Hey, barkeep. Their next round's on me." Others would take up the cry. We didn't buy a drink for a week.

When the Major left on a transport for San Francisco, I thought long and hard about stowing away . . .

❄ ❄ ❄

The American G.I. Chorus moved into Fort De Russy, an R&R camp located adjacent to Waikiki Beach. I soon became involved with several attractive young ladies and settled down to a daily routine with three of them—which almost proved to be my undoing. After rehearsals in the afternoon I would visit a beautiful Korean miss; in the early evening my tryst would be with a pretty peaches-and-cream blond SPAR from New

The American G.I. Chorus, 1945. I cannot identify myself in this picture. Can you?

Jersey; and then I would spend the night with a lovely librarian. I'd get back to camp barely in time to stand reveille—then stumble to the mess hall.

Early one morning, the strain of combat took its toll. The choir was scheduled to go to the "Big Island" of Hawaii for a series of concerts. About four in the morning, I began to shake like a Tahitian dancer and fell out of bed. Vacio, my roommate, called the medics, who rushed me to the hospital. For two weeks I drifted in and out of consciousness and awoke to find three doctors staring down at me.

"We've all separately diagnosed you and have come to the same conclusion, soldier. What are your duties in the Army?"

"I sing with the G.I. Chorus," I whispered.

"Very perplexing," one said. "We nearly lost you from complete exhaustion."

Don't tell me that stuff can't kill you.

❄ ❄ ❄

The Choir was invited on Christmas Eve, 1945, to a delightful party at the home of lovely Justine Van Oort, a gifted soprano who was high society on Oahu. Then the Jekyll and Hyde existence I always seem to lead took over.

On the transport that brought me to the islands had been a large contingent of the famed 442nd Regimental Combat Team, a heavily decorated unit of Japanese-Americans who had fought valiantly in the bloody Italian campaign. These men were inveterate gamblers who bet on me consistently in my shipboard bouts.

Now, on the way back to De Russy from Van Oort's party, I passed Oahu's largest taxicab stand. The owner of the fleet was a huge Samoan, a professional wrestler and now a philanthropist, who was throwing a wide-open Christmas party for any servicemen who wanted to join in. There must have been 1,000 people celebrating.

"Johnny Mitchum. Hey! Johnny Mitchum." My hailer in the crowd was a member of the 442nd. I went over to say hello.

"Hey, everybody. This is Johnny Mitchum. Best goddamn fighter you ever seen. Smooth, like oil. Goddamn!"

A sailor confronted me. "You don't look so tough to me!" he snarled.

"Oh, Lord, no," I protested. "I never said I was tough."

The sailor was not to be put off. "We've got Swede Larson here. Heavyweight champion of the submarine fleet. Ten dollars says you can't lay a glove on him."

The Swede hove into view. "What's goin' on?"

"This G.I. says he can beat you." The sailor sure knew subtle ways to trap a fellow.

A human ring formed around us as the Swede moved in on me. I caught him a sharp left hook to the ear and rocked him. I felt I'd earned my $10. I never got it.

Pandemonium reigned. Everybody started fighting. Tire irons. Jack-handles. Broken beer bottles. I bugged out of there in a hurry.

***

The American G.I. Chorus, a maverick outfit to begin with, caused great consternation to the Post Commander, a "regular army" Texan and an inarticulate major. "Singing" soldiers? Bullroar!

We often played our guitars and sang long after lights out. The Texan, in order to discipline us, tried like hell to catch us red-handed. We were General Blount's "pets," according to him, so he had to be careful of his charges. We didn't make it easy for him.

One of our group adopted a stray German Shepherd that we affectionately dubbed Poontang. One night, the major crept down the long, unlit hall that led to our barracks, hoping to nail us. The beer was flowing, the guitars were throbbing and ol' "Bear Down" Davis was bearin' down on his fiddle. The major had us at last.

That is, until Poontang bit him unceremoniously on his big ass. The major's war whoop could be heard as far as Canton Island. We were instantly in our rooms, sound asleep. Poontang was protectively jeeped to the lee side of the island as the Major still ranted noisily about getting his target pistol.

I wish I had kept a copy of the report the major sent to Island Headquarters. It spoke of "them singin' soldiers," their late hours and how he, in the line of duty, had attempted to "catch 'em red-handed after lights out. But a dawg by the name of Poontang bit me on the left rear flank and them boys hid that there dawg so as I could not shoot him."

A copy of the report mysteriously appeared on the bulletin board but was scuttled before I had a chance to retrieve it. Bless ol' Poontang.

A few months later I set sail for home and, except for the fact that we were entertained by Joe Maphis, the fabulous two-neck guitar player, it was an uneventful trip.

Joe and his wife Rose became an integral part of country music players in America. They eventually settled in Bakersfield, California, and were a popular singing team until Joe's death in the summer of 1986.

We steamed in under the Golden Gate Bridge into misty, mythical San Francisco. Every available man was topside. The sight of that lovely span brought cheers from our throats and tears to our eyes.

I was sent to Camp Beale for discharge, and was soon heading for Los Angeles, that great city of fabled contrasts, and home.

BOOK FOUR

POSTWAR HIGHS

BOOK FOUR

HOME AGAIN, HOME AGAIN

WHEN I LEFT Camp Beale, near Marysville, California, it was in the dead-heat of summer. The hills seemed barren and desolate after Hawaii. I swore never to return to the area—though in later years I would come full-circle, breaking this vow.

My first destination after my discharge in 1946 was West Los Angeles where my wife and daughter were living with her sister, Gloria Grahame, and Mother Hallward. When I arrived, no one was home. I stood disconsolately on the front porch until a voice boomed out: "You must be Mitchum."

I looked around to see a short, rotund fellow staring impassively at me. He stuck out his hand. "Bill Conrad," he grumbled. "Come on in and have a drink." Although he was later to star in TV's "Cannon" and "Jake and the Fat Man," in those years Conrad was a struggling radio actor who played occasional heavies, and damn realistic ones, in films.

As we sat sipping Scotch and soda, Conrad asked if I played chess. When I told him that I played a modest game, he set up the board. He didn't lose graciously. After eleven straight losses, he apparently made a solemn vow to himself. One night, I drank far too much Chivas Regal and lost my first game to him. He leaped up like a squat jumping jack. "That's it!" he cried. "No more!" and he left the field, victoriously.

* * *

The great Winston Churchill numbered among his vast accomplishments the art of bricklaying. Once, during a morning stroll, he stopped to observe three such artisans in the act of plying their trade.

"My good man," Churchill said, beaming at the first worker, "what are you doing?"

"I'm layin' bricks, I am."

"And you, sir," Winnie growled at the second bricklayer, "what are you doing?"

The man looked at Churchill oddly. "Why, I'm buildin' a wall."

The great leader sighed in exasperation. He then asked the third man the same question and was gratified when that fellow looked at him with a quiet awareness. "I'm building a cathedral," he answered.

Churchill went on happily. One out of three wasn't bad.

And now Lou Huston, an old buddy from the Long Beach Players days, had *me* involved in a bit of bricklaying for Bill Conrad. Lou had become a writer and, like so many of the breed, fought a constant battle with John Barleycorn—a fact that would figure mightily in our wall-building.

Bill Conrad made a deal with Lou that he soon regretted. Bill would supply the booze for the workmen needed to erect a brick wall in front of Conrad's house. It was to be three feet high and 30 feet long on each side of his walkway. In addition to myself, Lou found two other cronies and we set to work with a vengeance. With the wall only half-finished and a $400 booze deficit confronting him, the frustrated Conrad called a halt to the proceedings and hired a professional to finish the job.

The next morning, Bill stared out his front window to see the professional, a gnarled old bricklayer, sitting on the curb, staring at the half-finished, far-from-perfect wall. Bill went out to talk to him.

"My good man," he bristled. "I'm not paying you $15 an hour just to sit and look at that wall."

"No charge, Mr. Conrad, until I get started. But you told me to match *that!*" He pointed scornfully at our masterpiece. "There ain't no way I can do that."

Bill had him finish the second half in conventional style.

William Conrad

❄ ❄ ❄

Gloria Grahame, since 1945, had been married to actor Stanley "Stash" Clements. It was a rocky marriage and no small part of the difficulties involved our shared mother-in-law. Neither one of us was considered good enough for her daughters. Stash had to bear the fact that he was Polish and from Brooklyn.

To Mrs. Hallward (of London), the aforenamed combination put Stash one step beneath human dignity. Only the fact that Bob was my brother and that he had worked with Gloria in "Crossfire" saved *me* the ultimate snub.

Stanley Clemens

❄ ❄ ❄

Gloria called me at my apartment shortly after midnight, gasping that she wanted me to come to her rescue. Stash was royally drunk, armed with a butcher knife and threatening to kill his mother-in-law with it.

"Call the police!" I suggested—but no way. They didn't want publicity. On the way over to their place, I wondered how they could avoid it if the knife struck home.

When I arrived, Stash turned the knife on me. I tried to talk him into putting it down. He wouldn't so I threw a left hook that broke his nose and put him out cold. Gloria called their doctor who groggily and angrily agreed to meet us at his office on Westwood Boulevard. On the way, I pulled the car over twice to knock Stash out again because he kept waking up and fighting me. In the doctor's office, I was forced once again—with apologies to the distraught physician—to knock Stash cold one final time.

For the next two months, I heard nothing more about the incident. Then my phone rang one morning. It was Stanley. "Hello, Mitch?"

"Yes, Stanley." I braced myself for the tirade.

"I wanna thank you. When I was a kid in New York, m' bruddah broke m' nose. The docs all said I had to get it rebroke to set it right. No way. I never had the nerve. But you did it for me. You should see it now. It's bee-oo-itful."

Stash and I had always been good friends. I felt good that a little nose-breaking hadn't changed that.

❄ ❄ ❄

"Crossfire," produced by RKO in 1947 under Eddie Dmytryk's direction, was a very good picture. The three Roberts—Mitchum, Young and Ryan—worked beautifully together to make a difficult theme acceptable as entertainment. Anti-Semistism was at the core of the story (based on a novel by Richard Brooks, who became an important filmmaker himself) and Ryan played the psychopathic killer to the hilt.

All three Bobs are masters of underplaying. At one point, a very exasperated Dmytryk said, "Hey, fellas, I know what you're doing, but if you keep it up, even the sound man won't hear you." One would start at a low level, the other would come in under him. The third would drop his volume even farther until they were veritably whispering at one another. They finally agreed upon a point of acceptance and complied with it.

"Till the End of Time" was one in a spate of films Bob made right after he was released from military duty in October 1945. It depicted the adjustment problems servicemen were facing when they came home. Bob portrayed William Tabeshaw, a vet with a metal plate in his head who seeks a few bucks from his sympathetic buddy Guy Madison.

MY SCREEN DEBUT

THAT SAME YEAR, 1947, I joined the professional ranks of character actors in Hollywood. I was walking down Santa Monica Boulevard and an agent, a little worse for wear from a four-martini breakfast, stopped me to ask, "Are you an actor?"

I told him that I wasn't and he stared at me. "So do you want to be one?" His scrutiny was intent.

"Why not?" I eyed him quizzically. "Where do I go?"

He took me to a studio on Cahuenga Boulevard, explaining on the way that the director-producer of the film had just described the kind of man he wanted for a particular role. The director, Frank Wisbar—who had escaped the holocaust in Germany to start over again in America—stared at me from all angles. "Yes," he slowly nodded in agreement with himself. And I was hired to make my first picture, "The Prairie."

The film depicted a pioneer family attempting to cross Indian country alone. Alan Baxter was the young, heroic scout while Charles Evans played my father. I played Asa, a naive, nice guy in love with the young heroine.

One scene called for me to fight Alan. The assistant director asked me if I could fight, and I assured him I could. The stunt coordinator told me to throw a left and told Baxter to throw a right. We were then to go into a clinch, after which the fight would be broken up. I threw a left alright, putting a gash above Alan's left eye that required six stitches. I hadn't been told that I was supposed to "pull" my punches in accepted film-fighting style. Later, in a scene with Charles Evans, I found out why I had been chosen for that part. Evans sighs, "Asa, you're a very dull lad." My film-cousin eventually murdered me for a clear path to the heroine.

***

While I began my own film career, Brother Robert was climbing rapidly in status into the upper echelons of the business. With his penchant for attracting characters, he had assembled a swarm of them. Although he had "open sesame" to the homes of the Hollywood elite, his real love lay in the environs of those characters. You have heard of Elmer (the Swami) Jones, George (Grey Cloud) Fargo . . . Now enter "Seed Sacker," "Dusty Dirty" and "Tyrone." The latter was really Boyd Cabeen, a professional baby-sitter.

In movie parlance, a "baby-sitter" is a man hired by a production company to go into bars and restaurants with their charge, the star of the film. If a nose is to be broken in a brawl, the studio figures "better the baby-sitter's" than their star's. It's hard to match film on Monday if the hero's nose is badly bent over the weekend.

Boyd was something else. I walked into the Coach and Horses Tavern on Sunset Boulevard one late evening in 1948 to see him kissing a young lady in a booth to the right of the entrance. Kissing? He was swallowing her. The bartender, apparently having seen this performance before, came from behind the bar and bolted the front door.

Tyrone took the girl from the booth and, after placing her on the bar, started to eat her up. He cocked an eye to the admiring crowd, announcing his intentions. Upon completing that leg of his journey, he pulled up the girl's panties, placed her on the floor, leaped upon the bar and intoned, "Turnabout is fair play!" She complied. Tyrone went into never-never land to the plaudits of the crowd.

❄ ❄ ❄

In the late Forties, Bob bought a modest home on Clearfield Avenue in Panorama City for our mother and stepfather. It was there that I became aware of a family ritual of which I had been only subliminally conscious before.

The Major—who had sailed around the Horn on square-riggers, fought in the trenches of World War I, ridden a camel into battle against Bedouins in the Sahara, and partaken in the Philippine and Okinawan invasions of World War II—loved our mother with a quiet, fierce devotion.

Whenever he was at home, she woke up each morning to coffee, toast with jam, and a fresh flower on the table.

The flower was always there—even though, on occasion, a rose might be missing from a neighbor's garden . . .

❄ ❄ ❄

I started working with the Los Angeles Bureau of Music with Roger Wagner. The Bureau of Music was a farseeing enterprise that realized Los Angeles was a cosmopolitan city, including in its vast environs every creed, culture and race under the sun. What better way, the city fathers agreed, to join all those disparate groups cohesively than through their music?

With Roger as the head of the division, I conducted four youth groups. The most difficult was in Chavez Ravine. (That was long before the Brooklyn Dodgers moved there to create Dodger Stadium.) My work took me to the public school building there, across the street from an ancient Catholic church. For four weeks, I tried in vain to get the children to sing. They wouldn't cooperate. They weren't rowdy, just silent. It's an odd feeling to conduct music to forty bright-eyed mutes.

I told Roger I had failed him miserably, but he wouldn't accept my mood of defeat. "We need to get the Mexican children involved," he insisted. To this end, he came down to the ravine on my next rehearsal night. We went into the church and Roger introduced himself to the Padre. That worthy spoke no English while Roger, although totally conversant in French, spoke no Spanish. The two picked a common ground, conversing in Latin. I was fascinated to see them calmly dissecting a modern-day problem and putting it together in modern terms in ancient Latin.

Roger explained it to me. "These kids rely heavily on a 'macho' image. To them, a 'gringo' choir teacher doesn't carry that kind of meaning for them."

"What am I supposed to do then?" I asked.

He looked at the Padre, then at me. "Something will happen to cause them to see you in that light."

He turned to the Padre and spoke a few lines in Latin. The old man turned to me and beamed, nodding his head. Somehow, I felt that Roger's belief in God's mysterious ways would cause things to happen.

On the next rehearsal night, two young soldiers in uniform sauntered into the rehearsal auditorium. Both were smoking cigarettes, eyeing me with arrogant disdain.

"Fellows," I said, "it's against the city ordinance you see posted there on the door to smoke in a school building. You'll have to put your cigarettes out or leave."

One of them inched closer to me. "Who's gonna make me, teach?" He

A Young 'Prairie' Dog

These six photographs (all featuring me in "The Prairie") were loaned to Creatures at Large Press by Dan Faris, owner of San Francisco's Cinema Shop. He had received them from Robert L. Lippert, the producer of the film, shortly before Lippert died in 1976. They were the fine-grained photos used to make copies for the theatrical press kits. I have not been able to locate any of these photos elsewhere.

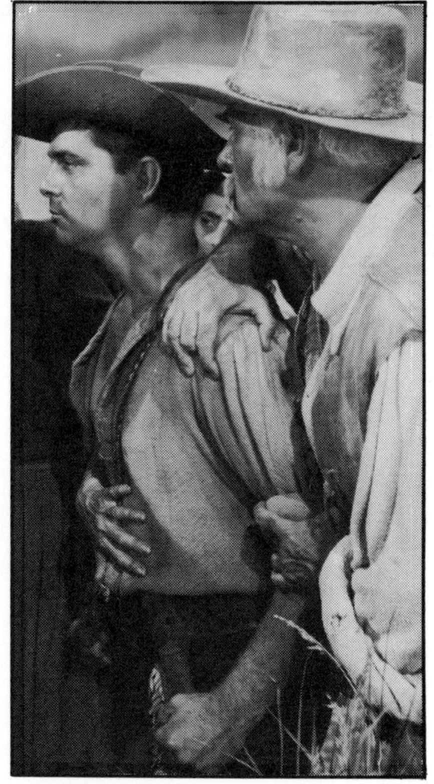

Orry-Kelly (an Australian born John Kelley) was famous for creating glamorous gowns for the stars and provided designs for literally hundreds of feature films (primarily for Warner Bros. and 20th Century-Fox) beginning in the 1920s and continuing until shortly before his death in 1964 (from liver cancer) in Sydney, Australia. He won an Academy Award for his costumes in 1951 for the Gene Kelly musical, "An American in Paris," and again in 1957 for "Les Girls."

punctuated his arrogance by blowing smoke in my direction.

"I guess *I'll* have to."

Magically, a ring of young people formed around us. I heard a girl whisper to her friend, "He's Carlos Chavez' nephew!" At that time, Chavez was a legend in Los Angeles, a fearful boxer who was heralded as the "iron man." My adversary assumed a boxer's stance, moving toward me.

"I'm a fighter too." I felt it only proper that I warn him. "But I weigh in at 190. What are you? 150?" He sneered, continuing to move in fast. I caught him with a left hook. He went down and out with one shot.

I looked at his buddy. "How about you?" I was ready to have at it.

"No, man, no!"

"Well then, get him out of here so we can rehearse."

After he dragged his comatose comrade into the open air, we had a great rehearsal. The old Padre was right. God works in wondrous ways.

❄❄❄

Homosexuals have never been a problem to Bob or me because we've always seen people as they really are. When Bob began his climb to stardom, he naturally became friends with casts and crews that had many gays among them.

One of these was the famed dress designer Orry-Kelly. An Australian, Orry delighted in explaining how he got to Hollywood, couching his words in a delightful Australian accent. "I wanted to be an opera star. I sang with the chorus in Sydney until we did 'Aida.' It was that bloody scene where a hundred spear carriers are shrilling their bloody guts out, throwing out high Cs in a sustained moment of exhalation. 'Hi-yee, hi-yee, hi-yee!' I was screaming at the top of my voice, but all the while I was concentrating on the beautiful behind of the singer in front of me. The conductor halted the chorus at the proper time. That is, everyone but a gay tenor. 'Hi-yee, hi-yee, hi-yee!' all by myself. And still staring at that beautiful ass! I was fired. So I took my last bit of money to find my way to Hollywood."

One of Orry's peers was a diminutive Nebraskan, Milo Anderson, a top designer at Warner Brothers, who was impish and gay as a quince. He truly loved my whole family. He'd come over to our house on Palm Avenue and talk with our mother until the wee hours. One night he came into the house, smiling like the cat that finally caught Tweety Bird, announcing he had just come from Ciro's on Sunset Boulevard.

"I've seen it all!" he chortled. "Anatole Litvak and Paulette Goddard were at the back of the club, kissing so passionately that the maitre d' asked them to leave. They started out of the club but stopped at the bar for a drink. Soon, they were at it again. Suddenly, Mr. Litvak dropped to his knees in front of Paulette and—in a swirl of taffeta—disappeared!"

The incident caused a momentary stir on the Hollywood scene but that's a place where something bigger, more exciting is bound to happen at any moment.

Brother Robert's arrest for pot-smoking wiped out that caper. Not that he wanted it to.

THE MARIJUANA CAPER OF '48

WHEN ROBERT was arrested in the fall of 1948 on his infamous marijuana charge, I was in sunny Sacramento singing with an octet at the State Fair. I was bombarded with questions from my fellow performers as to Bob's complicity when I arrived at the fairgrounds.

Bob had been invited to a party the night before in Laurel Canyon, a soiree also attended by actresses Lila Leeds and Vickie Evans and realtor Robin Ford. Two detectives burst in to find Robert smoking a marijuana cigarette. Bob is alleged to have remarked, "This is the bitter end of everything—my career, my home, my marriage."

For deeply personal reasons I cannot divulge the source of information, but I state emphatically that Brother Robert, under today's laws, would

Attorney Jerry Giesler representing Bob in Los Angeles Superior Court on Feb. 11, 1949, in a hearing to determine if he should be released from jail long enough to finish making "The Big Steal" at RKO.

have been declared innocent if through no other reason than entrapment. The house had already been bugged with hidden microphones before the bust, and rumors had it that the press knew about the event even before the cops so rudely crashed the party.

Bob was set up by those he thought were friends in order that the law enforcement agencies could arrest someone with a name. This lulled the public into believing the police were doing something significant about the problem of dope; the studio hierarchy used Robert as a sacrificial lamb. The major results were posted in the annals of history.

RKO and Selznick didn't want to lose their star so they hired a well-known lawyer, Jerry Giesler, and a capable advocate, Norman Tyre, before issuing the following statement to the press: "All the facts of the case are not yet known. We urgently request members of the industry and the public to withhold its judgment until these facts are known. Both studios feel confident that the American people will not permit Mr. Mitchum's prominence in the motion picture industry to deprive him of the rights and privileges of every American citizen to receive fair play . . . There are a

On Feb. 17, 1949, Brother Bob was a guest of the Los Angeles County Jail's honor farm for a week. He was making cement blocks seven hours a day and occasionally pushing a mop during the final part of his 60-day sentence. He emerged from this "scandal" none the worse for popularity.

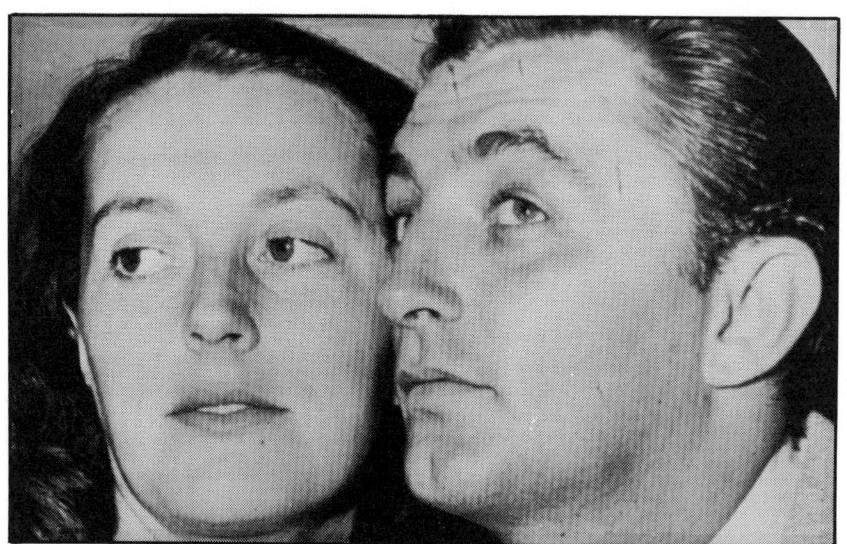

Dorothy and Bob, meeting for the first time since his arrest two days before. At home, in an atmosphere made casual by Bob's light-hearted quips, they posed for reconciliation pictures, two photographers at a time. She and her two sons had been driving across-country at the time of the bust, and had hurried on to Hollywood to stand by Bob.

number of unexplained facts and peculiar circumstances surrounding the raid made yesterday in which Robert Mitchum was involved. His many friends have expressed their opinion that, when all the facts are known, he will be cleared."

Dorothy Mitchum—temporarily separated from Bob—and their two sons were on their way to a reconciliation with the beleaguered Robert when the incident occurred. In a media-fest of attention Dorothy was quoted as saying: "Our differences were the same kind that all married couples get into. Everybody ought to be able to see that Bob is a sick man. Otherwise he wouldn't be mixed up like this. I am indignant that not only Bob but our whole family should have to suffer simply because he is a movie star. Otherwise I don't think all this fuss would be made just because a man may have gotten mixed up with bad company." Dorothy asked photographers and newsmen to ". . . not bother the children. They're very young. They love their father and they don't understand what this is all about."

Bob was put on two-year probation, provided he spent sixty days of it in jail. He was a model prisoner, living up to producer David O. Selznick's prediction that Bob would "come out of his trouble a finer man."

Robert became a huge success in spite of the reams of "bad" publicity, his next release, "Rachel and the Stranger," becoming a major box office hit for RKO Pictures. And dope—since those naive days—in all its chemical complexities and incredible megabuck profits has proven itself to be far beyond the control of conventional law enforcement—and tragically beyond the control of the legions of users.

If I were foolhardy enough to remind Brother Robert of that painful time in order to get some present day comment, I'd be lucky if he gave me only a terse "No comment."

WILD, HECTIC TIMES

THE LATE '40s were wild, hectic times for the Mitchum boys. In 1948 I worked at Columbia on "Knock on any Door" starring Humphrey Bogart and introducing John Derek. George Macready played a formidable prosecuting attorney, Derek a young man accused of killing a cop, and Bogart his defense attorney. I was the jury foreman and spent much of my off-camera time playing chess with Bogey. He played one hell of a game.

Frank Wisbar used me several times in his television series, "The Fireside Theater," and I did a small role in John Ford's World War II comedy, "When Willie Comes Marching Home." On that film I made a mistake: I snapped back at the great Mr. Ford after he barked at me that I was being paid to be seen, not hidden by an actor in front of me. I told him that if the big bastard blocking me would decide where he wanted to be, I could adjust, but that if he kept gyrating, I'd have to slow him down. Ford stared at me for some beats, and started the camera rolling again. The moose in front of me simmered down.

Around that time I also attended the Herbert Wall School of Music under the G.I. Bill, finding it to be a well-staffed establishment. The owner was a big Texan, Major Herbert Wall, also the head voice coach of the school. He was a magnificent teacher and, to this day, is remembered by his students, many of whom are still in show business.

The school boasted an excellent all-male chorus that enabled me to put on a well-reviewed concert at the Wilshire-Ebell Theatre. My friend, Dick Hunton, was the main soloist. As a result of our success, we were hired to appear at the State Fair again in 1949. The emcee for the Fair's last week was Rudy Vallee, the "My Time Is Your Time" singer from Yale University. He was a belligerent rascal, albeit charming.

One night, after a long, tiring rehearsal, Rudy invited a station-wagon load of us to a 2 a.m. breakfast in the old Lenhardt's Cafeteria in Sacramento. My friend Al Wadsworth, accompanied by three young female dancers, rounded out the party. Al and the girls went immediately to the food line while I waited for Vallee. He was talking to the help so he waved me on.

When I had my food and went to our booth, three strange men were sitting with Wadsworth and the dancers. The girls looked very uncomfortable at their obvious passes. I heaved a sigh. I knew it was going to happen.

I addressed the three invaders: "Gentlemen, this is our booth. Since the girls seem upset that you're in it, I suggest you find another one." I delivered my little speech matter-of-factly and wasn't a bit surprised when their ringleader became insolent.

"Well," he purred, "where are *you* from? Hollywood?" He looked at his two buddies for support.

"As a matter of fact, I am." I put my plate on the table.

"Well, Hollywood," he snarled, "let's go outside and talk about it."

The four of us got up from the table. As I stepped outside, I turned and swung as the first one—"Loudmouth"—came through the glass door. The solid punch took him right out. The other two didn't proceed beyond his sprawled form. I went back to the booth in time to hear one of the girls scream, "But he's out there with three of them!"

Wadsworth—6-foot-5, 240 pounds in weight—was coolly munching on a piece of ham. He sputtered out, "Son-bitch can take care of himself."

Just then, Vallee came roaring up to me. "You got in a fight!" he yelled. "Don't you know it's your duty to call on your fellow performers to help you? You've no right to keep us out of it."

Jesus, I thought. This man is serious.

Then I mumbled out loud, "Sorry, but it's all taken care of."

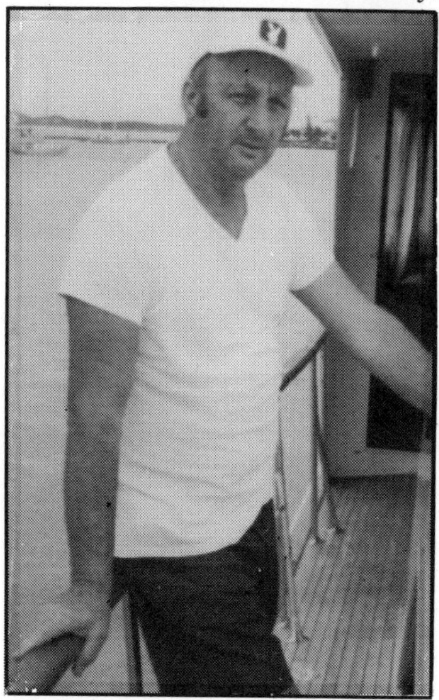

Tim Wallace, Bob's stand-in.

All the way back to our hotel, Vallee harangued me about my lack of faith in my peers. "It's not that, Rudy," I finally said. "It's just that I've never asked for help in a fight in my life. I just don't know how."

Later, when I told Robert about the incident, he heaved a deep sigh. "No, Brother John," he said, "they just don't look at *us*."

* * *

"Guys who pick fights are a pain in the ass," roared Big Tim Wallace. A huge Brooklyn Irishman, Big Tim was Bob's stand-in and friend for many years. He was a powerful fighter and a "no-nonsense" man who could put you straight in a hurry. It was Tim who once made the relevant observation to me that almost all men who pick fights can't fight. Really experienced fighters have nothing to prove; it's the bantam roosters who have to show their spurs.

One day, Bob and Tim were walking down Hollywood Boulevard when three men began heckling Bob. His hackles rising, Bob began positioning himself. Streetwise Tim saw the whole thing shaping up.

"Bob!" Tim, who is hard of hearing and feels he has to speak up, shouted his flat, nasal voice into Bob's ear.

"I'll handle this. You gotta stay out of it."

The ringleader stepped up to Tim, eyeing him amusedly. "Now *you're* gonna take care of it. Well, supposing *we've* got something to say about that?"

Tim hit him so hard the idiot sailed over the hood of a parked car. He landed in a heap on the boulevard and was out. Tim took Bob by the arm, leading him toward Las Palmas. In his loud, nasal voice, he let the world in on his philosophy.

"They gotta prove somethin'! They feel that they ain't nothing, so—if they can punch out Bogart, Mitchum, Cagney or the 'Duke,' they're really important." He shook his head sadly.

Bob nodded in agreement. "They see a screen image. It's too bad they never really look at *us*."

James Cagney, though short, was a very physical man. Brother Robert stands 6-foot-1 at a cool 205. John Wayne was 6-foot-4 and about 235. His trainer once told me in awe that John threw the straightest, hardest right hand he'd ever seen. He was of the opinion that John's right would kill most men. But John's pet word was "responsibility." Responsible men are loathe to misuse others.

Bob was right again. They never look at *us*.

TOUCHED BY MURDER

COMING BACK to Los Angeles from Sacramento found me up to my eyeballs in work. Not only was I involved in the Los Angeles Bureau of Music, but I also conducted a church choir and the Culver City Women's Chorus. The latter group inadvertently led me into a horrifying and bizarre happening.

On November 14, 1949, I held my usual rehearsal with the women's chorus from ten a.m. until noon each Monday. After that, as was my habit, I paid a visit to my friend Reuben Hausman, who lived close to Culver City. Reuben was a book publisher and we often had long, enjoyable conversations about writing over coffee or a drink.

When I arrived, neither Reuben nor his wife, Sylvia, were at home. Sylvia's father, Fred Stroble, whom I had met only a couple of times before, came to the door when I knocked. He kept the chain latch on and opened up only a few inches. I was nonplussed when he screamed "Go away! Go away!" I left, confused at his violent and unexplained outburst, and drove to my Hollywood apartment.

The next evening I was conducting a youth chorus in Westwood Village when two detectives came into the classroom.

"Are you John Mitchum?" one asked.

I assured him that I was and was told that I was to go along with them. I asked that I be allowed to talk to the children about the progress we were making, and the detectives agreed. After the rehearsal was over and the children had gone, I asked what this was all about.

"Just come along with us," one said. "If everything is okay, we'll drive you back to your car."

Mystified, and more than a little worried, I was driven to Reuben Hausman's address and ushered into the house. The living room was crowded with uniformed policemen, plainclothes detectives, a doctor, Reuben Hausman, and the acting chief of detectives, Thad Brown.

Brown, a huge man with a bland face and piercing eyes, who would soon serve as a prototype for some of the cops on Jack Webb's "Dragnet" series, sat in a chair stroking his chin slowly with his left hand. Somehow he made me feel guilty, and I didn't even have an inkling why. "Your car was seen here shortly after noon yesterday. Why were you here?"

I explained that after each rehearsal with my Culver City chorus, I would stop by to have a drink with Reuben and talk.

"What happened yesterday?" Brown waited for my answer.

I told him of Mr. Stroble's bizarre behavior. I had no sooner told my story when a piercing shriek came from the bedroom. "I knew it! I knew it!" screamed Sylvia, Reuben's wife.

I quickly learned that as I was standing on the porch, trying to understand Mr. Stroble's violent reaction to my knocking, little six-year-old Linda Joyce Glucoft, a girl who lived in the neighborhood, was lying in death on a bed in the house. Stroble had choked her with his hands, then he had strangled her with a tie. After I had gone, he stabbed her three times with an ice pick, severed her spine with an axe, then stabbed her in the back of the neck with a butcher knife. Police had found her mangled body dumped behind the Hausman's incinerator.

Newspaper articles printed that Stroble had begun seeking other women after his wife was committed to an insane asylum. When women turned him down, he found that ". . . little girls made me feel alive and strong." After a charge of child molestation, he jumped bail and was ordered out of the house by his son-in-law. Feeling that nobody loved him, he had chosen the Glucoft girl. Of Linda's murder, Stroble said, "I don't know why I did it. I liked the little girl very much. I deserve to die if anyone ever did."

Two and a half years later, at the age of seventy, Fred Stroble got his wish and died in the San Quentin gas chamber.

For years I've lived with the image of his face staring out at me from that front door. I've been haunted with the futile thought: My God, if only I'd known, I would have kicked the door down.

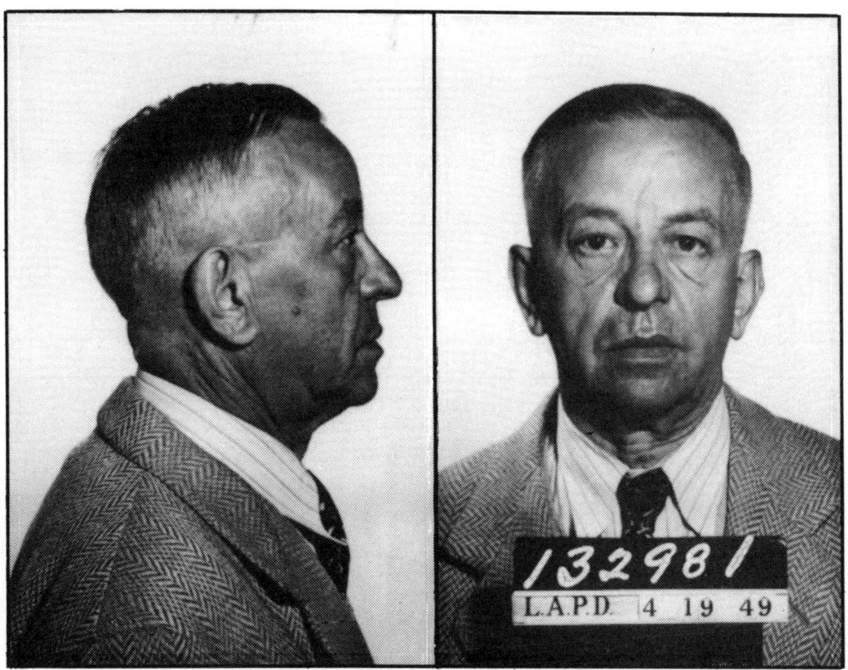

The Los Angeles Police Department's official "mug-shot" of Fred Stroble.

THE MAN WHO SAID HE WAS JOHN MITCHUM

ONE DAY I was visited by Lee Kendall, one of the Marine Raiders who worked with Bob in the 1943 film "Gung Ho!" As one of Carlson's Raiders, at 6-foot-7, Lee was a formidable opponent for most men. In this case, however, he wanted *me* to take care of a problem.

"There's a guy named Chuck Mitchell going around Hollywood giving you and Bob a bad name," he said. "Literally. He goes into bars borrowing money from the waitresses and patrons, telling them he's 'Bob's brother' and will pay them back when 'Bob gets home from location.' He even got a couple of the gals knocked up." Lee eyed me evenly. "You're his brother. You should do something about it."

Mitchell was using a bar on Cahuenga Boulevard as his base. I went there that same evening. When I told the bartender that I was John Mitchum, he said, "Oh, Christ! Not another one." Chuck came into a little L-shaped cul-de-sac at the end of the bar and the bartender nodded to me, calling out, "Say, Chuck, I want you to meet a friend of mine." Chuck rose, all teeth, smiling broadly. The barkeep said, "Chuck Mitchell, meet John Mitchum."

Mitchell froze in his tracks. "Can we talk? Can we talk?" he blurted out.

I said that if he kept up his present scam, he might never talk again. He promised he would never use Bob's name or mine in vain again. *(Much later, he became the proprietor of the restaurant that served as the location for the popular "Porky's" movie.)*

❄ ❄ ❄

My good friend, character actor Myron Healey, has been in hundreds of pictures that have left no impact on the screen, many of them horror pictures that received awful reviews. In Mick Martin's "Video Movie Guide" of 1987, he evaluated "The Incredible Melting Man" as: "Wild stuff: Rated R for terminal grossness." Now a review like that would seem to be a springboard for oblivion, but Myron keeps coming on strong.

Myron Healey

In 1949 I was singing at a night club called The Toddle House in Culver City, where Myron served as the show's emcee. On one occasion he tried to eject three noisy drunks who turned on him. I left the bandstand to lend a left hook. The three were subdued in quick order. Myron ("Mike") has always been quick to recall my saving him from a triple drubbing.

A few nights after that incident, Brother Robert came into the club with a singer who should have awed me into silence. He didn't though; I carried on bravely alone. Frank Sinatra turned to Robert and whispered, "The kid's pretty good."

That phrase carried me on a pink cloud for weeks.

FAME HAS ITS PROBLEMS

BROTHER ROBERT was now a thorough professional, riding high on a wave of success powered not only by his own talent but also by the strength of Katharine Hepburn, Robert Taylor, Harry Carey Jr., Robert Young, Robert Ryan, Gloria Grahame, Greer Garson, Loretta Young, Bill Holden, Myrna Loy, Janet Leigh, Walter Brennan, Ava Gardner and others of equal stature. Among his directors were Nicholas Ray, Don Siegel, Lewis Milestone, Edward Dmytryk, Raoul Walsh and others.

Siegel directed Robert in 1949 in "The Big Steal," a fast-moving caper and chase story that was partially filmed in Mexico. Bob was teamed up with Jane Greer (with whom he had starred two years earlier in that great *film noir* classic "Out of the Past") and they were in pursuit of Patric Knowles who was also being chased by William Bendix for the big boodle.

Years later I was directed by Siegel in Clint Eastwood's "Dirty Harry," portraying Harry's cop-partner, Frank di Georgio. While on location, Siegel told me that while they were filming "The Big Steal" Bob had "gotten drunk and obstreperous so Patric Knowles and I made the mistake of trying to force him into a shower. If Bob hadn't pulled his punches, he would have killed us. He obviously didn't want to hurt us. He just wanted to be left alone."

Jane Greer and Bob had been such a good team in "Out of the Past" in 1947 that RKO rejoined them in '49 for "The Big Steal," a good-humored chase film (the plot had as many twists as the mountain roads) set in Mexico. It was directed by Don Siegel, who would direct me in "Dirty Harry" in 1971 as Clint Eastwood's partner, Frank di Georgio.

Brothers In Harmony

Brother Bob and I have always had a penchant for music, and over the years we've both demonstrated it with our singing and playing in films and TV. In 1948 Bob sang and played the guitar (above) as Jim Fairways in "Rachel and the Stranger," a film that made a lot of money for RKO and proved that the marijuana caper had done no harm to his career as a box-office attraction. I'm still plunking away at the strings (left) and occasionally make personal appearances to present my oral and musical history of American folk music.

* * *

As Bob's fame grew, so did his problems. Basically a shy, introverted man, he became like a caped bull in an arena. Like the bulls following every move of the cape, Bob tried to answer the needs of every person around him. Strong and capable as he is, he found that he couldn't star in pictures, take excellent care of his family, and bolster his friends and fellow artists' demands continually. He went through a severe period of adjustment during the '40s and began to drink heavily. It never was a great psychological dependency. It was just that no matter where he went or with whom, the pleasant but inherently dangerous "What'll you have?" was the watchword of the day.

Bob and Dorothy rode through a stormy marital sea in those turbulent times.

* * *

In 1950 I worked for the first time with John Wayne in Howard Hughes' "Flying Leathernecks" as one of the Marine Corps pilots. At the location at Camp Pendleton, near San Diego, the set designers built a replica of Henderson Field that was so realistic that the pilots who had actually flown into the base on Guadalcanal shook their heads in amazement.

It was then that I met one of the fiercest men I have ever known, Johnny Bean, an Indian from Madill, Oklahoma. He had served with the Marine Corps in World War II and would soon be returning to war to fight in Korea. We became friends, for he swore that I looked exactly like his brother, who

Bob portrayed Dr. Mark Lucas in the 1951 antebellum melodrama "My Forbidden Past," which costarred Ava Gardner as a woman who couldn't keep her hands off even though the good doctor was married. Bob never has liked this film and was bad mouthing it to Hedda Hopper even before it was released. But that didn't matter to the public. When he and Gardner went on the road to publicize the film, he was mobbed. And there were plenty of fans clamoring for Ms Gardner as well.

Bob on one of his many hunting trips, bringing home the bacon to his sons, Jim and Christopher. This unusual photo was probably taken around 1950.

had been killed on Guadalcanal under grisly circumstances. When Johnny found his brother's body, it was apparent he had been tortured by Japanese soldiers. His body was still staked to the ground and ants were crawling through his remains.

Johnny and I were sitting next to a burned-out Nipponese tank that was part of the movie set when a young Marine started bragging about what he would do to the "gooks" when he got to Korea. Johnny told him to shut up. "The gooks," Johnny growled, "are a hell of a lot tougher than you are."

The kid bristled and challenged Bean. The young Marine weighed at least 190 while Bean was around 160. It was over in seconds.

They carted the kid to the hospital with a fractured skull and hauled Bean off to a board of inquiry.

The inquiry revealed that Bean should never have been called back into the Marine Corps: He had killed six American soldiers during the battle of Guam in 1944.

The incident occurred when Bean was on a routine patrol. He and his squad were held at gunpoint by six American soldiers who were in the process of raping the village chief's teen-age daughter. Bean had slewed his .45 holster to his backside because it chafed his hip, and the soldier watching him hadn't seen the handgun. When the dogface took his eyes off Johnny to get a better look at the rape in progress, Johnny yanked the .45 from its holster and shot him dead. Then he retrieved his carbine from the ground and coldly wasted the other five rapists. His court martial emphasized that he made no attempt to arrest the soldiers. He had blasted away without asking questions. He was discharged from the Corps immediately. And now he was booted out once again.

Bean came to see me in Hollywood. He called me "Windy," because I was always telling him stories, and we were still friendly, even though I had

In August, 1952, Dorothy and Bob introduced five-month-old Petrina (named after our grandmother) to newspaper and magazine photographers in their Mandeville Canyon home, just prior to leaving Hollywood on a vacation.

been warned about him by Gene Love, who had served on Guadalcanal with Bean.

Love was now an agent who worked with my agent, Jack Pomeroy. "Don't get too close with Bean," Gene advised me. "When he's drinking, he'll turn on anyone. I saw him on the Canal fight a sergeant to a draw. The sergeant outweighed Johnny by about 30 pounds. When it was obvious that neither could whip the other, Johnny told him he was getting his bayonet. 'When I come back, you'd better have yours!' The sergeant fled in haste for his own outfit. The argument wasn't worth dying over."

Gene held up a warning finger. "Here's another reason," he said. "One night a replacement looked at Bean quizzically as he was cooking some Spam over an open fire. 'They tell me you're an Indian.' The replacement probably meant no harm. 'That's right,' said Johnny. But the recruit went too far. 'You don't look like an Indian to me. Where're your scalps?' Johnny got up without a word and disappeared into the jungle. About four in the morning, he came back and threw two freshly severed Japanese heads onto the fire. 'Don't ever say that again,' hissed Bean."

I should have listened to Gene. One night Bean came to my house equipped with a bottle of bourbon. He started teasing my two-year-old son, Jack. "Hey, little girl." Bean thought he was being funny.

He kept it up until Jack started to cry. "I'm not a girl. I'm a little boy." The tears flowed now.

"There. You see. Only girls cry!"

I asked him to stop tormenting Jack and he became stone-faced, icy. I warily went into the kitchen for a drink of water and suddenly my mind recreated that chilling scene on Guadalcanal. *I saw the flickering campfire light dancing over the faces of the battle-hardened Marines hunkered around it, and then the awful sound of the two bloody severed heads hissing as they hit the flames.* I awoke to reality: I was standing in the kitchen with a big butcher knife in my fist. I turned the blade in my hand, in horror of what I must have been contemplating. I trembled as I put the knife back in its holder. I returned to Johnny and told him he'd better leave. He was angry but he gritted out "I'll see you around" as he left.

I never saw Bean again, but he did call me once from Havana, Cuba, where he was making his living as a dice-shooting gambler. He admitted openly that he was as crooked as a dog's hind leg. Apparently that's a very dangerous way to live with Cubans. Johnny Bean never called me again.

Brother Robert, who also knew Bean, told me that when he worked with Wilford Brimley in the 1986 TV production "Thompson's Last Run," they shot some scenes in the Oklahoma State Penitentiary.

"That is one grim hole," said Bob, shaking his head. "A prisoner I met reminded me so much of Johnny Bean. Oddly enough, both weighed about 160 and were not overly impressive physically—and both were deceptive as

"Macao" was one of two films Jane Russell made with Bob at RKO in the early 1950s (the other was "His Kind of Woman"). They hit it off well together, with Bob nicknaming her "Hard John." He never has told me why he chose that intriguing nickname.

hell personally. One of our crewmen laid a very nice jacket on a chair and when he looked for it, it had disappeared. He told a guard that the jacket had been a gift and it really hurt to have it stolen. The guard called the [Johnny Bean look-alike] prisoner over and quietly told him of the incident. In a matter of minutes, the jacket mysteriously reappeared on the chair."

Bob went to the guard and asked him how he had done it. The guard looked at Bob impassively. "The con [lookalike] is in here for murder. He's forty-eight now, been in here since he was seventeen. Killed his father, his brother and his cousin. On his first day out in the yard, a big con made the mistake of telling the boy that he was his, that he was gonna fuck him. The big con died within an hour. He's killed four more since then."

Bob whistled softly. "Jesus Christ, you'd never believe it."

The guard laughed. "Believe it, Mitchum. He's like E.F. Hutton—when he talks, people listen."

❄ ❄ ❄

In 1950 I worked on a William Holden picture, "Submarine Command," where I encountered a different kind of peril. One day we shot on a pier in the San Diego Navy Yard in which hundreds of extras simulated wives, sweethearts, mothers and daughters of submariners just returning from a long ordeal of sea duty. I was paired with a young lady who was so stunningly pretty I asked her to go to dinner with me. She was a natural blond, willowy, with beautiful breasts, lovely blue eyes and a peaches-and-cream complexion that almost defied description. When the company wrapped for the day, I rushed back to the downtown Grant Hotel to clean up for my anticipated evening.

As I was changing, a brick fell from the sky. I suddenly remembered that I had made a previous date with a young woman I had originally met while working on "Flying Leathernecks." For this very night. She was mighty attractive, and we had dated a few times since the film.

My roommate was another actor in "Submarine Command," Arthur Franz, who was sympathetic to my plight. He agreed that when the almost-overlooked young lady arrived, he would tell her that I had left for Los Angeles on an emergency. I was still in the bathtub when she knocked on our hotel door. I pantomimed to Arthur that I wasn't in. I closed the bathroom door, got back into the tub and tried not to make a sound. The dialogue I heard made it difficult to be still.

"Where's John?" Her voice had a brittleness that cut through the door.

"I do-do-don't know," stuttered the frantic Franz.

She spied a bottle of Scotch I'd left on the dresser, along with a bucket of ice and a bottle of soda. "Might I have a drink?" Her question was more like a command.

"Sure. Sure, of course." Franz got up and mixed her a portion. Silence reigned for a couple of minutes.

"Might I use your bathroom?" I wanted to sink under the cooling water.

"Why, why, why—yes!" Franz' voice raised to a shriek of despair.

The door opened and there I was, in all my glory. My resulting explanation was a masterpiece, but it backfired on me. I explained to the infuriated lady: "I have no money—a family crisis has arisen and I had to send everything home."

She melted visibly. "Oh, my poor darling," she cried. "You know that I have plenty of money. That's no problem. Why didn't you tell me, baby?" She went into her purse and brought out a hundred dollars and put it on the sink. "Now we can have a lot of fun with that problem settled."

We did. But I still have a twinge of sadness whenever I think of that gorgeous young blond. With my role in the picture over, I went back to Los Angeles and a home life with Joy that was becoming even more unbearable than it had been before.

❄❄❄

Early in 1951 my old friends Tom and Mary Hubbard put together one of the first live television shows to come out of Los Angeles. It was a family affair called "Adam's Spare Rib" in which I played the young husband and father, and Joy—who rarely got an acting job—played my neighbor. True to Joy's domineering nature, she even interferred with director- producer Hubbard's direction.

The great character actor Hal Smith emceed the show, which ran for 13 weeks—despite the fact that an elephant, used in the advertising to depict the solidity of our sponsor, Easy Air Mattress, stuck a foot through the product just as Hal explained the mattress could hold anything.

Hal Smith as Otis on "The Andy Griffith Show."

When the show was over, I had to face the truth that Joy and I were truly incompatible in every way. I started to drink more heavily than usual.

I was staring disconsolately out of my kitchen window when the phone rang. "Brother John," drawled that familiar voice, "what are you up to?"

"Starin' out my window." My voice seemed to carry with it the weight of the world. Joy and I had drifted painfully apart. Her dominant spirit on every possible subject had eroded my own until we were constantly at sword's point. I'd had enough dominance in the Army and didn't need any more at home. I wanted peace of mind. And love.

"How would you like to get away from it all and come to Colorado? I'm doing a picture and there's a part in it for you."

I came out of my depression. Fast. On the flight across the Colorado Rockies, I felt a swelling of pride as the clear, blue skies and the forests with their myriad hues rolled beneath me. I thanked God for such beauty and my brother for his understanding. A part in a picture was exactly what I needed in order to get away from my problems. However, that trip was to create new ones . . .

THE LEGEND OF CHARLES McGRAW

THE RKO PICTURE, originally titled "The Korean Story," became "One Minute to Zero," starring Robert, Ann Blyth, William Talman, Charles McGraw and Richard Egan. Our director was Tay Garnett, a veteran who had guided such films as "Bataan" and "The Postman Always Rings Twice."

Charles McGraw had a distinguished career playing tough guys good and bad. At left he's about to punch out Dennis O'Keefe in the 1948 film "T-Men." The portrait at right, taken in 1968 for "Pendulum," shows that Charley was still looking pretty good despite years of hard drinking and hellraising. Charley was also a popular voice on radio dramas in the 1950s.

Blyth was the epitome of sweetness, Talman was a quiet loner, and Egan was always coolly controlled. As usual, it was McGraw who kept the whole company in a state of turmoil.

Bob had first introduced me to McGraw one rainy night early in 1951. Bob had just finished "His Kind of Woman" (with Jane Russell, Vincent Price and Raymond Burr) and was having troubles with the RKO hierarchy, which had ordered McGraw to the set to take over the role if Robert should bolt.

When I came into the RKO dressing room suite with Bob, he knelt behind his desk and barked into what he thought to be a "bug." "Well, thin man," he intoned. "I'm back." "Thin man" was Howard Hughes who then was running the studio. Despite the boss-employee relationship, they got along famously. Now Bob's "threat" stalked into the dressing room in a way most impressive. His voice, an aggressive rasp, made him stand apart. Bob saw me looking hard at McGraw.

"Oh," Bob said, smiling, "most impressive, isn't he?" McGraw stiffened, taking a belligerent stance in my direction. "When I first met Charles," continued Bob, "I was terrified. Here was the man who was going to ease me out of RKO." It was easy for Bob to tell me of their initial meeting for McGraw was apparently behaving—for my benefit—in the same manic way.

"Get up!" Charles roared as he paced back and forth in front of Bob. McGraw wheeled and spun, throwing imaginary left hooks at my brother. Bob laughed and told him to relax. Fat chance. Bob told me that he was truly concerned until Charley took off his trenchcoat and his jacket. A little inward sigh of relief then swept over Robert.

Now McGraw was on his feet again in front of us, wheeling, weaving, diving, ducking. All the while, his left kept jabbing at Bob. "Get up!" he snapped. *"Get up!"*

"One moment, Charles, if you please." Bob turned to me. "Then he shed his sweater and I cried out in joy. Charley is a little man!" At this point, McGraw abruptly stopped his wheeling and ducking, put out his hand to

Charles McGraw and Bob (as Colonel Steve Janowski) demonstrate the effectiveness of the bazooka in "One Minute to Zero."

me and rasped, "McGraw. You must be Brother John."

In Colorado Springs, McGraw and I became fast friends. I found that his aggressiveness was continual; he kept going twenty hours a day and drank two cases of beer in the same time period.

McGraw became the key figure in a brawl between Bob and a fighter named Bernie Reynolds. Although he was in the Army, Reynolds was ranked tenth in the world at the time.

It started in a bar in Colorado Springs called The Red Fox, when McGraw was upbraided by an MP who accused the irascible actor for being out of uniform. "I'm an actor," rasped McGraw. "I'm not in your army."

The MP didn't believe McGraw and the air was clouded with vituperation and hostility.

At that moment Bob walked toward the exit, and Reynolds staggered through the door. The soldier-fighter had been drinking and chose Bob as his target.

Bob was up to his armpits with McGraw and would brook no nonsense from the bellicose Reynolds.

Reynolds threw a right-hand lead at Bob, who deflected the fist. It smashed into a brick wall. Feeling no sympathy for the injured hand, Bob knocked Reynolds down and, in a rage, banged his head against a handy piano bench, giving the pro boxer a concussion.

Robert was once again in deep trouble. But he was almost immediately rescued when Reynolds refused to obey the direct order to come to attention from two officers who walked in. Bob tried to intercede on the groggy Reynolds' behalf but was politely told to butt out. Apparently, Reynolds got off with restriction to Fort Carson for brawling. Robert and RKO breathed a sigh of relief when the incident was officially forgotten.

The Garden of the Gods is a beautiful place in Colorado Springs, a natural "garden" of breathtaking iron-red pinnacles. We were seated at the bar of the Garden of the Gods Hotel, a plush place owned by a group of wealthy Texans. One of these, a 6-foot-6 giant with a hat almost as big, came over, addressing us with self-importance. "You boys with the picture company?"

McGraw swiveled around. "Yep," he grunted. "I'm Charles McGraw, he's John Mitchum."

The man swelled up another two feet. "Name's Hallman," he drawled. Then he added, with great superiority, "Ahm in oil, m'self."

Charles glared at him. "What in the hell are you so proud of? All you did was poke a hole in the prairie."

I finished my beer in apprehension but the Texan just gaped a bit, trembled in frustration and walked out of the bar.

My role in "One Minute to Zero" was that of an artillery officer in charge of a battery of guns zeroed in on a road crawling with hundreds of refugees seeking asylum in South Korea. In the script I'm ordered to fire into their ranks because North Korean troops have mingled with the refugees and are using them as shields in an effort to penetrate our lines. (This incident actually happened during the Korean War, which made the film controversial at the time.)

As my commanding officer Bob kept ordering me to raise my rounds at a rate of 500 yards per salvo. Finally, I'm ordered to "fire for effect" and the shells (expertly simulated by special effects) tear the column to shreds.

"Cut. Print." Tay Garnett's laid-back voice signalled that the take was satisfactory. My stint in the picture was over.

Not quite. When the rushes were viewed, the production office was aghast.

McGraw, William Talman and Bob in "One Minute to Zero." Talman went on to star as prosecuting attorney Hamilton Burger in the "Perry Mason" TV series. He succumbed to lung cancer in 1968 after making some famous anti-cigarette TV commercials at a time when he knew he was dying.

Gloria Grahame gave Bob a lapel pin to signify his participation in the Crusade for Freedom Drive on the set of "Macao," a film they made together at RKO in 1951. I'm still wondering why I didn't give Gloria lessons in how to make love, as her mother once requested me to when she was still young and innocent.

There, in the jeep at the command post, was a uniformed John Mitchum, calmly obeying orders. (I had changed my name to Mallory in a short-lived attempt to further my acting career.) There, at the wheel of the jeep, was a recruited extra from the Air Force Academy, dressed in his formal Air Force blues.

"You'll have to stay over for a couple of days in order to get back to that area." The assistant director was most apologetic, although I didn't mind hanging around. I was in no hurry to return to L. A. and my life with Joy.

'WHY ARE YOU IN A PLACE LIKE THIS?'

"**ONE MINUTE TO ZERO**" called for Korea in the summertime. One day it snowed—and snowed—and snowed. Most unusual for Colorado in late September. My three-day bit turned into eleven weeks. The company did nothing but drink and play cards. There were some who met women; McGraw and I were among 'em.

At that time, the only Black night club in Colorado Springs was Duncan's, which made up for those that weren't there. Trains were still the main mode of travel; musicians on their ways East or West would often stop off and "blow" for their brothers. Charley insisted that I go with him to Duncan's—and it was there that I met Nancy Munro.

Nancy was a beautiful girl, a recent graduate of Colorado College who was working at an insurance company. She and some of her friends had stopped in to hear the music. And what great music it was, with a sax player from the East Coast rocking the place to its rafters.

When Nancy passed our booth to go to the ladies' room, I found myself pompously addressing her. "Why are *you* in a place like this?" I blurted it out before I knew what I was saying.

She surveyed me coolly. "I'm of age, I live in a free society, and I happen to like good jazz." She smiled sweetly at me. I sat staring dumbly after her. Her quiet dignity in this raucous place fascinated me, as did her large, hazel eyes. When she passed me again I could see why: She smiled again and that smile went far beyond a physical action—it came from within. I felt there was a deep and passionate love of life that burned within her. I had to know much more about her.

Good ol' McGraw. He insisted that Nancy and her friends join us and, with several others in the company present, we commanded a big booth.

Hal Baylor, who worked in such John Wayne films as "Big Jim McLain" and "Island in the Sky," and who worked with Bob in "River of No Return," suggested I hang this photo in my bathroom, on the theory that "it will move anybody." His postscript read: "Hang on to your teeth!"

One of the actors was Hal Baylor, an ex-fighter and ex-Marine who would later make movies with John Wayne. He and Bob were very good friends and respected each other tremendously. Hal had been a favorite sparring partner of the great Archie Moore and was a pretty good heavyweight in his own right. Years later Hal delighted in telling the story of my unimpressive debut as a romanticist and Beau Brummel in front of Nancy that night.

"Mitch was sitting there," Hal tells it, "waxing most eloquently about the charm and beauty of the young ladies present, the glory that is the Colorado Rockies, and the greatness of the evening. Suddenly, his upper plate fell out of his jaws and started clattering across the table. Mitch scooped 'em up without losin' a beat, put 'em back where they belonged and never stopped his dialogue."

When Hal later told my brother this story, Bob scarcely raised an eyebrow. "John had 'em since he was 15. Second nature to him now."

Baylor shook his head and muttered, "Never lost a beat."

ESCAPE FROM A WOUNDED TIGRESS

NANCY AND I fell in love. When I returned to California, Joy met me at the studio and flatly stated, "You haven't written. Is there someone else?"

Like a fool, I told her, "Yes, there is." She had often said that if I wanted a divorce, she would give it to me. She reversed her position like a wounded tigress.

I knew I had to sever myself from Joy. Her militant ego dwarfed mine; I was drowning in a sea of emotional forces beyond my control. In spite of a complete lack of compatibility from the beginning of our marriage, the "'til death do us part" vow wore heavily on me. I finally concluded that my dear, sweet grandmother was the one person I could rely on for a truly honest evaluation of my feelings.

One morning when Grandmother Petrine and I were alone, I announced with great inner tension my decision to divorce my wife. That venerable lady looked at me for a long moment, then spoke softly in her Norwegian lilt.

"I wondered how long you could stand it."

No one can imagine the flood of relief that swept over me.

Grandma Petrine Gunderson remains one of the sweetest women I've ever known, for she was often a guiding influence in my life, always speaking the truth, and always speaking it straight from her heart. In 1950, one year before she died of cancer at the age of 83, she and I took a trip along the Pacific Coast Highway and I stopped the car just south of Oxnard. There, drenched in sunlight as bright as the light that flowed from her free, loving spirit, I photographed her sitting on a rock watching the ocean.

My relief turned to panic when I found it impossible for me to get a divorce at that time in California. Fate stepped in again.

Tom and Mary Hubbard, with whom Joy and I had worked on "Adam's Spare Rib," were now in Dallas, Texas, employed at Gordon McClendon's Liberty Broadcasting Station. Tom called me in Los Angeles to ask me to come to Dallas and be a member of a stock company that was putting on three 15-minute shows a day. I gratefully accepted. I played various roles in two of the shows, and there are many people still living in Texas, Oklahoma, Kansas and Nebraska who have heard me introduced as "Brad Steele! Ace of Space!"

❄ ❄ ❄

Bob Bumpas was the vice president of the studio at that time and his lovely wife, Martha, worked in all of the shows. No nepotism there—Martha is a very talented actress.

We were all shocked at his death. A madman, intent on killing his own wife for her insurance, had planted a bomb on a passenger plane that exploded over the Gulf of Mexico.

Sixty-four people died—Bumpas among them.

The series was cancelled due to a lack of performance on the contractual level between the American Baseball League and the station. I was at liberty once again.

❄ ❄ ❄

On Tom Hubbard's recommendation I went on to Little Rock, Arkansas, to file for a divorce. He was from that state and was familiar with the laws. If I lived there just ninety days, I would be eligible to file.

I took an apartment in a rundown hotel overlooking the Arkansas River. It was called The Sherman so I romantically dubbed it "The Sherman by the Sea." Through Tom I met Jay Freeman, who had become a millionaire in the then-new frozen foods business. Jay and his lovely wife befriended me—without them, the days would have been bleak.

While my divorce proceedings were inching along, I managed to secure a job at Pine Bluff Arsenal, which was under construction. Because of my sheet metal experience, I naturally wound up employed in the sheet metal department.

I worked diligently, unknowingly incurring the wrath of the department. My fellow workers shunned me, then the foreman—a burly, glowering brute—bluntly warned me *not* to work as hard as I had been doing. "This here is the best payin' job we've had for a long time. We want it to last."

I looked at the two dozen men who worked under him. There wasn't a friendly smile in the pack. My time in Arkansas was almost over so I quit at the Arsenal while I was still ahead.

However, at the end of my ninety days, my heart sank when my attorney told me, "No one has entered a deposition for you. With no witnesses or depositions, I can't get you a divorce." Nancy and I were in constant communication by phone, anxiously awaiting the final decree. Nancy was the shining star to which I had needed to fix myself for many a long, lonely year—and I wanted to get on with a new life.

I went back to The Sherman by the Sea and mixed myself a vodka and seven. Then another. And a third. I could hear the community phone ringing out in the hall. "Johnny. It's for you." The skinny old manager had put down his bourbon long enough to answer the phone.

With sad heart, I plodded to the dangling receiver. "Hello."

The answer brought tears to my eyes. "Brother John."

"Where are you?" I gasped.

The answer came straight from Heaven. "Fifth and Main."

Bob and Tim Wallace had been on a fishing trip up in Idaho and Colorado in Bob's "Oochee-Papa-Poontang Wagon." Bob has always been admired by motion picture crews because he is totally aware of their contributions, so various craftsmen at RKO Studio had put together the forerunner of the modern motor home. Mounted on a Ford truck and beautifully appointed, it slept four comfortably, had a stove, refrigerator, an indoor bath and an ample supply of booze. Robert loved this gift from the hearts of his crews. I know I did when I saw that vehicle at Fifth and Main in Little Rock.

Bob and Tim had somehow drifted off-course into Arkansas. Bob avowed that he would most certainly be a witness for me, if necessary. However, he felt it better if Tim could testify to lessen the chance of any newspaper breaking the story. Tim agreed. We went to court together.

My lawyer was a tiny lady of 80 and the judge, just as diminutive, was 82. They had recently rekindled a childhood romance. The sparks that flew between them would cause many a younger couple to ponder.

Tim was on the stand now. The judge asked him if he had any knowledge of Joy's and my marriage difficulties. "Huh?" asked Tim, as he cupped a hand over his ear.

The judge cranked up and bellowed the same question.

"Oh, indeed, your Honor." Tim's voice could be heard in Pine Bluff. "The fightin' and yellin' was somethin' awful. It's a wonder they didn't kill each other!"

"*That's enough!*" yelled the judge. He looked at my lady lawyer and winked. "Divorce granted."

Within a week I married Nancy and we moved back to Dallas, Texas. Bob and Tim moved on in the Poontang wagon for a bit of Gulf fishing.

Life took on a different beat.

This photo was taken around 1950, when I was attending the Herbert Wall School of Music. Herbert's sister, Corinna Mura, bought coffee for me one afternoon and suggested that I was wasting some of my talent (and strength!) chasing every skirt that hove into my line of sight. Which was true, of course. When she told me women thought of me as being "easy," that shocked me for I had never looked at my pursuit of pleasure quite in that female-chauvinistic light. So I took Corinna's advice and slowed down for the next few weeks, chasing only half as many skirts as before.

BOOK FIVE

SECOND CHANCE

BOOK FIVE

WHO WANTS TO LIVE A NORMAL LIFE?

FOR SOME TIME after we married, I tried to live a normal life. Somehow it just never worked out. I landed a job at Collins Radio Company in Dallas, falling back on my old Lockheed experience as a sheet metal blueprint layout man. For at least a month, all went smoothly.

Although I worked in the sheet metal division, the foreman of the machine shop, Frank, often stepped over for my assistance as he wasn't too skilled at his work. I always said I'd help him if I wasn't busy with my own department's requests.

Frank was 6-foot-3 and weighed about 215; he was around 26 years old and arrogant as hell. One morning he slapped one of his department's blueprints down on my desk and *ordered* me to lay it out. I put it under several already scheduled prints. Frank roared, "You son of a bitch! I told you to lay out that print!"

I ignored his blast, but at lunch time he came into the same restaurant I frequented, sat near me and gave me the evil eye. He reached out and belligerently snatched a bottle of catsup from my table. "Frank," I said, "all you had to do was ask. I would've handed it to you."

He didn't bother to answer, but after lunch he stood outside the restaurant door waiting for me. "Now we're gonna find out just who the boss is around here!"

"Frank, are you serious?"

"You're God-damned right I'm serious!" He swung a ponderous right fist at me. I blocked it but the weight of his arm pressed my hand against my cheek and I heard my upper plate crack like an egg. Enraged, I ripped punches into him. He fell heavily to the parking lot pavement. I heard a siren wailing and realized it was coming closer. I went back to the plant and started working again.

In about an hour, Frank shambled in. I hadn't realized the extent of my fury until he stood in front of me, his shirt torn and soaked in blood. He leaned down, crying, "Look at my eye! They had to put six stitches in my eyebrow!"

"Frank, you hit me first."

"Yes," he blubbered, "but I didn't *hurt* you!"

After Frank left, a lean young Texan came over and stared at me for a long beat. "You know, you being from California and all, I'd thought about trying you myself." He took another beat. "No more." And he walked away.

On close inspection, I found that Frank's punch had almost cracked my plate in two. All day Saturday I tried to find a dentist to repair it; not one was in his office.

I had just been accepted into the Episcopal Church in Dallas and my confirmation breakfast was to be held Sunday morning; I wanted to be able

"Angel Face" (1952) was an unusual film for Bob, as he played an ambulance attendant named Frank Jessup who falls for a murderess (Jean Simmons) and comes under her spell working as her personal chauffeur while she plots the murder of her stepmother. It was directed by Otto Preminger and features a very bizarre ending.

to chew. Realizing my plate was made of plastic, I heated paper clips until they were red-hot and pressed them into the cracked sides of the plate. I finally made a reasonably secure weld over the cracks. That is, until I bit into a piece of cantaloupe at the confirmation breakfast. With that one bite, my plate fell in half. Choking and gasping like a stomped-on bullfrog, I ran pell-mell out of church and kept on going until I got to my apartment.

Nancy came home to find me dialing every dentist in the city. Only one agreed to help me. He was a Black man and he cautioned me to creep up his back stairs. "If my clientele finds out that I've worked on a white man's teeth, I'll lose half of them." I sneaked into his upstairs office and he did such a good job that I didn't replace the plate for thirty years.

Soon after that experience, I quit Collins and got a job selling life insurance for The Reinsurance Company of America. One day Elmer Jones stopped on his way from California to Pennsylvania to see us. I had to hand-deliver a check to a Black lady who had been in a car accident so Nancy suggested that the three of us go to dinner after I delivered the check.

I stopped the car in front of my client's house, leaped out with the idea that I would hand her the check, mumble a few words of encouragement and split.

"Come on in, policy man. Come on in." A party of some magnitude was going on. After all, she had barely escaped death. I explained that my wife and Jonesy were waiting in the car. Blacks are used to hearing excuses from Whites on such occasions. Mine was no excuse. When she said "Bring 'em in! Bring 'em in," I did. What a party: Mountains of fried chicken, biscuits, gravy, bourbon whiskey and Bull-dog ale.

Nancy, a Nebraska girl who had studied sociology at Colorado Springs, wondered at their high spirits and obvious enjoyment of life. She spoke to one of the young Black girls, asking if their obvious abandon was a result of new Federal laws banning discrimination. The young girl looked at her in amazement. Laws had nothing to do with it. "Lawdy, Miss Nancy," she laughed all the while, "if you were a Black girl in Dallas for just *one* Saturday night, you'd never want to be White folk again."

LIVING IN YOUR OWN SUNLIGHT

NICHOLAS RAY was a strange film director whom Bob dubbed "The Mystic." Bob told me that Ray would sit in his director's chair in such deep concentration that nothing could penetrate it. Suddenly, he would leap up and go into action with every detail straight in his mind. I first met Ray in 1948 at Columbia when I worked in "Knock on Any Door."

Ray also used me in "The Lusty Men," a moving story about modern-day cowboys in which I played a rodeo wrangler. Bob was the star (playing an aging rodeo rider named Luke) but he didn't know I had been cast in the picture when he arrived at Placerita Canyon in Newhall for a rehearsal. I watched Bob come out of the rodeo office as I sat on a corral fence and I called out, "Hey, Luke, I didn't see you on the entry list." It was one of my lines from the script.

Bob looked up in total surprise. "How the hell did you get here?"

We shot the scene smoothly. The Mystic went on record as saying that Bob's portrayal of the worn-out cowboy was the best, most poignant ever. It was. The essence of his force and his presence lies in something a film critic wrote: "The most poignant drama in the lives of rodeo riders was portrayed by Mitchum walking across an empty rodeo arena, the wind blowing rubbish behind him."

In late September, 1952, just when the film was opening, Bob and Arthur Hunnicutt, a character actor who specialized in Western roles and had just

"The Lusty Men," in which Bob played aging rodeo star Jeff McCloud, is still one of his best films—a fact that even he will agree with. It was written by novelist Howard McCoy ("They Shoot Horses, Don't They?") and David Dortort, who would go on to create and produce the popular "Bonanza" TV series.

Arthur Hunnicutt (left) was a wonderful character actor but in later years his career was slowed down by his drinking. He finally swore off and kept a half-filled whiskey bottle on a closet shelf as a reminder never to drink again. Nicholas Ray (right, in a 1977 photo taken two years before his death from cancer) was one of the top directors in the 1950s and directed Bob in "The Lusty Men."

been seen in "The Big Sky" in a role that would bring him an Oscar nomination, came to Dallas on a promotion tour for "The Lusty Men." (It coincided with the then-popular film company team of Dean Martin and Jerry Lewis appearing at the State Fair there.)

One evening, after appearing on the stage, Bob was met by a crowd at the stage door, where a woman suddenly threw her baby at Bob. Startled, he caught the infant in his arms and a camera flash went off.

Instant paternity suit.

Bob's lawyer settled a shabby amount on the shabby perpetrators, but right there Bob solemnly announced to the world that if anyone tried that again, the child would just have to take its chances on the pavement.

❄ ❄ ❄

Bob, Hunnicutt, and the comedy team of Martin and Lewis hosted a big party one night in a restaurant that set aside its regular routine to cater the special group. The bandleader was Ray Anthony. When Nancy and I, on Bob's invitation, came through the door, Bob's wife, Dorothy, introduced us to Mrs. Anthony. That poor woman, in her cups and totally forlorn, stood up on the counter, demanding everyone's attention. When the hubbub receded, she announced, "Ladies and gentlemen, I now want to introduce you to someone even *less* important than I am." She pointed at Nancy. "I want you all to meet Robert Mitchum's brother's wife."

The pathos of this has never left me. Bob's wife, Dorothy Spence Mitchum, never lived in Bob's shadow. She is a bright, resolute, completely whole person who has seen her husband through all of the trials and tribulations that beset any famous entertainer—and she has emerged undefeated.

Orchestra leader Ray Anthony with his wife Dee and their dog Gypsy. You have to learn to live in your own light and not be bothered by the tall shadows that threaten to engulf you.

Nor did Nancy ever live in *my* shadow; she was totally her own person, a much-loved and respected lady.

Poor Mrs. Anthony. How many people hide their own potential because their mate's or their parent's, their brother's or their sister's sun is too bright for them?

Stand in your own light. Should it not be dazzling, be aware that it is *yours* and you will grow in that light.

THE "ITCH" BECOMES UNBEARABLE

WHILE NANCY AND I waited for our son to be born, Brother Robert went far afield to film "White Witch Doctor" with Susan Hayward and Walter Slezak in Africa, and "Second Chance" in the then-trendy three-dimensional process with Linda Darnell and Jack Palance in South America. Bob and the director of "White Witch Doctor," Henry Hathaway, were not too fond of each other when the picture started. Hathaway, known best for big action epics, had a reputation as a screamer. He would, with unfailing acumen, find the weakest link in the chain of importance of cast and crew and target that link for vituperation and aggression. It seemed to be a form of therapy for the director.

Robert fights for the underdog so Hathaway found him a durable opponent. But at one point he had to concede defeat, being in the dark as to the real Robert, who is a quick study.

Hathaway was upset when Bob came onto the set for a long, difficult scene and asked what he was supposed to do. An assistant summoned up enough courage to give Bob a script. Bob glanced at it for about five seconds, then told the infuriated Hathaway that he was ready.

Hathaway cursed at him for not preparing sooner, then shouted, "Action!" Bob went through the entire scene without a flaw, speaking an African dialect for several pages. Hathaway was stunned into silence. Bob had spent plenty of time with the natives—eating and talking with them—to pick up their dialect without anyone being aware of it.

Hathaway had been had.

❄ ❄ ❄

In August of 1953, our son Jack II was born, but any thought of living the normal life of a father was far from my mind. The lure of California kept calling me. I had worked in a good many pictures and television shows and felt that I wanted to expand and learn more about the craft of acting.

I felt ready with a list of credits that included "The Prairie," "Knock on Any Door," "Flying Leathernecks," "When Willie Comes Marching Home," "Submarine Command," "Right Cross," "One Minute To Zero," and "The Lusty Men." Plus I had done many segments of "The Fireside Theater."

I had worked with Alan Baxter, Humphry Bogart, John Wayne, Robert Ryan, Dan Dailey, William Holden, Dick Powell and, of course, Brother Robert. I asked myself why I was working in a Texas radio factory. The answer came back: "Purely for the money."

Soon after Jack II was born, Nancy became frightfully ill. She was diagnosed as "extremely hyperthyroid," suffering from malignant exophthalmos. Her lovely eyes never did recede back to normal. She suffered much anguish as a result, and so did I. We decided that it was time for us to go back to California and sink or swim in the waters of the film industry.

Realizing that "man cannot live by bread alone," I followed the call. We moved back to Hollywood when Jack II was two.

It was not to be an easy venture.

WHO SAID IT WOULD BE EASY?

WHEN WE REACHED Hollywood, Brother Robert offered us his beloved Oochee-Papa-Poontang Wagon as a temporary haven. Within two weeks, we found a suitable apartment in the San Fernando Valley.

Bob had gone to the Cannes Film Festival prior to our return. The news media wallowed in reporting and photographing actress Simone Silva embracing Bob on the beach. She came bare-breasted at him in a deliberate attempt to create a wave of publicity for herself. Bob, seen throughout the world press with those uncovered breasts crushed against his chest, was totally unaware of her existence before the incident.

It might do skeptics well to ponder that the bizarre event didn't demean him. *Miss Silva's pathetic attempt to use Bob as a springboard to fame wound up in suicide in 1957 because that cherished "fame" she wanted so desperately never came her way. Bob was deeply moved when he learned that she had died by her own hand in London.*

❄ ❄ ❄

I started working again in the industry by doing three "Fireside Theater" segments in quick succession, but still had to supplement my income. Luckily, I had worked once for George Meyers, a contractor who built and hung garage doors. George was a former wrestler who stood 6-foot-6 and weighed 220 pounds. Despite all of that, he was a gentle, kind man who readily hired me again.

One day I jumped off a ladder without looking. A nail in a 2-by-4 pierced my boot, lodging so deeply in my left foot that a carpenter had to claw it loose with his hammer. Somehow I worked the rest of the day. A few days

At the Cannes Film Festival in 1953, photographers persuaded British actress Simone Silva to doff her upper pink veil and rush into Bob's arms. Six photographers reportedly fell into the ocean in the mad rush that ensued to get pictures for the newspapers of the world. Bob said later that he kept the girl crushed against his chest in order to cover her nakedness and save her added embarrassment.

Bob portrayed Clint Tollinger, a "town tamer" hired to clean out some gunmen, and Jan Sterling was his romantic interest in the 1955 Samuel Goldwyn Jr. Western, "Man With the Gun." This was the film Bob was making the night I came to him for financial help but couldn't ask for it and got so drunk I had to be subdued with the butt of a prop revolver applied to my noggin.

later I was hospitalized in St. Joseph's in Burbank with osteomylitis, an inflammation of the bone. While I was in the hospital, George brought me a bottle of vodka and a quart of 7-Up. He had no opener so he cracked the neck of the 7-Up bottle on the bed frame, waiting for the broken pieces to settle that he might pour.

Just then a Sister came into the room and caught us in the act of pouring. She harassed George, all 6-foot-6 of him, out the door like a wren pursuing a mastiff. The poor man didn't get a chance to say "Good-bye." I almost fell out of bed laughing. My laughter soon slowed to a dribble.

Workman's Comp paid me $35 a week. My funds disappeared rapidly. Soon, we were facing grim reality. I couldn't even pay the gas bill.

My foot was still heavily bandaged when I drove over to 20th Century-Fox Studios, where Bob was doing night scenes in "Man With the Gun," a formula Western which co-starred Jan Sterling, Angie Dickinson and Henry Hull. It was part of a five-picture deal bob had made with United Artists through his own DRM Productions.

In my quiet desperation, I kept hearing the dialogue that I thought would soon pass between us.

"Jesus, John! Can't you even come up with fifty bucks?" "Well, you see . . ."

"Well, dammit! If you'd only been more careful!"

By the time I reached the studio I was ready to blurt out, "Who needs your God-damned fifty?"

Edgar Buchanan, Bob and Arthur Hunnicutt in "She Couldn't Say No." The cast was a helluva lot better than the material.

When I pulled up to the gate, the guard told me where they were shooting. Bob was working in every scene so I went to his dressing room, where I found Big Tim Wallace. He was most solicitous but I ignored him.

"What's the trouble, John?" Tim pressed me for an answer.

A stout vodka served to aggravate my already vile mood. "It's none of your business, Tim." I was snarling.

He kept haranguing me until I told him that if he said one more word, I'd belt him. He said the one word and I knocked him into a corner. Just then Bob returned from the set, sized up the situation and gave me a tap with the butt of his prop revolver. It subdued me enough that I raged out of the studio without further violence. Instead of carrying my anger home to Nancy I had the good sense to park on a side street and fall asleep in my car.

I called Nancy from a phone booth at six the next morning. She was near hysteria. Bob had called her from his dressing room, informing her of my maniacal behavior. She told him I was trying to borrow fifty dollars before the gas was turned off.

Shortly after she talked to Bob, a messenger arrived at our house with a check for $2,000, a red rose for Nancy and a note which read, "Dear Nancy, If *ever* you need anything again, *you* call and tell me. Don't let the bull out of his corral, hurting. Love, Bob."

While I was lying around, waiting for my foot to heal and feeling sorry for myself, my old Army buddy, Natividad Vacio, who had kept me from going to Davy Jones' Locker back in '45, came to visit. He plunked a guitar in my lap, told me to quit moaning and learn something. Because of his insistence, I became a pretty good guitarist and folk singer.

❄❄❄

Lenny Geer was Bob's stunt double on "Man With the Gun." Lenny still relates the story of Bob's innate concern for his fellow workers revolving around the shirt that Bob wore in the picture. Lenny was doubling for Bob in a shoot-out sequence and after the final exchange of gunfire and stunt

My good friend Lenny Geer as he appeared in Walt Disney's "Spin and Marty" series. Lenny is one of those hard-working ubiquitous actors who's worked in hundreds of films and TV shows whose face (if not name) is immediately recognized. He's appeared in such films as "The High-Powered Rifle" and "The Great Locomotive Chase." Oh hell, name it and Lenny's been in it.

fall, the wardrobe department came to the fallen Lenny and started to cut a ragged hole—simulating a bullet hole—in his beautiful Pendleton shirt.

"Hold it!" Bob admonished from the sidelines. "That shirt looks good on Lenny." He ordered the wardrobe man to tear the inexpensive double's shirt *he* was wearing and re-exchange it temporarily with Lenny's good one. Lenny wore that Pendleton proudly for a long time.

THE FACTS BEHIND 'BLOOD ALLEY'

GEORGE COLEMAN, a burly teamster, was John Wayne's transportation manager on many of his films. He had that position in a film Bob was signed by Warner Brothers to make in 1954, "Blood Alley."

Fiction: Coleman refused to rent a bus to take the crew members from a Bay Area location to San Francisco for a night outing. Robert, indignant over George's lack of concern for his fellow crew members, took him to task at the end of a long pier. An argument followed. Coleman lost. The 278-pounder found himself floundering in the cold waters of the bay after what was publicized as "a little bit of horseplay." "Horseplay" my ass. Bob was mad.

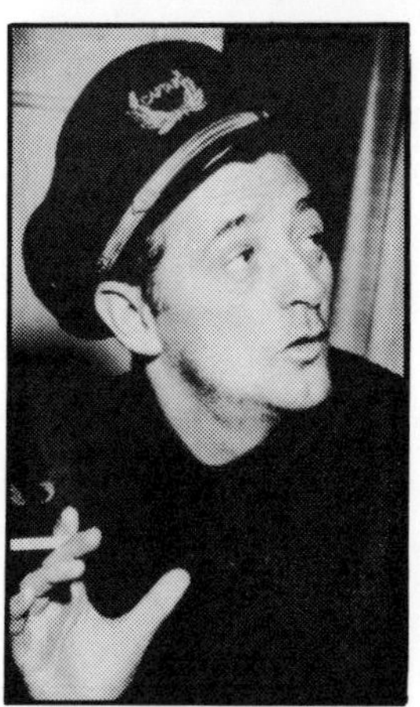

Bob defends himself during the "Blood Alley" controversy.

After Coleman dried out, he protested to director William Wellman and to the assistant director, Andy McLaglen, the son of actor Victor McLaglen. Bob was fired as—typically—he didn't elaborate any defense; besides, he didn't like the part. So, the story goes, John Wayne took over Bob's role.

Fact: "It never happened!" Brother Robert is adamant about it. The real truth lay in that John Wayne had a contractual glitch with Warner Brothers, needing one picture to fill out his obligation before contract renewal. When Warners told him that he could do "Blood Alley," Wayne said,

"Mitchum is doing that one."

The powers that be at the studio simply pushed a button. "Mitchum is doing that one" became "Mitchum *was* doing that one." The elaborate story of Bob's recalcitrance with George Coleman became fodder for the media. Both Bob and Coleman denied the story, but the studio heat was intense. Something that had never happened became a studio legend.

But now the record is set straight.

❄❄❄

Much has been written about Marilyn Monroe, but the thing that stays with me is Bob's comment after her tragic death: "Marilyn was much too fragile for Hollywood." He was not referring to her physical courage. When she and Bob were filming Otto Preminger's "River of No Return" in 1953, a beautifully shot Cinemascope Western, they rafted on the Bow River of Canada—without stunt doubles.

The raft started swinging out of control when the crew-manned security line snapped. They careened with alarming speed toward the turbulent rapids and could easily have been dumped in the rough water and jagged rocks. Bob insisted that Marilyn leave while she could with the help of the crew following on shore, but she refused until Bob could also be taken off the raft. "You shouldn't be out here," she told him. "You've got the flu so I don't get off until you do."

They got off—with a great deal of shouting and waving from the anxious crew. The raft didn't make it.

Marilyn's Achilles' heel lay in her caring too much.

Another member of that picture's cast was Western actor Rory Calhoun, known to his peers as "Smoke." Bob and Rory became instant friends, reflecting Robert's penchant for running with the mavericks. Bob told me about Calhoun once when a columnist wrote a disparaging remark about Smoke's "pretty face."

"His real name is Timothy Francis Duggan and he spent time in Oklahoma for a little thing called 'armed robbery,'" Bob said. A few years later, Rory was riding a horse in Griffith Park when a producer saw him and was impressed with the way he straddled a saddle. The producer asked Rory if he was in pictures. Smoke told him no. The producer suggested he should try the business. Smoke got an agent, and learned that the producer wanted him to change his name. And Rory Calhoun was born.

Rory Calhoun, known as "Smoke" to Bob, has come a long way since serving time at the Federal Reform School at El Reno, Oklahoma. Besides working with Bob in "River of No Return," he's been in countless Westerns and starred in the 1958-60 TV series "The Texan" as a roving gunfighter named Bill Longley.

Bob as Curt Bridges in the strangely allegorical Western "Track of the Cat," a 1954 color film (co-starring Diana Lynn, Tab Hunter and Teresa Wright) in which director William Wellman tried to keep the colors as muted as possible. The film was colorless in more ways than one.

In rapid succession Bob did William A. Wellman's "Track of the Cat" for Warner Brothers (based on a very strange allegorical tale by Walter Van Tilberg Clark) and "Not As a Stranger" for United Artists (based on a very popular novel by Morton Thompson). While making the latter film under director Stanley Kramer, Bob worked with Frank Sinatra and they became close friends. For years Bob would get a Mother's Day card from the singer that read, "Happy Mother's Day. You Mother!"

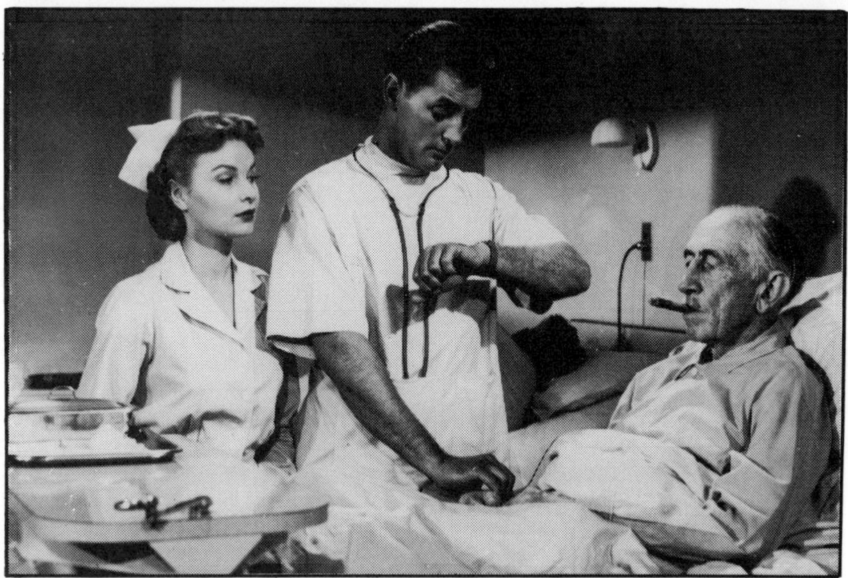

Bob as Dr. Lucas Marsh in "Not as a Stranger," 1955.

Following "Not as a Stranger," Bob did a remarkable film, "The Night of the Hunter." For sheer ability Bob deserved the Academy Award for his role as a psychotic hymn-singing preacher pursuing two small children for a hidden fortune. Unfortunately, the film was a financial disaster. I have long since shed the illusion that the Oscar goes to the "best actor" or the "best actress." The film has since become a popular cult classic.

It was the only picture actor Charles Laughton ever directed. I met him and he told me that Bob rated among the finest talents ". . . ever to perform anywhere." If you see the film, look and *listen* to Bob as he stands in the water, watching the two children drift away from him, escaping on the river. My brother is either stark, raving mad, or one fine actor.

That's Bob at the far left, on the set of "The Night of the Hunter," in the closing days of 1954. Actor Charles Laughton, directing for the first and last time in his life, is just to the left of the camera, and Lillian Gish is standing next to him. Bob is portraying the demented Preacher Powell, who is besieging Gish's home for wayward children in an effort to find a cache of stolen money. Powell is the evilest character Bob has ever played and his performance still holds up well today, for it was a finely crafted picture. Laughton deserved better treatment than Hollywood gave him after the film failed at the box office. Today he would be hailed as a hero.

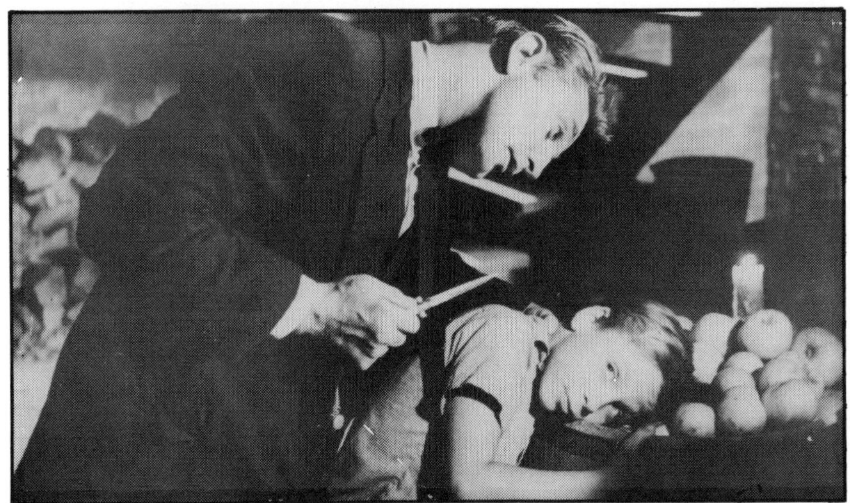

Charles Laughton got along well with Bob during the filming of "The Night of the Hunter," and would often praise his acting. Bob usually shrugged it off, and once remarked that as an actor he was always the same from picture to picture. The only thing he ever changed was his underwear.

CONFIDENTIALLY YOURS, NOT MINE

IN MAY 1955, Bob sued Confidential, a controversial Hollywood exposé magazine noted for its sleazy stories. The magazine alleged that Bob—attending a post-production dinner party in honor of Charles Laughton in producer Paul Gregory's posh Malibu home—stripped naked and poured catsup over himself, shouting that he was a hamburger.

This was a patently ridiculous story. As I've often pointed out, how many formal dinner parties are held with bottles of catsup on a table set with crystal and sterling? For more insight into the inner workings of such smut magazines, I'll relate the following adventure.

A little later that same year, I worked on "The Man in the Vault" (originally titled "The Lock and the Key"), a picture produced by John Wayne's brother, Bob Morrison. My segments were shot in Art Linkletter's bowling alley in West Hollywood. As we worked through the night, a security guard, an off-duty deputy sheriff, became very friendly toward me.

My ESP was working full-time; I wondered why he wanted to be my buddy. He kept calling me, dropping over to see me; he even invited me to his apartment for a drink. Here was a young deputy sheriff driving a brand-new Cadillac and living in a very expensive apartment complex. My curiosity didn't have to wait too long.

"How do you get along with your brother?" We were sitting in my house in Hollywood when he finally got to the point. The light immediately dawned. I went into my act.

"How would *you* get along with someone who is riding as high as he is when you have to live like *this*?" I indicated my surroundings. Actually, it was a very comfortable house on Genesee Avenue, but I made it out to be pauper's row. I appeared to be really bitter toward my brother.

"How would you like to get even?" He looked at me with eager anticipation.

I allowed that I'd love to, "But how?" (I already knew the answer, but wasn't prepared for the price range.)

"Fifty thousand dollars an article about any star you know in the business, but especially—your brother. You know what kind of article, but it has to be true and provable."

I could have been a millionaire in a week, but was never tempted—then or now.

Bob's attorney was the

I'm at far right as William Campbell and Barry Kroeger confront me in a tense scene in "Man in the Vault," the film which inadvertently led to my undercover activities against Confidential Magazine, the scandal sheet of the 1950s.

Once again Hollywood attorney Jerry Giesler came forward to represent Bob legally when my brother sued Confidential Magazine for an article that claimed he had danced naked on a tabletop in a posh Malibu estate. Bob's example was followed by Liberace and others who also sued. It led to hearings that finally did in the scandal rag.

late Jerry Giesler. After each meeting with the deputy, I'd inform Giesler. Meanwhile the officer was getting impatient with me, for no articles had been forthcoming.

"My boss is getting tired of your stalling," he told me one day as we drove around in his gold Cadillac. I assured him that I'd already written a number of pieces and would deliver them by the next weekend. He seemed placated; then I put in another call to Giesler.

I was talking to a friend on the phone that evening when a voice cut in on my line. The unknown eavesdropper told me that he had been observing me for some time. I laughed out loud.

"So, observe me. What's to observe?" I became a lot less jovial when he pointed out that he was observing me at that very moment. "You wife is at the sink, peeling potatoes right now and—ah—uh-huh, your son just came into the kitchen. He's wearing a pair of white shorts with a white shirt trimmed in blue. Yeah—he just grabbed his mommy's leg."

I looked over to see my son do just that. I didn't want to alarm Nancy, but I pulled the curtains on all the windows and called the telephone company. They notified the FBI; an agent came to my house. While I was on the phone, the unknown man cut in again. The FBI agent got on the line and warned the mystery caller that he was committing a Federal offense.

"You'll never be able to find me!" He roared with laughter as he switched off my line.

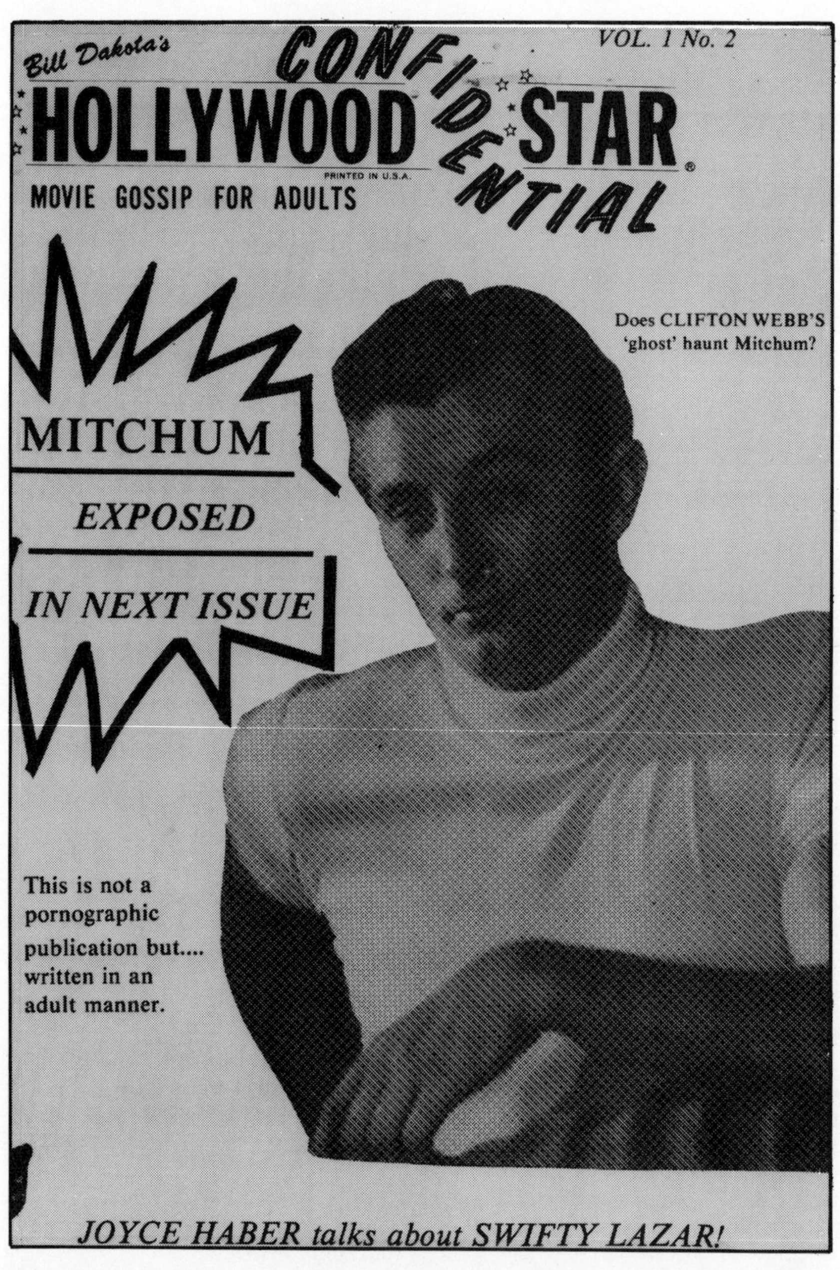

With the emergence of Confidential Magazine in the early 1950s, a whole new trend in "Hollywood Expose" was begun, as exemplified by this issue of "Bill Dakota's Hollywood Confidential Star," which featured Bob on the cover. Confidential folded but its mean spirit and lack of hesitancy to print anything scandalous (no matter how libelous) about a movie or TV star has been carried over into today's supermarket tabloids along the lines of the National Enquirer.

The phone company confirmed that he was right: "He has equipment much more advanced than ours." It was not very comforting to know that. *(Much later, I learned through a security guard at Paramount that the genius behind the electronic tap on my telephone was Reed Wilson.)*

Two days later, the deputy came by and he wasn't smiling. He drove me to a big apartment building, ushered me into a ground-floor apartment occupied by a number of hard-eyed men who weren't smiling either. The room was equipped with a lot of very expensive-looking electronics equipment.

It turned out that the head of the group was Fred Otash, a one-time Los Angeles policeman who had left the service under a cloud, then had gone into the private eye business. *(Otash and Wilson would later be implicated in the Marilyn Monroe-John F. Kennedy scandal, allegedly bugging the bedroom in which they held their trysts; Wilson was also one of those linked to the Watergate scandal.)*

I looked over at Otash's silent, glowering gunmen with the bulgy jackets. It was confession time. "I tried, God knows I tried." My voice was trembling and I started to cry. "But he's my brother and I just couldn't bring myself to do it."

Otash was thoroughly disgusted. "Get out, you sniveling bastard!"

I breathed a sigh of relief when I finally got back safely onto the sidewalk. It's a good thing he hadn't heard my brother tell a friend of ours, who had mentioned that I was a very sentimental person, "For Chris'sake, Jack can cry at card tricks."

Giesler called me that evening. "Stay in your house at night until this is over," he warned. "They'll jump the curb in a car, run you down, and that would be that. We'll make sure Confidential Magazine's dealings—and Otash—come out in the open, along with Bob's suit for slander, I can assure you." This was the first time I knew who Otash was working for. It was also the first inkling that—naive innocent that I was—my life had been in danger all along.

August 2, 1957: Hollywood private eye Fred Otash appears in Los Angeles at the Confidential Magazine hearings, to answer to charges that he had allegedly been hired by Hollywood Research Inc. to dig up the dirt on movie stars. Since I had met Otash firsthand, when he was trying to get the lowdown on Brother Bob, I knew there was no question of his involvement.

THE LAST OF THE GREAT COWBOY CLIFFHANGERS

FORTUNATELY, I was signed to do a picture shooting up in the Big Bear mountain area (now a lovely resort town). The image of the hard-eyed gunsels in Otash's apartment still haunted me so I brought my family along so we could live safely in the pristine mountains while Confidential was being driven out of business.

The picture was a milestone in film history, for it was the last of the Saturday afternoon multi-chapter serials ever made: "Perils of the Wilderness." Columbia, the only studio still grinding them out, had decided the matinee was a piece of Hollywood history and it was time to retire the cliff-hanger format. "Wilderness" was about girls jumping out of airplanes, Canadian fur trappers, bad guys, the Royal Mounted Police and Indians in war canoes. Just as bizarre as the Fred Otash caper, but it was legal and I was getting paid honest money for portraying a French fur trapper, *by gar.*

"Perils" was a production headed by Sam Katzman, who was one of the dying breed of filmmakers who shot films on such low budgets that his name became a Hollywood byword for frugality.

According to Screen Actors Guild rules, if an extra speaks he is upped in pay scale to the actors' minimum. There's a legendary story around Hollywood that Sam once avoided paying an extra the actors' minimum in a film sequence with the following ploy:

The hero goes into the saloon and asks the bartender (the extra) if he's seen any men ride into town. The bartender nods in the affirmative. "How many were there?" asks the hero. The bartender holds up six fingers. "Were

I'm at far right in this lobby card of "Perils of the Wilderness," the last of the movie serials. At left is Dinty Moore and in the middle is Pierce Lyden, who loaned me this photo from his extensive movie-still collection.

they white men or Indians?" The bartender spreads his fingers behind his head to imitate feathers. Maybe it wasn't art but it saved $40.

On "Perils" Sam hired a number of actors who had been the backbone of hundreds of Western films: Kermit Maynard, Terry Frost, Bud Osborne, Pierce Lyden, Dinty Moore, Don Harvey, Rex Lease, Lenny Geer, Rick Vallin and Richard Emory prominent among them. Most of them are gone now but all left an indelible mark on the history of Western films.

Two of the great unsung heroes of Western movies: Terry Frost and Bud Osborne. They represented an era that's long past.

ROBERT, TOUGH AND TENDER

BOB TOLD ME that Laughton, who spent years concealing his homosexuality, chided him gently over the publicity he had received from the "hamburger" article. "Bobby," he wheezed, "all of us have skeletons in our closets, but most of us stand by the closet humming a distracting tune while trying to edge the skeletons back into hiding by pushing them ever so surreptitiously with a foot. But you, Bobby! You drag your skeletons into the open and rattle them so all the world can see. You, Robert, must stop rattling your own skeletons."

❄ ❄ ❄

Bob showed me a letter he had received from a man in Marked Tree, Arkansas. The writer told Bob that he needed $10,000 immediately.

"If you don't send it to me," the letter continued, "I hope you die of the cancer."

That's a hell of a way to start your day. Bob had no connection whatsoever with the sick bastard whom I considered ripe for a mental institution. So much for the "glamour" of having a great deal of money.

❄ ❄ ❄

In 1957, Bob did a memorable John Huston movie with Deborah Kerr, "Heaven Knows, Mr. Allison." Bob played a tough Marine stranded on a Japanese-held island with Deborah, who portrayed a nun. Bob genuinely loved Deborah for her innate gentility and her inner beauty. After working with her in the mid-1980s in the TV-cable movie "Return to Fairborough," he told me that he still considers her the apex of the many stars with whom he has starred.

"Heaven Knows" was made on Tobago in the West Indies on very rough terrain. At one point Bob noticed that Deborah's feet were hurting her painfully. He knelt down, untied her shoes, took them off and kneaded her feet tenderly. She almost wept when, after gently replacing her shoes, he said, "Gotta have you around for the next shot."

This was after he crawled four times through stinging nettles to get a shot John Huston wanted done to perfection. Bob's bare chest and arms oozed with blood; Huston wanted to know why in hell he hadn't told him of the ordeal.

Bob's reply was terse: "That's the shot you wanted, wasn't it?"

Bob and Deborah Kerr in John Huston's "Heaven Knows, Mr. Allison."

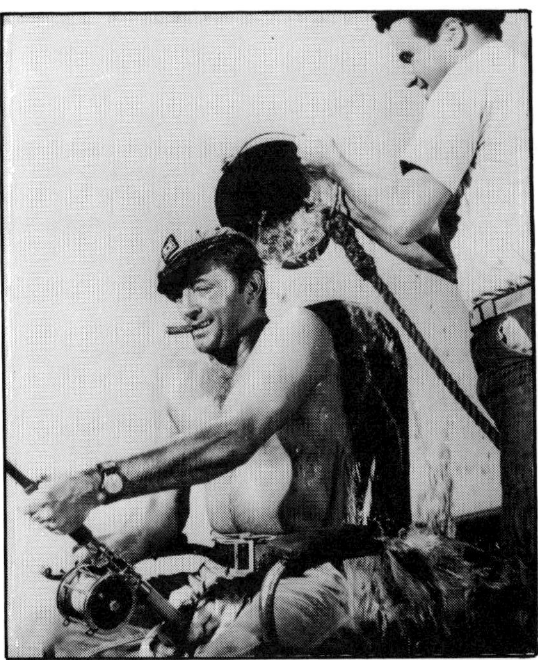

Bob gets dumped on anew—this time with a pail of water—in "Fire Down Below," a triangular Irwin Shaw melodrama set in the Caribbean that co-starred Jack Lemmon and Rita Hayworth.

Huston marvelled at him. Bob was matter-of-fact; he wasn't playing to an audience. He was just doing his job.

❄ ❄ ❄

In 1956 Bob went to Trinidad and Tobago in the Caribbean with Jack Lemmon and Rita Hayworth to make "Fire Down Below," a Columbia picture sandwiched between "Heaven Knows, Mr. Allison" and "The Enemy Below." Brother Robert started going on one tear after another, and got so drunk that he beat the hell out of two American sailors. Dorothy flew down to Tobago to put the lid on his roistering. It was no small chore for her to settle him down, but she accomplished it well enough to get the show finished—without any more head bashings and bloody knuckles.

❄ ❄ ❄

When we were children in Delaware, our uncle would often take us to the Atlantic Ocean at Bowers Beach, twelve miles from the Woodside Farm. Once, on the beach, I saw a small sand shark lying dead near the water's edge. Brimming with scientific curiosity, I thrust a small stick into its anal aperture—an incident that years later Bob would retell, his imagination truly reaching Andean heights.

In 1957 I played a very small part in "Operation Mad Ball," a zany military comedy starring Jack Lemmon. I wondered why Lemmon was always staring at me. I should have known: Brother Robert. A few months earlier, while shooting "Fire Down Below," he had walked the white coral sands of Tobago with Lemmon on a beautiful Sunday morning.

"Look at all of this," crowed Robert. "Azure sky, cobalt sea, white sands, green palms. Why, we're doing what we like to do, getting paid well, and working in Paradise."

Jack wasn't buying it. He offered guardedly, "We have to do water scenes. At night."

"So?"

"There're sharks out there," Lemmon quavered. "We have to work in the

Surrounded by beauty once again, Bob poses with Ingrid Tulean (Thulin) and Genevieve Page during the production of "Foreign Intrigue," a film produced-written-directed by Sheldon Reynolds, who had first made the idea into a popular TV series that was entirely shot on location in Europe. Bob enjoyed making the film and admired Reynolds' abilities to get the job done cheaply but efficiently.

water with sharks."

Bob waved that off. "Sharks, schmarks. I've got a brother who screws 'em!"

"My God!" Jack was astounded. "You're kidding!"

"No I'm not." Bob had him now. "My brother and I were at a party on Catalina Island and it got to be dullsville. I suggested we swim ashore to Malibu and catch some action there. We dove into the water and, several hours later, were within sight of the Malibu pier. Suddenly, in the moonlight, I saw a great dorsal fin appear and head straight for my brother. 'Oh, dear God,' I prayed, 'save him!'

"Not to worry. Brother John reached up with his left hand, grabbed that big fin and hauled himself aboard the shark. He started diddling the beast with his right hand and—before you knew it—the two were in love. A great wave caught them offguard, heaving them onto the sand. When I got ashore, John was astride the creature in full control. I swear the great shark turned her head back to him and grinned her approval."

I had forgotten Bob's tall tale until Lemmon's attorney called me on the phone to ask verification for Jack's autobiography. He wanted to know if the tale was true. I laughed and set the record straight.

I've kicked myself ever since then. I could have set another record: In "The Guinness Book of Records."

❄❄❄

While in the Caribbean, Bob, as usual, spent most of his spare time with the native people. The recording world was delighted to find that he could sing calypso like a native, and Capitol recorded a disc that was very successful. It was no great surprise to me. After all, we had harmonized our way into the hearts of those Alabama folks on Shades Mountain.

❄❄❄

"The Enemy Below" (1958), directed by actor Dick Powell, was a tremendous picture in that Bob and Curt Jurgens brought the sea war of World War II into a microcosm of human courage and valor under great stress. Bob portrayed the commander of a U.S. destroyer in pursuit of a U-boat

Germans Below, Americans Above

"The Enemy Below" was an excellent World War II sea saga that dealt with the theme of command. Bob played Captain Murrell, who engages in a cat-and-mouse game of war with a German U-Boat skipper whom he respects.

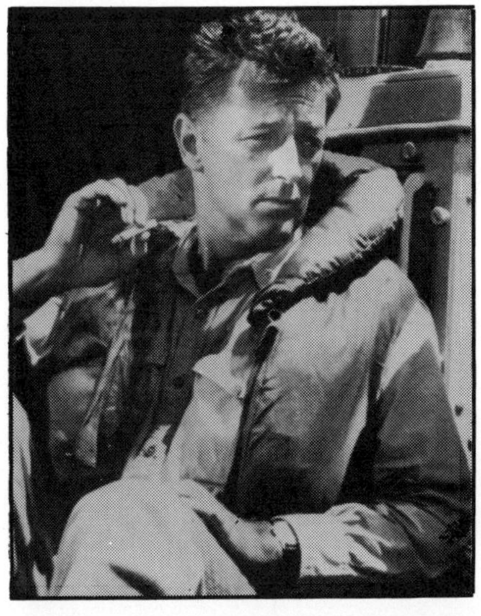

captained by Jurgens. It was the first picture of Doug McClure (who would later star on TV's "The Virginian"), whom Bob had affectionately dubbed "Hammerhead." Around the set Bob quietly became a mentor for the neophyte actor.

When they were returning by car to their respective hotels one evening, an assistant director turned abruptly to McClure, informing him that he was finished with his scenes and that his plane was leaving Honolulu Airport at eight o'clock that night. Bob looked at Doug to see tears coming into his eyes. "Why didn't you tell me sooner?" Doug cried. "My parents are flying in tonight to spend my birthday with me."

"Tough shit," snarled the assistant. "You're through, and that's that."

"Driver, stop the car," ordered Bob.

"What?"

"Stop the car!"

The car lurched to the curb.

"You," Bob said, "get out!"

"What?" The assistant couldn't believe it.

"Get out before I knock you out!"

The assistant got out.

When the car moved on, Bob turned to Doug and handed him a set of keys. "Here," he said. "These're to my suite. Use 'em as long as you like."

"What about you?" McClure asked.

"Oh," Robert answered cheerily, "I imagine that somewhere on this island, someone might take in a stranger."

THE LEGEND OF 'THUNDER ROAD'

BOB WROTE a beautiful song when he was 14 years old, "The Whippoor-will." I recall him singing it softly while we sat on a wooden swing in Rising Sun, Delaware. He had written it because of Dorothy and, later, he incorporated it into the soundtrack of the 1958 film he wrote, "Thunder Road," about moonshiners vs. revenuers. Keely Smith did a great job singing it; Bob sang the title song himself. He had finished the lyrics but couldn't come up with a melody until our Norwegian mother suggested an old Norwegian pavanne; it turned out to be the right one. "Thunder Road" the movie became a cult classic, while the title song sold into the millions. Listen to it in the driving melody that's so well known, then bring the tempo back to a stately 4/4 rhythm. You can see in your mind the grave Norseman dancing in courtly fashion to the pre-Mitchum melody.

❄ ❄ ❄

Carey Loftin was regarded as one of the best "car men" in the stunt business. *(If you saw Steven Spielberg's "Duel," a 1971 TV film that depicted Dennis Weaver being pursued by an enormous truck, you were watching Loftin at work.)*

In "Thunder Road," it was Carey who drove in Bob's stead in the chase that ended with the car turning over three times and stopping with its roof leaning against a power-line pole. Bob asked Carey if he could do it "just so." Carey allowed that he could.

Before the shooting, Carey dug a trench along the side of the road. When he was satisfied with his trench, he told Bob he was ready.

What the moviegoer sees is a perfect sequence of a car careening down a mountain road at breakneck speed. It turns over three times and lands

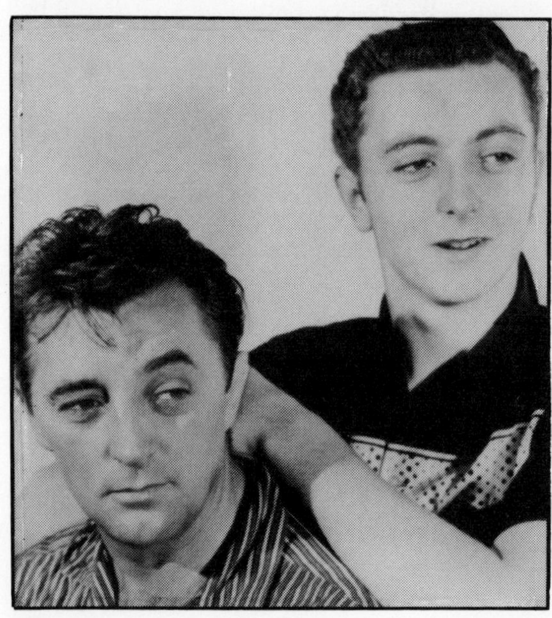

Bob chose his real-life son Jim, who was 16 during the production of "Thunder Road," to play his make-believe brother because of the striking similarity. The youth, who was already 6-foot-2, told reporters, "Pop says I go back to high school when the picture is finished." Jim's made many films since—"The Victors," "In Harm's Way," "The Money Trap" and "Trackdown" among them—but his career has never skyrocketed.

When Carey Loftin sent the photo at left, he told me: "On 'Thunder Road' when I went to Bob's room to talk about money for the stunts, he said 'What do you want to talk about it for? Just be fair. Don't fuck me or don't fuck yourself. Write it down and we have a deal. Now, would you like a drink?' I replied, 'I thought you'd never ask.' Later he offered me a part in 'Wonderful Country' but I told him I didn't trust horses and turned him down. He said, 'This is the first time you're ever going to be given a present for not doing a picture.' And he handed me an inscribed St. Christopher cigarette lighter."

exactly as Bob had wanted. When Bob ran over to the car, Carey grinned up at him. "Is this where you wanted it?"

"Later, I was watching the rushes," recalled Bob, "when I saw something I couldn't believe. I told the projectionist to roll it back, do it in slow motion. There it was: Carey was smoking a cigarette and, just as the car started to careen, he nonchalantly flipped the butt out of the car, leaning into the interior. He was the perfect picture of 'cool.'"

Bob's oldest son, James, played his younger brother in "Thunder Road." He did it well but, except for B Westerns and other low-budget genre pictures, he's never been able to build a real career in the business.

***

In 1959 Bob wanted a real change of pace. He bought a 300-acre farm above Chesapeake Bay in Maryland. It was almost 3,000 miles from Hollywood, a distance that would bedim most stars, but Robert moved there with Dorothy and their three kids—Trina was now part of the family too.

Bob began investing in quarter-horse racing. Many times I had been invited to his California home and allowed the privilege of watching him intensely pore over stud books and magazines for hours. I'd get up to leave and he'd ask me where I was going. Home, of course. Two hours and not a moment of conversation. Now, on his Maryland farm, he had quite a stable of beautiful stock. (Out of his absorbed interest, he bought Don Guerro, a big, solid horse who won the world's championship in 1974.)

Victor Buono, a classical character actor who was great at playing heavyset villains with feyish charms, was a very close friend of Bob's, and Bob related this story to me.

"I was reading through some stud books while Victor was watching his favorite football team, the Los Angeles Rams, play the San Francisco 49ers. At times, Victor would jump up like a frothing madman, shouting at the TV set. 'You fool!' he roared. 'You dropped the ball!' Then he'd yell, 'Idiot! You let him through the line!' Finally, I couldn't ignore his rantings. 'Victor,' I asked, 'how can you get so fired up over a professional football game?' He rose to his full height, glowering at me. 'I,' he answered imperiously, 'went to RAM!'"

❄ ❄ ❄

Dorothy really wanted to get away from Hollywood in more ways than just geographically. Their daughter Trina was now seven, Jim was 18 and Chris, 15. She wanted a more serene home life for them. Living in Maryland answered her needs for several years, but Bob was gone too much of the time, which eroded the serenity they both expected from the farm.

GROWLIN' CHARLEY McGRAW

BOB'S OWN production company, Talbot Productions, did a Western in 1959 called "The Wonderful Country." He portrayed a tough pistolero buying guns for a Mexican rebel played by Pedro Armendariz. Charles McGraw was once again teamed with Robert as an irascible town doctor and, not surprisingly, he again caused many problems for the company.

Bob, no stranger to McGraw's eccentricities, had chosen to film "The Wonderful Country" on location in Mexico. Fully aware of McGraw's penchant for attracting trouble, he arranged for McGraw's travelling companion to be Chuck Roberson, John Wayne's stunt double. At 6-foot-4, and over 225 pounds, Chuck made it appear that Charles had finally met his match. Not so.

Chuck Roberson, who was John Wayne's stunt double in many a Western, also did some serious acting in such films as William Wyler's "The Big Country," Sammy Fuller's "Shock Corridor" and John Frankenheimer's "99 and 44/100 Per Cent Dead." Chuck, after a long and distinguished career but one which remained relatively obscure to the general public, died of cancer in 1988.

When the plane landed in Juarez, Mexico, the mercurial McGraw dashed to a cab and careened into the nearest whorehouse. Roberson barely extricated him in time to catch the plane that would fly them first to Monterrey, then to Torreon.

In Monterrey, Charles made another mad dash for the nearest house of ill repute. This time, Roberson didn't extricate the determined womanizer from the inner rooms of that hallowed institution in time to board the plane to Torreon.

There was only one seat open on the next plane; it was beside one occupied by a very ill Mexican who had to carry his own oxygen equipment. McGraw ranted to such a degree that the airline finally took the sick man off the flight, giving the two seats to Roberson and McGraw.

Roberson said that he stared in stunned silence at the belligerent McGraw during take-off preparations. When the plane finally cleared the ground, McGraw bellowed at him, "What the hell're you staring at me for? He's a 'Denver lunger' and wouldn't have made it to Mexico City, anyway."

It was no easier for Roberson in Torreon. He had to ride herd on McGraw all the way. By the time they reached Durango, their location, McGraw had passed out from an overdose of beer. The transportation driver and Chuck carried the unconscious McGraw into a station wagon and drove to the set. They laid the now sleeping volcano onto a cot behind the set and finished the day's shooting undisturbed.

Back at the hotel, McGraw came out of his stupor and demanded to see Mitchum's room. Bob, in his infinite wisdom, had already anticipated McGraw's burning resolve not to take lesser accommodations than the star of the picture. "You're in it," Bob told him, having completely stolen McGraw's thunder . . . for the moment.

Three days later, McGraw's blistering tirade could be heard as far away as Mexico City. He was screaming at the hotel manager about the toilet in his room: It didn't flush. After three days of heavy beer-drinking, the man was beside himself. Bob, who bore witness to McGraw's tantrum, went

"The Wonderful Country," a beautifully shot Western made in Mexico, starred Bob as a gunrunner named Martin Brady who is buying arms for a revolutionist in the 1870s. The excellent supporting cast included Julie London, Jack Oakie, Pedro Armendariz and Gary Merrill. And our old pal, Charley McGraw.

along to inspect the facility.

"It was an abattoir," declared Robert. "Filled with three days of McGraw's deposits." All because "the idiot didn't recognize that the handle to the water closet was on the *left* side."

❄ ❄ ❄

Back in Hollywood after "The Wonderful Country," McGraw paced up and down the living room of his apartment like an enraged, caged tiger while I watched with a growing sense of awe. Divorced now, he was living with a girl friend I knew only as "Sam." She sat quivering like an exposed quail before the maddened McGraw. He had been gone for nearly an hour to a nearby liquor store to replenish his diminished stock of beer.

"What took you so long, Charley?" I thought my question innocuous enough.

"She!" He pointed at the distraught Sam. "My shorts!" he roared. Pacing like a madman he whirled and pointed again. "No clean shorts!" Now Charley was in high gear. "Hers! I put on a pair of hers!"

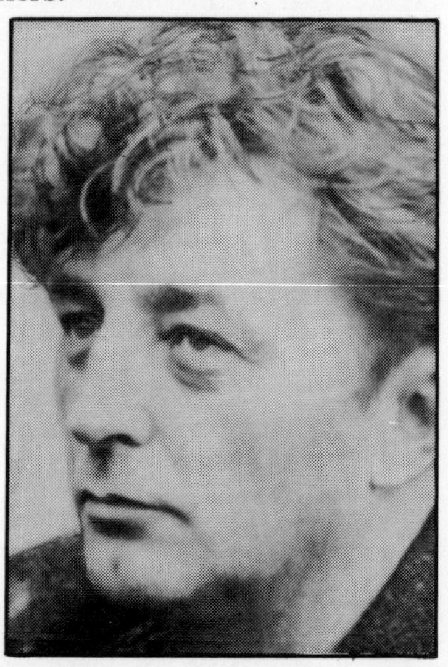

On August 2, 1959, Bob was in a pub in Bray, Ireland, signing a fan's autograph book, when suddenly the fan hauled off and slugged Bob from behind. Bob had a bad bruise over one eye . . . but you should have seen the other guy.

"Is that what held you up?"

Charley glared at my interruption. "The bathroom!" he bellowed. "No bathroom at the liquor store!"

Through his staccato tirade, I managed to interpret that he had asked the liquor dealer if he could use his toilet. The dealer explained that he didn't have one; he used the gas station's facility next door. Charley ran out of the store only to find the gas station locked. Desperate now, he stood behind the stone wall separating the two businesses. In the midst of relieving himself, a spotlight illuminated him. Two of Los Angeles' finest leaped from their squad car, guns drawn.

"You!" barked a cop. "Behind the wall! Come out with your hands over your head!"

"Not on your life!" Charley barked back.

The two officers looked at each other, momentarily speechless. Then one queried, "Is that you, McGraw?"

"Who the hell do you think it is?"

"Jesus, Charley, we could've shot you." The officer couldn't believe Charley's attitude, and Charley couldn't explain about the dainty underwear. He went back into the store, got his purchases of wine and beer and wended his way home.

McGraw finished his story and shouted, "Do you think I wanted them to go around saying I was a God-damned transvestite?"

***

McGraw, who was probably very drunk at the time, died in 1980 while taking a shower. He fell against the door of his stall, shattering the glass and severing an artery. His name is on a star on Hollywood Boulevard, in front of what is now Mann's Chinese Theatre. I advise anyone who walks in that direction not to tread on said star. I'm certain that somewhere McGraw is watching—and growling.

TWO CAMEOS - TWO NICE PEOPLE

MY DAUGHTER, CINDY, was born in May, 1958, the same week I was doing a Red Skelton television show. At the time Red's son Richard was terminally ill, but the comedian gave no hint of his deep sorrow. A true clown, he kept the cast and crew laughing at his antics. I wasn't aware of his pain until I came on the set with a box of cigars and pronounced gleefully that I had fathered a baby girl.

No one was cheerful. I was bewildered until a grip informed me that Red's son had died during the night of leukemia. The boy had been in the same hospital where Cindy was born. I felt that I had to say something to Red to apologize for my enthusiasm and, after knocking timidly on his door, was invited into his dressing room. He was lying down, staring at the ceiling.

"I'm sorry, Red. I didn't know."

He turned to me and, for the first time, I saw the inner man. "Sorry that you have a baby girl?" His voice was almost toneless.

"No, of course not, but I'm sorry that I carried on about it under the circumstances."

"Do you believe in God and in Jesus Christ?"

"With all my heart and soul," I said. "I believe so completely I suppose it's a terrible mistake I take it for granted that I'm one of God's children and that Christ is my Saviour."

Red lay back down on the couch again, sighing deeply.

"I've travelled all over the world searching out every belief existent. Constantly trying to find a spiritual explanation for my son's illness. Finally, I came full circle back to Christianity." He stared at the ceiling for a long moment. "It's the only religion of hope."

Whenever I see Red on television, the picture of him staring at the ceiling floods across me when he signs off by waving at his audience and saying, "God bless."

***

Cindy wasn't very old when she met Lee Van Cleef, who was then a heavy in Hollywood Westerns and crime dramas. Although the steely-eyed actor would go on to greater stardom as an anti-hero in "For a Few Dollars More"

Lee Van Cleef in a scene from "El Condor," one of the many action Westerns in which he has excelled. After working for years in Hollywood films and TV shows, his career really soared in Europe in the spaghetti Westerns, where he could play villains and good-guys-who-might-be-villains with equal believability.

and other hard-boiled spaghetti Westerns, he was still struggling to make a reputation for himself. He had made his debut in the great film "High Noon" as one of the gunman who stalks Gary Cooper down the main street of town. I had worked with Lee on a 1955 cops-and-robbers thriller called "The Big Combo" (directed by Joseph H. Lewis) and we had become close friends.

Lee came to my house at lunch time to deliver our three-week-old baby girl her first complete toilette set: Brush, comb, mirror, powder and perfume. The tenderness he displayed stays with me much more powerfully than his screen image of filling cantankerous people full of holes.

Lee, it could be said conservatively, had a drinking problem. On a sound stage in Hollywood, he took me into his dressing room and offered me a drink. I looked around and saw no bottle. Not to worry. From his flight bag, Lee took an elbow pad used to protect that vulnerable area in stunt falls. From its curved folds he extricated a beautiful silver flask molded to the same curvature of the pad. It was filled with vodka—but not for long.

JOHN THE GOOD DOES IT AGAIN

WHILE BROTHER ROBERT was coping with Charley McGraw in Mexico, I became reunited with a brilliant but obscure TV and film director, Richard Bartlett. Dick—who had made a few Jock Mahoney pictures at Universal-International and now worked steadily on TV's "Wagon Train"—had directed a play at the Santa Monica Theater in 1949 in which I had performed an olio. The star of the show was a then-unknown who was to become a great character actor, Strother Martin. His portrayals of Southern and Western lowlifes remain unsurpassed.

Strother and I also became reacquainted just about the time of my youngest daughter's birth. We had been living a half-block from each other and didn't know it.

Strother and his mother were at my house for dinner one evening when the old woman, who was in her eighties, surprised me by downing Jack Daniels straight. After a few shots she told me, "No one knows how great an actor my Strother is." She brushed past her son's objections, adding that she had visited Strother on a movie set that week, deploring the way the director treated him. She went to the director to lodge her complaint.

"Young man," she shrilled, "obviously you don't understand Strother's depth as an actor." When the badgered creature tried to voice an opinion, she marched away, casting her final barb over her shoulder. "No use in talking to you," she snapped. "You haven't got the sense of a turd in a punchbowl."

Strother Martin in a 1967 "Death Valley Days" TV episode. Among Martin's best films are "Cool Hand Luke," "Rooster Cogburn," "Shenandoah" and "Pocket Money." He also once starred in a horror film, "The Brotherhood of Satan," for his producer pal L.Q. Jones.

Strother is gone now (he died at the age of 61 of a heart attack in 1980 in Thousands Oaks, California) so it makes a story told to me by actor Robert Donnor all the more poignant. "I came out of my hotel to get in the car that was to take us to a location up in Montana," Donnor said. "I called out, 'Good morning, Strother,' and he answered, 'Good morning, Bob.' The driver, a local man, turned to Strother and snarled, 'What's good about it?' Strother eyed him steadily for a few beats, then drawled, 'Would you care to miss one?'"

❄ ❄ ❄

Brother Robert had worked with Edgar "Buck" Buchanan in 1955 in an RKO comedy, "She Couldn't Say No," co-starring Jean Simmons and Arthur Hunnicutt. Buchanan was another of those unforgettable characters to whom Bob was attracted. Buck had started out as a dentist and had been sidetracked into theater. It's a good thing; in his 36 years before the camera he gave people more pleasure as an actor than he ever could have bearing down on them with a dentist's electric drill.

I worked with Buck on the Ty Hardin television series "Bronco" at Warner Brothers in Burbank. It was one of many Western adventures the studio was turning out at the time to keep from going broke. One morning Ty and Buck were playing gin rummy and Ty was posing elegantly in his leather-tooled director's chair emblazoned with his name. Buck was crunched down on an applebox, glowering at his cards. Ty, under personal contract to Jack Warner, was being paid a comparatively low salary. Buck, under no contract, was getting his usual hefty sum as the guest star.

"Too bad you haven't got a chair like this one, Buck." Ty's voice had taken on an edge of smug superiority.

Buck squinted over his glasses and replied, "Difference in our salaries, boy, will buy me a lot of chairs."

During that same show, Buck told me that he had stopped his car at an intersection in Toluca Lake that morning just in time to see a very heavy woman come down her apartment stairs to pick up her morning paper. "Oh, she was big," rasped Buck. "She had a great head of frizzy red hair and was wearing one of those kigh-monos. She waddled across the lawn and when she stooped to get her paper, that kigh-mono popped wide open. For a minute, I thought she was ridin' a chow dog."

Edgar Buchanan

Slim Pickens had a role in that episode of "Bronco." One warm afternoon, he suggested to the folk singer Rusty Richards that he'd like to sing a parody to a cowboy song, "Cowpoke," that Rusty had just sung.

We were sitting outside, waiting for a stage set-up, when Slim, given the chord by Rusty, reared back and, to the obligato of his stamping foot, started in.

"I'm a rodeo cowboy and my name is Joe Gates.
I throw the best lariat in the 48 states."

At this point, Rusty took over the yodel that follows each stanza, but followed it by segueing up a half-tone. Four stanzas later, Slim was squawking like a sick soprano rooster, gasping for air.

"I don't know what's happened to my voice," he cackled. "I could always sing that sucker before."

Rusty wisely refrained from telling him why. Slim was awful big.

Rusty told me that Buck had taken him aside and given him his own philosophy of dealing with Hollywood. In his terse, clenched-teeth style, he said, "I've survived them for 20 years now, son. Just walk slow, drink lots of water, and stay in the shade."

❄❄❄

From the mid-'50s through the '60s, Richard Bartlett was under contract at Universal as a producer-director. He used me many times in his TV series, among them "Cimarron City" (produced by a dear friend, Andy Fennady); "Laramie," "Shotgun Slade" and "Riverboat." I was to have started as a regular on "Riverboat"—a series starring Darren McGavin and Burt Reynolds—on Monday but I self-destructed on Sunday afternoon.

My buddy, Abel Fernandez, had stopped by my house on Sunday morning, bringing a bottle of vodka and some tomato juice. Abel was a regular for some time as Agent Bill Youngfellow on "The Untouchables" (1959-63) with Robert Stack as its star. I had done a couple of the shows so Abel and I quickly became friends. He was a professional light-heavyweight fighter and could hit like a mule.

We had been working at Universal the previous Friday; Abel talked me into going to a bar across the street from the main gate. The Keys was a wild place, owned by a retired studio grip, Eddie Keyes. When Abel and I entered, the bar was so crowded we had to stand two-deep away from it. A big, burly, red-headed man seated at the bar was letting the world know that he was rough and tough. I looked at Abel and smiled.

"Pretty rough out, isn't it?" I didn't say it loudly. I thought it was funny.

The brute swung around on his barstool. "You want a piece of my action?" As he said it, all idle conversation at the bar ceased.

Abel Fernandez as agent Youngfellow in "The Untouchables."

"If it suits your fancy." I looked calmly at the man while he seemed bewildered by my taunting answer. Abel laughed, so the behemoth turned his attention to him. Abel is some 40 pounds lighter than I am, but I hasten to say that I want no part of him in any combat situation.

The aggressive redhead had a surprise in store for him. "How about *you*?" he challenged.

Fernandez took out his wallet and put a hundred dollar bill on the bar. "I don't fight for nothing." He eyed the man blandly as he added, "You match that and I'll fight."

The giant brute floundered around like a beached fish. He gulped several times then blurted out, "I haven't got a hundred dollars."

Abel went once again into his wallet and took out another C-note, proffering it to his antagonist. "I, sir, will lend it to you."

The astounded wretch jumped off the barstool and fled out the front door. He apparently didn't want to be misunderstood—no back door and into the alley for him.

Now, on that fateful Sunday morning, Abel and I were having Bloody Marys and getting around to some good fight-talk. Irritated, Nancy announced that she and the children were going over to Rusty Richards' house, implying that we could sit all day, drink and reminisce, if that was what we wanted. Abel apologized to her and insisted on leaving. My family and I went to Rusty and Amy Richards'—and to a disaster.

Rusty was a working cowboy, blessed with the purest tenor voice I have ever heard. He owned a beautiful, lively Arabian stallion named Barhund whom my son, Jack, asked if I could ride.

I have never proposed to be a Willie Shoemaker, but when my small son popped the question, my ego swelled.

"Of course I can. That is, if Rusty will let me." Unfortunately, he did. When I hit the rocky ground, the sound of my ankle snapping into multiple pieces could be heard a hundred feet away. Rusty looked somberly down at me and shook his head. "Third leg he's broke this year." (Barhund lived to be a ripe old 34, but he surely tried to shorten *my* life that day.)

Rusty helped me hop on my right leg to a bench outside his door. "I'll get a bucket of ice water for you to put your foot in." As usual Rusty was in no hurry or panic, and he explained why while I sat patiently, wincing from the pain. "Burt Reynolds is coming over with a song he might sing on 'Riverboat.' He doesn't read music and I don't either. Stick around long enough to teach me the melody so that I can play it on my guitar for him."

Rusty Richards

When Burt arrived, wearing a T-shirt and jeans, I taught them the song, sweat popping from my forehead, my ankle only slightly numbed from the icy water. Neither of the two had any apparent concern for my pain; then I realized they were both so accustomed to pain—Rusty being a working cowboy and Burt having taken many a jolting tumble on the football field—that *my* pain was a matter-of-fact thing. Burt was so charming and affable that for awhile I forgot my aching and worked enthusiastically at teaching them the melody.

After I left the hospital, I called Bartlett to tell him my sad news. That delightful man waited until my "coming out" party on my 40th birthday when the cast was off my leg. He told me he had written a much better part for me than the original one.

So I became Pickalong, a guitar-playing river rat, and the boat's cook, for a whole season (1959-60) on "Riverboat."

Playing Pickalong was some experience. I did eleven segments and got to know Burt. He told he had been an All-American halfback at Florida State,

Experienced pro Darren McGavin co-starred with TV newcomer Burt Reynolds in "Riverboat," but seemed to always go out of his way to make things difficult for the fledgling actor. The antagonism became a cause celebre around Hollywood in 1960, but I could never understand why Darren behaved as he did. What a delight it has been to watch Burt rise to become a star that has far outshined McGavin's own luminescence.

Jack Lambert: Not one of my favorite people

but had to quit football when a huge tackle shattered his spleen. While I hit it off with Burt I never could feel a camaraderie with McGavin. It seemed apparent to most of us on the series that McGavin wanted to shatter Burt's confidence as an actor, for he rode Burt unmercifully. No one was happier than I to see Burt's star rise to the heights it has.

On "Riverboat" I sang folk songs that fitted the period and the particular episode. Bartlett asked me to pick out the songs, keeping in mind that he wanted public domain music to keep costs down. It was because of that factor that Jack Lambert's smoldering resentment of me fanned into flames.

Lambert, who played the Scotsman Joshua in the series, was a friend of McGavin's and of Lew Wasserman, the head of Universal Studios; Wasserman was also the godfather to Lambert's children. Bartlett gave me more to do than Lambert. And Lambert, a veteran in the business with scores of Western films to his credit (including "Vera Cruz") resented it.

It erupted in the open in Leo Lotito's makeup room early one morning while Lambert was being made up; part of his ritual was the coiffing of an elaborate hair-do.

We were filming an episode in which the riverboat is stolen and the crew has to travel overland to retrieve it. I was experimenting with songs and started singing an old chain-gang tune, "Take This Hammer." I tried my best to be unobtrusive.

Lambert turned to me, saying ever so sweetly, "Why don't you take the fucking hammer to the captain yourself?"

I got up stiffly, put my guitar in the corner and stalked out into the hall. In about ten minutes, Leo came out to tell me that it was my turn. Lambert brushed past him to take a taunting stance in front of me. "Ba-a-a-b-y-y-y. We're angry, aren't we?"

"Yes, Jack, I'm angry!"

"Well now, what're we going to do about it?"

"I'm going to knock you on your ass!" I gritted, setting out to do just that. Lambert ran down the hall, stopping about thirty feet away to let me know that the head office was going to "hear about this." I was astounded at his about-face because he had told the entire company several times that he had been touted to be the heavyweight champion of the world. Until that time I always thought you earned a shot at the title by *fighting* through the ranks. *Touted?*

A few nights later we were shooting at the old fort on the Universal backlot when I heard a voice call out, "Hey, John! Johnny Mitchum!" The voice belonged to a visitor, a man with whom I'd been in the army at Camp Crowder, Missouri. He turned to the company, telling them that I was the smoothest fighter he'd ever seen. "Like a panther," he crowed.

Lambert was strangely silent.

TRIMMING THE MINGE

WHILE FINISHING "Fire Down Below, "Brother Robert went over to London to film interiors. He met a young lady who most certainly would rank high in the stories pertaining to "most unforgettable characters." Mavis Purvis was born within the clear sounds of the Bow Bells, and was as Cockney as an English lassie could be. Mavis deserves a chapter by herself, but I shall condense her story—which is like attempting to stuff a rhino calf into a kangaroo pouch.

Bob related the whole story to me: "I was driven to the studio in a furious downpour of rain when I saw this pathetic little wren of a girl standing by the front gate, water streaming down her face, and hunched against the rain like a bird on a telephone wire. I rolled down the window, inquiring what in God's name was she doing outside in that terrible rain.

"'Oh, Mister!' she cried out. 'I've never seen the inside of a studio. Could you 'elp me to see the inside of the studio?'

"I opened the car door. 'Get in.' When she was settled and the car moved inside the studio, I asked her name.

"'Mavis Purvis.' she rang out. 'From London.'"

The English crews are not noted for their manners; the gentlemen on "Fire Down Below" were no different. They would pass by Robert, asking him bluntly why he'd picked up such a pathetic creature. "Why a bird like this?" asked one. Another chimed in, "You can get any bird in England. Why do you bring in a sad little sparrow like this 'un?"

Bob threw up his hands in despair. How could he relate to them the innumerable times in his life that he had been on the outside of the candy store looking in? How could he explain the many untold incidents in his life that had left scars on his inner being?

Mavis needed desperately to be recognized as a person and Robert instinctively knew it. He even went so far as to get her a job in the wardrobe department.

"I was in my dressing room with Brian Owen Smith, my personal wardrobeman on the show," Bob continued. "Brian was a gay but double-tough. Mavis' timid knock came on the door so I bade her to come in. She paused like a frightened deer as she looked at Brian. 'Go ahead, Mavis, say what you want to say.'"

Bob realized that she wanted to confide in him.

Brian heaved a resigned sigh. "I'm a bloody fag," he snorted. "Couldn't care less about your personal life!"

Mavis explained to Bob that she was now 19 and had never been laid. "Oh, they muck me about. But they never go the 'ole route."

"Well," Bob pondered, "would you let us see it?"

"See my minge?" Mavis was appalled.

"How can I make a judgment if I've never seen it?" Bob and Brian nodded in agreement. Demurely, Mavis lifted her skirt and pulled down her panties.

She waited for their judgment.

"Dear Mavis!" Bob cried out. "How can you expect a young swain to wade through that jungle down there? It's like being on safari. You've got to mow that thatch before any sane man will look at you twice."

"Trim my minge! You wants me to trim my minge?"

"It's not what *I* want. It's what *you* want."

Mavis was two hours late the next morning. When she came demurely to Bob's dressing room, he reminded her of that fact.

"It's all because of Mum and my minge," she explained. "I was in the bath

A portrait of Bob, taken around the time he made "Fire Down Below."

when Mum sang out, 'Mavis, what on earth are you doin' in the bath? You'll be late for the studio.' 'Trimmin' my minge,' I yelled through the door. 'Oh,' she said perplexed. 'Trimmin' your minge? May I see?'"

According to Bob, Mavis' mum was so delighted by the neat appearance of Mavis' minge that she wanted her to trim *hers*. "That's what made me late for the studio," she told him. "Hair everywhere! It was a complete turmoil. But when I finished, Mum held up a mirror to see the results. I couldn't help but think of you, Robert, at her reaction. Mum gave a deep sigh and breathed, 'Dad'll like that.'"

❄ ❄ ❄

In 1974 I took Nancy and Cindy to Europe. We stayed in Marbella, Spain, on the Mediterranean Sea, and after a visit to Cadiz, Frontera de la Jera (where they produce a lovely sherry wine), Seville and Cordoba, we wound up in London. Dutifully, I called Mavis. "Oh, John," she bubbled, "My husband, Lex, is playing tonight at the Prince of Wales Club in Tottingham Hale." She proceeded to tell me the way to the club.

In our party of American tourists was Martha Adams, a young lady who had been Bob's consort at the Player's Guild in Long Beach, and who was now Mrs. Martha Fisher of Sacramento. Although divorced, and again on her own, she was still wonderfully naive.

When our party arrived at "Tottin'am 'ale," we were whisked to the club where Lex's band was playing. The headliner that evening was a female impersonator. Martha, who was from Long Island and had a distinctive New York nasal accent, looked at the long-armed, almost truck-driver-like entertainer for some time. "Mavis, is that really a man?" She had to speak loudly to be heard.

Mavis looked at her incredulously. "Yuz never sees a female impersonatin' a female, duz ya?"

The Trim-the-Minge girl Mavis Purvis and her husband, Lex Evans, taken in the Bahamas in 1976.

The band was roaring mightily so it seemed that any conversation would be confidential. "But Mavis," Martha droned, "the gown is so tight!"

The band stopped abruptly.

"Where does he put it?" Martha shouted at the top of her voice.

Mavis was not deterred by the silence. "Tucks it up 'er ass, dearie."

Martha gulped down her martini, nearly choking on the olive.

While I was still in London, Mavis told me that the place she wanted to see in America, more than any other, was the Grand Canyon in Arizona. "I suppose you'll laugh at that," she told me earnestly. "I've seen it in the flicks and in the rotogravure. Scientists say that it's one of the world's most remarkable sites for viewing the eons of the time that're etched on its walls. Civilizations risin', civilizations fallin', and all the while the mighty Colorado River's cuttin' its way to the sea."

Bob used to date Martha Adams Fisher back in the middle 1930s and it's not hard to see why.

She became pensive for a moment. "I can imagine that standin' on the edge of that great chasm could make you feel kinda small. Just think of it. Flyin' 9,000 miles—just to be made to feel fuckin' small!"

***

When she and her husband, Lex, finally flew to America, I took them on an extensive tour of mountain and desert country. Ben Nevers is the highest peak in Scotland; at a little over 4,000 feet it would be only a foothill in California.

I drove them to Big Bear Mountain which hovers some 5,000 feet higher than Nevers. We drove down the mountain on the Mojave Desert side.

The day was glorious; you could see forever across the desert.

Lex was aghast at the awesome distances. "How far be that peak?" he asked, his Scottish burr very pronounced.

"About 200 miles away," I answered.

"Half the length of England!"

It was about 9 p.m. when we arrived back in the San Fernando Valley. I was driving up Coldwater Canyon when Lex asked if we could stop to look down at the Valley floor. We all stood silently on a ledge while Lex drank in the sights of the sixteen-mile-long valley.

"There must be a million people down there. Trucks, fire engines, cars. All the while up here, ye hear nae sound but the soughin' o' the wind and a few crickets."

Just then Mavis rent the air with an uncontrolled spate of flatulence. "Well, I've done my bit!"

"And killed six crickets along the way, n' doubt!" Lex roared.

—BOOK SIX—

ADVENTURES IN THE '60'S

—BOOK SIX—

IT WAS A VERY GOOD YEAR

NINETEEN SIXTY was a good year for Robert. He starred in "Night Fighters" (Irish rebellion action story directed by Tay Garnett), "The Grass Is Greener" (Deborah Kerr-Cary Grant comedy directed by Stanley Donen) and "The Sundowners" (Fred Zinnemann's sensitive portrait of Australian sheepherders).

It was while Bob was in Australia on "The Sundowners" that I became aware that he, too, was vulnerable. He genuinely adored Deborah Kerr, which whom he had first worked in "Heaven Knows, Mrs. Allison." It was far beyond anything that could be related to infatuation or flirtation. Deborah, to Bob, was an actress of such heights as to defy the imagination. No matter what the critics might say, it was a picture that was held together by the magic of their caring.

While in San Francisco, getting ready to fly to Australia for "The Sundowners," Bob's back hurt unmercifully. Brian Owen Smith, the big English wardrobe man who was going with him, chided him for not calling a

Bob and Deborah Kerr played married sheepherders roving the Australian countryside in "The Sundowners," based on Jon Cleary's wonderful novel and photographed on location by Jack Hildyard. It was one of Fred Zinnemann's finest directorial achievements. What a cast: Peter Ustinov, Glynis Johns, Dina Merrill, Chips Rafferty.

masseuse. Bob got on the phone and called the desk. "Send me up a masseuse—a legitimate one. My back's killing me."

In a few minutes, Brian opened the door to a tall, gaunt, redheaded woman who was about 70 years old. Bob's description was graphic: "She was raw-boned with a bull-dog thrust to her jaw and her obviously hennaed hair was done up in early armadillo. She brusquely ordered me into the bedroom, had me disrobe and get on the table she had set up. A light sheet was thrown over me. She started kneading me like so much dough. I soon noticed that her breath was getting shorter. At the last second, I reached down to protect my 'store.'

"'Why not?' she gasped, 'Glenn Ford lets me!'"

Back in Hollywood, Bob stopped by Paramount where Ford was working, went to his dressing room and told him that he'd met an old friend of his in San Francisco.

"Oh," said Ford, "who was it?"

"An old beldame masseuse in her seventies," Bob leered.

Ford blurted out his inordinate confession. "She's only 63!"

Bob roared, "You let her. You *let* her!"

He turned to leave, then looked back to see Ford standing forlornly in front of his dressing room. The poor man held up his fingers in the Marine Corps salute. "Semper fi?" he implored.

Bob didn't respond to the plea. After all, he had been in the Army.

❄❄❄

On the flight down to Australia to film "The Sundowners," Bob met Jimmie Rodgers—the singing sensation who made "Oh, Oh, Fallin' in Love Again" and "Honeycomb" pop music chart history and household concert material in the late '60's.

Something was amiss with the plane. After a stopover in Hawaii where mechanical work was done on the wing, the Qantas flight continued on to Nandi Fiji, where the wing was worked on again. While they waited, Bob and Jimmie were loaned a jeep, some fishing rods, and a flagon of vodka and orange juice. No great amount of fish were caught, but Jimmie and Bob sang songs, drank screwdrivers and whiled away the hours.

In his not-too-alert condition, Jimmie dove into the cove in his white shorts. Later, on the reef, he started to swish them in the water to rid them of sand. A shark darted in, ripping them out of his hands. "Dear God!" said Jimmie, aghast. "I swam in there!"

A Fiji islander sitting nearby grinned at him. "Oh, they go for anything white."

Eighteen hours overdue, the plane landed in Australia in the early hours. An intrepid newscaster burst into the

Jimmie Rodgers

Bob hugs France Nuyen in "The Last Time I Saw Archie," an odd service comedy directed by Jack Webb in 1961. It depicted the experiences of a real-life G.I. named Archie Hall. Bob played the role of a service conman and Webb was a goldbricking buddy. After the film was finished, Archie sued!

compartment with lights and camera where Jimmie and Bob were sleeping. With hot lights glaring in his eyes, and a microphone shoved into his face, Bob woke to the maelstrom of the media. And roared "Fuck off!"

The announcer froze, then sputtered, "You're on telly, you know."

Bob was fearful of the consequences, but Jimmie said they loved him in Australia. "They don't like pretenders," Jimmie went on. "In Robert, they got the real thing."

Jimmie's concert was a smash. "The Sundowners" wasn't too bad, either.

❄ ❄ ❄

Immediately after "The Sundowners" Bob filmed "The Last Time I Saw Archie," directed by and starring Jack Webb. I had been featured in several episodes of "Dragnet" so I was inured to the staccato dialogue for which Webb was known in those days.

I was not surprised when Webb put out an edict that "No one will leave the lot for lunch." Nor was I surprised when, the instant the lunch-break began, Bob drove his car straight to the gate. When informed that he would have to eat in the studio commissary, he promptly backed up, stopped, hit the gas and drove his car through the the road barrier. He spent a leisurely hour at The Backstage, sipping martinis. When he returned to the studio, Webb said nothing. The incident was closed.

❄ ❄ ❄

In 1962 in Savannah, Georgia, Bob starred in a film now considered a cult favorite, "Cape Fear," based on John D. MacDonald's novel "The Executioners." Gregory Peck co-produced and starred; Polly Bergen played Peck's wife. Bob played an ex-convict who, to avenge himself against Peck, whom he thought had sent him to prison unjustly, plays a cat-and-mouse game with Peck in which he insinuates that his revenge will come at the expense of the man's wife and daughter.

Peck is forced to break the law himself and does so by hiring three goons to maul Bob so badly that he will leave the area. Instead, Bob beats the three unmercifully and Peck is more terrified than before.

In one scene Bob is in the police station, stripped down to his boxer shorts so the police can search for anything that could lead to his re-arrest; he's also wearing a hat and smoking a cigar. Bob noticed that in all the jail sequence takes, Peck never looked directly at him. Finally Bob's curiosity got the better of him. "Greg," he asked. "You never once looked at me during that sequence. Why?"

Greg grinned a slow, expansive smile. "Because of the condition you were in, I was afraid you might try to fuck *me*!"

DOUBLE MURDER AT CROOKED RIVER GORGE

WHILE BOB was in Georgia creating his great menace in "Cape Fear," I was in Bend, Oregon, filming two "Have Gun/Will Travel" episodes. Andrew McLaglen, son of actor Victor McLaglen, was directing the popular series starring Richard Boone as Paladin, an intellectual gunfighter for hire. Once again time, people and events were wrapping concentric rings around both of us.

Bob and Polly Bergen on the set of "Cape Fear," in which Bob portrayed a psychopath named Max Cady, who was second only to his killer preacher in "Night of the Hunter" for sheer scariness.

Bend is an idyllic location. The Deschutes River winds through the town, which took its name from wagon train drivers heading eastward who took one long last look at that pretty stream before heading their wagons into the Oregon desert. "So long, Bend," they would call to the bend in the river.

On May 11, 1961, the discovery of a shocking double murder cast a dark pall over the entire area of Bend. A family on vacation from Washington State stopped on a bridge that traverses the Crooked River Gorge about 20 miles north of Bend. The children looked over the edge of the bridge's railing down into an awesome chasm that drops almost vertically 350 feet to the river's edge. "Daddy," one child cried out. "There's two dolls down there."

The father took one look and ran to his car for his binoculars. The grim scene came into focus: The figures were not dolls; they were the corpses of two children.

The park rangers of the Gorge hauled the small bodies up to the highway. They were identified as Martha Jackson, four, and her six-year-old brother, Larry.

Our TV production company anxiously awaited for the chilling drama to unfold—but this drama wasn't scripted for entertainment. The children's mother, Gertrude Mae Jackson, 25, had a lover, Jeannace Freeman, 19, a "bull dyke" lesbian. They were spotted driving a 1952 Mercury sedan in Oakland, California, and were extradicted to Oregon within a few days and put in the Bend slammer. Police searchlights arced through the long nights illuminating the entire area around the jail. The police thought the bright bath of light was justified: Silent men in pickup trucks with telescopic hunting rifles ringed the area.

It was ascertained through their own sworn statements that the two women decided to murder the children because the kids cramped their style and mobility. Gertrude stated that little Martha was asleep when she was dropped to her death. "I said a prayer over her before I let her go. I knew she would be in peace."

The boy was another matter. He had seen his sister hurled to her death and he clung to his mother's hair so fiercely that Jeannace, in order to force his grip loose, had reamed out his anus with a tire iron. He was then thrown screaming into the dark void. Bits of his mother's hair were still in his clenched fists when his body was examined by the coroner.

Freeman originally claimed she had had nothing to do with the murders, that Jackson had "disciplined" the children with the tire iron, then thrown them over the bridge.

Attorney Chuck Johnson, a former college roommate of my brother-in-law Robert Munro, introduced himself to me on the "Have Gun" set, along with his lawyer friend, Bill Holmes. Chuck was selected to defend the mother. Holmes was given the impossible task of defending the bull dyke lover. Holmes told me that he had no remorse when Freeman got the death penalty. "I had to take hour-long showers every night to get the smell of her off me," he confided to me later.

The Governor later reprieved Freeman's death sentence but she became so aggressively hostile, and came on so blatantly sexually to women inmates, that the Federal Government kept her for some years in a Federal Penitentiary in the Virginia area. She was released on probation several years ago and now both Gertude Jackson and Jeannace Freeman are walking the streets again.

As recently as 1988 Freeman was reportedly living in the Eugene, Oregon, area and was filing a petition to change her name legally.

"Life imprisonment," said Bill Holmes, "isn't life."

(Chuck Johnson died of a heart attack in the summer of '86. "Pressure," said Holmes. "Too much pressure.")

❄❄❄

Brother Robert later had occasion to ask Bill Holmes for assistance. We were working in 1966 around Eugene, Oregon, on "The Way West" and eventually the company moved across the Cascades to finish the picture in the Bend area. Since Bob had his own car, he left Eugene a day ahead of the company, arriving in Bend in the late afternoon. After putting his clothes away in his assigned motel room, he went to a local restaurant, The Copper Room, for an early dinner.

"I ordered a Scotch and soda and a steak," Bob told me. "As I sipped my drink, a woman came over to my table, plunked herself down and boldly announced that I could put my shoes under her bed any day. I told her that I wasn't remotely interested in her offer and would she be so kind as to leave me alone. At this point, she rose angrily to her feet and stalked off to corner a cowboy in conversation. He kept throwing dark looks at me, finally coming to my table.

"'I want you to apologize to the lady.' He was bellicose as hell."

Bob looked up and told him that he hadn't met any ladies yet. The cowboy became increasingly antagonistic. Bob took out a $10 bill, laid it on the table and started for the door.

The cowboy backed out ahead of him to make a stand in front of Bob's car door.

"You ain't goin' nowhere, mister, not until you apologize to the lady."

Bob's voice became brittle. "That's my car you're standing in front of and I'm getting into it—through you, over you, around you, whatever route you want me to take."

The cowboy still tried to bar the way. Bob knocked him clear over the hood of the car into the street. Then he casually started up the engine. The stunned 'poke rolled out of harm's way as Bob motored off. When he got back to his hotel, Bob called me in Eugene and asked if I had any connections in Bend. I told him about Bill Holmes and said I would call him.

Bill just happened to be the City Attorney, exactly the right man to call.

In the morning, the cowboy belligerently came into Bill's office, planted

A 1956 photo of the Major (our stepdad, Hugh Cunningham Morris), Bob's good friend E. J. Jones, and our mother Ann Mitchum Morris. I'm unable to identify the couple at right.

his butt down on the desk and demanded that Bob be arrested for assault and battery.

Bill told me that he looked up at the fellow and said, "Number one, you're sitting on my desk. Get off it immediately. Number two, I went down to the Copper Room last night and got a detailed report of all that happened. Number three, it was your lady friend who solicited Mr. Mitchum's person. That constitutes a misdemeanor, aided and abetted by your threatening behavior. Now, in light of all of this, I suggest you leave my office immediately or I'll have you arrested for trespassing." The cowboy left in great haste.

❄ ❄ ❄

Bill Holmes figured in our lives again in 1969. One of Bob's quarter horses, Bull's Eye Bee, a handsome young gelding, was pastured near Bend, where Bob was training him for picture work in "Young Billy Young." Now he wanted to move the horse over the Fourth of July weekend, but horse trailers were hard to come by. I called Bill to see if he knew where one could be rented. He did. It was owned by a gas-station owner at the edge of town and he held it for Bob as a favor to Bill.

Driving a borrowed pickup, I attached the trailer to the hitch and drove it to the motel where Bob was staying. Once there, "big brother" came to the fore. He took over the wheel of the pickup.

In charity, I must say that he plain forgot that the horse trailer was at-tached to the vehicle. Bob drove the truck under the slanted roof of the motel entrance. The heavy steel trailer hit a beam that was an integral part of the structure, completely dislodging the trailer from the pickup and three-quarters of the motel's guests from their beds. Fortunately, the portico stayed put. I hurriedly reattached the errant trailer to the truck.

Once the transfer of the horse was made from old pasture to new, we returned the trailer, but the owner had left. In his stead, a teenager had taken over the station's duties.

He eyed the horse trailer with bland suspicion.

"Say," he drawled. "That dent weren't in that trailer when you got her."

"No, it wasn't," I agreed.

"What are you gonna do about it?" he asked. He was watching out for his boss's interest.

I had an inspiration. "Do you know Bill Holmes? Just tell him about it. He can arrange for it to be fixed, then send us the bill."

He eyed us apprehensively. "Do you mind if I call him about it?"

"No, no, of course not," Bob assured him.

After a few minutes, the youth told us that Bill would attend to the details of the trailer's rehabilitation. Then he eyed us squarely. "Do you mind telling me how you did that?"

We looked back to the large indentation in the forepart of the horse trailer. "As we came over a ridge just north of Redmond," Bob drawled, "a ninety-pound robin came hurtling through the skies at us."

"Like a jet plane," I added.

"Couldn't escape it," Bob added.

He stood in the doorway to the station, muttering to himself as we drove away. *"A robin? Ninety pounds!"*

❄ ❄ ❄

Brother Robert is a paradox: He is as tender as a buttercup with children, old people and the needy; but he is hard as steel with those he feels are power-hungry or callous toward others. This attitude came from a childhood that saw him falsely imprisoned, fighting physically for his well-being if not for his life, and from a constant threat of poverty. Through it all, he retained a great compassion for the weak and the helpless.

Imagine then how he must have felt when, in India to film "Mister Moses" in 1964, he would be picked up at his hotel in a sleek limousine, only to see hundreds of children staring at him with sunken cheeks and hollowed eyes as he cruised by. He saw the dead being swept up by the hundreds, people of all ages who had died in the night from starvation.

He told me that tears filled his eyes, for he was cruelly aware that he couldn't do anything about it.

While filming "Mister Moses," he met Jomo Kenyatta, then the president of Kenya. Throughout the meeting, Bob became keenly cognizant of the great difficulties that the African nations face, not only from the terrible droughts but also from ancient tribal animosities that perennially erode any hope for unity.

Kenyatta held a meeting of tribes whose representatives had agreed to meet unarmed, ready to listen. The council was to rendezvous in a place where the Kikuyu tribe, made up of Bantu who are sworn enemies of the Massai, was predominant. The Massai are feared warriors; they face lions with their spears without quailing. Now fifty of them were in the Kikuyu village—unarmed.

"The meeting got out of hand," Bob related to me, "and 2,000 Kikuyus started after the fifty Massai, who ran into the bush just a short distance away from the village. Just as the pursuers reached the edge of the bush,

In early 1964 Bob went to Kenya to film "Mister Moses," playing a diamond smuggler named Joe Moses who stops running from authorities to help a native tribe evacuate its endangered village.

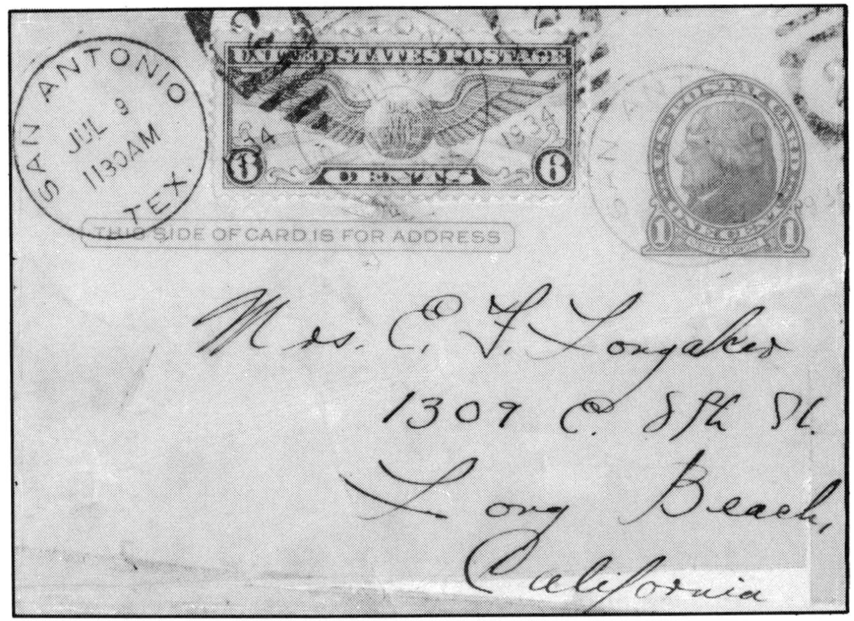

Dear Net 'n Ernie
So we're
just lazin' along,
takin' it easy.
Grabbed the wrong
freight out of Birming-
ham and rode to N. Orleans
'stead of Dallas, so
I haven't been to
Dallas for my dough.
P'raps Jack has, tho,
he left me in
Lake Chas. La. Will
grab a hot shot outa here
tonite for El Paso. Write
me in El Paso. Love
Bob

This precious 1934 postcard, addressed to our sister Annette (Mrs. E. F. Longaker, 1309 E. 8th St., Long Beach, California), was mailed to her by Brother Bob from San Antonio, Texas, on July 9 at 11:30 a.m. when he and I were making a cross-country trek to California. It reads: "Dear Net 'n Ernie—So—we're just lazin' along, takin' it easy. Grabbed the wrong freight out of Birmingham and rode to N. Orleans 'stead of Dallas, so I haven't been to Dallas for my dough. P'raps Jack has, tho, he left me in Lake Chas. La. Will grab a hot shot outa here tonite for El Paso. Write me in El Paso. Love, Bob." I hadn't exactly "left" Bob, since two deadly weapons were pressed against my head when we were separated in a freight yard. I guess Bob didn't want to take any heat for getting separated from his younger brother. Oh well, to each his own perceptions.

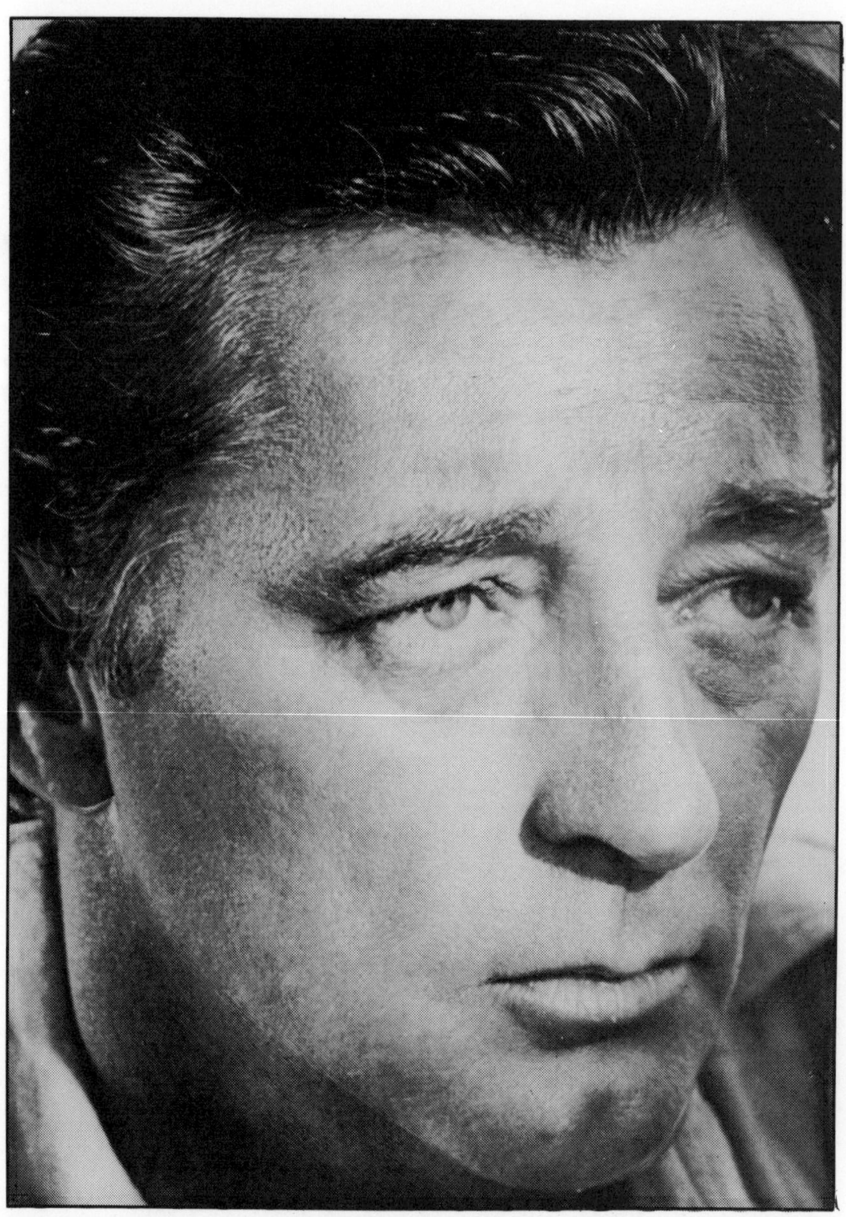

This photo of Bob was taken around the time he went on the road to promote "Mr. Moses." Although he often grumbles about having to do press and television interviews, and avoids them when he can, he occasionally acquiesces and spins some very colorful and fanciful yarns to the media once he's in the mood. The greatest Robert Mitchum interview occurred when the limousine in which he and movie critic Roger Ebert were riding in to a movie location got lost and never did reach the filming site. I guess you could call that the Mitchum touch.

Of our sister Julie, columnist Walter Winchell once wrote: "Julie Mitchum—four stars, four orchids." As a singer and pianist, Julie became known to servicemen of World War II as the "petite blonde lass" who could sing their favorite songs in no less than 11 languages. As part of the Army Special Services in '45-46, Julie collected battle ribbons, wings, insignia and other military decorations and adorned her hat with them (see inset). In the picture above she's performing in Joe Wright's Palladium with Sam Butera, Jimmy Blunt and Bob Hennandy. Her beloved husband of many years, Elliott Sater, is now dead and she lives in Tucson, Arizona, taking care of our mother Ann.

Cousin Louise Tetreault and Bob's good friend, Elmer Ellsworth Jones, have had a mutual admiration society going since the late 1930s. This snapshot of them was taken around 1941.

In 1984 I decided to thin down and dropped from 240 to 178 pounds in about three months. I was going through a divorce with my third wife, Dorothy McCoy, around that time and I guess I was psychologically getting rid of several encumbrances at once. It was an emotional debacle because such a severe weight loss left my neck looking scrawny and the rest of my body looking old. I felt harassed about losing my all-important love handles and regained the lost weight in about four months, and decided to stay that way.

Although Bob and I have worked many times in the same film, I could find no photographs of us side by side taken by location or studio photographers—an oversight I will correct when we do our next picture together. However, there are some snapshots, such as this "brotherly" scene at left, taken at a surprise birthday party that was thrown for me on September 6, 1986, at the Jewish War Memorial on Ventura Boulevard in Studio City. I was lured there for an alleged music taping, and arrived a full hour late to find 60 disgruntled surprisers wondering where the hell I had been.

At the same surprise birthday party, attended by a wonderful collection of family members and friends, my daughter Cindy posed with Bob. She now lives with her husband Steve Azbill and two children, Vanessa and Corina, in Nevada City, Calif.

It was a grand birthday party, one which I will always remember warmly, even if I did arrive late. Here I'm with Bob, his wife Dorothy and Tom Corrigan, son of Ray "Crash" Corrigan, the famous cowboy actor and stuntman. Tom has become quite a restaurateur in the Thousand Oaks area. That's his wife Marilyn peeking out from behind my shoulder.

A rare shot of myself (very thin, when I was going through my weight change phase), my sister Julie (very petite) and Brother Bob (very casual), taken when we threw a party to celebrate our mother's 90th birthday in 1984. We filled the receiving hall with 160 splendid guests.

My mother Ann and I posed together on the day of my marriage to Bonnie Duff in 1986. Also in attendance as flower girls were my granddaughters Vanessa and Corina Azbill, children to my daughter Cindy.

My son Jack II on the day of my wedding, flanked on the left by Chalice Hilyard, soon to be his bride, and on the right by my new bride, Bonnie Duff-now-Mitchum.

two hundred Massais who had been waiting in concealment suddenly stood up with their deadly spears poised and ready. The Kikuyus turned and fled in terror. Man, they wanted no part of those lion hunters!"

STANDING ON THE VIETNAM FRONT LINE

UNHERALDED, Bob went to Vietnam twice during the war. He asked to be helicoptered to the outer perimeter of the battle sites. He spent much time with Green Beret units, arriving by chopper and alighting with a quart of Chivas Regal in each hand. The men, when they finally recognized him, would always ask, "Why, in God's name, did you come here?"

Bob's answer? "A way to get out of the house."

Once he asked a Green Beret captain where the front line was. He was a bit wary when the captain stated flatly, "You're standing on it."

"The Hunters" (1959) is but one of many films in which Bob has played a military role. The combat became real when he began making trips to Vietnam in the 1960s.

He hastily withdrew into a tent when the captain added, "And that red shirt you're wearing won't help you any, either."

Bob talked at great length to the men, finding that they genuinely cared about their mission. Despite the torrid controversy that goes on—and will continue to go on—around the Vietnam War, Bob is firmly convinced that the Green Beret were extraordinary men.

"I sat and talked with many of them under extremely difficult conditions," he related to me. "Certainly they were a superbly trained fighting team, but they carried a deeper dedication . . . One officer voiced it perfectly: 'We feel it's our moral duty to explain to these people that there are options in the world. They don't have to always live in fear and suppression. Basic sanitation, irrigation, cultivation and a host of other advances could free them for a better life. We in the Beret want to fight for their liberty as much with those weapons against ignorance as we must do with guns.'"

Bob sighed deeply. "I know this sounds like State Department rhetoric, but I was there. Those men meant it." Bob returned to the States filled with admiration for them—and with a growing coldness toward those at home who marched against our soldiers fighting the war.

❄ ❄ ❄

I can imagine the look on Brother Robert's face when—back at the farm in Maryland—his son James came to him with an unbelievable request. Jimmy informed his father that henceforth he would require $100,000 a year to "keep up my image."

"What 'image' are you talking about?" Bob's eyebrows must have raised at least half an inch.

"I'm a Mitchum." James couldn't understand why his own father didn't immediately fathom that importance.

"Just what does that entail?"

"I should have a complete wardrobe for every occasion; maitre d's should be impressed whenever I enter a dining room; my car should be first in line in a parking lot; my—"

"Hold on a minute, James. Your Uncle John is a Mitchum and I *never* heard him say that *his* image needed all of those trappings. I gave you an Aston-Martin, did I not? Well, I'll tell you what."

He rose, went to a closet, got out an Indian blanket and handed it to James. "You take this and a gasoline credit card, go back to Hollywood, wrap the blanket around yourself and stand in front of Schwab's Drugstore because *that's* your image."

Angered, James left Maryland to return to Hollywood.

George Fargo filled me in about what happened next. "I heard a knock on my door in the early morning hours so I opened it to see James standing there with an Indian blanket draped over his 6-foot-4 frame. He asked if he could come in, stay with me for awhile. I agreed, on the condition that he *not* sleep in my bed.

Two weeks later, at about four in the morning, he rolled up from the floor onto one elbow. 'George, are you awake?'

"'I am now. Whatta you want to talk about?'"

James said that he couldn't understand why his father, one of the highest paid actors in Hollywood, wouldn't afford to give him a 'mere' hundred grand a year. "'Think of it, George. He's worth millions—while *I'm* sleeping on your *floor*!'

George, a product of a Chicago ghetto, wasn't buying any of it. "So if you don't like my floor, there's the door. By the way, you're pretty handy with the knife and fork. I shook out the Wheaties box this morning—nothin'! Say—I got the telephone bill this morning. Fifty-two clams for long distance. I'm just an extra, James, not a star. I can't afford fifty-two Abraham Lincolns for the phone."

George brightened. "Ah, the solution. I'll go down to the phone company today and tell them the good news—*Jimmy Mitchum* put the fifty-two bucks on the bill. You know what Ma Bell's gonna do? Well, she'll give me a Dixie cup and a string."

Ever since then, that's become a by-line between myself and all of my friends. Phil Crosby, one of Bing's recalcitrants, is a dear friend who falls over laughing at the phrase. Actors are prone to be fitful in their employment. Whenever one's telephone line would be "temporarily disconnected," Phil would grandly announce that they had been "Dixie-cupped."

Does anyone remember the stringing together of two tin cans and trying to emulate Alexander Graham Bell?

HAVE SHOW, WILL TRAVEL

THE SIXTIES were busy years for both of us. Bob filmed nineteen pictures during those ten years while I worked in countless television shows, toured the country with James "The Virginian" Drury, and sandwiched in the development of Father Garrett's Boys' Home, a political tour with Senator Barry Goldwater, a half-dozen movies, and an RCA record album, "Our Land, Our Heritage"—and a little personal life, too.

Bob journeyed to the Malayan jungles in 1963 to make "Rampage." Here he's clowning around with some of the "locals" as they beat out a popular U.S. tune on their canteens. Bob portrayed big game hunter Harry Stanton, who is assigned to bring in some killer cats with Jack Hawkins but gets entangled in an affair with Hawkins' wife, Elsa Martinelli. Sabu the Jungle Boy co-starred.

Bob was filming "The Longest Day" in France in 1961 when our mother and stepfather were in a horrible car wreck that nearly took their lives. Mother received a life-threatening gash in her head that led to lifelong complications; the Major was literally flayed from head to toe as he was hurled onto gravel.

While Bob was flying from Paris to Los Angeles to be with them, I went to the Lancaster Hospital to see Mother and the Major. The two doctors in the emergency ward eyed me wearily. "Your mother might make it. But the old man is fading fast."

After seeing Mother and knowing there was nothing more I could do, I went to the Major's side. As I looked down at the 80-year-old patrician swathed in bloody gauze, he suddenly opened his cornflower blue eyes. "How did you get here?" he barked.

"Heard it on the radio," I answered softly.

"Oh well, I suppose it'll be in all the papers then." He seemed not to like the idea.

"Dad, when you get out of here, you've got to promise me you'll stop by my house for a great big glass of brandy."

He reared up and roared, "Only one?"

I looked at the doctors; their weariness was gone. The Major lived thirteen more years.

The CHP officer at the accident scene told me, "I was writing out a death report when I looked down to see him staring at me. 'Where's Dan Matthews?' he asked [Broderick Crawford's character in the old ZIV-TV series, "Highway Patrol"]. 'Sorry, old timer.' I stopped writing and tried to get my wits about me. 'He's—uh—busy and can't be with us today.'"

"Ten-four!" shouted the Major, passing out again.

When you consider that our mother is alive and well in 1988, and that the old man was thrown a hundred feet from the point of impact when a hay truck hit them, then you have to believe in miracles.

Bob was back in California by the time our parents were moved to St. Joseph's Hospital in Burbank. One dark, rainy evening, Bob and I sat in their hospital room for a long time, listening in silence to their shallow, steady breathing and the driving rain. About ten o'clock, our fifth of brandy was gone so we left the hospital to face the elements.

Bob told me he was going to stop in Toluca Lake to visit his old friend George Fargo, alias Grey Cloud. George was alone in the house and, since it was going to be sold, it was furnished with only a refrigerator and a tiny night-light. The three of us sat on the kitchen floor in the dimness and discussed life over a bottle of red wine that kept my heart moving along to their tempo.

Bob had recently spent some long hours with a group of French Algerian dissidents and they, in their passion to have their voices heard in America, poured their troubles out to him. A sympathetic Mitchum promised to make their cause known. In turn, they gave him the only present they thought worthwhile: A block of hashish. Bob was now sharing what he had left with Grey Cloud. I don't smoke at all and I was spellbound at their dialogue which took them from Algeria to Paris, from Paris to Saturn, from Saturn to Jupiter, then suddenly—back to Earth.

"Well, that's the last of it," muttered Robert.

"One moment, Goose." Fargo sprang to his feet and disappeared into the dark bowels of the house. (He had always called Bob "Goose" after the bird that lays the golden eggs.) He reappeared in a short time with a Bull Durham sackful of marijuana.

Bob sniffed it appreciatively. "Where did you get it?"

"Grew it myself." George's voice had a ring of pride.

"Where?"

"On the freeway." They broke up laughing.

"Vroom—vroom—vroom!" they roared, imagining minions of the law zooming down the freeway on motorcycles, searching out wrongdoers. All the while, the city sprinklers were nurturing the glistening leaves of Canabis.

April 27, 1968: Phyllis Jacqueline Mitchell and TV actor James Drury were finally married at the Westwood Hills Christian Church, after being prevented from doing so because Phyllis' ex-husband was criminally insane, and they feared reprisal until he could be put safely away. Behind Drury is Doug McClure, who costarred with him in the long-running NBC series "The Virginian."

* * *

In one segment of "Laramie," a long-running NBC series that starred John Smith and Robert Fuller, I had the distinct privilege of singing while Hoagy Carmichael, a series regular who portrayed a character named Jonesy, played the piano. Hoagy's role was to take over the entertainment duties at a saloon in town after I threw out the previous piano player. Both my character and I, privately, were impressed by Hoagy's playing.

"Now that's *real* music, boys," I roared. I drunkenly sang a chorus of "Genevieve, Sweet Genevieve" until I "passed out" into the crowd. Having Hoagy as my distinguished accompanist is one of my favorite memories.

PISTOL-PACKIN' JIM DRURY

JIM DRURY and I became fast friends when he was at the height of his popularity on "The Virginian," an NBC-TV series based on the famous 1902 novel by Owen Wister. Drury played the title role of the laconic Shiloh Ranch gunfighter for almost a decade.

We had much in common: Jim drank enough to drown most men, and I kept up a pretty fair pace myself. Neither of us would ever back down in a fight, although I must confess that Jim was a bit more radical than I. He had a penchant for guns, while I have always relied on a left hook and a right cross.

Jim's love affair with weapons often got him into trouble. Once, while living in West Los Angeles, he became increasingly hostile after a bitter dispute with his wife. While sitting on the john of his second-story apartment, he fired his .357 Magnum into the floor by his side. The bullet went through the tiles and smashed into the bathroom floor below him, just missing the john, on which the apartment's occupant was seated. He ran screaming into the street. The police, who came to his rescue almost immediately, deciphered his babblings sufficiently enough to collar the

James Drury (shown here in a "Virginian" publicity still) divorced Phyllis after a few years and moved to Cypress, Texas, where he is now happily married to a full-blooded Texan named Carlann. He has a successful business in which he recycles used asphalt and readies it for new roads and parking lots. He told me in 1988 that "I haven't tasted Who-Hit-John in six years." Carlann must have really reformed him.

morose Drury and bring him to bay. The studio used its influence to free their fledgling "Virginian" back into the fold.

His next bit of gunplay occurred in an elevator in Virginia. Jim was on a personal appearance tour when he decided to fire his .357, with a full load of blanks, in the elevator. A passenger literally had a heart attack and, once again, studio money was brought to bear to get Jim's release from jail.

In 1963, he asked me to put together a road show for him because he was being flooded with offers from all over the country. My job, to develop a format, was a tough one. Jim couldn't sing at all, played no instruments and was not a joke-teller.

I finally found the solution: I researched every area or town we were to tour and wrote a glowing show opener about the history of each place. To the recorded strains of "The Virginian" theme, Jim would ride into the arena, circle the track and wave to the people. As he dismounted, Jon Locke, a singer and banjo player, would join me in singing in harmony the words I had written to the Nebraska fight song: "Let us present The Virginian, dark, handsome and tall." (Since Jim was about 5-foot-10, balding ferociously and myopic, we felt we did quite a selling job.) Drury would then thrill the civic pride of his audience with "his" glowing speech.

We broke the act in at Bob Heilman's 6-B Ranch in Grass Valley, California. Jim had a vested interest in the ranch; he and Heilman were raising Appaloosa horses then and Jim had a young colt that was exceptionally blanketed. He wanted to use it in his shows but it remained too skittish for arena work. At a big party to celebrate the ranch's opening, Jon and I went into our "Let us present the Virginian." We were a smash hit. Soon we were on our way to the rodeo in Hastings, Nebraska.

Jim had recently divorced his wife and was going with a lovely girl, Phyllis Mitchell. They wanted to marry but Phyllis was married, and her husband, diagnosed to be a homicidal maniac, was committed to a state insane asylum. At that time in California, a divorce under those circumstances could not be granted for a seven-year period. This factor added to another of Jim's injudicious bits of gunplay.

Jim, Jon Locke and myself were appearing on a TV interview show to promote the rodeo while my wife, Nancy, and Jim's girl were on the sound stage, just out of camera range.

The handsome young announcer beamed at Jim. "I know that John's charming wife, Nancy, is seated here in the sound stage. Is that lovely lady with her your wife?"

In an angry flash, Jim drew his converted .357 Magnum from its holster and held it under the poor man's nose. It was loaded with full blanks, the hammer cocked. (At that range, a full blank load of black powder could have been lethal.)

"That's none of your damned business," snapped Jim. The cameraman immediately zoomed in on Locke and me. The emcee's eyes were crossed, sweat pouring from his brow.

Thousands of Nebraskan television viewers thought it was part of our act. I knew better and thanked God that Jim hadn't let the hammer go on that big gun.

That night we did our first Nebraska rodeo show. The people who had witnessed Drury's adroit gunplay now looked forward to his horsemanship. They were unaware that the Virginian had a fifth of Johnnie Walker Red Label under his gunbelt. He came prancing into the arena on a beautiful big red horse and promptly pulled it over on himself. He was nearly crushed but managed to roll clear. Jon Locke, our comedian, deadpanned, "And now for my next act . . . "

Fortunately, Jim thought it was funny.

The next morning the Lions' Club of Hastings gave us a breakfast in their lodge, a huge cavernous room, and it was filled with local celebrities. "Let's give our guests a big Lions' roar!" shouted the emcee.

"Roar—roar—roar!" went the Lions.

"Blam—blam—blam!" went Jim's revolver.

Hastings' leading banker, who was also its mayor, fell over backwards in panic. It quickly became apparent that he had wet his pants. Once again, Drury had scared the pee out of somebody.

CROSSROADS TO AMERICANA

WHILE we were in Hastings, a member of the Chamber of Commerce approached me, saying that since I seemed interested in American history, he'd like to show me a bit of it. He drove me eleven miles south of the city, stopping at an isolated crossroads. At the northwest corner, he pointed out a weathered stone obelisk about four feet high.

"Over a thousand wagons a day passed this spot on their way to Oregon and California in the 1840s." He pointed to the winding hills to the west. "You can still see the tracks left by their wheels."

A strange feeling came over me. That feeling was intensified when he pointed out the graves of settlers killed by Indians, and even a few graves of Indians who had died in the battles. To the south, a branch of the Blue River ran clear and sparkling in the sunlight. The aspen, barely starting to turn to autumn colors, made the whole scene come alive and planted the germ of an idea: Of tying American history together with songs that originated all over the world, songs which helped form the happenings. But it would be many years before the idea would become a reality as my "Songs of History."

On the night of our final show in Hastings, we were given a lavish pool party at our motel. Jon and I sang songs, played our instruments, and were generously lauded by the party guests. Jim, unable to join in as an entertainer, stole the limelight in quite another way. He suddenly appeared at poolside dressed in his cowboy hat, boots and six-gun. Since that was all he had on, the conservative Nebraska folk had a lot to recall about "picture people" after we left town to return to Hollywood.

❄ ❄ ❄

In the fall of 1963, after my stint as a rodeo entertainer in Nebraska, I worked on the film classic "My Fair Lady." I was cast as one of the quartet of singers with Cecil Holloway in the "Get Me to the Church on Time" sequence. During a long set-up, I found that I had picked up a pen and written a song that had been spinning around in my head ever since I saw the stone obelisk and the wagon tracks on the Oregon Trail. Lorne Greene liked it enough to record it on an RCA album.

All The Pretty Horses

The wagon band rolled along,
Wheels creakin', singin' a song
Of a land of freedom lyin' ahead,
When all of a sudden, a little boy said,
"Look at all those pretty horses!"

In stark silhouette against the sun
The wagon master saw them run
Their ponies from the shadowed dale
To the high ground flanking the Oregon Trail
On all their pretty horses.

When the little boy's voice
Cut through the air,
His father rode close, he was lean and spare,
He said, "Son, you lie down in the wagon bed
And don't you dare to raise your head
To see all those pretty horses."

Then the wagon master made a circle round
And for such a long time there was no sound
'Til a man said aloud, "They're the Brule Sioux,
And they're circlin' down by the Little Blue
On all their pretty horses!"

With lances high and carbines flashing,
The Indians sent their ponies crashing
Against the guns of the wagon band
And blood spilled over the prairie land
And over all those pretty horses.

On the next day when the sun climbed high,
A lone hawk soared through the brazen sky
While down below a boy could but stare
In horror as he knelt in prayer
'Midst all the pretty horses.

The cavalry came and found him there,
His head still bowed in bleak despair,
His lips were cold, his face was gray,
And through his tears they heard him say,
"They were such pretty horses!"

HOSS PLAY

ONE OF MY best friends was Dan Blocker, the big lovable Texan who became Hoss on the great television series, "Bonanza." Our first meeting was on "Cimarron City," the George Montgomery starrer, and by "Bonanza" time Dan and I were fast friends. Dan became increasingly interested in my folk singing—and we decided to make a record together.

Brother Robert and record company executive Joe Reisman were friends from a long way back. When Joe asked Bob to write liner notes for the back cover of "Our Land, Our Heritage," he readily agreed, and titled it

Brother John . . . Texan Dan . . . And a Monument to the Enjoyment of American Music

" . . . It has long been my contention that survival itself is, in the arts, a measure of merit; that intent and content are the inner statures which surpass the mere physical form of expression—often the immediate reason for acceptance. In short, it is a banal truism that a forty-inch bust and a beautiful face are no more guarantee of immortality in an actress than is a resonant and mellifluous voice in a politician.

"Happily, this also was evident to brother John, and, as he collected the essentially American songs, which more and more he favored, he dug back into their histories to learn not where *they originated from but* why. *He finally compiled a spiritual and emotional anthology of native expression which surely must be one of the most impressive extant.*

"Accompanying himself on his guitar, John found himself sought by groups to whom the legacy of our country was a source of pride and an exercise in enjoyment.

"And so it happened that one evening, invited to a beer and barbecue gathering (the typical "wild" party of contemporary Hollywood), he hauled along his guitar, and, far into the warm night of the San Fernando Valley, they all sat around singing. They sang and talked of the heroes of American music, and John's host, Dan Blocker, proposed to introduce him to Joe Reisman at RCA Victor Records for the purpose of discussing the merits of the whole concept of American musical tradition.

". . . Joe says now that he had allotted ten minutes of his busy schedule to listen to the idea, but two-and-a-half hours later, brother John walked out committed to a project which overwhelmed him by its magnitude."

—Robert C. Mitchum

❄ ❄ ❄

Reisman wanted Dan to sing two verses of "Erie Canal" for the recording. Dan stated emphatically that he couldn't sing. "Just say the words to the rhythm," cajoled Joe. Finally, Joe stood in front of Dan, snapping his fingers methodically to keep Dan in tempo.

"Dammit, Joe!" Hoss exploded. "You know I've got the rhythm of a one-legged spider!"

'Our Land, Our Heritage': A Rare, Forgotten Album of Americana In Story and Song

"Our Land, Our Heritage: Stories of America's Great Songs" was recorded in 1964 in the Music Center of the World in Hollywood and issued by RCA Victor on Stereo, LSP-2896, with liner notes by Brother Robert. Side One contained "Springfield Mountain," "Roll Out, Heave That Cotton!" and "The Battle Hymn of the Republic." Side Two yielded "The Erie Canal," "Paiute Sunrise Chant" and "Charles: Steal Away; He Never Said a Mumblin' Word." Part of the album cover showing Dan Blocker and me working on the album at the Music Center is reproduced above.Backed by a 23-piece symphonic orchestra and the Ken Darby Choir, I felt a special thrill to be working with such distinguished artists. I was especially impressed with the concert violinist in the "Springfield Mountain" rendition, as he astounded me with how much "country" he gave to the piece. I sang the songs and Dan narrated special material I had written about their origins. Many hours of research went into uncovering the roots of these songs.

Dan Blocker, at the peak of his popularity in the 1960s when he was portraying lovable Hoss Cartwright of the Ponderosa Ranch on "Bonanza." Since he had done very little before the series, Dan came to epitomize the heights to which a personality can climb in the vastly commercial medium of television. However, some "Hoss" lovers might have objected to the stream of colorful language which quite often flowed from his lips while he was working on the set. "Colorful" is right!

During one of the recording sessions with Blocker, Father Latimer Garrett, an Episcopal priest and a dear friend of mine, came down to observe. Dan had become a close friend of Father Garrett's during the formative times in the development of Father Garrett's Boys' Home. One morning I saw Father walking in apparent despair across the courtyard of St. Mark's Church in Van Nuys. He told me that he had dedicated himself to building a home for boys. He had found the ideal spot: Eighty acres of desert land near the town of Acton, just forty miles from Los Angeles and close to Palmdale. It was his for just $5,000, but akin to the great majority of clergy in America, Father didn't have $50, let alone $5,000.

I blurted out a commitment before I knew what I was saying —"I'll get you the $5,000." I was then reminded of the old adage: "Better to put mind in gear before putting mouth in action." Too late. The die was cast and I plunged into a new adventure.

The Devonshire Downs Fairground in Northridge could be rented for $600 a day. I called up Brother Robert, asking him to donate six big ones. "What for?" he asked. I told him that Father Garrett needed $5,000 to buy land for a boys' home. "What kind of boys?" he wanted to know.

Father had told me that his charges were "deprived," so that's what I told Bob. "Deprived?" he snorted. "What are they? Geldings?" Despite his flair of cynicism, he gave me the $600 to rent the fairground.

Bob Finney, a top mathematician with the National Aeronautics and Space Administration, a close family friend for years and a fellow church member, figured out that, at a dollar a ticket, we could flood the stands with customers who would buy hot dogs, soda pop, cold beer and popcorn. From pre-sales organized by Doris, his zany but brilliant wife, Finney calculated that we would net $5,280 for the day.

Dan Blocker appeared at the all-day gala. So did the Sons of the Pioneers, The Frontiersmen and Joanie, the Stroud Brothers, Lenny Geer and his

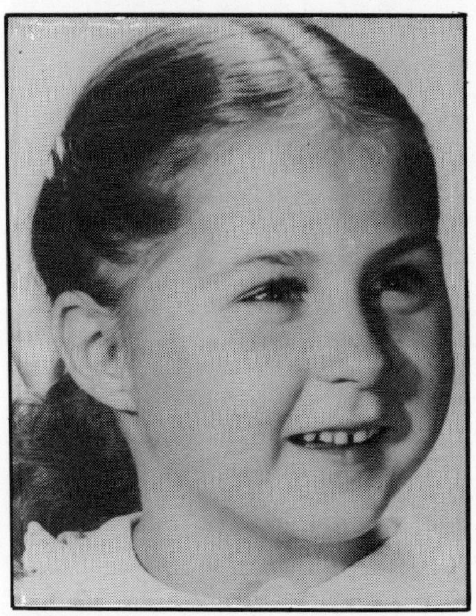

My daughter Victoria at the age of seven. Today, she's a beauty with three sons and makes a wonderful living as a landscape designer in Chatsworth, California. She's my living doll.

Frank McGrath

Doug McClure

stunt group, Frank McGrath of "Wagon Train," John Smith and Bob Fuller of "Laramie," James Drury and Doug McClure of "The Virginian." The grounds were awash with many more celebrities. The crowd must have had a wonderful day because that evening I brought home a bulging steel box—the day's receipts. I counted the entire amount to the penny. Bob Finney had missed his mark by $168. We had made $5,448.

The next day I called Father Garrett, telling him that I had his $5,000. "However," I admonished him, "I'm not giving it to you unless you make me a solemn promise."

"What's that?" He seemed vaguely alarmed.

"You've got $448 over that amount. But you don't get any of it unless you promise to buy some new clothes. You look terrible."

* * *

Now, at midnight, we were all sitting in a restaurant taking a break from the "Our Land, Our Heritage" recording session. Dan Blocker heard Father order a hamburger so he chided him about eating meat on Friday. Father looked at Dan pertly, turned his new collar backwards and announced, "For the next half-hour, I'm not a priest."

When we left the restaurant, Dan noticed the threadbare condition of Father's tires. "Good God a'mighty!" he exploded. "You don't drive to Acton every day on those, do you, Father?" Father said that he did. "Well, you go down to Mark C. Bloome on Sunset tomorrow morning. Tell Mike to fix you up with a set of tires and put it on my bill."

Dan always considered himself an agnostic. I figured that God continues to work in wondrous ways . . .

TRAGEDY AT HUNTSVILLE

EARLY IN 1964, Blocker invited me on a junket to Huntsville Prison in Texas. Each year, the prison hosts a rodeo that is part of the rodeo association's schedule. At one time Huntsville had been regarded as one of the worst prisons in America—guards were given truncheons and advised to use them often. Prisoners working in the fields drank from garbage cans that more often than not had dead mice, rats and insects floating in the water. If they complained, the truncheons would sing. The present warden, Mr. Moore, had done much reform there but it was still no girls' school.

On the plane flight, Dan asked me if I could write something special for the prisoners. Armed with the knowledge of the prison's past reputation, I wrote a parody to "Beautiful, Beautiful Texas."

Beautiful, Beautiful Huntsville

Beautiful, beautiful Huntsville,
Nestled in warm Texas air.
Where the guards are all soft-hearted
And the warden is always fair.

You may dream of the "Rock" or San Quentin,
Carson City and all the rest.
But beautiful, beautiful Huntsville
Is the bucket that I love the best.

When we arrived at the prison we were given red-carpet treatment. Dan was riding high then as Hoss on "Bonanza." The world adored him.

The skies were darkening ominously by the time the rodeo started. Dan, who was introduced while a prisoner readied himself to ride a saddle-bronc, received a great ovation from the 2,000 inmates. They were in a fenced-off section, enjoying Dan's comments about their stay at the "Huntsville Hotel," when all hell broke loose. The prisoner was thrown from his mount while still in the chute and the terrified animal plunged and reared furiously. Frantic cowboys opened the chute. The crazed bronc leaped out into the arena, bucking insanely.

The cowboys dragged the fallen rider out of the chute into the arena where the prisoners could plainly see that he was dying: His lungs were pierced by broken ribs, his head crushed by the flying hooves.

My guitar was abruptly thrust into my hands as Dan shouted, "You're on, buddy." I started "Beautiful, Beautiful Huntsville" and the prisoners calmed down and listened.

"Don't touch the microphone," a guard whispered, as sheets of lightning flashed in the distance and the darkness grew more intense. I understood the guard's concern; the microphone was now a lightning rod.

By the time the dying prisoner had been removed, I was into the second chorus of my parody:

Now the gun-towers here at Huntsville
Are tidy and neat as well.

The guards, armed with automatic weapons, could be clearly seen silhouetted against the dark sky.

And the gentlemen who watch o'er them
Are peachy-keen and swell!

The rest of the lyrics were lost in a bedlam of screaming, yelling prisoners. The guards looked at me with something akin to pure hate while the storm swept over us. It was like a scene from a Frankenstein movie—darkness blanketed the arena; rolling, crashing thunder roared from the sky. Terrifying flashes of lightning made the arena brighter than day for seconds at a time; in those seconds, the prisoners could be seen being herded back into their cell blocks.

We were soon on our way to the airport to fly to Houston, escorted by a motorcycle patrolman dressed in a yellow sou'wester; it rained in a steady, heavy downpour all the way.

We stopped over for a day in El Paso because Dan wanted to see some friends. One was James Parr, a war buddy Dan had known in Korea in 1950. On the flight from Houston to El Paso, Dan explained Parr as best he could.

"We called Parr 'Colonel' because he was the least likely man in our division to ever get over the rank of private. Our outfit was dug in on a mountainside in North Korea, overlooking the Yalu River. It took a long time to melt enough snow for drinking water so 'Colonel' Parr volunteered to sneak down to the Yalu to fill a five-gallon can. We rigged up a knapsack-like strap to put the can on his back and, with that secured, he started down the mountainside.

"He picked his way to that ice-cold river and filled the can while we watched through our binoculars. We didn't realize it, but we weren't the only ones. On the way back he slipped and fell backwards on the snowy slope. The heavy can acted like a sled and Parr rocketed downward. We could hear him shouting 'Whoo—whoo—whoo—whooeeeee' all the way to the river. He made it back but man, was he lucky."

Dan was sent on patrol to investigate a Korean farmhouse the Reds had studiously avoided shelling. Dan went down into the valley with a squad of six men and, nearing the farmhouse, told them that he was going inside. "If there's any trouble, come a-bustin' in. Otherwise, just stay put."

He found the floor littered with old, sick Koreans who just stared at him. Sympathy was flooding over him when he heard a door fly open and he looked up to see a Chinese soldier with an automatic rifle. The soldier tried to fire but the weapon jammed.

"I pulled my .45 from its holster, pointed it straight at his eyes," Dan recalled. "I couldn't think of what to do so I yelled out, 'You're under arrest!' The Red didn't understand English but he shore savvied that .45! We took him prisoner and sent in medics to help those old people."

On another patrol, a member of Dan's party was presumably lost in a snowstorm. The next day was clear so Dan and his squad took turns looking through powerful binoculars they had placed on tripods overlooking the valley. Suddenly, one of his men shouted, "Dan, it's him!"

"Him" was an Oklahoma Indian named Charley, and he was drunk. Through the binoculars, they saw him sit up in the snow and take a whiskey bottle out of his overcoat. He took a great slug, replaced the bottle carefully in the coat, and started off the *wrong way* up the steep mountain slope. The squad kept track of him through the glasses until he disappeared about a third of the way up the incline.

In about three minutes, he came back into view as if shot from a cannon and started down the mountainside, falling, rolling, running for his life. Then the entire mountain seemed to open up on Charley. The rifle and machine-gun fire was tremendously heavy but the now thoroughly sobered Indian was climbing "our" side of the canyon with great speed.

When he reached the perimeter, the command took him in for interrogation. They forgot to punish him for his infractions when he told them what he had seen.

"Charley"—Dan shook his head in amazement as he recollected the story—"had fallen into an elaborate defense system when we lost him in the scopes. The deep trench was filled with Chinese soldiers, many of them wearing bits and pieces of American uniforms. Because of Charley's Indian appearance, the soldiers took little notice of him until he wandered into a command post run by Mongolian officers, some of whom, according to

Charley, 'were seven feet tall.' They stared at Charley in disbelief, long enough for him to run for his life.

"From his misadventure," Blocker said, "the American command pieced together enough information to realize that the territory now contained over a million Chinese! Charley saved the lives of countless G.I.s—maybe mine, too," mused Blocker.

Dan looked into some dark space for a long moment. "Charley died on that mountain. He wasn't killed by the enemy. One of our own mortars fell short of its target and blew him to pieces."

❄ ❄ ❄

In the spring of 1964, Jon Locke and I once again teamed up with James Drury to do the Fat Stock Show in Fort Worth, Texas. We swelled our ranks by adding the venerated Sons of the Pioneers to our cast and they were a great plus. Rusty Richards was their top tenor at that time, Dale Warren, baritone, Pat Brady played the bass and Lloyd Perryman was the leader.

The guitar player, Roy Lanham, is a legend in country music. He has performed with some of the greatest names in the field and has been with the Pioneers for nearly three decades. A host of stories have sprung up around him. He was born in Corbin, Kentucky. Since the famed "Kentucky Fried Chicken" Colonel is a Corbin-ite, the two were friends. Roy told me that "Everybody in Corbin loved Colonel Sanders. All the townspeople got

Roy Lanham and his wife Marianne Lanham: Legends in country music.

together on his birthday and licked each others' fingers."

Roy told me that when he was born, his folks were so poor that "My mother had to go next door to have me."

A famous story among his country music friends stems from a gig he played at a club in Burbank. Roy can't drink too much and he had imbibed beyond his limit that evening. His wife, Marianne, was playing the cocktail drums, doing the vocalizing and trying unsuccessfully to slow down his imbibing.

Fortunately, his brother Ray and sister-in-law Freida were with them so Ray took over the wheel of their Cadillac when the gig was over. The cocktail drums and Roy's guitar were in the trunk.

Just before they got to the Ventura Freeway, Roy's carburetor caught fire and flames spread rapidly to the entire engine. Ray, Marianne and Freida could not put the fire out by fanning the flames with their coats—they only made it worse. Finally, Marianne turned to Roy and, to her amazement, found that he was just an interested bystander.

"Roy!" she screamed. "Do something!"

Roy, a slight man, teetered forward. "About what?"

Marianne was frantic. "The car is on fire!"

Roy stopped teetering and squinted at the car. "I can see that."

Now Marianne was beside herself. "But your guitar's in the trunk!"

Roy shook his head, eyeing her blandly. "I don't feel like playin'."

DRURY'S NEVER DREARY

IN FORT WORTH, Drury once again got heavily involved in hanky panky. He had been romancing a lovely young Texas miss, the Miss Cotton winner at the State Fair. His embroilments swept me into the rapids when my phone rang at one o'clock in the morning and Miss Cotton was the caller.

"John," she sobbed through the instrument, "where's Jim?"

Jim was in his room with another lady from St. Louis. He had put a "no phone messages" on his line and was not to be disturbed. I evaded her question with an "I don't know" response.

The motel was crowded to the gunnels with rodeo guests; there was no room at the inn. Miss Cotton had started to drive to her home in Amarillo but dense fog had forced her to turn back to Fort Worth. I told her that she could stay in my room as I had two beds; rather than sleep in her car, she leaped at the chance.

All went well until my phone rang. It was my wife, Nancy, calling from California. In two seconds her voice changed from "Hi, darlin'" to "There's a woman in your room!" I felt that it would be nigh unto impossible to explain that I was just being kind.

"No, n-n-not on your life!" We talked with me stuttering and her being icily distant, then she hung up. When I got back to California, I told her the truth. Happily, she believed me. If the culprit had been anyone other than Jim Drury, I would have had a harder time selling my story.

❄❄❄

From Fort Worth our rodeo troupe went on to St. Louis for a ten-day stint at the Police Circus Show. There we met Major Daugherty. This famous police officer had volunteered to step into a cell with the giant heavyweight

Charles "Sonny" Liston, who had been arrested for shooting a St. Louis policeman. The two had fought it out and Daugherty broke the feared fighter's leg. (Liston was the champion of the world from 1962-64.)

Daugherty invited us to visit the jail to see an eerily beautiful thing. In one cell was an unfinished portrait of Christ. Daugherty explained that during the Depression, an unidentified transient had spent a cold winter night in that cell. The next morning, after the penniless vagrant had been given a hot meal and sent on his way, a jailer had discovered the incomplete portrait, sketched in black and sepia tones on the white wall. It affected him so that he brought in the police commissioner and the chief. They too saw its magnificence. No prisoner has been in that cell since. To this day, no one has been able to determine what medium was used or the artist's identity.

THE ONE-ARMED WOMAN WITH A BASEBALL BAT

THE CIRCUS PEOPLE we worked with included a wild animal trainer—a French Basque whose name was Johnny Zebrini, though he was billed as "Tarzan." He wore only a leopard skin bikini and a sheath knife when he entered the cage of lions.

Tarzan, whose sister Mimi was a petite, elfin creature, had a birthday party during our stay and we were all invited. The Sons of the Pioneers sang a number of their old favorites from a vantage point on a hill overlooking St. Louis.

The goat cooking on a spit over an open fire filled the air with a delicious fragrance while the rum cake Tarzan's mother made started mouths watering. Mimi sang "Lonesome Me" in French while Jim Drury showed Tarzan how to twirl a six-shooter.

Tarzan was ready to trade his entire act to become a "cowboy." He admired my Stetson hat so much that I gave it to him.

A few shows later, Tarzan and his father owed their lives to Mimi. A huge male lion attacked Tarzan, and in seconds he was fighting for his life. Tarzan's father leaped into the cage to beat the lion off when the two other males jumped him. The beasts were well on their way to mauling father and son to death when Mimi, who had been sitting in the stands with a broken arm in a cast (the result of being accidentally stepped on by an elephant) rushed into the cage and beat the animals so fiercely with a baseball bat that they stopped mauling their prey to escape into their individual cages.

Hell hath no fury like a one-armed woman with a baseball bat.

❄❄❄

We finished our road tour in Harrisburg, Pennsylvania, where we performed for the Shriners' Circus. Our troupe was asked to visit the Shriners' Hospital and tour the wards. Hundreds of children with afflictions and deformities caused tears to well up in the eyes of the strongest among us, but we still entertained them. One terribly deformed little girl with the face of an angel asked me if I'd take her home with me. To this day, I see that pitiful body with her angelic face, imploring me . . . God bless those Shriners. They are not heralded nearly enough.

Jim Drury may be hell on wheels but he is an outstanding stage actor. In a variety show, however, he's at a terrible disadvantage because he can't sing and he can't do standup comedy without lines and material.

His father, a professor at New York University, came one day to see the show in Harrisburg. Afterward, he spoke gruffly to his son. "Jim, John here sings a hell of a song and Locke is very funny. Roy is a fantastic guitar player. Why don't you have John sing more and give a special spot to Lanham?"

Jim bristled. "I never said I could sing," he snapped defensively.

His father shook his head in disgust. "For Chrissake, you can't even clap."

❄ ❄ ❄

Brother Robert did two pictures in 1963. One was "Man in the Middle" (directed by Guy Hamilton, famed for some of the James Bond films) with the beautiful France Nuyen as his leading lady. But Bob was hard-pressed to keep apace with Trevor Howard. "Every scene I played with him, he stole it from under my nose." But Bob felt that it was right for the picture: "I'd like to teach young actors one thing: Worry about whether or not the picture as a whole is good or bad, and whether or not your performance in any small way is contributing to its being good. Only the amateur worries whether he looks right and is getting a big enough share of the lens."

In 1958 I had worked in a film called "Five Steps to Danger" starring Sterling Hayden and Ruth Roman and featuring William Vaughan. My role was that of a desert sheriff. When I went to Western Costumes for my fitting, the costumer greeted me happily and steered me to the dressing room. My clothes were hanging on a rack. I tried them on and, as they fitted me comfortably, I said they were fine.

Bob spent several months in England and India to make "Man in the Middle" with the late Trevor Howard (far right). After Bob's character, Lt. Colonel Barney Adams, shoots and kills a British soldier, he's placed on trial to determine his sanity. It was based on Howard Fast's novel "The Winston Affair" and was directed by Guy Hamilton, famous for "Goldfinger."

"You'll never make it in the picture business," said a handsome young man also being fitted in a uniform.

"Why not?"

"You're not careful enough about your clothes."

I found out later that he had demanded that his shirts be tapered to his slim waist and that his trousers be fitted to show off his narrow hips and race-horse legs. The last time I saw him, he was tumbling down the steep sides of a desert arroyo. Under the dust cloud he created, I could scarcely make him out, let alone the tapered shirt. I worked thirty years more in the picture business and I never saw him again.

❄❄❄

In Bob's second picture that year, "What a Way to Go," Shirley MacLaine was once again Bob's leading lady. In it he tries to milk a bull and consequently is kicked through the barn wall to an ignominious finish. It brought back to me the memory of Brother Robert on Woodside Farm in Delaware milking one of our cows and dreaming about the fortune in diamonds that must lay beneath his feet.

While Bob was surrounded by all that beauty and glamor, I was gracing an outdoor show for San Jose's annual prune festival. Our stage was a huge flatbed truck decorated for the occasion. The local papers had advertised the event with the unfailing reference that "John Mitchum, Robert Mitchum's brother" would be a featured entertainer.

I have long been used to the inevitable association but was a bit astounded to see an ancient crone standing in the audience and making minuscule wavings while grinning at me from toothless jaws. When I got off the stage, she darted at me, gave me a pinch on my shoulder and cackled, "Say hello to Bobby for me."

When I next saw Bob, I told him that a toothless old woman in San Jose had asked me to say "hello" for her. Being fresh from the close proximity of gorgeous Nuyen and shimmering MacLaine hadn't slowed him a bit. His instant riposte was, "Oh yes. I had her. She was very good!"

HOW TO PICK YOUR OWN POCKET

FOR MUCH of 1964, I toured the country in Senator Barry Goldwater's aborted effort to become President. The fact that several studios bluntly warned us to cease our efforts only caused us to work all the harder for him.Senator John Tower, a man of moral strength and courage, and now the new Secretary of Defense under President Bush, was the principal speaker in our group while Phillip Crosby, Jon Locke, James Drury and I did the entertaining.

I shall never forget the sadness in Senator Goldwater's face as he looked at a huge crowd that had assembled in Wichita Falls, Texas, the home state of his Democratic opponent, President Lyndon B. Johnson.

Goldwater, knowing that the polls had Johnson ahead by a tremendous margin, spoke softly. "When are the people going to learn that the United States Government is not a money-making institution? It cannot give monies to one faction of the government without taking it away from another."

His words come back to me whenever I hear the statement, "The government should do it." Since we *are* the government, we are constantly picking our own pockets.

A recent photo of Senator John Tower

❄ ❄ ❄

In the early summer of 1965, I received a bizarre phone call from Hong Kong. It was about four in the morning (California time) and the operator's crisp, British voice confused me for a moment. "Are you John Mitchum?" she chirped. "Hong Kong calling."

Suddenly a familiar voice roared through the system, filling the line with song.

"Hawg Junior High! Hawg Junior High!" It was the school fight song for the junior high named in honor of James Steven Hogg of Texas. The singer was the then Senator John Tower of the Lone Star State, one of the ablest men to have hailed from that bigger-than-life grazing land. He had called to simply keep in touch by singing his alma mater; he must have been lonesome in that exotic land.

Now, in the waning days of August, 1988, I had the chance to sing his alma mater back to him via telephone. "You remembered!" he marveled.

"Who," I asked, "could ever forget James Hogg, a man who had the temerity to name his daughter Ima? And who could forget a man of your stature, a distinguished State Senator, the head of the Armed Forces Committee, and a pretty good baritone?"

We both laughed and he said that we should get together to sing the song more fully. And soon. Now we would have to meet at the White House.

❄ ❄ ❄

Dan "Hoss" Blocker and I had been very close friends until I toured for Goldwater. I didn't know it at the time but Blocker, a democrat, had developed a political bent that would be more correctly labeled as Socialist.

On the "Bonanza" set one day, Blocker was waxing eloquently on his political theories to a group of what we actors called the "split-tail suit" set out of Paramount's New York offices.

"Government is big business," exhorted the giant Hoss, "and government should *run* business!" He looked around for confirmation and his gaze settled on an extra, Eddie Moon. "Ain't that right, Eddie?"

Eddie look at Blocker calmly. "No, it isn't right."

Dan became apoplectic. The big boys from New York started to look restless. "What? What do you mean, 'No'?"

"Dan, your publicity says you came from West Texas, from humble beginnings. That right?"

Dan snorted. "Yes, that's right."

"And you graduated from Sul Ross College in Texas and then taught school in Odessa for a little over $4000 a year. Is that right?"

Growing more red-faced and angry by the statement, Dan agreed that it was all true.

"Then," continued Eddie, "you came to California and started teaching in South Pasadena for a little over $6000 a year. Is *that* right?"

Dan had to nod again.

"You started doing picture work and later became Hoss on this show. Now your salary is $10,000 a segment. That, plus road shows and pictures during your hiatus have made you a millionaire. Right outside this sound stage is a bright red Ferrari automobile. It's yours, Dan. And you know why you bought it? So that everyone who sees it *knows* that Dan Blocker 'made' it. From a dirt-poor Texas boy to multi-millionaire. The American Dream, Dan. You've made the American Dream come true. Now I want to become a great writer. Of course, I don't know if that will happen, but it's my dream, Dan. No matter how late I work on the show, I dedicate four hours a night to writing. I cherish my dream, Dan. It saddens me to know that now that you have made *your* dream come true, you want to install a form of government that will take away *mine*."

Eddie Moon stood up and surveyed Blocker and his open-mouthed entourage from Paramount. "No, Dan, I don't buy it." And he walked away.

William Vaughan

***

For a number of years in the 1960's, my actor friend William Vaughan had a tidy little business on the side. He had contracts with department stores, private parties and the Van Nuys Chamber of Commerce to supply snappy Santa Claus outfits during the Christmas season.

Occasionally William would call me to fill in for a St. Nick who was unfit for duty from a bout with John Barleycorn. I would find myself assigned to a day of ho-ho-hoing up and down Van Nuys Boulevard or darting into banks, department stores and restaurants with a large bag of candy canes on my shoulder and a desire to spread good cheer.

One afternoon, two young thugs tried to wrest away my bag of goodies and were stunned into momentary inactivity when, in my best Saint Nick delivery, I told them, "This is one Santa who just might knock you on your asses!" They hoofed it away. I then went into a department store to see Lenny Geer's wife, Dotty, who was avidly looking over some jewelry items. I pinched her on the fanny and whispered an inviting "Ho-ho-ho" in her ear. She whirled on me like a tigress.

"Who are you?" she demanded. "I'll have your job!"

"John Mitchum says 'You can have it,'" I whispered.

Dotty almost fell down laughing. She quickly forgave me.

One night, two police officers asked me if I would go to the Van Nuys

Police Station right after I got off work. It seemed that their watch commander, a family man with four children, was morosely unhappy. It was Christmas Eve and he couldn't be with his family. I agreed to bring Santa Claus to the station.

On the way there, the officers asked me if I could play a drunken Santa. I assured them that I could. They brought me, handcuffed and weaving tipsily, into the station, where silence immediately fell over the personnel. They uncuffed me and plunked me down in a chair before the watch commander, who froze in place. He turned away from me and stared out the window. "Why didn't you dump him off in North Hollywood?"

Just at that moment, a pretty lady cop walked past, so I tugged pathetically at her sleeve.

"Would you like some candy?" I gurgled in my best wino-ese.

She disgustedly pushed my hand away. "No, thanks."

The watch commander turned back toward me. "You're the most despicable man I've ever met. Thousands of little children go to bed on Christmas Eve believing that Santa Claus is real. What in God's name do you think went through the minds of those kids who saw you like this on the street tonight?"

His body tensed as he whirled and barked at the two officers, "Book him."

I took off my wig and beard and smiled at the astonished commander. In a sober voice, I told him there was no cause for that. The two officers burst into laughter and then the commander joined in.

"Thank God," he sighed.

The lady officer graciously took some candy canes for her family and I dumped the half-empty bag on the commander's desk. "Tell your kids that Santa Claus gave you these. Straight from the North Pole."

I was driven back to my car by the two officers. They were delighted with their night's work.

So was I. I hadn't been booked.

CONFRONTATION

HATRED IS A WORD that confuses me, for I am a man of quick passions. I can become angered in a searing flash but the anger soon dissipates into a bemused reaction whose primary element is one of acceptance of the *status quo.* My philosophy is best put in the Serenity Prayer:

God give me the serenity to accept
The things I cannot change,
The courage to change the things I can,
And the wisdom to know the difference.

My wife Nancy had an uncle, Charles Munro, who lived in Sherman Oaks. Charles' wife, Lida, was a Norwegian woman active in the Lutheran Church. I visited them rarely for Lida was consumed with a hatred for Roman Catholicism that was so vitriolic it permeated the air around her. She purely hated all Catholics. Books, pamphlets and newspaper articles were strewn about her house, all breathing hate. It left me troubled and concerned.

God give me the serenity to accept the things I cannot change . . .

Charley Munro was the same, but different. His slurs were couched in terms that avoided direct bigotry, but their meanings were unmistakable.

"Lincoln only did half his job" was an indicator of his leanings. "I feel that I should have the right to live in a white neighborhood" was another. It did absolutely no good for me to bring up to Lida or Charley that the very strengths of America came from her building a foundation on the emancipation of all mankind.

. . . The courage to change the things I can. And the wisdom to know the difference.

When Lida died of cancer I was called to do the driving for the pathetic remnants of Charley's family. His own sister Bessie and her minister husband Herman came from Wyoming for the funeral. Lida's sister Martha was weeping unconsolably as we left Charley's house for the funeral parlor.

"Oh, Lida. Oh, my Lida," she wailed as I guided her down the brick steps to the car. "Oh, my Lida."

Her pitiful voice wrenched the air. She suddenly turned to Charley and in a voice as cold and brittle as an icicle snapped out, "She promised me the diamond ring!" She immediately returned to caterwauling about "My dear Lida."

Bessie and Herman went into Lida's well-stocked bar and poured out all of her liquor. Jack Daniels. Chivas Regal. Schmirnoff. I learned a lesson in intolerance from those supposedly religious people.

I kept getting telephone calls from Uncle Charley Munro. Facing infirmity, old age and the revelation that his deceased wife had often cheated on him, he phoned one night to tell me that he was going to kill himself.

I drove to his home, entered the back door, crept into his bedroom and

My second wife Nancy and I were asked to be the celebrities of the afternoon at Hollywood Park in 1965, on a day when my favorite horses were not trotting quite fast enough.

unloaded his Colt .45. As I tiptoed toward the front door, the yard came alive like a carnival midway. A bullhorn voice ordered me to "Come out with your hands on your head!" I faced ten squad cars with spotlights blazing.

I told the man in charge who I was. "I've got a bizarre story to tell you, but I warn you, it'll be hard to believe."

"I've heard a lot of 'em," said the cop. "Go on."

I was showing them the cartridges I had dechambered from the Colt when the front door burst open and Charley—6-foot-2, skinny as a rail, toothless, in a flannel nightgown and cap—called in his quavery voice, "John, what's going on?"

The cops melted into the night.

With considerable irritation, I told Charley what I had done. He looked at me with heart-rending pathos. "John, I decided I'd never kill myself. My sister would cry."

When Charley died, the only people who came to his funeral were some friends of mine who decided to give me a helping hand. His tearful sister-in-law decided to stay in Redondo Beach with the diamond ring.

A LESSON IN BIGOTRY

THE PREPONDERANCE of hate and bigotry in our world surfaced almost comically when I was doing "Magnum Force" in San Francisco in 1973. I received an invitation to dinner from an old friend, Beverly Eagleson, and since I was the godfather to her two daughters, I gladly accepted. Beverly and I were having an after-dinner drink when she got a call from a nurse stationed at the Presidio Hospital. Beverly invited her down, explaining who I was and that I was a guest.

When the woman arrived, I noted that she was wearing a sleek evening dress, much too dressy for our simple occasion. She had an Irish accent that was thick enough to cut into slabs and she started pouring out her woes to us. Her husband was a major at the Presidio and not only did he have a young Japanese girl friend on the side, but a male sergeant as a backup lover. I granted her that she had emotional woes but when she planted herself in my lap, I made a wry comment as to her husband's errant choices.

"Why, you're a bigot!" Her eyes flared wide.

I hadn't said anything that came close to touching the reality of her husband's complications but I immediately saw that she had many problems herself that were none too well disguised. I decided to find out what they were.

"Of course I'm a bigot."

Again those Irish eyes opened wide. "Just what are your prejudices?"

I looked at her somberly. "I hate Jews, niggers and fry cooks." I honestly expected the last target of my supposed hatred to elicit a laugh, but none came. I decided to plunge on:

"Of course, the Chinese should be done away with."

She gasped convulsively. "A billion people?"

"Gas 'em all," I snorted. "And the Samoans—all that long hair under their arms—ugh. The Eskimos—eating whale blubber all summer long; imagine how they must smell. The French must go, too; a lustful nation—attacking little girls all the time. Germans—all they want to do is kill you. The Scandinavians? Stupid; "square-heads." And Mexicans—lazy. Have you

Playing One of the Bad Guys

Ever wonder who plays the nameless hired guns who take out after the hero when the villain commands them to ride? In the 1963 MGM Western, "Cattle King," I was one of Ray Middleton's henchmen. At right I'm holding Robert Loggia while Arthur Batanides pummels him. Below, I'm the fifth rider from the left, next to Batanides as he shoots it out with Robert Taylor.

That's Ray Middleton leading the posse in the riding photo above, with Batanides to his right. I'm directly behind Batanides. "Cattle King" (also known as "Guns of Wyoming") was a minor Western directed by Tay Garnett but it had a wonderful cast that included Joan Caulfield and William Windom. With Taylor below, sitting on the fence, is character actor Ray Teal, who became best known for his role as Sheriff Roy Coffee on "Bonanza." Before that the gentle-mannered actor (who always looked sunburnt and leathery and shrewd on film) had small but pivotal roles in such features as "Streets of Laredo," "The Men," "Along the Great Divide," "Distant Drums" and "The Command."

ever heard of a hard-working Mexican?"

"My God! You're a terrible man." She clutched her heart.

I laughed. "Don't you realize that I'm pulling your leg?"

She rolled her eyes back. "Thank God for that."

I became serious now. "There's only one race of people I hate."

She stared at me again. "And who might they be?"

"The coldest, cruelest, most cold-blooded race under the sun."

"Who are they?"

"The English."

She leaped to her feet, her eyes blazing with fury. She pointed a shaking finger at me, her face contorted in hate. "You're right! You're right!"

She became confused. I was rolling on the floor laughing.

Prejudice exists strictly in the heart of the beholder. Since I am Norwegian, Scots-Irish and Blackfoot Indian, I find it hard to decide which part of me I don't like.

A VISION OF CIVIL WAR

WESTERN WRITER Gordon Sheriff gave me a copy of "The First Maine," a paperback about the famed Civil War regiment that fought so gallantly at the battle of Gettysburg. The entire James Drury troupe was invited to that hallowed place during our stay in Harrisburg.

I went to Little Round Top, feeling an intense chill when I realized I was standing on the very ground where the 6th Alabamans had used rifles, bayonets and their bare hands to prevent the 1st Maine from taking and controlling Round Top. If the Southerners had secured the position, Rebel artillery would have been directed at the entire Union line. In the book, the author described the creek below as "running red with blood" for three days.

When I surveyed the peach orchard where Pickett's famous charge met with withering fire from the Union lines, I had an uncanny vision of General Robert E. Lee astride his horse Traveller, somberly viewing the Confederate disaster.

In "America, Why I Love Her," the only album narrated by John Wayne, I wrote: "A land forged by the hot steel of raw courage and formed forever by the awful crucible of civil war." My inspiration came from Gettysburg, Pickett's Charge and Little Round Top.

Inspiration can come from strange places and things. Two examples still return to me through the mists of the past. One was a tall vase, beautifully adorned with graceful flamingos, which Grandfather had picked up in Japan shortly after World War I. As an eight-year-old, I held it in awe as a sacred thing, as I did all things from that mystic island.

The other was a book that Grandfather kept on a table in what we called "the front room." In colors so vivid that I see them now, the exquisitely done paintings were of Prussian lancers, French cannoneers, English infantry, and American West scenes of Indians and U.S. Cavalry.

Brother Bob was apparently not so deeply imbued with inspiration. When I spoke to him recently about that book, he said his only lasting impression was a scene of Attila the Hun. When I reminded him how awed I had been to learn there was a lot more than Delaware out there, he snorted, "You were more impressionable than I was."

I guess I still am.

DOUBLE DEATH

IN THE LATE 1950's I successfully sold policies for the Prudential Life Insurance Company, even though it really wasn't what I felt I was best suited for. If there was a reason for my distaste for the job, it was my supervisor.

Still, I retained the Prudential job and I found myself working consistently in television and films, almost always in Westerns: "Gunsmoke," "Bonanza," "The Virginian," "Laredo," "Shotgun Slade," and so on. My beard and long hair helped me to land many of the roles.

I would sit on the sound stage of whatever show I was working on and while away the long hours of waiting by working out comprehensive insurance plans for likely prospects. Invariably a fellow actor would wander over and ask what I was doing and I'd launch into a sales pitch. In this manner I sold a $200,000 policy to Rory Calhoun, a complete hospital-and-income protection plan to Lee Van Cleef and various amounts of insurance to many other actors.

This meant nothing to my supervisor. He'd run his hands through my long hair and snidely ask me when I was going to start looking like an insurance salesman. To him this meant suit and tie, hairless face and trimmed hair. What business I brought into the office apparently carried little weight in his evaluation. I wasn't about to shave or trim my "movie" hair, so Prudential and I eventually parted company.

One of my potential clients was a very good young actor, Tom Pittman. Tom and I had been in serious discussions about an insurance program for him when suddenly he was reported missing. The mystery was solved when two hikers found his car at the bottom of a ravine off Mulholland Drive, the windy mountain strip that divides the San Fernando Valley from Hollywood and Beverly Hills. Tom was still in his car. A four-by-four piece of guard rail had pierced through the windshield—and his body.

By then I was a good friend of Tom's father, radio actor and comedian

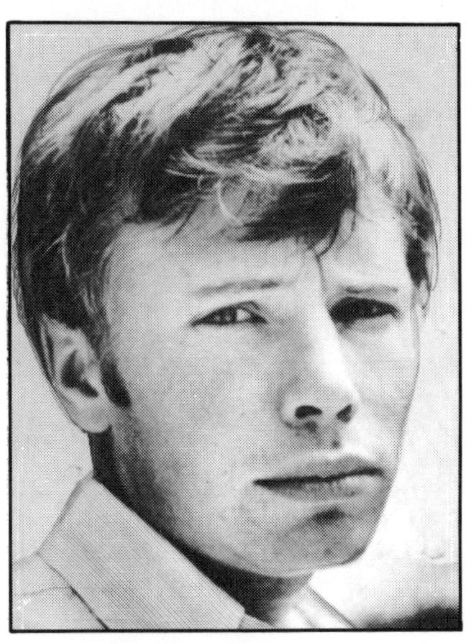

My friend Tom Pittman was considered one of Hollywood's most up and coming young actors when he burst on the scene in 1957 in "The True Story of Jesse James" and "The Young Stranger." Suddenly, Tom disappeared on October 31, 1958, and wasn't found until Nov. 19. His body was discovered in the wreckage of his sports car, which had plummeted into a mountain ravine in the Hollywood Hills. Shortly before his death he had completed roles in "The Proud Rebel," "Apache Territory" and Samuel Fuller's "Verboten."

Frankie Alton, and my heart went out to him. He spoke with a decidedly Austrian accent and he had an irrepressible sense of humor. Tom's death shocked him deeply.

I now jump ahead to 1966. Alton, a member of the Optimists' Club, was contacted by the Fresno chapter to arrange a fund-raising show at the city's Civic Auditorium. And so it was that in January of that year I went to Fresno with Roy and Marianne Lanham to be in the show.

When we arrived at our motel in Fresno, the band members who had preceded us were packing their instruments. When they heard Roy warming up, they asked if they might join in. Within minutes my modest group grew into a large one. Their percussionist was Spider Webb, a fantastic drummer. Their bass player Thumper McDowell certainly lived up to his name. And lead guitarist Bill Malouf could swing with any of them.

My friends Doris and Bob Finney came along just to enjoy the show, but Doris was to become involved in a bizarre happening.

Mickey Rooney had been asked to be a guest star at the fundraiser, but, due to previous commitments, couldn't make it. His 17-year-old son, Tim Rooney, came in his place.

Simultaneously, on January 29, the papers, radio and television media

The Mickey Rooney Tragedy

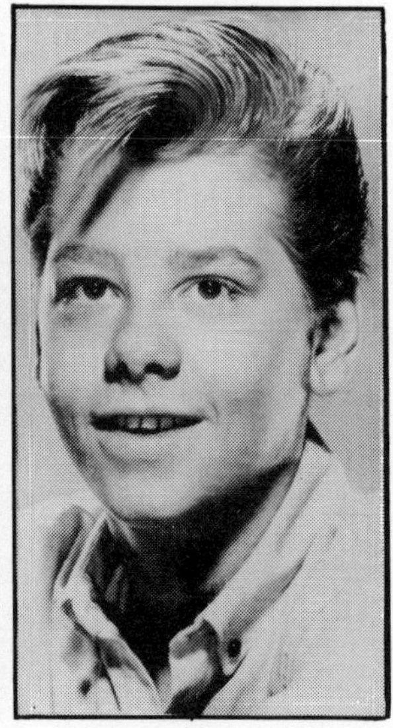

Actor Milos Milocevic (left), who had played a memorable character in "The Russians Are Coming, the Russian Are Coming" under the name Milos Milos, shot and killed Mickey Rooney's estranged wife Barbara (actress Barbara Thomason, shown with Mickey above left) and then killed himself on January 31, 1966. Tim Rooney (above right) had begun his career at 15 in TV's "Make Room for Daddy" comedy series.

exploded the news that Mickey had filed a divorce suit against Barbara, Tim's mother. That afternoon, for some insane reason, her lover, Milos Milosevic, shot her through the head, then took his own life by inserting the powerful handgun in his mouth and pulling the trigger.

On the night of Tim's show, only Doris Finney's comforting arms kept Tim from losing control. The audience watched the teen-age actor on the stage and laughed at Frankie Alton doing his act from the balcony with a rubber chicken.

I watched them closely as they performed. Both did their stint perfectly. The audience had no inkling that Tim's mother had died brutally and that Frankie's only son had lain alone for days at the bottom of a ravine, horribly mangled—a tragedy that had never lifted off Frankie.

Truly, the show—and life—must go on.

REVELATION IN BLACK

CHANGE IS INEVITABLE. It is in the nature of things. Now and then, one is led to wonder whether all change is for the good.

The National Association for the Advancement of Colored People has been around since its charter was founded in New York State in 1909. Subtly, its programs have been attacked by "the young Turks" of each generation, those Blacks who have become Moslems, turning away from Christianity. In a broader sense "young Turks" has come to stand for the constant assault on old values by each succeeding generation. "Colored," "Negro," "Negroid," "Black" . . . each term is haggled over, bickered over and even fought over, in order to find a definition suitable to the generation of the moment.

In 1965 the underlying current of change blew to the surface in the Watts riots and became crystal clear to me in its aftermath. Dick Menser, an executive with the Screen Actors Guild, received a plea for help from a Black minister in the Compton-Watts area who witnessed a murder during the riots. (He must remain anonymous because of continuing threats to his life.) The good reverend had a dream to create a haven for young Blacks, a complex that would house a gymnasium, library, social hall and recreation room that would give the young people of the area a place to find themselves. But there was a major drawback: It would be under Christian leadership, antithesis to the rebellious young Turks.

Dick, aware of my involvement with many charities and my ability to raise monies, told the pastor to call me.

I agreed wholeheartedly to help.

My inspiration was a book I had read, "Angel Mo." Written by Roland Hayes, the Black American concert artist, it described how his mother had washed windows, scrubbed floors and cleaned offices to earn money for his music studies.

Hayes learned and sang in nine languages before the crowned heads of Europe. He was a great artist and he accredited his mother for his success.

Hayes' book told of his great-great grandfather, Aba Ouigi, an African of the Dohemy tribe, captured after a battle with the Porto Nova tribe and sold by Arab slave traders to the British. He was brought to America in 1790 and sold on the block in Savannah, Georgia, to Charles Weaver, a man whose wisdom saw Aba Ouigi for what he was: A man of strength, moral courage and leadership. Weaver made Aba Ouigi an overseer on his plantation. Aba (the word means Prince) became known as Prince Charles, and he led his people as might a Messiah.

Methodist missionaries from the North taught Charles of God and of Christ. Later, those missionaries were forced to leave the plantation workers alone, for the slaves began reasoning that if the White man's God said that all men were equal, then the "Colored" man should not bear his chains.

For a while, there was a vacuum in the development of the Coloreds' religious beliefs. Prince Charles inaugurated field singing as a method of keeping Christ's teachings before his fellow slaves. He would go down the cotton rows singing "Steal Away, Steal Away, Steal Away to Jesus." The song would give signals as to where they would meet; in the meetings, he would exhort them to greater faith. He was eventually beaten to death by frightened plantation owners, but not until field singing was an established means of communication between the slaves and their newfound Lord.

Now, in 1965, to help raise monies for the proposed asylum for the Black youth of the Compton-Watts community, I wrote a play on the material I read from Roland Hayes' life.

The great singer, Herb Jeffries, was to portray Aba Ouigi; Charles McGraw was to be Charles Weaver; Martha Fisher was to have played Mrs. Weaver; Jim Drury was to play a sympathetic plantation owner, and I would have directed the show and conducted the music—had I been allowed.

I informed the Compton police that I had received life-threatening calls from the young Turks of the area who didn't want my "kind" of Christian help. If my group appeared on the stage, I'd been warned, we would be sprayed with automatic rifle fire and killed. The message was made very clear:

"Whitey, stay away!"

The police underground informed me that my house was under surveillance. "Stay away from your picture window and see that your daughter Cindy is escorted to and from school."

Despite fierce protestations by McGraw and Drury, I cancelled the show. Herb Jeffries solemnly told me I had done the right thing; I was dealing with an extremely violent element.

I couldn't help but think of Lilly Mae and Mack Chase from my childhood days. Somewhere along the line, progress has turned its back on innate graciousness, gentility and love.

I had to withdraw my efforts to help in a desperately needed venture. I have never doubted that I would die for a cause in which I believed. It's quite another thing to ask your friends and family to do the same.

In the winter of 1987, I had a surprising call from the Screen Actors Guild informing me that the same Black minister—now a bishop presiding over several counties in Washington State—wanted to contact me. I phoned him immediately and listened in stunned amazement as he said he wanted to share his good fortune with me in return for what I had tried so earnestly to do for his community in 1965.

He wanted me to produce and emcee a fund-raising show. A month of hot long-distance calls between four states to verbally commit several great country and jazz talents I know came to naught, for the fear of reprisal apparently remains with my would-be benefactor.

TENSE MOMENT ON THE OREGON TRAIL

"THE WAY WEST," an epic Western depicting the problems of a Westbound wagon train, was filled with happenings that never showed on the screen. Of course, this is true of many pictures, but I single out this production, shot on location in Oregon, because the unusually large cast and crew contained characters who created as much excitement as screenwriters S. Ben Maddow and Mitch Lindemann.

Bob and Kirk Douglas were at pistol barrels most of the time and director Andrew McLaglen did his best to keep the peace. Only their professionalism kept them from open warfare.

In a major scene for the movie, the entire cast, except for Robert, had enclosed itself behind the barricade of the circled wagon train, along with 200 extras who had been called in as "Indians." The huge setup, under the towering, snow-capped Mount Bachelor, was an impressive sight.

During a rehearsal for the scene, Douglas grabbed Richard Widmark by the arm to show the veteran actor where he wanted him positioned.

Widmark instantly went into an attack position, staring at Douglas with an intensity that went through the whole company like an electrical shock. Douglas lost composure for a moment, but struggled mightily to get it back.

Widmark, once a very good Golden Gloves middleweight fighter, is a thorough professional, but he is also an introvert who does not mix readily. Widmark pushed Kirk away from him, eyeing him coldly. In a tight whisper he said, "Don't direct *me*, Kirk!" He pointed to McLaglen. "There's our director. If he wants to tell me something, I'm prepared to listen. But—*you*—don't—direct—*me!*"

The tension was so great that Paul Lukather, a young actor in the film, tittered in embarrassment. The son of production manager Lee Lukather,

Kirk Douglas, Bob and Richard Widmark on the Oregon Trail in "The Way West," the 1967 epic Western that was never deemed a great success—West or East of the Mississippi.

I played one of the Henry brothers in "The Way West," and Brother Bob portrayed frontier scout Dick Summers, who is slowly going blind. I am sorry to report that most of my delicious scenes and lines of dialogue ended up on the cutting room floor, which frequently happens when you're a character actor. Because the part was so heavily cut, I became one of the faces in the crowd everytime Kirk Douglas and Richard Widmarked argued about which way was West.

Paul was trying hard to make his folks proud of him, which only added to his own inner tension.

Now Douglas turned his withering sarcasm on the youth. The whole scene was ugly and uncalled for. The crew, by tradition, never take sides openly, but their attitude—to a man—was contempt for Kirk's behavior.

Harry "Dobe" Carey (nicknamed "Dobe" because of his red hair) remembers the incident well for he was standing next to Widmark when Douglas grabbed him. "Dick's mouth had a thin white line around it from his intense anger." Dobe said. "You could have heard the proverbial pin drop out there on the meadow grass."

Bob was not present during this unsavory incident. When a break was called, I hurried to his trailer. "You're the only one who can do anything about it," I reasoned.

Bob sighed a deep sigh. He had worked with Douglas before. "We'll see about it tomorrow."

We returned to the same set-up the next morning. I watched in anticipation as Bob left his trailer and strolled toward our group. When he arrived he started talking, apparently to no one in particular.

"On my last picture, a young man came to me and said, 'Oh, Mr. Mitchum, I envy you. You've reached such a pinnacle that now you can call the turn. You've become one of the world's best-known actors; now you can write, you can direct, you can do anything you want in films.'

"I asked the young man what he wanted to do. 'Oh, I want to be a director. Is there any way you could help me to be a director?'

"I said, 'Sure. It's very simple.'"

Bob stopped, turning to stare pointedly at Douglas. "I told him, 'Just put on your wardrobe and appear on the set. It seems that that qualifies *anyone* for the job.'"

A frustrated Douglas couldn't say a single word. Bob "outranked" him in every way possible.

I was recently asked how Brother Robert and Kirk Douglas get along now that they are supposedly mellowed. When I put the question to Bob he fended me off in his usual oblique way by telling me a story:

In 1987, Kirk filmed "Queenie," the story of Merle "Queenie" Oberon's marriage to Alexander Korda. Kirk played Korda and Olivia de Havilland played Oberon. Larry Peerce was the director.

Two weeks into filming, Kirk approached producer James Begg with a complaint. "That young actor I'm working with is taller than I am."

Dig that dimple on Kirk Douglas for his role in "Queenie." Any other actor with a dimple is in clear defiance of the star's wishes.

Begg was mildly amused at first. "But you've known that for two weeks."

Kirk's answer changed the aura of humor. "No one is taller than I am! There will be an adjustment made for that."

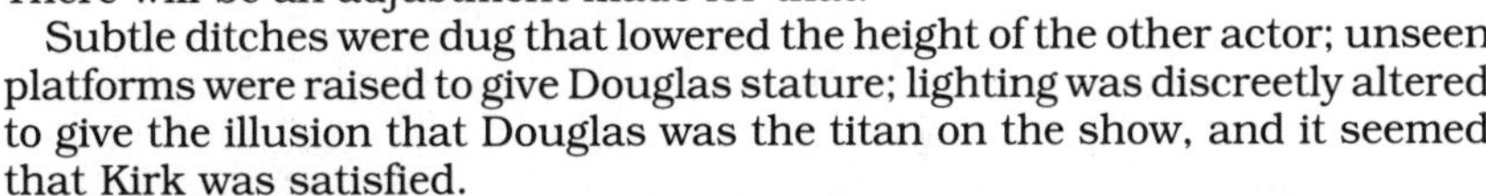

Subtle ditches were dug that lowered the height of the other actor; unseen platforms were raised to give Douglas stature; lighting was discreetly altered to give the illusion that Douglas was the titan on the show, and it seemed that Kirk was satisfied.

Two weeks later another conference was demanded. "What's the problem this time?" asked Begg.

Kirk surveyed him coldly. "The man has a cleft chin."

Again Begg reminded him that he had obviously observed that weeks ago.

Douglas shook his head: "*I* have the cleft chin."

After days of conferences, it was agreed that something in the dialogue would explain the existence of the actor's chin resembling Mr. Douglas'

Richard Widmark driving his wagon to Oregon in "The Way West." That's lovely Lola Albright next to him, hanging on for life.

Harry Carey Jr., son of the famous cowboy actor Harry Carey, followed his father into films after World War II in "Red River" and (opposite Bob) in "Pursued," which remain among his best pictures. He worked in numerous John Ford films, usually opposite John Wayne, and remained close to Wayne until the death of Ward Bond in 1960. After that Wayne turned cold to him, and didn't reactivate their friendship until one day in 1976 when Harry was on the Paramount lot and accidentally ran into Wayne, who was making "The Shootist." Wayne treated him like a long-lost son, as if nothing had ever happened. To this day "Dobe" isn't sure why Wayne behaved the way he did.

prominent dimple.

"How can you compete with that kind of an ego?" asked Robert.

He finally answered my question: "We get along perfunctorily. I say 'Hello' and the emperor acknowledges my greeting."

* * *

Harry "Dobe" Carey Jr. is one of the nicest men in pictures. He is a gentle, kind man and among the steadiest actors in the business. He resembles his famous father—a popular Western actor in silent and sound films—to a remarkable degree. Much of his innate gentility is a genetic tribute to his mother, Olive Golden Carey. Brother Robert knows her well and states, "Everyone who has ever known her has a warm word for Ollie Carey."

JOHN TREADWELL AND HIS AMAZING OXEN

ON THAT SAME meadow location, I saw two amazing incidents involving oxen. The herd of thirty massive bovines was under the care of John Treadwell, a huge New Englander who was as taciturn as he was gigantic. One day the front wheels of the Chapman, a huge motor-driven camera crane, lodged in a narrow stream and could not be budged free.

"Can your oxen pull it out?" the camerman asked.

"We'll see," snapped John, starting off vigorously. His favorite team was lying quietly on the grass. As he passed them (without touching or looking at them) he ordered, "Tim, Tom, follow me." We all looked in amazement as the beasts got to their feet, obediently following John like docile dogs.

They pulled the Chapman out of the ditch so easily that we all shook our heads in awe of their strength.

A few days later I saw an ox standing alone, staring off to the east with a great tear rolling down his cheek. Treadwell was walking nearby so I called to him. "What's the matter with your ox?"

"Homesick."

"Homesick?" I looked around at the truly grandiose setting of mountains, streams, meadowland and forest. "You've got to be kidding."

"No," said John somberly. "He wants to go home."

I suddenly realized that an ox from Massachusetts might not give a hoot about the grandeur of the Cascades.

❄ ❄ ❄

In "The Way West," Roy Glen, a fine Black actor, played Kirk's servant. One day we were shooting in Christmas Valley, located in eastern Oregon's high desert country.

Stubby Kaye, a rotund character actor who was best known for his comedy roles, sat in a director's chair absorbing the hot sun. "Ah," he crowed, "I live most of the time in either London or New York. I never get a chance to sunbathe like this. Why, I'm getting as black . . . " He froze in embarrassment, for Glen was suddenly standing in front of him. Stubby looked up at Roy, his eyes wide with concern. Roy just walked slowly by, stopping at the last moment to deliver his riposte: "Stubby, ain't you got enough trouble just being Jewish?"

Comedy character actor Stubby Kaye.

❄ ❄ ❄

One Sunday morning Stubby asked me if I'd drive him to the Safeway store in Bend. "I'm on a diet," he moaned. "I need to get some yogurt."

When we entered the store, Stubby was confronted by a large, florid farmer wearing bib overalls, a much-washed blue shirt and red bandanna. He towered over the thickset actor.

"Mah whoman wants yore aw-der-graph." The farmer pointed at his "whoman"—red of face and holding two squirming offspring under her arms like sacks of flour—who half-hid her face. "She's too 'mbarrassed to ask, but I ain't too 'mbarrassed."

Stubby shook his head in disbelief. "Why in the world would she want *my* autograph?"

"I know who you are. Yep. I know." The man winked at Stubby, nodding his head in smug affirmation.

I looked at Stubby and saw a gleam come into his eyes. "Who am I?" he asked blandly.

"Ah, hell!" The farmer stuck his jaw out aggressively and proudly responded: "Yore Choby Checkers!"

Somewhere in Oregon, "Choby" Checkers' "aw-der-graph" is a treasured keepsake, for that's the name Stubby Kaye penned on the envelope that the farmer thrust on him.

GRIST FOR THE MOVIE MILL

HAL GRIST HAS probably signed more autographs than anyone in the film business. On "The Way West" location, autograph hounds swarmed over the territory like army ants on a march. Now, in the Oregon desert, the film company was inundated by carloads of folks who had discovered that a picture was being shot where normally there were only sand dunes and rattlesnakes. Their cry—pen and slivers of paper in hand—was invariably, "Are you anybody?"

Hal Grist would answer these queries with solemn gravity: "*The* most important man on the location." The pens would be thrust forward with startling vigor.

Hal wasn't lying. His function was to furnish the "honey wagons," large, departmentalized portable toilets. Without him, those distant barren locations would be—uh—difficult.

❄ ❄ ❄

Autograph seekers should be more keenly aware that the stars they approach are human beings often beset with problems of their own. Just as Stubby Kaye bridled quietly at being labeled "Choby Checkers," so did

Hal Grist, posing with one of his all-important Honey Wagons. Believe me, there's nothing sweeter than a Honey Wagon when the urge comes upon you on those days when you're out in the middle of the prairie with no gas stations around.

Brother Robert take umbrage against a young man who worked in a 31 Flavors ice cream parlor in Santa Barbara.

The youth realized that he had seen Bob on the screen but had no earthly idea *who* he was. So, he bravely thrust a pen and paper at Bob, asking for the signature while confessing ignorance of his true identity. Bob sighed deeply and penned a forgery. I saw the progress of the flowing pen and heaved a sigh of my own.

There, on the white paper, was boldly written a grand name: "John Foster Dulles."

"Are you anybody?"

CLIFFHANGER AT CROOKED RIVER GORGE

THE CROOKED RIVER Gorge played a frightening role in "The Way West" in a manner unforeseen by the production company. In the story the wagon train must be dismantled piecemeal, then lowered down the side of the gorge. The production unit actually set up a primitive crane device—much like the original settlers must have used—that would lower people, equipment and farm animals into the canyon.

Loggers working as extras on the film tried to advise the production people that they should not use a pine log as their gin-pole. "Use fir," one of them warned. "Fir'll start to unravel before it breaks. Pine'll snap and do it without warning."

The loggers were ignored.

The second unit cameraman and his assistant were lowered over the canyon rim to their destination—a small ledge about 200 feet down. From that vantage point they filmed cattle, horses, wagons and people being lowered over the side. Finished with the filming, the second unit signalled to be pulled up.

The two men and the wagon bed had been raised some twenty-five feet from their precarious ledge when the gin pole broke. Without warning.

Stuntman-director Hal Needham.

By a miracle, the plunging wagon bed did not bounce off the ledge but turned over, pinning the men beneath it. Had it not held fast, it would most certainly have plummeted them another two hundred and fifty feet to their deaths. Those of us at the bottom of the gorge were horrified when the log snapped. We didn't know for some time if the two men were alive or dead.

The stunt foreman was Hal Needham, the daredevil who later became famous for his directorial work on "Smokey and the Bandit" and "Cannonball Run" with Burt Reynolds. Needham and his crew, with the aid of several young Oregon mountain climbers, raced up those perilous slopes to aid the stricken camera team.

When they scampered onto the ledge, they found the cameraman in shock, crawling about on his knees, groping for his glasses with an enormous gash on his head. He was within inches

Kirk Douglas and Bob on the set of "The Way West": Back together again for the first time since that 1947 film noir classic, "Out of the Past." When Kirk wrote his memoirs, he never even mentioned this film.

of crawling into eternity when the rescuers pulled him back. The assistant was still pinned beneath the wagon; one leg had been almost torn from his body.

The stuntmen and the mountain climbers ingeniously devised two stretchers and lowered the injured men to the bottom of the canyon. In the meantime we cleared a path on the makeshift road by moving all the wagons by hand. A station wagon took the injured cameramen to the local hospital and they were flown to Los Angeles.

Just the day before the accident, the director, Andy McLaglen, had asked Bob to stand on a great, wedge-shaped rock on the canyon rim to simulate peering down at the route the train would be taking.

"No way!" protested Robert. "Not on that mother!"

McLaglen huffed and puffed about it but Robert prevailed.

In the morning, the rock wasn't there . . .

***

While still in Eugene, I met with folksinger Michael Whitney to tell him that the producer of "The Way West," Harold Hecht, wanted him to introduce the film with a song. We were in the Eugene Hotel's cocktail lounge when a local man—uninvited and most offensive—sat at our table.

"You boys are good ol' boys!" he claimed. He gave us his name, which I promptly forgot. I introduced him to Michael and told him that I was Herbert Witherspoon. (I've found that this ploy saves me from much explaining and a few knots on the head.) The local went on until he stepped into deep water.

"Now you boys are alright," he said. "But that Robert Mitchum—he's a no-account."

"How is that so?" Whitney asked quietly. Michael was a soft-spoken Huron Indian, standing at 6-foot-3 and weighing about 195.

"Well," went on the local, "I used to work in the service station across the street." He beamed at us. "I own it now." His smug superiority was getting a bit hard to accept. "That Robert Mitchum was doin' a picture ["River of No Return"] up here with Marilyn Monroe. He wanted his car washed so I washed it for him. He said I didn't do a good job. Why, that sorry s.o.b. He knew I did a good job. He— "

Whitney interrupted. "We were just kidding about 'Witherspoon.' That's not his name at all."

The station owner looked hard at me. "I thought that was a made-up name. What's your real name?"

"Let me introduce you to *John* Mitchum," said Michael.

The local reached out to shake my hand, panic in his eyes. "Ain't Bob a good ol' boy?" he cried out, promptly fleeing from the saloon. Mike and I clinked our glasses in a silent toast to his departure.

Reporter Al Reiss

While we were filming "The Way West," Al Reiss, who at that time was working for a Medford radio station as an entertainment reporter, and writing freelance for the *Medford Mail Tribune,* tried to get interviews with the series principals; he was actually too shy to be successful. So I lined up interviews for him with some of the cast. As a result we became great friends.

At that time Al had already won the Western States Playwriting Competition Award for "The Smallest Giant," a political satire that had been staged the year before at the Very Little Theater in Eugene.

Al also interviewed John Wayne when The Duke filmed "Rooster Cogburn" up at Grant's Pass, and came on the set of "Paint Your Wagon" while I was up at Baker, Oregon. He also came to San Francisco in 1976 to cover the making of "The Enforcer." An awful lot of fine radio interviews and newsprint came out of our lucky meeting on "The Way West."

When I contacted Al in 1988, he informed me that he had written eleven regional plays, of which six had been produced. And in 1970 he won the John Masefield Memorial Award for narrative poetry. He was still with the *Tribune* writing movie and drama reviews, interviews and consumer stories related to the entertainment field.

He reminded me of the time when we were making "The Way West" and how I had climbed out of my car late one afternoon, dressed in my pioneer's costume, all dusty and grungy. A motorist in a nearby car gave me the once-over and remarked, "Traveled a long way, did you?"

He also reminded me how Bob would occasionally come to the motel where Nancy and I were staying to chew the fat. One day the maid recognized Bob's car outside and knocked on the door, under the pretext of delivering fresh linen. "Always a magnet, always drawing attention," said Al. "Bob can never escape it."

A Splinter Group Member

Here I am as "Elmer," the crooked bartender in Howard Hawks' "El Dorado," right after a simulated rifle bullet fired by Bob has driven several bartop splinters into my hand.

PRACTICAL JOKE— HOWARD HAWKS STYLE

IN 1966 I worked in "El Dorado" (the loose remake of Howard Hawks' 1959 film "Rio Bravo"), playing the part of the bartender in the saloon frequented by the "bad guys" Ed Asner and Christopher George. Bob played the drunken sheriff who had lost his pride to booze, and John Wayne played his friend who brought him back from the brink of disaster.

James Caan had the role of the jester and Arthur Hunnicutt was, well, Arthur Hunnicutt.

When Brother Robert comes into the saloon to confront the "baddies," I inch my hand across the bar top toward a gun I have beneath the bar. He barks a command at me.

"Elmer, keep your hand away from that gun!"

(Bob always used to sneak Elmer Jones' name into a film somewhere, as a tribute to our life-long friend.)

I once again try to move my hand off the bar and go for the gun. Bob fires a rifle bullet under my hand. When I pull it up, pre-set splinters obstensibly are imbedded in it. Of course, the rifle bullet's "impact" is a special effects powder squib implanted in the bar.

Hawks had told me the squib would go off on the count of three. He had it set to go off on "one." The look on my face was *not* acting.

Mick Martin, the author of the best-selling "Video Movie Guide," told me that although he has seen the picture a dozen times, he still laughs every time he sees my expression.

In that same film, Wayne belts Bob over the head with a copper spittoon. The look on Brother Robert's face is priceless. His *was* acting. No one could ever look like that for real.

Time magazine wrote of Bob and Duke in "El Dorado": ". . . with crutches as swagger sticks, they limp triumphantly past the camera; two old pros demonstrating that they are better on one good leg apiece than most of the younger stars are on two."

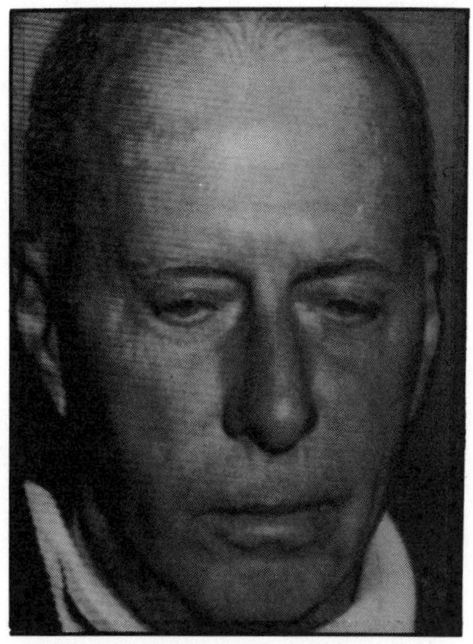

Director Howard Hawks.

❄ ❄ ❄

Bob worked in "That Championship Season" in 1982. One of his co-stars was Bruce Dern. I asked Bob what Dern was like to work with. His reply was succinct. "He hasn't yet learned that acting is not a competitive business."

❄ ❄ ❄

When "El Dorado" was released, Elmer Jones came down to see it, delighted to find that I was "Elmer." The last time Bob and I had seen him had been during the Watts riots in '65. Jonesy had owned a used car lot in Venice at that time and his cars were more than used; they were one step away from being pitiful.

The majority of Jonesy's clients were Blacks. He sold his cars for as low as $15 a week, but if they missed one payment, he'd pick the car up. He put a .38 in his belt whenever he saw an irate customer come onto the lot, then he'd meet him with both the revolver and his huge Shepherd dog in plain view. Bob and I fell down laughing when we visited his lot one time, for Jonesy had put up a huge banner on butcher paper. It read in great black letters:

SOUL BROTHER!

Now he had his right hand heavily bandaged, the result of a fight with his ex-wife's new husband. Elmer's son had called, telling him that the stepfather was beating both him and his sister. Jonesy drove from Watts to Bakersfield to confront the new husband. He was a Marine, half Elmer's age, and had won the "Physical Fitness Award" of the year. He made the mistake of challenging Jonesy. The leatherneck wound up crawling on his hands and knees in a terrified effort to get away from the enraged Elmer.

Jonesy had broken his hand on the Marine and he was still wielding it like a bloody club on the man's head when the police came just in time to keep the stepfather from being killed. There were no charges against Elmer.

THE SUPER CHIEF

"F TROOP," a television comedy satire on cowboys and Indians, was in full swing at Warner Bros from 1965 to 1967, starring Forrest Tucker, Larry Storch and Ken Berry. In intermittent segments, I portrayed Hoeffenmueller, a German who spoke no English but was still the translator for the Indians.

Tucker, who played a con man named Sgt. Morgan O'Rourke, became a good friend. I am happy to say that the tales about his sexual prowess, so legendry as to sound apocryphal, are true. One revealing incident—told to me by Tuck himself—took place on the 18th green at the Lakeside Country Club, where he was golfing with Phil Harris and Phil Crosby.

Tuck reached down on the green to pick up his ball—it was only two feet from the cup—when Harris ordered, "Sink it!"

Tuck fumed. "I've been giving you guys 'gimmes' all day. You mean I have to sink this?"

Crosby nodded along with Harris. "Sink it."

Tuck, so endowed by nature that he called his appendage "The Chief," now angrily avowed that he could sink the putt with The Chief.

Forrest Tucker was one of the more flamboyant characters in Hollywood and steadily made films and TV shows from 1940, when he debuted in "The Westerner" with Gary Cooper, until his death in 1987. The "film noir" photo at left clearly shows his dramatic side, which he displayed in "The Sands of Iwo Jima," "Warpath" and "Bugles in the Afternoon." That's him at right, showing off his comedy abilities as O'Rourke of "F Troop."

"Let's see you," challenged Harris.

Tuck unzipped his trousers, knelt on one knee, positioned The Chief, and swung. He sank the putt.

❄❄❄

I once did a show for Tuck at a golf tournament in Phoenix, Arizona, with Phil Harris as the emcee. When he came to the mike, it was a foot too high, and he had a great difficulty loosening it up. Phil looked at the crowd and remarked, "This is the first time I'd ever had trouble gettin' it *down!*"

❄❄❄

Phil told me that one night Tuck had imbibed too much Scotch at Phil's house in Beverly Hills. Because Tuck lived across the Santa Monica mountains in Toluca Lake, Phil insisted that the inebriated Irishman spend the night with him. He called Marion, then Tuck's wife, explaining the situation.

Marion was most grateful that Phil wouldn't allow Tuck to traverse the canyon roads in his condition.

When Tuck came out of the shower that next morning, Phil did a double-take. "Tucker," he said, "do me a favor. Every night, before you go to bed, put out a bowl of warm milk for that thing or some night it's gonna turn on you."

❄❄❄

Phil Harris, who's been married to Alice Faye since 1941, has proven himself to be an all-around talent in radio, TV and movies—not only as a comedian but as a dramatic actor as well. His radio comedy show of the 1940s still holds up as a classic.

Tucker's personality permeated the entire "F Troop" company and made it a pleasure to be working. And Bob Steele added a nice codicil to the aura. Bob, a popular cowboy star in the 1930s who had turned into a damn good character actor in later years, had given up drinking for some time by then. In one scene Tucker, as the owner of a saloon, had his troop line up to drink beer and add to his coffers. Beer can't be faked. Foam is foam and tap beer must be real. Bob raised his stein in a toast. "Only for Forrest Tucker."

Thank God we did it in one take.

CONFRONTATION WITH LEE MARVIN

In 1958 I had filmed two segments of "M Squad," a network crime series set in Chicago and starring Lee Marvin. Granted, Lee was a tough ex-Marine, a hard-drinking bastard, but I liked him.

Now in 1968 I was working on "Paint Your Wagon" in Baker, Oregon, with Marvin starring. A helicopter flew me to the location that I might be ready for the next day's shooting. I played the part of Jacob Woodling, the Mormon with two wives, one of whom was the exquisite but tragic Jean Seberg.

Dressed in my Mormon's costume, I was approached by Lee, who was very drunk. He grabbed me by the lapels and snarled, "Well, *Mitchum!* Tonight, when we wrap, why don't you wear your wardrobe down into Baker so people will know you're an *actor*?"

Many thoughts coursed through my mind, mainly about my dear friend, Jon Locke, who had been badly misused by Lee. Jon played the banjo and sang barroom songs. Once, at the China Trader in Burbank, Jon had been

Lee Marvin wasn't the easiest guy to get along with after he'd had a few too many, but I always respected his talent. That's him playing Lt. Frank Ballinger on "M Squad" at left, in the episode "Dolly's Bar" that aired on NBC on Feb. 7, 1958. And that's him sitting in the window at right, in a scene from "Paint Your Wagon," the musical Western in which I played a Mormon miner.

performing when Lee, swaying like a cobra in front of him, suddenly launched a karate chop in Jon's direction. The blow destroyed Jon's antique banjo—and broke his cheekbone. They settled out of court. So you can see why I had my reservations about the bodacious Marvin.

Now, what in the hell is the sane thing to do? I can hit with the impact of an anvil. Should I upend this actor? No, I'd immediately be on a plane heading for Los Angeles, blackballed from the industry. You don't cold-cock a "star" without paying a price. I shook myself gently loose from the belligerent Lee and walked away.

Later, I found out the reason for Marvin's violent challenge—Tyrone Cabeen had dressed him down. "Lee," Cabeen had said, "I baby-sat for [Robert] Mitchum at MGM and he'd drink until six in the morning. He'd arrive on the set at seven and not miss a line. *You* have two beers and you don't know your ass from the Grand Canyon. For Chrissake, why don't you recognize your limitations?"

Lee gave no heed to his limitations but the name "Mitchum" had its effect. Ol' Tyrone had come close to getting me mightily involved.

The confrontation resolved itself when the rushes of my scenes as the Mormon were shown to the company. Marvin stood up before the entire cast and roared, "At last we've got somebody on the set with balls!" It was his oblique way of apologizing.

George Fargo told Jean Seberg that the hordes of little white flowers growing on the surrounding Oregon hillsides were psychedelic when smoked. She believed him and picked a bushel and dried them in her

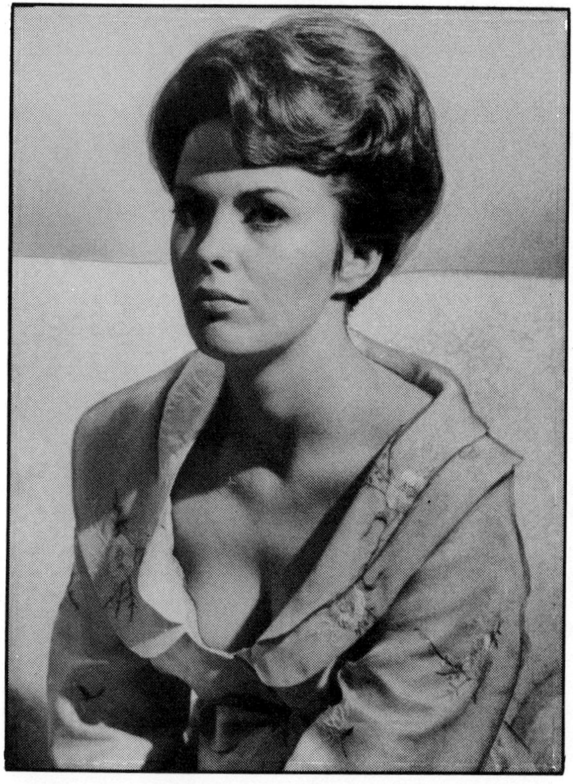

Jean Seberg was a homespun Iowa girl who was picked from thousands of hopefuls by Otto Preminger for the lead in "St. Joan." That film failed but it launched Jean on a career that took her to considerable popularity in Europe. She was married three times in her frustrated search for happiness. One wonders if she wouldn't have found it in Iowa, without all the stardom and hoopla. Or was she doomed either way?

When Bob and I were making "El Dorado" at Paramount in 1966, we were visited by our stepfather, Major Hugh Cunningham Morris, and our mother Ann. They struck a rather stately pose while Bob looks like he stayed in character as Sheriff L. B. Hurrah, who was usually getting over a hangover in the picture. Did I tell you that the Major once captained a refrigerator barge during World War II? He used to make his own fruit brandy aboard ship and then exchange it for fresh ice cream from battleships and destroyers passing by. He had the greatest ingenuity of any man I've ever known.

company-rented house oven. The crew had a good laugh over that—which is now a sour memory. In 1979, on a Parisian sidestreet, she was found dead in her car—victim of a self-intended overdose. She had been lying there on the seat for several days. Whenever I remember her beauty, her charm and talent I can't help but wonder why.

Why are people driven to such inner despair that they die by their own hand when everything is out there for them to savor and to love? Why are not the mountains, the deserts, the seas, and the stars enough to make us aware of the immensity of God's love?

Eddy Little Sky

❄ ❄ ❄

During the filming of "Paint Your Wagon," Eddy Little Sky, a full-blooded Oglala Sioux and a fine professional actor, asked me one beautiful Sunday morning to drive him to a powwow in Le Grande, Oregon. I eagerly agreed. Since I'm a quarter Blackfoot, I have a great deal of interest in all things Indian.

Eddy introduced me to a Modoc standing in front of his teepee. The Modoc eyed me passively. "You got any Indian?"

I assured him that I did.

"What tribe?"

"The warmest, nicest, kindest tribe of all the nations," I crooned.

"What tribe?" It was a command.

"Blackfoot," I stated proudly.

He glared at me fiercely. "You don't know those sons o' bitches like we do!" And he kept on glaring.

I was not exactly a smash hit at the powwow, but I was Eddy's friend so I was grudgingly accepted.

RIDING AGAIN WITH JOHN WAYNE

IN 1969 I worked in a Western titled "Chisum," starring John Wayne as John S. Chisum, the famous New Mexico cattleman who figured prominently in the Lincoln County War of 1878. Other historical figures in the story were William Bonney (Billy the Kid) and the English-born cattleman John H. Tunstall. Tuck played the bad guy who starts the range war while Bob Donnor and I played crooked deputies in his employ. In the re-enactment of an infamous scene from Western history, Bob and I waylay and murder the gentle Tunstall, played by Patric Knowles.

Brother Robert had worked with Patric in "The Big Steal" and "The Way West," introducing me to him while we were on that epic Western.

While shooting "Chisum" in Durango, Mexico, Patric and I would often walk from our motel into town for the exercise. He had been a close friend to Errol Flynn, so I told him of the only time I had met the hellraising New Zealander.

I'd been working on a boat called The Memory, *anchored off Avalon. Flynn came aboard to join the ongoing party while my friend Elmer Jones and I washed dishes.*

Flynn appeared at the galley door, stuck his hand out to our sudsy grasps and grinned at us. "Goodnight, you chaps," then he was gone.

"That was Errol," said Patric, nodding as I finished my story. "Didn't like the fluff, always felt more at home with the workers."

Patric launched into a story of his own. "Errol and I were at a garden party in Beverly Hills. It was a huge estate, complete with every kind of tree and flower . . . When Flynn was thoroughly surrounded by gasping females, he found himself in desperate need to pee. No way could he get away and into the house.

"Suddenly," Patric continued, "he disappeared and only I saw him duck into the folds of the pampas grass at the end of the garden. That is, only I and a large English sheep dog frolicking around the yard. The dog followed Errol in, then came out from the hidden area shaking his hairy head.

"'What a lovely animal!' cried one young starlet. She was stroking its massive head when a glazed look spread over her face. Wordlessly she rose and floundered off toward the house, her hands glistening in the sunlight and held well away from her lovely gown. I looked at Flynn," chortled Patric. "He looked as though he were about to wet his pants again, laughing!"

❄ ❄ ❄

While I was in Durango, Tuck phoned, asking if I'd come over to his suite. He explained that a friend had written a song about Chicago.

Patric Knowles, a distinguished British actor who has also been a novelist, a community leader, a lecturer on films and directing, a Shakespeare scholar and a student of horticulture.

"I'm from that area so whenever I do a stage show there, I'm asked to sing 'Chicago.' I'm getting tired of it. I want a new song. This friend of mine in Hollywood sent one. I want you to hear it, give me your opinion of it."

I went over and heard the song. It was a namby-pamby and Tucker saw my negative reaction.

"Damn!" he exploded. "I knew it. It's no good, is it?"

"It's not that, Tuck." I groped for the right answer. "It's just not *you*."

"Damn!" the 6-foot-4, brawling Irishman burst out again. "I'm really disappointed."

"I'll write you a song," I said without thinking.

"You will?"

"Yes, I will." I left for my room. Within two hours, I called him back.

"I've got a song for you, Tuck. Do you want to hear it?"

"Hell, yes, John. Bring it over."

I went to his suite and sang him the song. He liked it so much that I gave it to him.

As they say in show business, it goes something like this:

CHICAGO — MY HOME TOWN

It's a giant of a town—it's a roilin,' broilin' town,
Where a thousand rails of steel scar the earth.
It's a fun-lovin' town—it's a hard-workin' town.
Where a man can be proud of his birth.

There's a lake by the town—it's a giant of a lake,
Where ships from every nation come to call.
And those men off those ships walk her streets in admiration
For Chicago! It's the town that runs it all.

(CHORUS)

They call her the Windy City
But I call her my home town.
I can't even say that she's pretty
But she's mine—and the best that I've found.

Well, hello! to old Chicago,
Where the lights from the Loop light the night.
Where the wind off the Lake really does blow
With a nip and a zip and a bite.

Now the Gold Coast of Chicago
Will never ever let you down.
Your love for her will grow and grow—
It's Chicago—my home town.

Tucker beamed. "It's mine? You're giving it to me?"

"Absolutely. I don't know anyone other than you that it fits."

Tucker expressed so much interest in my writings that I recited my poem "Why Are You Marching, Son?" which I had written after my fourteen- year-old son flung down a newspaper, exploding in anger over a photograph of dissidents burning the American flag in Central Park.

I unabashedly love my country. I have travelled it in such a manner as to rub elbows with every strata of society, finding the great majority of my countrymen to be a warm and generous people.

My son had thrown down the gauntlet. I couldn't rush to New York, wielding a sword against the ingrates, but I took pen to paper. "Why Are You Marching, Son?" was formed. Tuck was visibly impressed.

John Wayne in "Chisum."

WHY ARE YOU MARCHING, SON?

Why are you marching, son? . . . I'd really like to know!
Is it because of Valley Forge . . . or perhaps the Alamo?
"One if by land—two if by sea,"
A trumpet's call . . . the will to be free?
And what of a man who stood straight and tall,
Who wept silent tears when he saw brave men fall?

No matter—no difference—the blue or the gray,
All were his brothers . . . how often he'd pray.
And what of Antietam . . . that now peaceful stream
Where the water, blood-red, glittered and gleamed?
Appomattox . . . Chickamauga . . . Vicksburg . . . Bull Run,
Cumberland . . . Gettysburg . . . and then Washington.

Why are you marching, son?

In Flanders Field . . . how proud were they,
Whose forms beneath the poppies lay.
Men who saw Verdun . . .
And died at the Marne . . . Soisson . . .
And those who tried the fearful foe at Chateau-Thierry,
Who fought and bled . . . whose hearts grew weary,
But in whose minds one thought kept churning . . .
That the torch of liberty keep burning.

Why are you marching, son?

The planes swarmed in . . . and the rising sun
Glowed fiercely on the evil done
To men whose blood runs through our veins.
Men who died, and whose remains
Lie forever locked in waters deep.
Now is it right that they should sleep
While the warm sea laps at a twisted hull
And see the torch of liberty grow dull?
Anzio . . . Cassino . . . and the Po!
St. Mere Eglise . . . Le Mans . . . St. Lo!
Gardelagen . . . Buchenwald . . .
On and on the roll is called!

And why . . . Why are you marching, son?

Bugles shrilled in the frozen night
And at first dawn, the awful sight
Of seas of men . . . row after row,
Left to die on blood-stained snow!
Pusan . . . Pyongyang . . . Suwan . . . Kyongju!
And blood-red ran the swift Yalu!

In South Vietnam the big guns roared,
And once again we fought a war
To honor a pledge our nation gave
To help that little country save
Her people from the certainty
That she'd be ruled by tyranny.

No matter where the big guns roar,
Our fighting men, like those before,
Take the torch we all held dear,
And face freedom's enemies without fear.
Our fathers died from sea to sea,
And blessed the torch of liberty.

Why? . . . Why are you marching, son?

RIDING AGAIN WITH JOHN WAYNE

THE NEXT MORNING, Tuck took me by the arm and marched me straight over to the Duke. He was playing a game of chess with my nephew, Chris Mitchum. Wayne looked up at Tuck as he planted himself before him. "Duke, you've got to listen to what Mitch has written."

Wayne stopped the chess game and drawled, "Well, go ahead. I'm listenin'."

I recited "Why Are You Marching, Son?" Halfway through it, the battle-hardened Duke had tears in his eyes.

Tucker looked intently at him. "If it means that much to you, why don't you record it?"

John reached out and took my hand. "I will," was his answer. And he did.

Two years later, during one of many recording sessions at RCA in Hollywood for what had grown into a major record album, "America, Why I Love Her," Wayne and I were having lunch at the Brown Derby. He excused himself to go to the men's room. When he returned he was looking down at his trouser leg in exasperation.

"It happens every time," he groaned as he sat down. "I'm at a public urinal and some joker is going full force next to me. He'll see me out of the corner of his eye, recognize me and whip toward me in uncontrolled excitement. 'Why, you're John Wayne!'" Duke shook his head ruefully. "Every time. Right in midstream!"

Billy Liebert, a very good musician and composer, handled the recording sessions. Wayne had a difficult time recording the lyrics. He would take sips of Jack Daniels to ease his pain. Most of the time he would spit the whiskey out, but once in awhile he would look at us apologetically and say, "Oops, that one slipped away."

In hindsight, it is obvious that the cancer that finally took him in the summer of 1979 was hindering his breathing and his ability to talk in long sentences. The man was dying, but he had said he'd cut the record, and he did. His word was always his bond.

There was a great tenderness in John Wayne, exemplified when he read the lyrics from "Taps": ". . . and the savagery of the conflict was grimly evident in the river of wounded that wound through the green hills. Now a

John Wayne's "America, Why I Love Her" (RCA, LSP-4828), which today is coveted by collectors, included ten cuts, nine of which I wrote or co-wrote: "Why I Love Her," "The Hyphen," "Mis Raices Estan Aqui," (My roots Are Buried Here), "The People," "An American Boy Grows Up," "The Good Things," "The Pledge of Allegiance," "Why Are You Marching, Son?" and "Taps." In 1977 Simon and Schuster issued a special book edition, filled with photographs, sheet music and a foreword by John Wayne.

new sound drifted in the soft, evening sky. On July 2nd, in the year of 1862, its strains floated over the graves that scarred the dark Virginia earth."

(At this point, all that is heard is a purely clear, single trumpet playing "Taps." The notes soar into the sky, then, halfway through it, Wayne's voice comes back in.)

"It's been more than a hundred years since that sound was born . . . "

John looked at me with tears welling from his eyes. "Mitch," he whispered softly, "aren't the people gonna get mad at me for talkin'?"

***

At the James Peninsula, the Seven Days' War laid the groundwork for the story of "Taps." Colonel Dan Butterfield, a New Yorker, was a man of music and letters. In order to forestall his men being killed by Rebels while firing volleys over their dead, he penned the now hallowed notes. "Play these," he informed his bugler, "at our next funeral."

THE SIGNS OF WINTER

BOB ADMITTED to me in the late '60s that he was getting tired. He had done eight films in three years (1967-'69) and they had entailed a great deal of travelling—with little artistic satisfaction for his actor's ego. "Anzio" (directed by Edward Dmytryk) was a World War II epic about the disastrous landing in Italy in 1944. Did I say disastrous? Bob had never been happy with the script, and he felt the end result was not a good one.

He rode aimlessly through "Villa Rides" with Yul Brynner and Charles Bronson. In "Five Card Stud," a Western remake of a story first told in the 1950 feature, "Dark City," Bob once again played a villainous brimstone preacher, "elected by God and Mr. Colt," named Reverend Jonathan Rudd. Katherine Justice, with whom he had worked on "The Way West," and his old friend, Dean Martin, aided and abetted him on that one, along with Roddy McDowall, Inger Stevens and Yaphet Kotto.

In "Secret Ceremony," directed by Joseph Losey, he came away quite bewildered. In the George Tabori script, he played a bathtub scene with Mia Farrow. When the film was released, Bob was startled to see that same scene now featured Farrow with Elizabeth Taylor. No Mitchum in sight.

"There was Mia, licking Elizabeth's back," Bob snorted.

"Apparently lesbianism had become the in-thing. I wouldn't have known how to handle that!"

Bob on location in Spain, looking very bored as he waits for his next call to camera while making "Villa Rides!" He never cared much for this picture, in which he plays an early aviator-adventurer who joins the Mexican Revolution to become a one-man air force. In his study of Western movies, Brian Garfield writes: "The acting by everybody, even including Mitchum, is distressing."

Western Action in the Mitchum Style

"Young Billy Young" (1969) starred Bob as Ben Kane, a lawman searching for his son's murderer with the help of a young gunfighter nobody much likes. It featured the offspring of several established stars: Robert Walker Jr., David Carradine, Deana Martin and my nephew, Chris Mitchum.

In 1969's "Young Billy Young"—which Bob co-produced through his Talbot Company—he worked with Angie Dickinson and David Carradine. Bob, who portrayed a cowboy, Ben Kane, out to avenge his son's death in the town of Lordsburg, found Angie to be one of the nicest gals one could work with. However, he was wryly amused at David Carradine's ineptness as a horseman—on the first take that required David to mount a horse, he put his right foot into the stirrup. The director, Burt Kennedy, yelled "Cut" and Bob chided him for stopping the scene.

"Why didn't you let him carry on? It would have been interesting to see him riding into the sunset backwards."

Carradine was also in "The Good Guys and the Bad Guys" with Bob, George Kennedy, Martin Balsam, Tina Louise and Lois Nettleton.

My only meeting with Carradine became a confrontation. He came over to my house once with Billy Records, a studio technician. David stretched out on my living room floor and asked me for coffee.

He watched me pour it from the pot into a cup, took a big swig then spat it out. "Christ!" he exploded. "This is boiling hot!" I told him that since he had watched me pour it, I assumed that he would have deduced as much.

"You spoiled my acid, man." He took off his neckerchief, digging three coffee-stained sugar cubes from its folds. I told him that I didn't allow drugs in my home. David had the audacity to tell me he had already laced my sugar bowl with LSD. I poured the sugar into the sink, brought out the machete I kept around the house and said, "David, if you'd do a thing like that, I'd have your head on a pike pole in my front yard as a warning to anyone else who might think it's cute."

He looked at me with that unfeeling look I saw so many times on "Kung Fu." "Man, you come on strong, don't you?"

I looked at the machete. It was a deadly thing. "Just try me!"

He never did. And that was the last time he came over.

Bob spent only ten days shooting "Secret Ceremony" in England and Holland. It was a strange psychological drama starring Elizabeth Taylor and Mia Farrow that did okay at the box office, even though Bob didn't think much of it. For its television showing, Universal re-edited the film, cutting some scenes and adding others. It was directed by Joseph Losey, an American film maker blacklisted in the '50s who escaped to England where he continued a successful career.

"The Good Guys and the Bad Guys" was an amusing comedy directed by Burt Kennedy that teamed Bob with George Kennedy in a fight against a gang of young kids led by David Carradine. Lois Nettleton (in scene at right) provided the love interest. Others in the cast: Tina Louise, Douglas Fowley, Martin Balsam, John Davis Chandler and John Carradine.

MAYHEM—IRISH STYLE

SCREENWRITER Robert Bolt called Bob, asking him if he would play the part of a schoolteacher in David Lean's "Ryan's Daughter" with Trevor Howard, John Mills and Sarah Miles. Bob liked the role but he wasn't interested in working as hard as the script hinted at. Bob begged off, even going so far as to tell Bolt that he had plans to commit suicide in the immediate future. Bolt's answer got to Bob's funnybone. "Well, if you will just do this wretched little film of ours, you could *then* do yourself in!"

His resolve broken, Bob soon found himself off to Dingle, Ireland. He worked on the film almost a year. When it was released, he was the only actor acclaimed in it. The other thespians emoted so heavily that *his* gentle approach to the role made the character of Charles Shaughnessy stand out like a rose in a herd of water buffalo.

"In Dingle, I was invited to a lovely cocktail party and buffet," Bob told me. "I was head-down, concentrating on carving a piece of turkey when—for no discernable reason—some clown hit me a thunderous shot in the eye. The pain was so great that I was momentarily stunned, but I tried to pierce him through with the carving knife. He ran down the stairs but my stunt-double, a big, double-tough Englishman, tackled him and brought him to bay.

"Down at the Constable's office, I pressed charges against the idiot, but the complacency of the constable made me aware that not much would be done about it. In a sprightly Irish accent the lawman burbled, 'Down here they call it mayhem. It happens all the time.'"

Bob never did find out the reason for the cowardly sock in the eye.

I guess it was another example of those "Let's get the big star when he's not looking" acts.

* * *

In the spring of '70, my nephew Christopher met a ship's radio operator on a London-to-America voyage. His name was George McMichen and he told Chris that he had a screenplay based on the career of Lieutenant William Calley, who was then being held at Fort Benning, Georgia, on charges of taking part in the 1968 My Lai massacre in Vietnam.

Chris, who was considering the idea of playing Calley, asked me to contact McMichen, who by that time had graduated from a law school in Georgia and was a practicing attorney in Atlanta.

I telephoned McMichen, who asked me if I would fly to Georgia and interview Lt. Calley. It was McMichen's opinion that Calley, who was faced with almost 100 counts of premeditated murder, was a scapegoat being used by the U.S. Army to cover up higher ranking officers.

I met McMichen at the Atlanta airport and we drove straight to Fort Benning, but when we arrived we were politely informed by the Army that Calley would not be allowed an interview with us. We were both sorely disappointed; we felt Calley's story would have made a powerful film. (A few months later Calley was found guilty.)

❄ ❄ ❄

McMichen, a physical double for James Cagney, was a flamboyant personality. He took me to a nightclub owned by one of his clients, a man who had been involved in over 750 burglaries. Somehow, George had got him off and the goniff was extremely fond of his lawyer. At two in the morning, he closed the doors to his bar and we sat down to talk, only to be jarred by a thunderous pounding on the front door. The owner opened it to face a squad of somber policemen. Heading the group was a huge Black man,

Bob as schoolmaster Charles Shaughnessy in "Ryan's Daughter."

their captain, who crowed that he now had caught the owner red-handed serving liquor after hours; it was obvious that he would try to get the dismissed burglar on any charge possible.

"I'm his attorney, sir," said McMichen. "As you would have to testify, his door was locked in order that the general public not be allowed in. Therefore, this gathering must be construed as a private party and, as such, it exempts him from your harassment."

All of this flowed from McMichen with the stentorious pronouncements of courtroom rhetoric. The Captain furiously contended that it was not so. In his too-stiff cap and bright new uniform, he reminded me of a Gilbert and Sullivan line: "A policeman's lot is not a happy one."

"Do you wish me to call Judge Ball at this moment on that issue?" asked McMichen. Judge Ball was a powerhouse name in the local courts. As McMichen reached for the telephone, he casually stated that the Judge might be a little short-tempered at 2:30 a.m. The Captain and his squad melted into the night.

That same year I also worked on a film called "Big Foot," a bizarre tale of the legendary Pacific Northwest creature that has supposedly been seen in short glimpses in the deep woods. "Big Foot" starred John Carradine, a gentleman who is world's apart from some of his offspring.

I have been in several movies that could be labeled "Worst Picture of All-Time," but "Big Foot" qualifies as *The Worst*. It was directed by Robert F. Slatzer, whose major claim to fame is that he was married to Marilyn Monroe before she became famous. Big Foot was played by a seven-foot-tall Italian in an ill-fitting gorilla costume. Chris Mitchum and Lindsay Crosby headed a motorcycle gang attempting to snare the monstrosity.

Big Foot's offspring were enacted by midgets from Hollywood. One midget took off his gorilla suit to air himself out after climbing our phony mountain. "This is too fucking much!" he shouted.

He was absolutely right. How in the name of all that's good can funding be found for such horseshit when *good* films take years of hard work to get on the screen? And many *excellent* screenplays never make it at all.

Carradine played a promoter trying to capture B.F. and put him on exhibition. The only thing worthwhile on the shoot was watching Joi Lansing, a very voluptuous blonde who often played sexpots, run around the forest in a Baby Doll nightie. And Carradine's off-camera storytelling.

Late one night we sat up on top of the Hollywood Reservoir, in a dripping rain, exchanging past theater experiences. Carradine's was a classic.

"John Barrymore and I were performing 'Othello.' While we were in the makeup department, I asked him, 'John, I've often wondered, what was the last thing your father was in before he died?'

"The great star paused, then said, 'I'll ask Sam!' [Sam, in this case, was his sister, Ethel.] When he called down the hall to Ethel, he said, 'Sam, Carradine wishes to know what was the last thing father was in before he died?'

"Ethel's soft, elegant voice floated back, 'Mary Boland!'"

❄ ❄ ❄

"Big Foot" was previewed in a Reseda theater. After it was over, I furtively slunk out but a youngster stared intently at me, blurting out, "Hey, you were in— !"

I held up a warning finger. "Cool it!" and kept going until I was safely wrapped in the dark of night.

—BOOK SEVEN—

DAYS OF DIRTY HARRY

—BOOK SEVEN—

DIRTY HARRY IS BORN

IN THE SUMMER of 1971 I worked in "Dirty Harry" starring Clint Eastwood as a hard-edged cop, Harry Callahan, who packed a .44 Magnum. The director was Bob's old sparring partner, Don Siegel. We shot on location in San Francisco, a city I dearly love. George Fargo (Grey Cloud) had recommended me to Clint for the role of Frank di Georgio, the detective who would also serve as Harry's partner in the next two sequels, "Magnum Force" and "The Enforcer."

The filming of "Dirty Harry" was light years away from "Big Foot." Siegel was a top-notch director, Clint Eastwood was superb as Dirty Harry, and Harry Guardino as the mayor played his role flawlessly. A newcomer to films, Andy Robinson, was perfect as the maniacal Scorpio Killer and Reni Santoni blended in as Clint's partner who dies in blazing action.

Clint and George had been friends long before Clint's success in spaghetti Westerns, including "A Fistful of Dollars" which springboarded him to stardom. Back in the 1950s, even before Clint was a Universal-International contract player, doing bit parts in such films as "Revenge of the Creature" and "Tarantula," they had been journeymen carpenters together. On one job, Fargo was fired because of his never-ending joke-telling. The foreman looked up to see Clint putting on his shirt. "Where do you think you're going?" he snapped at the lantern-jawed actor.

Clint looked at him evenly. "You fired Fargo—you fired me." That incident was a good indicator to Clint's character. Not only is he a tremendous actor, he is a strong person, both physically and emotionally, with an incredible sense of loyalty.

While "Dirty Harry" was hard work, it had funny moments. One cold night at the old Kezar Stadium, near Golden Gate Park, Clint and I were to climb over the locked gate to enter the stadium grounds and track down Robinson (the killer), who is living in a deserted building. Clint climbed the wire gate easily. Fortunately the writers had foreseen the possibility that it might not be as easy for me. Clint points to my middle and I admit ruefully to "Too much lasagna" and search for an easier way.

That same night, while working at the stadium, our assistant make-up man, Bernie Abrams, went to a tiny all-night grocery to surprise the cast and crew with potato chips, dips and doughnuts. The store owners were small, dark, wiry men who looked at him indifferently while he put his purchases on the counter. He paid for the goodies, then erred. "Moseltoff," he chirped. (In Yiddish he had said "good luck" to the owner.)

"You Jew! You Jew!" one man screamed. "Me Ahrabb! Me Ahrabb!" The screamer promptly snatched the potato chips and other sundries to his chest, creating crackling sounds as the chips became sawdust.

Bernie asked him how long he had lived in America. "Born here! Born here!" the hysterical man shouted.

Harry Callahan, Badge #2211

Clint Eastwood as Dirty Harry Callahan (firing his trademark, a .44 Magnum, "the most powerful handgun in the world") in the climactic shootout filmed at a rock quarry near San Anselmo in Marin County. This is the sequence in which he throws Inspector's Badge #2211 into the water and walks away from law enforcement. Well, not really because it became the quintessential Eastwood role and Dirty Harry has returned in several sequels, though none of them has topped this great 1971 release.

"Then you and I're Americans. What's your problem?" The man's partner calmed the insanely furious clerk and made him release the treats.

"Not these!" said Bernie. "I paid for whole ones."

Bernie exchanged the crushed chips for a new bag. As he left, he could feel the knife in his back that the enraged Arab wanted to put there.

❄❄❄

During the filming it became apparent to Don Siegel that Clint's destiny involved his becoming a director. To that end Don insisted that Clint get his director's card and Don helped him to do so. Now Eastwood would be wearing two hats: He was primarily an actor, soon to be a director, and he had a vested interest in the films he would star in.

"We were shooting late at night in the south part of town," Don related to me. "I remember a big sign that dominated the street corner we used; it read 'Jesus Saves.' The special effects crew, a crack team, was laying miles of electric wires throughout the area to simulate a shoot-out effect. It was getting late and Clint came to me more than a little agitated. He wanted to know why we couldn't hurry up the process."

Don told Clint that the men on the job were the best and that if they weren't, he'd let them go. "'But I don't want anyone hurt on this picture, and this is one place where an accident could easily happen. So Clint, go to your trailer and close those baby blues of yours until we're ready for you.' Some time later, I was in my director's chair engrossed in the script. I felt just a featherlight kiss on my cheek and looked up just in time to see Clint disappearing in the darkness. It was his way of saying that I was right and he was wrong."

Siegel told me that one of the scenes in "Dirty Harry" filled him with

An image that has become a 20th Century icon: Eastwood and the .44 Magnum. And it can blow your head clean off. Are you feeling lucky, punk? . . . Well, are you?

Don Siegel only became one of Hollywood's finest directors after failing as an actor. He started by cutting montage sequences for films at Warner Bros. and graduated to directing in 1946 with "The Verdict," which starred Peter Lorre and Sydney Greenstreet. He's great with action and crime dramas: "Riot in Cell Block 11," "The Lineup" and "Hell Is for Heroes." He also directed John Wayne in his last film, "The Shootist."

apprehension. It was where I talk to Reni Santoni about Harry's umbrella of dislike for any partner he might be forced to work with. In it I covered a lot of people, for the dialogue refers to their ethnic backgrounds. Don told me that he feared the scene would label Clint as a bigot but that my delivery of the lines suddenly made him feel secure.

"He [Harry] hates everyone: Limies, Micks, Heebs, fat Dagos, Niggers, Honkies, Chinks. You name it."

Santoni asks me how Dirty Harry feels about Mexicans. Clint throws me a wink that belies the whole situation. "Especially Spics," he answers.

It becomes clear that his partners die on the job and he doesn't want to get too emotionally close to them. According to Siegel, my underplayed delivery and perfectly timed wink made it crystal clear to the viewer.

When the reviews of "Dirty Harry" came out, Siegel got the lion's share of the plaudits, and deservedly so.

* * *

One morning before shooting, George Fargo, Don Siegel and I were walking down the street to breakfast. A skid row derelict came up to panhandle us for a quarter. Fargo grabbed the bum by the collar, pulled him up close, thrust three dollar bills in his hand, then snarled, "Don't let me catch you buying coffee!"

George, a product of one of the toughest sections of Chicago, had a heart that surpassed most people's concept of love. I'm sure that his father had a great deal to do with his concepts, for George told us that his dad was "old world" Polish. He came to America seeking a better life, but spent most of it emptying garbage cans in apartment buildings. On his deathbed, he grasped George's hand, whispering a condemnation of all of those faceless people who had taken him for granted.

"They steal your effort," he said, sighing. Then he died.

The phrase haunts me to this day.

* * *

George's mother became an instant celebrity because of an unfortunate accident on the Hollywood Freeway. A truck carrying thousands of chickens overturned and the birds scattered in all directions. A few hundred took refuge in a wooded enclosure formed by the Ventura and Hollywood freeways. Beverly Garland's Hotel created the northern barrier to the chickens' range and Universal Studios, the southern.

Mrs. Fargo and an old friend of hers kept feeding the birds with leftovers from the garbage pails of a Chinese restaurant on Lankershim Boulevard in North Hollywood.

Eventually the birds became a potential traffic hazard. "What if they should fly into freeway traffic?" a bureaucrat downtown had asked. So the confrontation began.

Mrs. Fargo and her friend were intercepted by some of Los Angeles' bluecoats and told to cease and desist feeding the fowl. "How can the Animal Regulation Department catch them if you continue to feed them?"

Mrs. Fargo had an answer—in her thick Polish accent. "The chicken are hungry. The restaurant supplies free rice and sprouts. So jail the chicken!"

"Well, ma'am," a slick young minion of the law drawled, "if you continue to feed these chickens, I'm going to have to run you in."

Mrs. Fargo drew herself up to her 5-foot-1 and exploded: "Murder. Rape. Robbery. Steal. You want arrest me for feeding chicken?" She glared into a TV news camera for the world to see. "Go ahead!" She held out her arms to be manacled. "Arrest!"

The big cop did the only thing he could do: He sidled off into the growing crowd and became *persona non grata.*

MOONED BY ROBERT MITCHUM

BERNIE ABRAM'S confrontation with the two Arabs in San Francisco pinpointed the validity of the poem Howard Barnes and I wrote for the John Wayne album, "America, Why I Love Her." The poem was "The Hyphen" and describes how our nation is weakened when Americans hyphenate their heritages. As Wayne recites on the album, "We're Americans, and that says it all."

Barnes wrote the lyrics to a country classic, "But I Really Don't Want to Know." It has been recorded to date by over 720 artists. His lyrics, so tender and deeply reaching, bely his personality on occasion.

One day Howard and I drove over to Bel Air to see Bob, whom Howard had never met. Dorothy rather tersely explained that Bob was showering in his den bathroom. We went up the stairs to find the shower was going. When the water was turned off, I called out to let my errant brother know I had a guest with me.

Bob stepped out of the shower stall, hidden from view by an ell-shaped partition, and mumbled something about having to shave. He soon strode into the den, his face a grotesque mask of numerous nicks covered by blood-soaked dabs of toilet paper—which was all he was wearing.

He bent over and mooned the great composer. Much as a photographer might instruct a subject to look at the lens, Bob ordered Howard to "Look at the movie queen!"

Later, repentant and recuperating, Bob sat on a couch to explain that he suffered from a monumental hangover. We left him there, sipping from a bottle of port wine, so that he might recover in solitude.

As we drove away, puckish Howard told me that he had considered letting Robert know that he had a "nice smile."

On the San Diego Freeway, a sports car cut sharply in front of me, held for a moment, then darted off like a scared rabbit. Its bumper sticker read, "Have a nice day!"

Howard groused for ten miles. "'Have a nice day! Have a nice day!' Everybody in the damned country wants me to have a nice day. If I want to have a nice day, I'll have it. I don't need some silly bastard to tell me to have a nice day."

"Howard, the guy's probably in Bakersfield by now."

He grinned at me evilly. "Well, let's see *him* have a nice day *there!*"

❄❄❄

In 1949 Brother Bob had co-starred with Myrna Loy in Lewis Milestone's "The Red Pony," based on the John Steinbeck story. In 1971 I had my chance to work with Loy when I played an apartment house manager in

The triumphant triumvirate: Helen Hayes, Mildred Natwick and Sylvia Sydney in "Do Not Fold, Spindle or Mutilate," in which they carry out a practical joke that backfires.

the TV movie, "Do Not Fold, Spindle or Mutilate." Vincent Edwards, old Ben Casey himself, starred as a psychotic murderer who rented an apartment from me. Ted Post, whom I would work with again in '73 in "Magnum Force," was the director.

But I did Bob one better when I had the remarkable opportunity to work with not only Loy but three other great ladies of the stage and screen: Mildred Natwick, Sylvia Sydney and the immortal Helen Hayes. They were all such consummate pros that I found myself beaming inwardly to have been asked to work in such exalted company.

It has since occurred to me that someone should have been on the sidelines with a camera, photographing those four ladies. Their unobtrusiveness, poise and awareness of the process of filmmaking would be a valuable lesson for all aspiring actors. They funneled all of their energies to the camera. Nothing was wasted offstage.

Much later Ted Post told me that before the picture began, he had received a phone call from Loy (famous for playing Nora Charles in the "Thin Man" series), who was in New York City. For some moments, Ted felt that it must be impressionist Rich Little putting him on, but Myrna finally convinced him that it was really her. "I hear," said Loy, "that the Queen [Hayes] is doing a TV movie and that you're directing. I want to be in it."

Ted vowed that he would work it out, called the producer and found that he would be delighted to have Loy in the cast. A half hour after he relayed the good news to Loy, his phone rang again. "Ted Post? This is Sylvia Sidney calling from Connecticut. Myrna tells me that the Queen is doing a TV movie and you're directing. I want in."

❄ ❄ ❄

George Fargo called me to say that he had just heard from Lee Marvin, who had moved to Arizona so that he might be far removed from the temptations of the big city.

Loneliness would creep over Marvin from time to time, for he had wanted to talk to Fargo for no other reason than just to hear a familiar voice. This conversation, however, took a bent that only Fargo could have engineered.

"What are you doing these days?" Lee's voice seemed listless.

Sunny Buono in Mexico

In the still at right from "The Wrath of God" (1972), Bob is in Mexico with his good friend Victor Buono. Once again Bob played a priest, defrocked and with a gun concealed in his Bible. Once asked why he made such a terrible film with director Ralph Nelson, Bob replied, "I'll do anything to get out of the house." Buono, a brilliant wit and poet, weighed 300 pounds and fell victim to a heart attack on January 1, 1982, at the age of 43.

"Jerkin' off," replied the mercurial Fargo.
"Did you come yet?" asked the equally volatile Marvin.
"Not yet!"
"Why not?"
"Somebody stole my Betty Grable poster," snarled Fargo.

❄ ❄ ❄

Bob, playing another priest (one who slung a gun and slugged whiskey), teamed up with Victor Buono in late '71 to make "The Wrath of God" in Mexico for director Ralph Nelson, who had won an Oscar for "Lilies of the Field." While working in an old mine shaft, Victor rapped his head solidly against a beam and was taken to the company doctor, who soon pronounced him ready for duty. A short while later, Buono whacked his poor pate again. This time they took Victor to Mexico City for X-rays. When Buono came back to the location, Bob asked him how he was.

"Upset!" said the roly poly thespian, best known for his roles as oleaginous but articulate villains. "The doctor told me that I was surprisingly healthy and—for a man of 45 or so—was in excellent condition."

"What's so sad about that?"

Victor looked at Bob sorrowfully and said:

"I didn't have the heart to tell him I was only 32."

A MAN AS BIG AS A BONANZA

ON MAY 1, 1972, Dan Blocker underwent routine gall bladder surgery in Inglewood's Centinela Valley Hospital. He regained his strength quickly, so doctors sent him home. On Saturday, May 13, he began complaining to his wife Dolphia of a shortness of breath and excruciating pain. Dolph rushed him to Daniel Freeman Hospital, also in Inglewood.

By 4 p.m. that afternoon he was dead of a blood clot in his lung, a pulmonary embolism. It was a tremendous shock to all of us who knew the 6-foot-4, 260-pound actor. It happened so suddenly, it took a long time to register that the star of "Bonanza" was gone. Dan was a warm-hearted man, a very liberal man.

❄ ❄ ❄

Dan once told me of an incident during a "Bonanza" promotional tour in Louisiana, where the cast had been invited to a party hosted by a politically powerful man named Leander Perez, a fierce Louisiana segregationist who defied an order to desergregate parochial schools and was excommunicated from the Catholic Church as a result.

"Mr. Perez was a huge, bloated toad of a man who held all the reins in his parish," explained Dan. "One of his servants walked by so Perez looked at my empty glass and drawled, 'Niggah, get Mr. Blockuh a drink.'

"It offended me to hear him say that and I told him so. He stared at me with round, bulbous eyes and wheezed out, 'Mr. Blockuh, Ah could have you killed—jus' like that!' He snapped his fingers to accentuate his meaning. 'Ah don' tell folks what to do in *their* place. Don' you presume to tell me what to do in mine.'

"Perez then turned to the manservant. 'Are you a niggah or are you not?'

"The well-conditioned servant answered, 'Oh yes, Mr. Perez, Ah is a niggah.'

"Perez then turned to me. 'Mr. Blockuh, *he* knows *his* place! Do *you* know *yours*?'

"I excused myself from the party and took a cab back to my hotel. I've been acting so long, I'd forgotten that people like Perez ever existed for real."

Dan was haunted by Perez's arrogance and hatred. That great heart, so soon to be stilled, was as big as his body. He was only 42.

A 1962 photo of Judge Leander Perez: He looked as mean and unpleasant as he behaved the day "Bonanza" star Dan Blocker attended his party in the state of Louisiana.

THE DAYS OF DUSTY DIRTY, THE SAGA OF SEED SACKER

TIME steadily takes its toll . . . Two of Bob's oldest friends died during this period. One was Desmond Slattery, known to all of Bob's cronies as "Dirty Desmond," alias "Dusty Dirty." In the late '50s, Desmond had made a great pitch to get the leading role in a Robin Hood TV series. He purchased a jeep, had an artist paint a portrait of "Dirty" as Robin Hood on the wheel cover, and paraded around Hollywood dressed as the hero of Sherwood Forest.

Riding with him was an Irish wolfhound of magnificent proportions. The beast ran afoul of the law when it leaped from the jeep onto the back and finally the throat of a German shepherd. The quick demise of the shepherd brought wailing waifs onto the scene and, subsequently, the law. The damaging publicity squashed any chance Dirty Desmond might have had at stardom as an English hero in green.

Dirty's next ill-fated adventure was to fly to Ireland to purchase four bales of shamrocks, with the intention of selling them at the opening of the now-famous Shamrock Hotel in Houston, Texas. The hot, humid weather was decidedly uncooperative. Desmond's shamrocks became a sorry, wilted mass of damp green leaves.

To the surprise of no living man, Dusty didn't sell a single one.

His next adventure was to fly to Taiwan to buy 20,000 tiny cricket cages. The phrase "cricket on the hearth" had been immediately translated into "a cricket on every hearth" by the nimble-witted Dusty Dirty. Alas—to everyone else, it was common knowledge that crickets are insects and are more often met with the flat of a broom than with loving-kindness. Ask anyone in Fresno.

Desmond Slattery, alias "Dusty Dirty," passed away in remote Belize, Central America, ". . . trying to run a scam on the natives," Bob drawled. "You don't do that south of the border."

❄ ❄ ❄

Sed (Cedric) Onstatt, "old Seed Sacker," also quit the scene. "Never," said Bob, "have I ever known a man with more integrity than the Seed Sacker." His nickname was derived from his habit of saving marijuana seeds in Bull Durham sacks. "He was a frugal man," Bob explained. "He had to be."

Seed Sacker was an impish fellow with a slow, warm smile. He charmed the ladies everywhere he went. Although never overburdened with the green stuff, he never allowed that to sway his thinking. On several occasions, women who were quite wealthy wanted to keep him in lavish style. Bob was always delighted when that slow grin spread over the Sacker's face as he'd tell them, "You don't buy me, ma'am. I either come free and willing, or I don't come at all."

Scott Brady

Now Sed lay in his coffin, felled by a heart

attack. Scott Brady, the brother of Lawrence Tierney and a good actor in his own right in scores of B pictures during the 1950s, had been asked to deliver the eulogy for his old friend. Scott, a little the worse for wear after a forty-year bout with John Barleycorn, lurched up to the bier and solemnly shook his head. In his best actor's voice, he spoke his piece. "Sed—dead." He did an about-face, almost toppled, then sat down in the pew. Another of Bob's folk heroes had bit the dust.

❄❄❄

I have a particular philosophy that gives me a complete acceptance of death. When Red Skelton asked me of my belief in God, I answered, "Of course."

I wrote a song called "The Trout" and its message is that Life, not living, is eternal. The line, ". . . no matter how hard he tries to leave the stream and touch the skies, he'll fall right back into that running stream," depicts how I feel about mankind's vain attempts to leave the stream of infinity. He just can't do it.

When I see a movie or a television show studded with performers I have worked with who are long gone, I feel that they are still with me. I've often caught myself saying a few words to an old friend on a screen. I suppose that anyone who has ever overheard me say "Hi, Duke" or "Howdy, Buck" thinks I've flipped my cork. To me, those friends are very much alive in spirit and have never left that stream of Eternity that we are all in.

GNATNOOP

MY TELEPHONE RANG on a lazy summer day. When I picked it up, that familiar voice intoned, "Brother John." I asked him where he was; he told me that he was staying at the Beverly Hills Hotel for a few days while on business. He asked me to come over for a visit.

Living in Van Nuys, only six miles away across the Hollywood Hills, I soon arrived at Bob's suite and was surprised to find three men in his living room. I was further surprised that this trio of strangers didn't bother to acknowledge my arrival.

The leader of the group was earnestly advising Bob that they could get him laid.

It crossed my mind that Bob's getting laid has never been an insurmountable problem, so I wondered where this sortie was going. It turned out that the three had seen Bob in the lobby and had followed him for the obvious purpose—to bask in the presence of a star.

Bob told these men that I was his brother, that he hadn't seen me for a considerable length of time, and that he would like the privilege of talking with me privately.

"Oh," the ringleader announced, "I can get *him* laid too."

Bob looked at me with a leer that I've long been aware of as meaning, "Stand by." "John," he barked, "hold his head."

I made a lunge for the guy and he yelped, "What're you doing?"

"You wanted to get me laid? Well, you're it. I'm going to lay *you*!"

I was laughing hard as the three bounded for the door to freedom and made their accelerated escape down the hall.

I looked at Brother Robert through my tears. He was laughing to the point of exhaustion.

"The Yakuza" (a reference to the Asian Mafia) remains one of Bob's most unusual films, depicting his efforts to rescue a friend's kidnapped daughter in Japan. Written by Robert Towne and Paul Schrader, it contained an odd blend of underworld violence and Eastern mysticism and philosophy. It wasn't a big hit when released in 1975, but it has slowly developed a cult following ever since.

Bob worked next on "The Yakuza" in Japan. It was a very intriguing film directed by Sydney Pollack and written by a dynamite team, Paul Schrader and Robert Towne. It was about a kind of Asian Mafia whose basis in Oriental mysticism was lost on most American audiences. It was a very good film and will be viewed for a long time to come.

While in Tokyo, Bob was introduced to one of the top geisha girls of Japan. Over warm saki one evening, Bob asked her about John Wayne. The Duke had known the geisha well on his last sojourn to the Orient, so Bob's question was overly impertinent. She had smilingly murmured politely, "Too much licky-licky." Ah tact. Bob's eyes widened in mock horror.

THE RETURN OF DIRTY HARRY

IN THE SUMMER of 1973 I was back in San Francisco, playing Frank di Georgio again in "Magnum Force," when a call came from Brother Robert. He had just finished "The Friends of Eddie Coyle" on location in Boston, Massachusetts. That picture, in which Bob plays an aging loner, a small-time hood who meets disaster, left me saddened. For the first time I saw the deep scars that had long been hidden in Bob's life take over on the screen. But now, on the telephone, he was titillated by an idea.

"While you're in San Francisco, call Laurette LaRue."

I didn't believe the name. "Laurette LaRue?"

"Oh, indeed. She's for real. Call her."

I went back to the bar at the Quality Inn where we were staying on Van Ness Avenue and told some members of the cast and crew of Bob's suggestion. The make-up man was intrigued and insisted I call. Within the hour, Laurette graced our company.

Laurette was a big woman, very attractive, with a tremendous appetite for Scotch whiskey—and sex. After she downed a dozen drinks without a sign of slowing, I realized I couldn't afford her. The make-up man found that to be true too; Laurette and he became intimately inseparable all during the filming—often literally. His wife finally left him.

❄❄❄

The theme of "Magnum Force" centered around a few young policemen who, under the guidance of police commissioner Hal Holbrook, actually formed an elite band of assassins. It was filled with gunfire and violent murders and became a box-office bonanza.

During the production I met David Soul, who would go on to star in the television series "Starsky and Hutch." He also plays the guitar and sings, and one night we had a folk song session that lasted as long as the Heineken beer on hand.

The director was Ted Post, a delightful and gentle man whose nature seemed opposed to the violence in the script. Clint and Ted had last worked together on "Hang 'em High." Post had been asked to direct "Dirty Harry" but had already committed to another film. Considering the positive background of the Eastwood-Post relationship, their subsequent falling out over directorial problems seems sad indeed.

In his "Video Movie Guide," Mick Martin writes "Clint is iron-jawed and athletic, but the film still lacks something." What something? I asked Post to give me his side of the story.

Hal Holbrook (above left with Eastwood) was never happy with his role as Lt. Briggs in "Magnum Force," and later came to regret giving in to Clint's wishes instead of sticking to the director's. David Soul (above right with Eastwood) went on to star in "Starsky and Hutch" and has pursued a career as actor and director since those successful TV days.

"I had directed Clint in twenty-four 'Rawhide' episodes," Post began, "and found him to be, at that time, a quietly determined and earnestly dedicated performer absorbed in mastering the craft of acting.

"His co-star Eric Fleming was gifted with a deep, resonant voice (something Clint wished he had) and a surface grasp of the technique of acting. Eric, in self-centered and unrelated stentorian tones, overcooked the emotional delivery of his dialogue.

"Clint was just the opposite. He would understate with intelligence. To Clint's credit he always managed to ferret out the reason for the character's behavior and in his soft, unobtrusive and seemingly egoless manner, effectively deliver the scene's emotional demands. He took direction well. Eric didn't or, most of the time, couldn't. It ended tragically for him—he drowned in the rapids of a river while making a picture in Peru in 1966, the same year 'Rawhide' went off the air.

"When I directed 'Hang 'em High' [a critical and box-office success], the exhibitionistic, egotistical co-writer and producer Leonard Freeman took it upon himself to exercise his power. In a childishly, compulsive way, Freeman would flamboyantly stride on the set, slashing a quirt in his hand, Cecil B. DeMille style, wreaking havoc by interrupting and derailing everyone's train of thought with unworkable suggestions that slowed up production.

"Clint was then slowly coming to grips with his confidence and importance as the star of his first American-made movie following the success of his spaghetti Westerns made with Sergio Leone in Italy. In an unprecedented action he pulled Freeman aside and told him quietly, in no uncertain terms, that if he saw him again anywhere near the vicinity of the set, the production would cease. Freeman never showed up again. We finished the film on time

Ted Post has enjoyed a prolific career in directing, alternating between episodic TV and feature films. He helmed a great many segments of the "Peyton Place" series, and among his features are Chuck Norris' "Good Guys Wear Black" and "Beneath the Planet of the Apes." He feels that the Burt Lancaster film he directed in 1978, "Go Tell the Spartans," is among his best work.

and on budget.

"With time and success in his favor, Clint became afflicted with a touch of megalomania that he dissembled with great finesse and charm. The characteristics in Irving Berlin's song, 'Anything You Can Do, I Can Do Better,' began to manifest itself in Clint's conduct.

"Anybody can be a boss; the proof of this is that he became one. He wore this 'prejudice' like a halo. His intense desire for financial security and control assisted Clint in structuring his deals so that in a fifty-fifty proposition, he would insist on getting the hyphen too. This approach took its toll on meaningful scenes that were ruthlessly shortchanged and even excised. Clint's greed and ego began to affect his sensitivity and judgment. It was painful to watch.

Clint Eastwood as the Man-With-No-Name in "For a Few Dollars More," a famous spaghetti Western directed by Sergio Leone.

"Clint, at that time, had obviously been influenced by Sergio Leone, who had directed him in three successful Westerns. Leone's ponderous directorial style ["A Fistful of Dollars," "For a Few Dollars More" and "The Good, the Bad and the Ugly"] had rubbed off on Clint. He started doing long, lingering close-ups on principals, well after the point of the scene had been made, interferring with the narrative flow and thrust of the story.

"My own directing styles were influenced by John Ford, Frank Capra, Orson Welles, William Wyler, Ernst Lubitsch, David Lean, Elia Kazan, Billy Wilder, George Seaton. And I had learned, among many complex principles built into the craft of directing, that (1) there are no rules in filmmaking—only sins—and the cardinal sin is dullness, and (2) never underestimate the intelligence of the audience; doing so stimulates restlessness and boredom and taxes the audience's patience.

"On 'Magnum Force,' Clint was sensing his oats as a budding director. In the opening scene, I had Buddy Van Horn [Clint's stunt double] play a news-cameraman. I wanted him to actually photograph with a 35mm Arriflex camera as a labor leader exited the courtroom doors at City Hall. In the story the labor leader had been accused of being a co-conspirator in a murder trial and has just been exonerated on a technicality. He was hurrying toward the staircase leading down the courthouse exit. I instructed Buddy to get a moving shot of the labor leader who, in turn, was directed to *viciously* knock the camera out of Buddy's hands so that it would spin in the air a bit and Buddy would then barely catch the camera before it hit the floor. We did several takes before the scene was accepted as a print. This piece of business was injected into the scene so that the audience would viscerally see and sense the twisted, uncontrolled feelings and *violence* inherent in the freed killer, and symbolically justify his murder scene to come.

"I never saw the scene in the dailies. When I asked about it, I was told (among other lame excuses) that the lab had lost the footage. It was confirmed later that Clint had decided the scene was a waste of film and had ordered Van Horn not to have the camera loaded.

"Another unprofessional act was Clint deciding to make editorial changes without consulting me. The results of those editorial decisions were visible to me and to the perceptive critics who felt, as I did, that the picture was, in the main, sluggishly paced and incomplete in some of its pictorial choices.

"For instance, missing in the film was an establishing master tie-up shot of two inactive, aged naval aircraft carriers docked alongside each other (one much lower in the water than the other). This was an important scene because on one of the decks a cop-killer on a motorcycle was chasing Eastwood, who was also on a motorcycle. Both are traveling at fast speeds and literally fly off one carrier's deck onto another. Seeing the entire geography in advance of the action would've spelled out for the audience the visual and physical relationship of the breathtaking action.

"Eastwood the producer said the shot was unnecessary, the audience wouldn't miss it—silently implying the shot was too expensive despite the fact that the film was days ahead of schedule and enough under budget to finance another film.

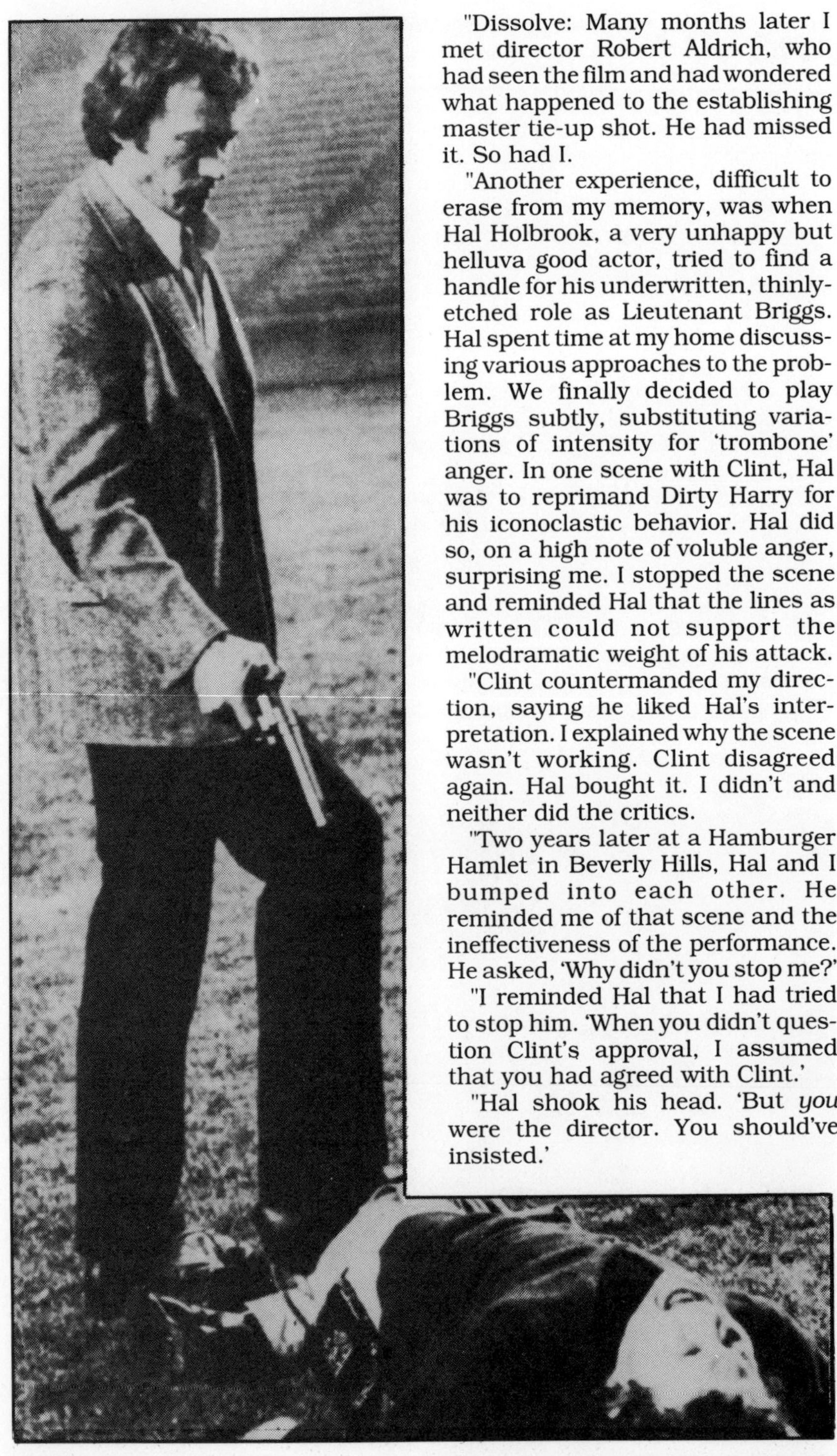

"Dissolve: Many months later I met director Robert Aldrich, who had seen the film and had wondered what happened to the establishing master tie-up shot. He had missed it. So had I.

"Another experience, difficult to erase from my memory, was when Hal Holbrook, a very unhappy but helluva good actor, tried to find a handle for his underwritten, thinly-etched role as Lieutenant Briggs. Hal spent time at my home discussing various approaches to the problem. We finally decided to play Briggs subtly, substituting variations of intensity for 'trombone' anger. In one scene with Clint, Hal was to reprimand Dirty Harry for his iconoclastic behavior. Hal did so, on a high note of voluble anger, surprising me. I stopped the scene and reminded Hal that the lines as written could not support the melodramatic weight of his attack.

"Clint countermanded my direction, saying he liked Hal's interpretation. I explained why the scene wasn't working. Clint disagreed again. Hal bought it. I didn't and neither did the critics.

"Two years later at a Hamburger Hamlet in Beverly Hills, Hal and I bumped into each other. He reminded me of that scene and the ineffectiveness of the performance. He asked, 'Why didn't you stop me?'

"I reminded Hal that I had tried to stop him. 'When you didn't question Clint's approval, I assumed that you had agreed with Clint.'

"Hal shook his head. 'But *you* were the director. You should've insisted.'

"I painfully answered, 'You're right. I should have insisted.'

"However, in all fairness to Clint's choices, 'Magnum Force' made fifty million dollars at the box office, beating 'Dirty Harry' by three million. So there was something Clint was doing that had the approval of the god Mammon. *Chacun a son gout.* Everyone to his own taste."

Post went on to give me further insight into the business:

"Your brother did 'Nightkill' under my direction. His costars were Jaclyn Smith, James Franciscus and Mike Connors who were terrific with Bob. The wildcat crew was something else again. Due to incompetence, several reels of precious dailies were lost and never recovered.

"To complicate matters, Tony Richmond, a talented, romantic, passionate cameraman, was undergoing an emotional crisis that was affecting his work. He had fallen in love with the beautiful Jaclyn Smith. (Both happened at that time to be inconveniently married.) Tony's problem was compounded when his very attractive wife and their two gorgeous, intelligent children arrived on the set from England. To quiet his conscience he took the familiar Hollywood B picture 'cure' to settle his upset heart—the bottle.

"Since he was also camera *operator* on 'Nightkill,' Tony had to execute some very agile and tricky moves. On more than one occasion he had to pan 180 degrees and several times he ended up on the floor flat on his keester. Buster Keaton couldn't have done it any better, or funnier. Only this was not a laughing matter but a rather sad and disturbing sight, especially for those who knew of Tony's talent and saw it being embarrassingly wasted on drink."

Brother Bob differs with Post about Richmond's behavior. He told me "We were shooting in Scottsdale, Arizona, but Richmond had somehow discovered a direct pipeline to Columbia, South America. Tony would drink a little brandy while working, but it was the cocaine that caused him to lose his balance. We were all amazed when Jaclyn married him. She is straight-arrow. Somehow she got him straightened out. They're still happily married and have two nice kids."

Ted Post, whenever he has the time, teaches a master class in film directing to a select group of professionals at UCLA-Extension. One of his students was James L. Brooks. Since then, Brooks won Academy Awards for writing and directing "Terms of Endearment" and was nominated again for directing "Broadcast News." It might be concluded that Ted Post has not lost his touch.

❄❄❄

The sadness that Post feels about the subtle change in Clint Eastwood's manner does not alter in any way the real gratitude Ted feels for Clint's sticking by him in his transition from television to major motion pictures.

David Picker, the former head of United Artists, was vociferously and even violently opposed to Post directing "Hang 'em High."

Ted was primarily a stage and TV director and Picker didn't want to take a risk.

Picker pulled every string he could to get another director but Clint stubbornly stuck to his six-shooters.

No Ted Post—no "Hang 'em High."

Finally Picker had to accept Clint's determination and Ted directed the picture.

It drew rave reviews, the director received accolades and the picture made a lot of money.

David Picker? He responded by telling all who could hear that he didn't want that "goddamned genius" anywhere near him.

❄❄❄

Memories of that murder I had witnessed at Rehobeth Beach so many years before came flooding back to me while I was making "Magnum Force." A young man working in the film began relating to the cast and crew an incident that happened to him at San Quentin Prison. He was a professional boxer who went to prisons to explain to convicts his belief that a clean, healthy body was a prerequisite to a clean mind. He was invited to the mess hall for lunch and was regaled about the phoniness of the movie business by an inmate who sat next to him.

"Dat was a good speech you give us," the con said. "But dat stuff about blowin' a guy backwards is crap. Clint takes dat great big .44 Magnum and—BLOWIE. The guy goes sailin' back about ten feet. I killed three of 'em. One—BLAM! Right between the eyes!

"He keeps stumblin' at me an' then falls over. Another one—three shots in the chest. He comes walkin' at me.

"The las' one? Bloom-bloom-bloom-bloom! Four in the gut and he walks forward about six more feet an' down he goes. Not one of 'em blowed backwards. Dat's a lot o' crap."

The boxer, who looked on with growing horror while the cold-blooded inmate laved his steak with catsup, left in a hurry, grateful to be going back to the comfort of a phony movie set.

❄❄❄

"JOHN THE GOOD" RIDES AGAIN

IN THE FALL of 1974 I worked on a segment of "The Little House on the Prairie" in Sonora, a fascinating town in the Sierra, filled with memories of the Gold Rush days. One saloon has a magnificent mahogany bar that was brought piecemeal up the mountain from a clipper ship moored at San Francisco. The area abounds with antique shops, a must for anyone who wants to relive a turbulent time in our history.

I had just passed my 55th birthday and had put all thoughts of wild abandon out of my mind, but fate ruled it otherwise.

Bobby Doyle, who was 32, played my son in the episode, which had us attempting to steal wagons loaded with nitroglycerine that Michael Landon, Victor French and Lou Gossett were driving to the railroad. In one scene, Victor fumbles with a nitro vial, terrifying Doyle and me as we ride as fast as we can away from an impending explosion. The filming went well enough—but in town, matters exploded.

One night Bobby had too much to drink. On the way back to the hotel, he insisted on one more for the road. I finally gave in. We stopped at a quaint little place called The County Jail. We were at the bar sipping our drinks when a big blond fellow, about 6-foot-3, 200 pounds and around 30, sat next to me. He asked if we were with the picture company and I avowed that we were.

"Stuntmen?" he asked.

I told him no, we were not stuntmen.

"You look like you could be stuntmen."

I was rather flattered. "No, we're just poor ol' actors."

He rose and walked further along the bar, stopping to talk to a big, dark Indian. The Indian glared down the bar at us, absorbing whatever Blondie was giving him. The blond fellow returned to say, "I think Sugar Ray Robinson was the greatest fighter that ever lived, don't you?"

I bluntly told him, "No. I don't think so."

"How can you say that?" He appeared astounded.

"First, you asked me. Secondly, what chance would Sugar Ray have had against Rocky Marciano? Forty-six fights, 46 wins. 42 knockouts."

"Hey, man. He's a heavyweight!"

I knew this guy was trouble. "We weren't discussing weights, were we? How about Willie Pep, or Archie Moore, or Billy Conn? Are you discounting Joe Louis or Jack Dempsey? How about Marcel Cerdan or Rocky Graziano? Are all of *them* 'chopped liver'?"

Blondie went back up the bar and got the Indian's ear. The menacing redman dreadnought came stalking down the bar, planting himself directly in front of me. "Get up!"

"Why?"

"We're gonna fight."

"I don't know you. What've we got to fight about?" The bar was strangely still now. He stepped into a position I suppose he thought was commanding. I looked at him somberly. "I have to tell you that if I fight you, I'll hurt you. I see no reason for that."

He sneered. "Wait'll I take my coat off!"

I smiled up at him. "Go ahead, take it off."

Bobby and ninety percent of the crowd thought I'd surely "Sunday" him while he was in the process of removing his coat. I've never done that and

In 1972 film columnist Hal Boyle wrote about Bob's 30th year as an actor, and this is the photo that accompanied the article. "After 61 pictures," read the caption, "Mitchum has become one of the most durable box-office names in an industry in which short-lived fame is commonplace." Amen to that, brother.

I never will. He turned back to me as I held up my hand. "Are you sure you want to do this? I don't want to hurt you."

"Get up. Now!"

I did.

(The next day Bobby Doyle said, "My God! I've never seen a man hit harder and as often as he was.")

The Indian sank to the floor. Blondie rushed out the front door; he *knew* that *he* was the one I wanted.

The police came, questioning the bartender and the patrons. An officer suggested that Bobby and I get into the squad car. "Officer, I haven't done anything wrong. You talked to the people here. You know that."

He was young, efficient and adamant. "Of course, we know that. But you just disposed of the town bully. Now they, like the old gunfighters, are going to keep trying you."

He heaved a sigh. "And we don't want to be that busy."

THE COLONEL WITH THE BIGGEST REVOLVER IN KENTUCKY

THAT SAME YEAR I got embroiled in another threatening situation while doing an acting stint in "The World Through the Eyes of Children." Bob's old friend, Jimmie Rodgers, a dreamer whose sensitivities show in everything he does, had long dreamed of filming his allegorical script, and he had proceeded with almost child-like faith and innocence.

We filmed in Wondering Woods, a lovely location outside Cave City,

Kentucky. An eccentric millionaire had built a town that duplicated a late 19th century village, complete with blacksmith shop, church, schoolhouse, drugstore and a white gazebo. In this idyllic setting, Rodgers had surrounded himself with a fine cast: Bill Mims played the town mayor, Gregg Palmer was the blacksmith, and I was the local pastor. Russ Tamblyn played the Devil, while Jimmie was the symbolic figure of Good. But the crew was another matter, made up of technicians who constantly misused Rodgers.

The intrusion of pot-smoking and cocaine use especially stood out as sordid. The first crew, for the most part, was continually high; the photography and lighting were subsequently atrocious. Finally, Jimmie fired the lot of them, bringing in a thoroughly professional group from Hollywood.

One of the people I still wondered about was a bodyguard named Bobby Phillips. That, in itself, was odd. Why would anyone need a bodyguard if he had nothing to worry about?

Phillips, once a third-string fullback at the University of Southern California, took great pride in his karate training. He would kick at the back of someone's head with such great control that his foot would stop just before contact; the purpose was obviously to intimidate the cast and crew.

The makeup man was tall, slender Bobby Romero. I had worked for years with Romero's father, who had served in the makeup departments at several Hollywood studios. Bobby asked me to stay close to him one morning. When I asked why, his simply delivered answer popped my eyes open: "I've killed more men before breakfast than Phillips ever dreamed of killing."

Phillips came around with his usual stretching and preening, letting us all know that he was a deadly threat. Romero, while making up one of the actresses, asked him where he had taken his karate training. Phillips pompously named his mentors. Phillips then made the mistake of asking

Gregg Palmer was the new kid on the block in the early '50s, and groomed by Universal-International to be a star under his real name, Palmer Lee. Stardom never took hold so in '54 he took the name Gregg Palmer. Fame still eluded him but he's enjoyed a distinguished career as a character actor in such films as "To Hell and Back" and "40 Pounds of Trouble." This is how he looked in 1956 when making "The Creature Walks Among Us."

Romero if he knew anything of the art.

Romero described his own schooling. I have never seen a man cowed as quickly as I saw Romero strip Phillips of his arrogance. Romero had reached a peak of competence far surpassing Phillips' elephantine antics.

That evening, Romero explained that, for the past four years, he had been in Central America as a mercenary fighting for the American Fruit Company. Insurgents were trying to wrest the banana trade from AFC and the company, through low-key ads in magazines, had recruited soldiers of fortune like Romero. Those who passed the mental and emotional tests were trained to a James Bond perfection in the arts of killing.

"We had just laid a trap for the insurgents," Bobby told me, "so I sat on a dead log to look over the completed work. I felt a deep, searing sting in my rear end and thought for a second that I'd been shot. It turned out to be a bushmaster that struck me, fanging so much poison into me that I almost bought the store. A helicopter picked me up, carried me to a U.S. naval carrier that was offshore. Their doctors saved my life. Since some of the poison was still in my fatty tissues, I had to leave the jungle. Small bits of it washed into my bloodstream and affected me like malaria. That's why I went back into the makeup department."

That same morning I discovered that the second assistant on the show, Wayne Douglass, had been a mercenary in Africa, had taught weaponry and hand-to-hand combat in Israel, and had been a fighter pilot in England. He too had been watching Phillips in wry amusement. That benighted wretch had no idea how many people were *not* intimidated by his "macho" bravado. (Wayne became one of my closest friends and his wife Addie—AKA Nellie—became my literary agent.)

The producer was constantly making fun of the local people and particularly of Colonel Handy, a man who lived in the motel we stayed at in Cave City. Colonel Handy was an intense man, very thin and wiry, who incessantly "dry-smoked" by chewing on cigarettes. Gregg Palmer and I liked him very much. It turned out that he was the magistrate of Barren County. He also owned the Cave City bank. Obviously, he was not a man to be taken lightly.

He told us that Kentucky is saturated with caves that few people even knew existed. "You can find hundreds of places here where you can drop a body into a small hole in the ground and God alone knows how far it will drop. Down here, we take care of our own. Somebody steals from my people or hurts my people—I take care of 'em myself."

Gregg, who is 6-foot-4 and weighs 285 pounds, looked at the skinny Colonel and laughed. "You're kidding!"

The Colonel whipped his coat back, displaying the biggest revolver I'd ever seen. "I'm the magistrate of Barren County. I've used this before and I'll use it again."

Gregg quit laughing.

I became embroiled in a sticky situation myself when the producer gave me my first check. It was short by over a thousand dollars. It showed none of the things demanded on any legitimate studio check: FICA, Social Security, permanent charities, etc. The producer told me that because of my salary, I wasn't entitled to overtime. I had put in twenty-eight extra hours that first week, and his statement was news to me. Gregg came by at that moment, just as perturbed.

I started across the street. The producer told me I was due on the set. I told him that I was going to the bank. Gregg decided to tag along. At the bank the manager declared that he would have to call a bank in Lexington before he could cash our checks. Just as we came out of his office, Colonel Handy came in.

"Frank," the Colonel boomed, "these are good boys. Fine boys. Their checks are good."

"No they're not, Colonel." There was a heavy silence. "I've just checked with Lexington. There's no money there."

The now-bristling Colonel turned to me. "John, that producer fellow just wrote a check to Dan Roby at the hotel for $10,500. If your check and Palmer's check are no good, then he's trying to cheat Dan Roby." He looked at me somberly. "You tell that producer fellow that in the sovereign State of Kentucky, any amount written over $25 with obvious intent to defraud is two-to-five in the Kentucky State Penitentiary. And I can make it stick. How many checks do you suppose he's written?"

I told him that there had to be at least forty of them floating around.

Handy growled. "He'd better know then that if he doesn't come up with the cash by Monday morning, he'd better plan on spending the rest of his life as a guest of our State. Will you tell him that?"

It would be a pleasure, I told the Colonel. I went back to my room and called Brother Robert to tell him what had transpired. Then I asked a favor: Should I be killed somewhere in the Kentucky woods, would he see that my death be avenged? He assured me that it most certainly would be. I went down to the production office.

"Why aren't you on the set?" The producer glared at me while bodyguard Phillips also eyed me hostilely. It became obvious who had hired Phillips.

Harold Shillman was a world-weary private eye whom Bob played in the 1982 TV-movie "One Shoe Makes It Murder." He's a lucky dog—in that one he got to make love to Angie Dickinson. Some people are born blessed, I guess.

"Because I haven't been paid yet."

"I gave you a check this morning!"

"It's no good! And Dan Roby's is no good either! And Gregg Palmer's! Roby's is for *ten thousand dollars!*" I felt like a walking exclamation point.

Now he looked startled. "How do you know that?"

I told him what the Colonel had said. Out of the corner of my eye, I saw Phillips sidling toward me. I spun on him. "If you kick my brains out while I'm in the woods, you'll be having a sandwich one day when a .38 slug will go in one of your ears and come out the other. It's already been arranged."

On Monday morning, I was paid everything that was owed me. In cash. Once again I was thankful for Brother Robert.

"The World Through the Eyes of Children" was never released. Jimmie's negative had so many liens against it that it became a white elephant around his neck. He was so innocently unaware of what was happening that many of us wanted to take the miscreants who misused him and boil them in oil.

THE GRASS WIDOW AND THE SONOFABITCH

I ENDED THE YEAR in ignominious fashion. My nephew James Mitchum called me from Las Cruces, New Mexico, where he was doing a picture called "King of the Mountain." He cajoled me into playing a part so I agreed to fly down to El Paso, Texas. At the last moment, I realized that he had sent me a one-way ticket. I began to feel uneasy.

On a Saturday afternoon a company driver picked me up at the airport in El Paso and drove me to the Rodeway Inn in Las Cruces in record time. I checked into my room, hung my clothes up, surveyed my immediate domain, and retired to the downstairs bar.

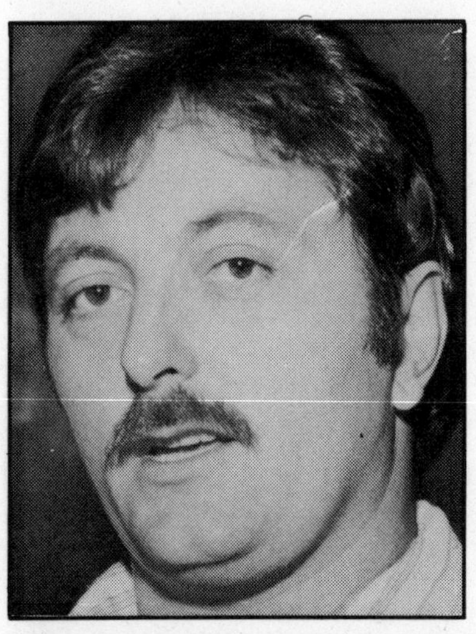

Jim Mitchum in one of his starring vehicles, the 1976 "Trackdown."

I had been seated about 20 minutes when a man sat down next to me dressed in a Pendleton shirt with Levis and cowboy boots. "Who're all these boys in here wearing beards?" he asked me suspiciously.

I looked around to see a dozen young bearded cowboys around the bar. "We're doing a picture here starting Monday," I said. "I don't know them, but I suppose they're with the movie company too."

He looked at me with smug superiority. "I'm a rancher myself." We had another drink in silence, then he blatantly threw out a challenge. "When I get a couple of drinks in me, I get mean!"

I shrugged. "Join the club."

He told me he was waiting for a "grass widow" and that he was going to sweet talk her out of a hundred thousand dollars. "You know how those gals are. I'll give her a little fun on the way," he assured me, punctuating his remark with a sly wink that irritated me.

The widow under discussion arrived. Her name was Pona Lynch, a lovely lady of Greek descent. She became very interested in "King of the Mountain," going on at length about her interest in filmmaking. I wasn't aware of the rancher's anger at playing second-fiddle until he suddenly challenged me. He thrust out his right arm, placing his elbow on the table. "Ever play this game?" I arm wrestled him down easily. He tried the other arm, which was no better. Then he started getting nasty.

I'd had it with him so I turned to Pona. "This bastard told me he's going to hit you up for $100,000. He intimated that since you're newly divorced, you'll be easy pickings. You take it from there, but I felt I had to tell you."

The rancher jumped up. "You sonofabitch! Wait'll I get my gun!"

I laughed. "If you think I'd let you leave to get a gun and come back and shoot me, you're crazy. I'd break your neck before you got out the door."

He grabbed Pona by the hand and half-dragged her out of the bar. Her eyes pleaded with me to do something but I didn't know what.

In a moment, I was surrounded by the dozen bearded cowpokes. "Your nephew told us what you were like," said one. "By God, he was right!"

Another added, "If that asshole had come back in here with a gun, we'd have shoved it where the sun don't shine."

Pona called me early the next morning. She had slapped the rancher across the face and sent him on his way. She thanked me for exposing the guy for what he was.

❄ ❄ ❄

"King of the Mountain" was woefully underfunded from the start. It folded less than halfway through its schedule. Bob had to bail Jim out of serious trouble. The oldest statute in law refers to "defrauding an innkeeper." Bob paid the Rodeway Inn over $11,000 to keep his son out of jail.

On the way to the El Paso airport in a driving snowstorm, I remembered that nagging feeling about the one-way ticket. I made a vow that I'd never accept another one.

INDIANS, ACTORS AND ESTONIANS

IN THE EARLY 1960s, at CBS, I worked on a television daytime drama, "Clear Horizons," playing a Russian sailor who gets done in by a comrade because he wants to defect to America. In the cast was Narda Onyx, a beautiful, statuesque lady from Estonia, a country taken over by the Russians after World War II. Narda and her husband George became close friends. Sometime between the making of "Dirty Harry" and "Magnum Force" I invited them to Thanksgiving dinner. Will Hunt, a fine character actor and close friend, was also there with his girl friend, Caroline Richter, a singer-dancer and comedienne. I had also invited Eddy Little Sky and his family. When Thanksgiving came, Eddy was out of state on a picture location but his wife Dawn came with her sister Fern, Fern's husband Bill Jones and their granddaughter Fawn.

Dawn and Fern are Hunkpapa Sioux, while Bill is an Arikara. A former hard-drinking, hard-riding rodeo man, Bill was a "born again" Christian and a Methodist minister to boot, which created a few problems.

After Jack and Cindy served hors d'oeuvres, I thought it would be a unique idea to have Thanksgiving prayers said in English, Estonian and Siouan. Narda gave a prayer in Estonian, I gave a prayer in English, and Fern started in Siouan. I saw a look of horror on Dawn Little Sky's face. Later, she explained that since Fern's husband's tribe was Arikara—traditional enemies—Fern was calling him terrible names. But Bill didn't understand Siouan and was blissfully unaware that her "prayer" was an excoriation of him and the entire Arikara tribe.

Fern was an alcoholic. Within minutes of arriving she had secretly stashed four half-pint bottles of vodka. The rest of us were drinking wine with our sumptuous turkey dinner. Then Bill took little Fawn for a walk. They never came back. Bill called a cab, took Fawn with him to the airport and flew to Oklahoma City without a by-your-leave to his wife or to Dawn.

That left Fern free to dig up her caches of vodka. The next thing I knew, George's voice came from the kitchen, excitedly explaining that there was "no air" in him. I went in and found Fern, with my sharpest paring knife in her hand, threatening to let the air out of the big Estonian. She had decided

If that face at the left looks familiar, it's because it belongs to Herbert Quatermaine, a leading character on "General Hospital." I know that face better as Will Hunt, a wonderful actor who's had recurring roles on "Somerset," "In the Beginning" and "Gimme a Break." He's also done a slew of features, "The Karate Kid II" and "Cheech & Chong's Next Movie" among them. And would you believe many repeats as Elwood P. Dowd in "Harvey" among his 200 productions in stock companies, dinner theaters and off-Broadway?

to commit this mayhem simply because he was a "white eyes."

He danced around the kitchen with his shirt open to his bare chest, all the while pointing to his middle. "There is no air! See, there is no air!"

"Fern," I suggested, "let's go have a drink, then call Eddy." She had no desire to talk to Eddy, but she sure wanted that drink.

Now Caroline Richter held the floor. She had just returned from a dance tour of Europe, China and Russia and was explaining about the Russians she had met. "What a wonderful time we all had," she chirped. "We danced together, sang together, drank together—I loved the Russians."

She looked up to see Narda towering over her. In her rich, contralto voice, Narda stopped the dancer's enthusiastic conversation cold. "So, you love the Rahssians—dahling! During the war, the Germans came. They robbed and looted Estonia. We could not imagine a worse people. Then the Rahssians came—dahling! They shot my father, they shot my mother, my brothers and my uncle. I ran to the swamps and, at eleven years of age, crawled many miles, many days. I hid in the swamps and at night, continued

Her beauty still dazzles me, everytime I see her picture. Yet Narda Onyx remains an obscure actress, who went out of my life under odd circumstances. She and her husband were trying to raise money to produce films, but apparently were so broke by the mid-70s that they came to my doorstep, luggage and all, expecting to move in with us. Fun is fun, but Nancy and I had to turn them away. And I've never seen Narda since.

crawling until I crossed the Finnish border. All the while, the rifles rang out, night and day, while the soldiers killed my people. Oh yes, you love the Rahssians—dahling. They will sing with you, dance with you, drink the night away with you, and *cut* your throat in the morning!"

Will Hunt and the subdued dancer went home early, but Dawn and her tribe spent the night. Cindy found Fern sitting on the john, putting up a totem on the bathroom floor while chanting incantations against the white eyes. She was building her totem pole from the turkey bones I had planned on using for soup.

❄ ❄ ❄

Narda's outburst against the Soviets brought sharply to my mind a conversation Brother Robert once had with the great jazz trumpeter Louis Armstrong. "Satchmo" had also entertained in Russia and in China.

Bob had put it to him straight. "Louie, you just came back from a world tour. You met a great many heads of state. What do you think the chances are for a world peace?"

"Bobby," Louie rasped out in his famous style, "after World War II, all of them big cats got together and smoked the Peace Pipe." He eyed Bob with those well-known orbs getting bigger and bigger. "But they didn't inhale."

SLUGGING IT OUT WITH CHARLIE BRONSON

BACK IN 1968, Brother Robert starred opposite Charles Bronson in "Villa Rides," a Western depicting the Mexican Revolution of 1916. Bob told me that he got along well with Charlie, who was a product of a tough ghetto district in a Pennsylvania mill town. Bronson had gone back to his birthplace after his success in films to avenge himself on those whom he fancied had misused him. According to Bob, Bronson went up to the rooftops of several apartment houses in his old neighborhood and urinated down into the ventilator shafts.

In 1975 I worked with Bronson in "Breakheart Pass," a whodunit action Western which was shot in Idaho. I was surprised and delighted to see old acquaintances on the cast roster: Richard Crenna, David Huddleston, Ben Johnson, Ed Lauter and Eddy Little Sky—men who are always delightful to work with.

Bronson, on the other hand, remained true to his own image. He was taciturn and surly, never joining in with the rest of us.

I couldn't help but picture him peeing in the air shafts.

In a long scene we did together, Bronson cheats me at cards and I catch him. I slap him an open-handed swat to goad him to fight. The director

This was taken the day I had my on-screen fight with Charles Bronson. We almost had one off-screen, too.

That's me in the foreground, entertaining the troops with my guitar on the set of "Breakheart Pass," a film we shot in Idaho in '75. It was a Western whodunit from a script by Alistair MacLean.

—Tom Gries of "QB Seven" fame—told me to look as if I was really giving it to him.

On the first take, I had to pull my slap because Bronson didn't move a muscle. (An open-handed whack can be dangerous; a fingernail can rip an eye wide open, and I had no desire to do that.)

"You missed him," Gries said. "Why?"

I took him aside and explained that unless Bronson moved with the slap, I had no choice but to pull it. "You told me to really let fly. I punch fast. If he doesn't move right, I have to either land on him or pull it away."

I hadn't seen Bronson come up behind me. He spoke with a sneer. "So, you're pretty fast, are you? Let's see!"

I couldn't believe it. He assumed a fighting stance, holding his left way down and away from his body, seriously ready to slug it out with me. It's a great style for street fighting but against a professional left jab, it can be disastrous. I got into my stance, told him that this was the way *I* fought. He backed off. The next take was perfect. He flowed with the slap.

Later, when I supposedly hit him with a right, Charles did a beautiful take and fall.

I weighed about two hundred and fifty pounds at that time and Gries took me to task. "John," the director admonished me, "you have to start exercising. Look at you. You're too heavy."

(He was most sincere. He played tennis every day he could. And dropped dead on a court in Chicago in 1977, while in the final editing stages of his last film, "The Greatest," the story of Muhammad Ali.)

That morning during breakfast in the hotel, one of the actresses, Sally Kirkland, asked if she could join me. I agreed, but was surprised when she verbally attacked my food choices.

"Sausage, eggs, toast! All bad for you!" She proceeded to spread about 30 different pills across the table, clicking off the names of the vitamins and supplements. She sounded particularly ecstatic over kelp.

"You should live in Malibu," I replied. "Look at the money you'd save. Every morning you could chew your way through the kelp beds for no charge." She downed her pills and left in a huff.

I told Crenna and Huddleston, who were sitting outside the trading post we used for the fight scenes, about the incident. When the same young lady sat next to them, Crenna began talking about peanut butter. She chimed in enthusiastically, extolling its virtues. Crenna and Huddleston feigned mounting interest.

Dick turned to Dave. "Dave, I love peanut butter."

Dave answered eagerly. "So do I, Dick. So do I."

Dick asked Dave if he preferred the creamy or the nutty.

"The creamy," Dave drooled. "I love to fuck it."

Participants of the Creamy Peanut Butter Incident: Richard Crenna, Sally Kirkland and David Huddleston.

Sally dashed off to the safety of her dressing room. She neither sat with us nor criticized our eating habits again. I wish I had taken her dieting advice. She won an Oscar as best actress of 1988 in the picture "Anna."

I was given another reminder of what folly it is to judge someone prematurely. An extra on the set added atmosphere by chopping kindling wood outside of the trading post. As I watched him through several takes, I became fascinated by the precision of his axe stroke. He would cut a large log into precise sticks, each piece coming from a single stroke.

Until then I had discounted him as a man who needed a few extra bucks, but I found that he was a well-off gentleman of Finnish descent who had once been a bush pilot in Alaska. I asked him if he still flew.

"Oh my, yes," he answered, telling me how he had acquired his latest plane. In a bar in Lewiston he overheard a man discussing an airplane he wanted to sell, a type with which the Finn was familiar. The man was willing to take only $2,500—if the sale was immediate. Since the aircraft was worth $65,000, the Finn was at first skeptical. The man produced the pink slip and proof that he was a prominent Boise physician who had flown his pontoon-fitted plane into a high mountain lake to do some idyllic trout

The Ordeal of an Irish Hoodlum

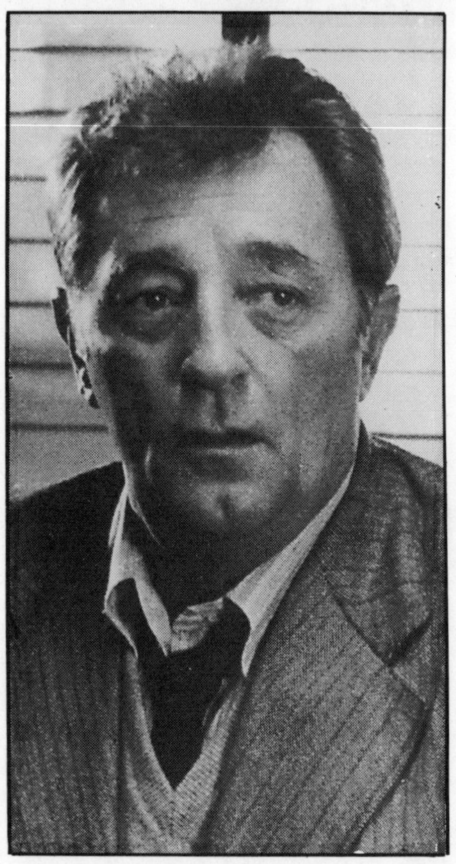

Usually Bob has portrayed strong men going up against overwhelming odds. In "The Friends of Eddie Coyle" (1973) he played a weak-willed small-time hoodlum in Boston who has to rat on his pals, even though he hates doing it and knows it will label him a "fink." Again, Bob accepted a challenging role and proved his versatility. The critics loved him in it and so did I.

fishing. His only problem: He couldn't fly out; the lake was not long enough for him to get airborne.

The Finn wrote him out a check for the $2,500 and took possession of the airplane, which lay on a little jewel of a lake some six thousand feet above sea level.

"I knew that lake well," said the Finn. "I went up there with a tent, a Coleman stove and enough provisions to last a week. On my sixth day, a big, black cloud formed at the north end of the pass above the lake. I packed my gear into the plane, untied her and started her up. When she was really warmed up, the wind swept toward me at about 50 miles an hour. I went full throttle into it and was airborne in less than 200 feet."

I looked at the man I had brushed aside so lightly. Live and learn.

The film company was invited to visit the Nez Perce reservation for a barbecue and rodeo on a Sunday. It was a tremendous spiritual feeling to be with them and to remember Chief Joseph's vow: "I will fight no more, forever!"

Being in that country—with its steeply rising canyons and high mesas—made me aware of the tribe's rich inheritance. Wild horses would often appear high up on the slopes, standing like sentinels against the blue sky.

❄ ❄ ❄

Shortly after finishing "Breakheart Pass" I threw a party at home that lasted two days. Harold Hensley, the great country fiddler, Roy Lanham of the Sons of the Pioneers, Rome Johnson, the group's tenor, and a half dozen more fine musicians kept the festivities going far into the wee small hours. Police came to investigate—and stayed to listen.

I proudly paraded around my house with a name tag that my Sioux friend, Eddy Little Sky, had pinned to my shirt. I almost wept; I had been accepted as a brother.

I asked another Sioux friend the meaning of my tag, "Chay-mazza." He grinned when he told me. I'd been strutting around like a peacock under the banner of "Iron Prick."

GETTING SHOT BY JOSEY WALES

LATER IN 1975 I worked with Clint Eastwood on "The Outlaw Josey Wales." On the flight over to Kanab, Utah, we flew in a single-engine plane owned and operated by Navajo Indians. Our pilot was excellent and the plane was in great shape, but Charley Tyner was preoccupied with the fact that he had been offered a commercial which was to be shot in the next two days. "Do you think we'll be out of here today?" he kept asking.

Although there is no guarantee on a picture as to when you will finish, for *anything* can go wrong, I assured him that I would do my best to facilitate matters. I saw his eyes widen as he looked out of the plane window and pointed toward the ground. "What're those?"

I looked down at the mounds that even from the air were huge. "Anthills." I looked back at my magazine.

"Anthills? *Those* are anthills? Are you sure?"

The pilot turned to him. "You don't see any livestock walking around there, do you?"

Charley turned pale. I'm sure he envisioned crash-landing on one. Later,

That's me as the grizzled killer in "The Outlaw Josey Wales."

it became apparent that it was still very much on his mind. I was one of two trappers "raping" a little Indian girl when Clint, as Josey Wales, stalked into the trading post. Charles Tyner nervously played the owner of the post.

Clint told us to be gentle with the girl during rehearsals but to be "savage" during the take. We did just that and Clint came in, stared at us, then at Charley. Now Charley, who was aware that the stranger was Josey Wales, was to say "We've got some fresh-brewed choc" to Clint. ("Choc" is apparently a homemade brew.) As Clint prowled by him, Charley said, "We've got some bresh-chewed frock." Josey/Clint slowed, stopped, slewed around, then gritted out, "What did you say?"

Nine takes later, Charley managed to say "We've got some fresh-brewed choc" perfectly.

When we finished the "rape" scene, the little Indian girl hissed at me, "Don't ever go to Tucson. My mother will kill you and put you on an anthill!" Charley had been thinking about that all along.

I died again, this time at the hand of Josey Wales. He shot me between the eyes and then spat tobacco juice on my forehead.

HELLO, FRISCO, HELLO

BROTHER ROBERT had first worked with Tony Curtis in 1962 on John Huston's "The List of Adrian Messenger." Bob, Frank Sinatra, Burt Lancaster and Curtis are all in disguise so that the audience is surprised when their true identities are revealed. Bob told me that Curtis had to put on so much make-up to alter that handsome face that he almost bolted.

"Oh no," drawled Robert. "If *we* have to put up with this shit, so do you."

While "Messenger" was in production, I brought a young girl onto the Universal lot so she could see a movie being filmed. I had met her briefly in Colorado Springs years before while I was doing "One Minute to Zero." We were having lunch in the commissary when Tony came by. He sat and had coffee with us and on leaving, kissed the girl's hand.

She sat as if paralyzed, staring intently at the receding Curtis. She was so rigid I asked if she was all right.

"I can't move," she whispered. "I just came all over myself!"

❄ ❄ ❄

In 1975, Robert starred in Elia Kazan's "The Last Tycoon" opposite Tony Curtis. Bob and Tony worked together smoothly and Robert told me that Tony had become a very polished actor. He was light years away from the time at Universal-International when he had done the Ali Baba line in pure Brooklynese: "Yondah stan's the castle of m' foddah."

Instead of a starring role Bob accepted a supporting part in 1976's "The Last Tycoon," based on F. Scott Fitzgerald's last novel. He played a movie executive named Pat Brady. Although written by Harold Pinter and directed by Elia Kazan, and starring Robert De Niro, the film turned out to be a bomb, and even Bob acknowledged that he had been "dull."

Philip Marlowe Lives Twice

"The Big Sleep," the 1977 remake of the great 1946 Humphrey Bogart classic with Bob in the role of Raymond Chandler's cynical private eye Philip Marlowe, was strangely set in London instead of Los Angeles, and this threw the film off-kilter. The plot was basically the same, but it was updated to modern day and didn't work as effectively because our standards have changed so much. It was directed by Michael Winner and co-starred Sarah Miles, Richard Boone and Joan Collins.

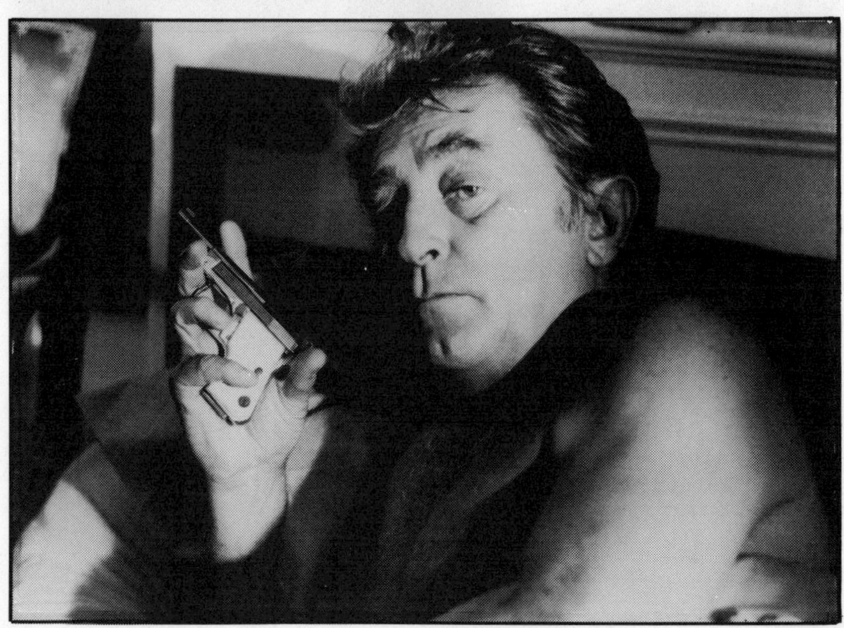

A Film Noir Classic

Bob also played Philip Marlowe, but with much greater effectiveness (he was putting those hooded eyes to better use) in 1975's "Farewell, My Lovely," a remake of the Raymond Chandler novel that had first been made in 1944 with Dick Powell under the title "Murder, My Sweet." Bob co-starred with Charlotte Rampling (above right), who had agreed to do the film only because Bob was in it. This time the setting was right: Los Angeles 1940. A classic example of film noir.

In his droll manner, Forrest Tucker once told me of the early days when the great stuttering comic, Joe Frisco, had stood on the corner of Hollywood and Vine with Denver Pyle and Claude Akins. They were bemoaning the fact that between them they didn't have the wherewithal for a jug when Tony Curtis wheeled around the corner in his white Cadillac. Frisco hailed him down to borrow the double sawbuck for which he was famous.

Curtis stopped and Joe slipped into the front seat. Tony drove around the block, obligingly digging his change out of his pockets. He left Frisco off at the same corner and departed.

Akins and Pyle were exuberant as they watched Joe count out the money. "Fuh-fuh-five, te-teh-ten, tuh-tuh-twelve, fuh-fuh-*fourteen!* Why, the suh-suh-suhn of a gun sh-sh-short-changed me!"

Joe Frisco was a legend in Hollywood. As a standup comic of the 1930s, he was the undisputed king. His humor, never raw, was as subtle as a feather. His stuttering was real and brings to mind a legendary story.

Joe Frisco, as he looked in 1927.

A friend met Joe on Vine Street one day and asked how he was. In a strained, stilted manner, Joe answered, "I am fine, thank you."

The friend was astonished. "Joe," he said, "what's happened to you?"

"I am un-der con-tract to RKO Stu-dee-oh," carefully replied Joe. "They are tea-ching me el-o-cu-tion."

"You! Elocution?"

"Yes," said Joe gravely. "I say, 'How now, brown cow.' Buh-buh-buh-but ha-ha-have you eh-eh-ehver fah-fah-fah-found a w-w-way to use tha-tha-that in a con-con-conversa-sa-tion?"

Our sister Julie used to live in a hotel on Whitley Avenue just north of Joe's Hollywood Boulevard place. Even though he earned as much as $25,000 a week, Joe was always broke because he and racehorses seldom agreed. When he ran out of money, he would borrow a twenty from his myriads of friends. He made it a point of honor never to pay it back.

On the reverse side of that coin, he gave away thousands of dollars to friends in need. He never considered repayment. Once a down-and-out actor friend stayed with him at the Whitley Hotel. As usual, the management carried Joe, knowing that when he went back to work, they would be amply repaid.

A new night clerk stopped Joe one evening and reminded him that although he could stay as long as he wished, his friend had to go. "More towels, more water, more electricity." Something would have to be done.

Joe called his agent and told him to book him in Vegas. Knowing Frisco, the agent asked him how much advance he needed. Joe stuttered out, "Tuh-tuh-tuh-ten thousand."

He picked up the advance, paid the night clerk the eleven hundred he owed the hotel, tipped the astounded wretch a hundred and said, "And b-b-b-be kind enough to b-b-b-bring up another Bu-bu-bu-Bible for my f-f-friend."

—BOOK EIGHT—

DEATH IN THE FAMILY

—BOOK EIGHT—

A NUMBING SADNESS

EARLY IN 1975, Brother Robert went to London (then on to Amsterdam and Hong Kong) to portray a retired narcotics agent in "The Amsterdam Kill." It was not a memorable picture but I do remember Bob calling me from his hotel one evening, telling me that his face was pressed against the window as he stared down at the cold, wet streets with a great tear sliding down his cheek. Bradford Dillman and our old friend, Richard Egan, were with him, helping to make his stay a little less lonely.

While I tried to sympathize with him, my heart was heavy with dread for my Nancy was now very ill. Although her doctors said that she was only suffering from influenza, I hesitated to accept a two-day junket to Arizona to do a charity show. The doctors assured me that it would be all right, so I went.

I must now pause to elaborate on a painful part of my life, so that events to come will be clearly understood. I must flashback to 1953, to the summer shortly after our son Jack was born in Dallas. I awoke one morning and looked over at Nancy's sleeping form, appalled by the sight of her right eye: The entire lid had swollen to the size of a tennis ball. The doctor diagnosed it as an "allergy." I clearly remember paying fifteen dollars for a useless prescription.

Within two days her left eye looked identical to her right. And her behavior pattern was developing a rapid change. She asked me that morning what I wanted for breakfast. When I told her, she angrily snapped "Fix it yourself!" She broke down into a helpless, sobbing wreck. My faith in local doctors badly shaken, I called my doctor brother-in-law in Nebraska for advice. He called a Dallas bone specialist who had been in med school with him. That doctor came to our home at 2 a.m., after working on six teenagers in a horrible car smash-up.

He took one look at Nancy and diagnosed her as suffering from hyperthyroid; her thyroid gland was secreting antibodies into her system at an alarming rate, creating an eye condition called malignant exophthalmos, or Graves' disease. Later we learned that her case was "one in a million." Small comfort. Her eyes never did return to normal.

A specialist at Baylor Hospital in Dallas gave Nancy radioactive iodine which killed the thyroid gland permanently. Still later, we found that the medical profession had discarded that treatment as being too radical.

In California, she again became a guinea pig for doctors who tried to relieve her eye condition. One doctor injected so much cortisone into her that I came home one day to find her slumped in a corner, almost in a comatose state. It was some time before she could function as a human being again.

Three years after Jack was born, Nancy went through a terrible ordeal. In Denver, Colorado, her surgeon uncle removed panels of bone from her temples and literally dug out fatty tissues that caused her eyes to fall out of their sockets at the slightest touch. I flew to Denver to be with her over the weekend, but had to be back in Hollywood on Monday morning for a "Gunsmoke" episode; there was no way they could shoot around me. Her mother, Alta Munro, flew in from Nebraska to be with her, but it was a lonely time for all of us.

Although the doctors had warned Nancy against it, she wanted another child. After losing one prematurely, she finally gave birth to Cindy. Her doctor put her in the UCLA hospital so she might have a better chance of pulling through.

Nancy started drinking heavily after she came home from the Colorado surgery. As I have always been a drinker, I didn't notice for some time that she relied on alcohol more and more to get through the day. I was working steadily in an assortment of movies and TV shows and was unaware of her growing dependency.

One night she asked me to go to the store to buy more wine. I told her that neither of us needed another drink and suggested we go to bed. She came at me in a rage, clawing at my face with the ferocity of a wild animal. I slapped her lightly to get her off my eyes and—dear God!—my fingers hit the boneless section of her left temple. The eye had to be removed. Nancy spent weeks in the hospital and years in a specialist's office where he rebuilt her eye so that it would move in precise correlation to her right one. We were married for twenty-four years and I can honestly say that during that time we were in doctors' offices and hospitals a large amount of that time.

Before malignant exophthalmos took its toll, Nancy was an exceptionally beautiful woman. Her eyes were especially attractive. It is not hard to imagine how she felt one night when a woman in a restaurant remarked to her escort, "That woman has the ugliest eyes I've ever seen." Nancy began to shake violently and I had a hard time restraining myself from giving both that inconsiderate wretch and her escort eyes to match Nancy's.

Gradually I became submerged under a sea of problems. As often as possible I took Nancy and the children with me when I travelled, either for films or road shows. I could never save any money when on the road and, until the Screen Actors Guild finally negotiated a hospital plan, I spent a small fortune on doctors and hospitals.

❄❄❄

When I came home from that 1976 Arizona junket, my 18-year-old daughter Cindy was near hysteria. I rushed into the bedroom and found that Nancy couldn't even lift her head from the pillow. I called for an ambulance. A medic checked her pulse, then stared at me as though I were a wild beast. "She should have been in the hospital yesterday," he growled.

Cindy told me that she had called the doctor in charge and he had assured her that it was ". . . just the flu."

On the way to the hospital, Nancy's pulse was zero over zero. Finally, the learned doctors informed me—much too late—that Nancy was terminal with cancer. It was incredible that no one—*no one*—knew before now.

For eight days she lingered and suffered in mechanical suspension, causing within me a great numbness of spirit.

I was standing in the hospital corridor, staring out of a fourth floor window in deep depression. I had about made up my mind to jump to my death. Frankly, the fact that we had two children didn't register with me at that moment of blind, dumb grief.

And then a figure came walking down the hall toward me, swinging a silver crucifix that hung from his neck. It was our friend, Father Thomas Vaughan, the Episcopal "jazz" priest, wearing his collar and a jaunty black beret. He stopped beside me, cast a searching look and asked a totally irrelevant question: "John, do you know Dick Foran?"

I pulled myself away from the window, managing to mumble, "I've met him. Why do you ask?"

"Well," said Father Vaughan, "he's very concerned about his old friend, Andy Devine."

Now he had me thinking of someone else's problems. "What's the matter with Andy?"

"Well, Andy has a pacemaker in his heart. Being curious, Dick asked him if it ever gave him any trouble."

Andy squawked out his answer in that inimitable voice of his. "Oh no, Dick, everything's fine."

Dick asked again, "No trouble at all?"

Andy squeaked out his reply. "Oh, no, Dick." Then he stopped short. "Except when I fart, then the garage door opens up."

I couldn't help but laugh. Sacrilegious as it sounds, inappropriate to the occasion, time and place, I laughed.

Father Vaughan took a deep look at me and saw that I was going to be all right. I suddenly realized my responsibilities to Victoria, Jack and Cindy, to my mother, brother and sisters, and to my friends. I had no right to ease my way out of my sorrow. I had to fight my way out. I had to live.

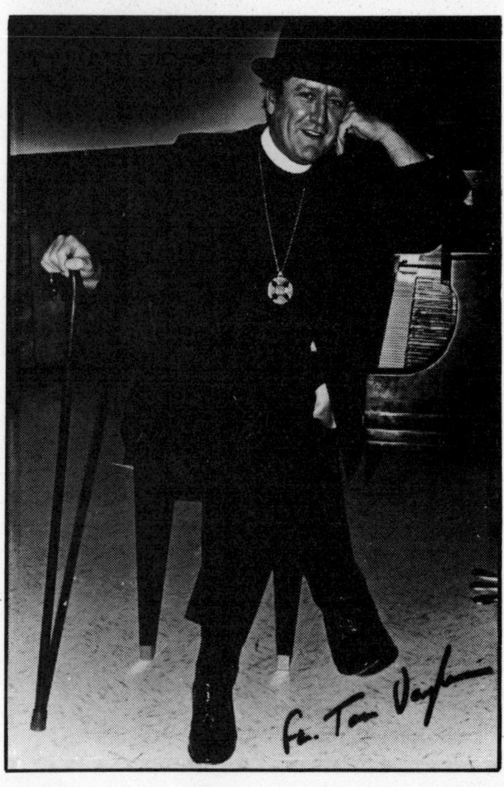

Father Thomas Vaughan, also known as the Episcopal "Jazz Priest," is presiding bishop at St. Martin's in the Fields in Northridge, California. Father Vaughan calls me periodically, usually to pass along some new stories he's heard. These narratives are frequently offcolor and they never fail to get a laugh out of me. There have been several crises in my life that Father Vaughan has helped me to surmount. No one has made me laugh more. He also does a pretty good imitation of John Wayne.

THE NIGHT FRANK DI GEORGIO DIED

CLINT EASTWOOD, transmogrified into a knight in shining armor, came to my rescue in those difficult days following Nancy's death. It was time to make "The Enforcer," the third film in the Dirty Harry series, and for me to play his partner, Frank di Georgio, for the last time. That summer of 1976 I flew to San Francisco and plunged with relief into the make-believe world of movies.

As di Georgio, I meet my doom in a warehouse filled with sophisticated weapons. Young revolutionaries are stealing military weapons that they might take the mayor of San Francisco hostage and hold him for ransom. I catch them red-handed and while I hold them at gunpoint, their leader stabs me in the back. I "die" later in the hospital.

I was thrilled when the technical advisor, a nurse for some 25 years at San Francisco General, turned white when I finally bit the dust.

"My God!" she gasped. "That man *died!* I've seen people die for 25 years, and *he* died!" (Unfortunately, the camera closeups of my death scene ended up on the cutting room floor.)

Well, I've had enough practice: I died in "The Outlaw Josey Wales," in "Chisum," in "Telefon," in "The Virginian," "Bonanza," et cetera, et cetera, et cetera.

But "The Enforcer" was the first movie in which I died in bed.

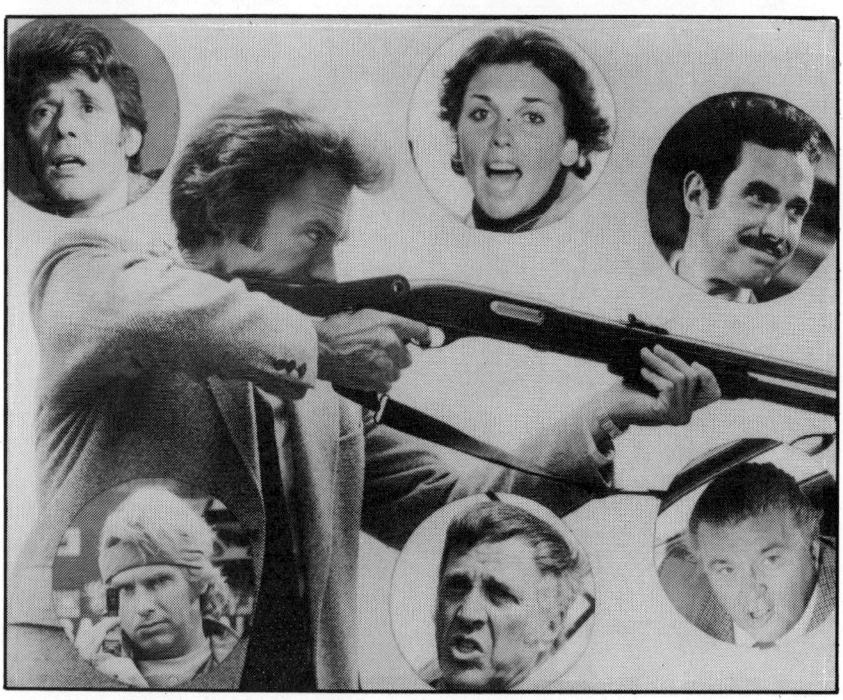

This publicity photo for "The Enforcer"—the third release in the Dirty Harry series—features assorted co-stars in the insets. Clockwise around Clint Eastwood, from top left, are Harry Guardino, Tyne Daly, Bradford Dillman, yours truly, John Crawford and DeVeren Bookwalter.

The photos on this page and the next are of me in "The Enforcer," the third and last film in which I portrayed Clint Eastwood's partner, Frank di Georgio. There's some confusion about the spelling of the name. In the closing credits of "Dirty Harry" my character's name is spelled "de Georgio." The later films spelled it "di Georgio." It's the latter spelling we've stayed with for this book.

JOHN MITCHUM

One lonely evening after a hard day of acting I walked into the hotel bar. As I was singing to the Musak, a woman took my hand and said, "You sing beautifully." Dorothy McCoy was attractive, tall, and had a compelling personality. The bitter loneliness that lay over me like a shroud made me vulnerable. I needed love. We married in haste.

❄❄❄

Big Tim Wallace was right. "They never look at us" sank in once again when I was in the Old Vienna Inn in Linda, California. Dorothy and I were invited to dinner at the Inn with a friend of Dorothy's, Ray McAllister, his wife Dolores, and their mutual friend, Betty Nicolaus.

Coincidentally, a huge bash was in progress celebrating the 20th anniversary of a high school graduate group, now forty-ish and partying it up in grand fashion. When we started to leave the Inn, it became increasingly difficult to find passageway through the mob. Holding sway in the center of the aisle was a man at least 6-foot-3 and weighing around 225. His sycophant entourage fanned out from him in waves while he recounted his glory days on the gridiron. I asked him if he would step back to allow the three ladies and me passage and he grandly told me to "Go around me!" I held back an impulse to step *over* him and finally found a way out.

Once in the parking lot, McAllister asked me what the man had said. When I told him, he spun around and marched back into the restaurant. Ray is 6-foot-3 himself.

Soon we heard the crash of broken glass to the rising cacaphony of women screaming. Dolores wailed, "Ray's gotten in a fight!"

Indeed he had. When I got there, Ray was on the floor with half a dozen men holding him down. "Go Around Me" was being held back by two of his cronies; he was screaming "Let me at him" at the top of his lungs. I walked up to him.

"You don't have to go very far to get at me." I was right in his face.

One of his buddies shoved me rudely and said "You stay out of this." I whacked him in the head and he went down and out. Silence prevailed. "Go Around Me" stood staring at me like a gaping fish.

"Well?" I motioned for him to make his move. It became apparent that he had no stomach for a fight. Some two dozen of his classmates stared at me, not moving. Then the manager stepped around the group.

"Can we talk?" he asked nervously.

I assured him that we could and soon our little party was once again in the parking lot. It seems that people who can't fight like to pick them. And they never *look* at you.

❄❄❄

Dorothy McCoy had four children when we wed. The oldest at the time of our marriage was 21, the youngest, 14. The less said of those eight tempestuous, lonely years of ill feelings, the better. I finally decided that I'd had enough when I came to the long-delayed conclusion that the now 29-year-old was still in our home—and still as pampered as ever—as was the now 22-year-old who had added a wife and daughter to the unhappy household.

My children were never accepted. I finally realized that I hadn't been either. I never got the love I needed, nor was I allowed to give it. Dorothy McCoy and I were divorced—not without a few complications.

Charles Bronson and Lee Remick in "Telefon," the film in which I've been programmed to act as a Communist saboteur and blow up a chemical warfare factory by driving into it with a truck of TNT.

THE LADY WHO DIDN'T LIKE CHARLES BRONSON

I WORKED WITH Charles Bronson again in 1977 in "Telefon." My segment, with Don Siegel directing, was shot in Great Falls, Montana. The character I played—a Russian terrorist living in America—had been implanted with a post-hypnotic suggestion that caused him, on receiving a telephone "suggestion," to carry out an act of sabotage. Donald Pleasence, who had worked with Bob two years previously on "The Last Tycoon," was the evil genius causing me and others like me to destroy strategic targets.

A demolition team was brought in to destroy the condemned school building that was doubling as a chemical warfare plant. When I apparently drove my truck into the building, it blew to smithereens without a brick landing in the street.

I was even more impressed by the Charles Russell Museum in Great Falls. A visitor cannot help but come away from there in awe of that man's enormous talent and capacity for work. Charles Marion Russell (1864-1926) lived in close proximity to the Plains Indians in the wilds of the Montana Territory. He became one of the great chroniclers of the American West through his realistic oil paintings and dynamic bronze sculptures of cowboys, horses and Indians—with only three days of formal training. Thousands of Russell's paintings are there, each depicting frontier life as Russell had lived it. This artist had transformed a rugged existence into delicate beauty.

While filming "Telefon," Charles Bronson was having dinner one evening with co-star Lee Remick when a middle-aged woman approached their table. "Could I have your autograph?" she asked Miss Remick. "My children would love to have one." Lee was charming and cooperative.

"How about mine?" Charles seemed nettled that she hadn't asked him. The lady surveyed Bronson coolly. "I don't like you."

"Well, I don't like you either!" snapped Charles as he sulked back into the booth.

❄ ❄ ❄

In that same film, Bronson "kills" Roy Jensen by choking him to death with a scarf. Roy is—at 6-foot-2, 230 pounds—a man of power. When he was an All-American on UCLA's football team, doctors on the campus were amazed at the thickness of his skull.

Roy played Canadian football; during a game he had broken the hand of an opposing player. That night the two met accidentally at the head of the stairs in their hotel. The lineman, who had his injured hand in a butterfly splint, told Roy, "When this hand heals, you sonofabitch, we'll find out who's the best man!" Roy took the broken hand in his and crushed it, then hurled the wretch down the stairs, following after him. "If you ever call me that again," he warned, "I'll kill you!"

I found out that years before, Brother Bob and Roy Jensen, while working on "River of No Return," had had words. I'm glad that's as far as it went.

Less bounce to the ounce: Whatever possessed Bob to make "Matilda" remains one of the great mysteries of our century. He played newspaperman Duke Parkhurst, who hopes to use a boxing kangaroo to eliminate the criminal element from the fight game. At left is Elliott Gould and in the middle is Gary Morgan, in "drag" as the battling jumper. I warned Bob that he would 'roo the day that he made this stinker.

❄ ❄ ❄

Brother Robert bounced along in "Matilda," a picture with Elliott Gould and Harry Guardino that featured a boxing kangaroo. Part of this fiasco was filmed in Reno, Nevada. I was living in Sacramento at that time and I asked why he hadn't motored down the mountain to visit me. He told me that the wardrobe department had mislaid his clothes and there were none in his hotel room. "I ran around in my 'jammies' for three days," he explained. (That is an image I cannot imagine.)

OH, THE DIFFICULTIES OF RAISING PRODUCTION CAPITAL

NOR HAD I IMAGINED the difficulties of getting my own pictures funded. Taking a hiatus from acting, I started writing my own scripts, undeterred after some professionals warned me that the average time from conception to "getting it in the can" is twelve years.

While Bob was working on a series of less than distinguished features—"Breakthrough," "Agency," "That Championship Season," "A Killer in the Family"—and the first part of the much-viewed eighteen-hour TV miniseries "The Winds of War," I spent my time in Texas, California and Ohio with characters that even now seem unreal.

At one point I met a man who promised he could get me $20 million to do three pictures. There was only one drawback: I was to give him $10 million under the table and pay 20 percent interest on the twenty. Considering that I would have to pay out $4 million within a year, that would leave me only $6 million to make three pictures. Since I couldn't guarantee a return for at least eighteen months, I could see myself wearing cement boots at the bottom of Los Angeles Harbor. Incidentally, the last time I inquired about my would-be benefactor's health, I learned that certain elements in Chicago were trying to learn his whereabouts so that they might fit *him* in the same stylish footwear.

In "A Killer in the Family" (a 1983 TV-movie) Bob played a psychopathic murderer who is broken out of prison by his sons Eric Stoltz (left) and Lance Kerwin. A killing spree and nationwide manhunt follow the breakout. It was based on a true story.

In Dallas, Texas, I met Larry Gillum, who grandly informed me that he could acquire unlimited funds to do the pictures. Gillum lived in Brownsville and had an associate there who had access to such monies. That associate was Sergio Lerma, an outgoing, delightful young Mexican who was very active in the gold business. Lerma invited me down to Brownsville for a weekend. After picking me up at the airport, he took me to his office. I had not informed Gillum of our rendezvous.

Sergio sat behind his desk and smiled at me. "Larry tells me that he has to handle any deal between us himself. He tells me that you won't deal directly with me."

My jaw dropped. "Why did he say that?"

Sergio smiled again but it was not really a warm smile. "He says that you don't like Mexicans."

I shook my head in bewilderment. "Do you mind if I make a phone call?" He pushed the phone toward me, looking expectant. I explained that I was going to call an old friend in California and have Sergio talk to him. I wouldn't say a word until he finished. I dialed Natividad Vacio, then handed the phone to Sergio.

He spoke in Spanish to Vacio and was soon laughing and relaxing. Sergio was still laughing when he hung up. "That Larry Gillum. You 'don't like Mexicans'! The first thing Natividad said was, 'Where is my brother?'"

Just then, by purest coincidence, Gillum called. Sergio casually invited him to come over. When he hung up the phone, he reached into a drawer and took out a nine-millimeter Luger. He tucked it in his waistband and leaned back in his chair. In a few minutes Gillum came in. Naturally he was startled to find me there.

Sergio wasted no time in calling Gillum a liar. Gillum gasped like a beached fish but Sergio went on. "I've caught you in too many lies, Larry. We have nothing to say to each other any more." Larry was big, but no match for

In "Promises to Keep," another TV-movie, Bob portrayed a man tainted by wanderlust who left his family 30 years before and now wants to return and enjoy his children. It was distinguished solely by the fact that it costarred Bob's son Christopher and his grandson Bentley Mitchum (right).

the prominent Luger. I never saw him again.

Sergio, who thought he had kicked the heroin habit, started in on it again. He now lies in his grave in Brownsville, Texas.

My next encounter in this ill-fated venture was with a Mexican film producer, a friend of Sergio's, one Rojelio Agrasanchez, just when the Mexican peso dropped out of sight and was almost six hundred pesos to one American dollar. Financing for the picture faded rapidly.

A brother-in-law at that time was Bill McCoy, who lived in Arlington, Texas. My wife at the time, Dorothy, introduced me to him at four in the afternoon. By four-thirty, I had been told that he had a "deal going in Waco that was a million four," another in Fort Worth that was "two million five," a "little deal going in Tyler that was only a million two," but he was really working on a big one in San Antonio—"seven million six!"

A short time later a service representative came to the front door and I overheard Bill explaining why the water and power hadn't been paid. I gave him close to $1,000 and told him it was not a loan; it was a gift. He told me he'd "shoot it back to me." I told him again that it was a gift. (I've learned that loans lie like a dead weight on friendship. Just give and there's no further transaction needed—as long as the generosity isn't abused.)

He introduced me to a group of real estate people who wanted to raise money for films. One of these, Lee Harmon, was a man in his late forties who prided himself on his physical fitness and his way with the ladies. He also fancied himself as an astute businessman, attempting to lay a few traps to see if I were for real. I couldn't blame Lee. There are so many con artists trying to raise money for films it certainly behooves any prospective investor to be sure of his ground.

One of these traps involved Roger Wagner. My resume had included the fact that I sang with the Roger Wagner Chorale and had worked for him with the L.A. City Bureau of Music.

"You sang with Roger Wagner, didn't you?" Lee asked me in his office in Arlington. I nodded. He continued, "I've got two tickets to a concert he's

When Barbara Walter interviewed Bob in the Bahamas in 1983 for one of her ABC-TV specials, she thought she was getting a great story. But the truth is, Bob told her nothing. It was the damnedest thing. He kept adroitly side-stepping all the topics. I don't think he gave her one straight answer.

giving in Dallas. Want to go?"

I knew what his motives were so I jumped at the chance. The concert was held in a huge, beautiful church in the Highland Park district. The first half was typically Roger: Exquisite ancient church music in Latin, followed by French art music which tapered into Bach chamber that ended the half-session.

"Let's go back and meet Roger." Lee was pushing it.

We threaded our way backstage and Roger, with his back to us, was talking to one of his baritones. When he finished, I spoke up. "And then John Mitchum said . . . "

Roger spun around, threw his arms around me and roared, "You old sonofabitch! Where've you been?" He turned to Lee, a perfect stranger, and told him, "The last time I saw John, he knocked the hell out of a man who was making dirty passes at my wife."

I introduced Lee to him. When we went back to our seats for the rest of the program, Lee was subdued. He was also enthralled by the concert. He had never heard music like that before.

Forrest Tucker was starring in a play at the Granny Theater in Dallas, "Captain Outrageous"—a natural for ol' Tuck. Lee had tickets and put me to the test again.

"You worked with Tucker, didn't you?" he asked. I was dying to say "Let's go!" but held my tongue. "He's doing a play in Dallas. I've got a party going. Like to come along?"

Tucker was great in the play as a rapscallion in a hospital who scandalizes the institution with his outrageous antics. When it was over we went backstage. Lee cleared his throat and spoke up. Tuck was just putting on his boots.

"John, here, is apparently a hell of a good writer."

Tuck looked up at him. "I'll do *anything* that he writes." Once again, Lee sank into subdued silence.

❄❄❄

Lee had been working hard in West Texas oil field exploration. He lost his shirt when oil profits plummeted to rock bottom. That ended my sojourn in the Lone Star State.

Sergio Lerma is dead; Lee Harmon has faded from my horizons and I have

"That Championship Season": Paul Sorvino, Stacy Keach, Bob, Bruce Dern and Martin Sheen.

long since divorced myself from the McCoys.

One bright spot remains among my associates in Texas: Glen "Chuppa Chuppa" Heath, a man whom I still look forward to doing a picture with one day in Texas.

Glen will forever be "Chuppa Chuppa" to me. When he was a little boy on his grandmother's farm in Midlothian, Texas, Sunday afternoons were always fried chicken, potatoes and gravy, and homemade ice cream. His folks were death on smoking so he and his brother would stash their Bull Durham tobacco behind the barn, where they could "roll one" unseen and unhurried.

On one such Sunday, they were enjoying their ice cream when their little, almost bowlegged, dog came trotting across the lawn to the serenely happy boys. Glen tells that his little bowlegs made a "chuppa chuppa" sound as he went across the porch. Serenity turned to panic when Glen's parents and grandparents saw what Chuppa Chuppa had in his jaws: a telltale Bull Durham sack, complete with a half-full pouch and a sheaf of roll-your-own papers.

❄ ❄ ❄

A picture I had written—about an evangelist who is a womanizer and a drinker—met a strange fate at the hands of an Ohio preacher. Through the now long-defunct associations with Bill McCoy, I met a gentleman from Vandalia, Ohio, who flew me to that city to meet a preacher who wanted to fund the film.

I signed a contract with the preacher and accepted a sizable "good faith" advance, then heard nothing more from him. I finally found out that the holy man was in a Federal Penitentiary for laundering cocaine money. He got eleven years. It was his second time around.

Lots of folks who cross themselves at dinner don't really mean it.

I've always adored my nephew, Christopher Mitchum, a gentle, thoughtful, concerned young man. When we were making "Chisum" he came to work with a black eye and I asked him how he got it. "I was walking through Durango when a gang of tough guys jumped me," he replied. "I finished them off with my karate." Since Chris has a black belt in karate I didn't question his story—until I heard later the truth: He had been watching a pretty girl and walked smack into an awning post.

Gloria Grahame on the night of March 19, 1953, as she proudly clutched her Oscar for Best Supporting Actress as the sexy Southern belle in "The Bad and the Beautiful." She was all of 27, but had been nominated five years earlier for her role in another fine film, "Crossfire." Among her other memorable movies were "In a Lonely Place," "Sudden Fear," "The Big Heat," "Human Desire" and "Not as a Stranger," the latter with Brother Bob.

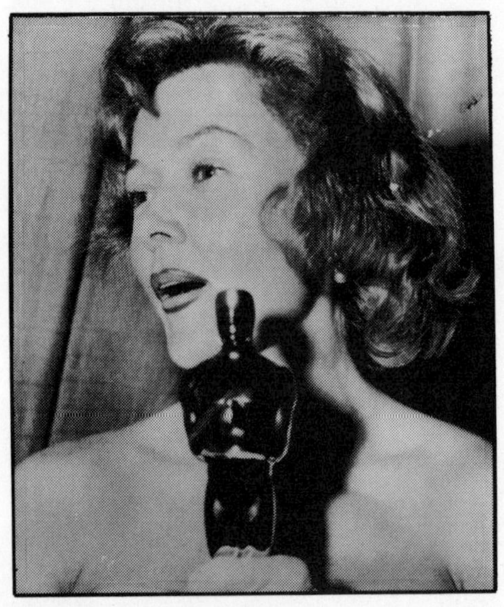

THE DEATH OF A STAR

IN 1981 the theater and motion picture world lost one of its brightest lights. Even though Gloria Grahame was my *former* sister-in-law, she had always held a dear place in my heart. A grim sequence of events began when Gloria, whose roots were firmly implanted in the stage, had flown to Liverpool, England, to star in "The Glass Menagerie."

Prior to her flight she had seen a Dr. Grace in New York City for a condition he strongly suspected to be cancer. Her tests came back negative but the doctor explained to Gloria that he had a gut feeling that all was *not* well; he should do exploratory surgery and find out the true nature of her condition. Dedicated to her profession, she refused and prepared to leave for England.

Meanwhile she made several trips to a hospital to drain off fluids that caused her stomach cavity to swell—a tricky and dangerous procedure. She arrived in Liverpool and began performing, but still needed the draining procedure periodically.

The hospital suggested she stay an extra twenty-four hours. Once again that bulldog tenacity I'd so often seen in her sister Joy surfaced and she left the hospital to return to her apartment near the theater. It turned out that the needle used to drain off the fluids had pierced her colon and peritonitis rapidly spread throughout her body. Gloria was close to death. Dr. Grace's gut feeling had been all too correct—a cancerous condition was responsible for the ascites.

A friend went to her apartment and found Gloria delirious. She still refused the hospital. The friend called Joy in California and insisted that someone in the family fly to England and take her back to Dr. Grace in New York.

Gloria's son Tim (whose father was the late Nicholas Ray, the director) and daughter Polly (whose father was producer Cy Howard) left for London immediately. On the flight home, Gloria slipped into a death-like coma on the plane and Tim brought her back to life with CPR. In the New York airport, Gloria sank to the floor in complete exhaustion. Some onlookers assumed she was drunk.

In the hospital, Dr. Grace told Gloria that he would have to operate immediately. From her wheelchair, Gloria smiled wanly. "I'm dying and I know there's no hope. So, no operation. Please wheel me to the window so I can see the city."

The doctor did so. With Tim holding her left hand in his, she gave a "thumbs up" sign with her right hand and slipped away into death. It was October 5, 1981.

I had known Gloria since she was a bubbling, energetic and delightful child of fourteen. She grew to great heights, both in the arts and as a person. I felt a deep loss, the sting of which hasn't lessened as I write this farewell to a great lady.

Here's Gloria Grahame when she was at her sensuous peak in the early 1950s. She was great at radiating a naughty sexuality, but there was a fragile, vulnerable side to that persona too. When I think about her it's hard to believe that she's gone.

The year 1984 found me back in Northern California in an area close to Camp Beale, the spot I once said I never wanted to see again. David Steensland, a bright young producer-director from Sacramento, had put together a "Twilight Zone" type of anthology and wanted me in one of the episodes, "Coffee Break." Vincent Price was the host introducing each of the stories. The finished product, "Escapes," became a successful videocassette movie.

David laughed softly after the filming was finished. "When I met you, John, I found you not only accessible but so cooperative as to overwhelm me. I expected both you and Vincent to have a superior attitude toward me. The reverse stunned me. I learned a great deal from the two of you. I shall be forever grateful."

❄❄❄

Recently my sister Julie sent me two poems that Brother Robert had written on our friend Elmer Ellsworth Jones' twenty-first birthday. She had kept them for years, unwilling to toss them away because of their poetic content. Julie recognized much of Robert's striking contrasts in the two odes he penned so long ago.

The first, simply titled "To Jones," came from the heart and exposed the tender core of Robert Mitchum. Allegorical in text, it likened Jones to a rock in a stream: solid, steadfast and responsible. Bob couched it beautifully—Jones, "unafraid and laughing." The words "deep and gentle" startled Jonesy; they brought unaccustomed tears to his eyes.

Bob had looked deeply into his inner being.

❄❄❄

TO JONES

By Robert C. Mitchum

Gleaming stream
Of living
Giving colored contrast
To the sylvan banks
Smooth and hushed
Through ranks
Of rushes,
Meets a shining stone
Which stands alone
Its steady feet
Set deep
In sandy bed,
Its head
Making ripples
Breaking velvet flow
And shaking off
The jeweled cascade
Unafraid
And laughing.

Tiny crystal sparks
Descend
And crown
A friend.

Around the bend
The quiet pool
Where waters gather
Deep and cool and gentle,
Marks
The melody
And echoes
Softly then
Its tune.
Mark then
How the stone
Is ever adding
Harmony—
Gentle—
Pleasant—
Mark it there
Forever.
Softened voice
To buff the swirls—

It's Good Girl's!

Mark them well
These noble stones—
The voice—this stone's—
Rejoice—Miss Jones.

Wonderful chap,
So everyone thinks—
Truly a marvelous fellow!
(Stinks!)

This second poem sprang from the rogue side of Bob's character.

He had shown the depths of feeling he had for his best friend and now he had to camouflage that tender sentiment with an expose of Jonesy's rough exterior.

Bob's referring to Jonesy as being "queer" and exhorting him to take his hand off his hip was a shield against exposing *both* of their innate gentility from prying eyes.

Jonesy had so many young ladies after him that he might as well have had a revolving door in his house to take care of the traffic. Thus the "sneaky gigolo" and "always on the make" phrases. "Mother Jones" was Bob's not-too-subtle reminder to E.J. that, although Bob was aware of his true soul, he was not unaware of the warts and bumps that debecked E.J.'s all-too-human exterior.

TO JONES

Greetings to you, Mother Jones,
Bless your aged creaking bones.
Haggard puss, lined deep with care,
Varicosed old derriere;
Box-like body, squat and square,
Forehead bare—receding hair;
"Nature Lustre" upper plate,
(What a scurvy thing is Fate)
May you be without neuralgia,
Pleural aches and dread nostalgia;
May the next year find you free
To cut your gusts in musty glee.
May your astral aspect shine
Now that you are sixty-nine;
I'm convinced you'd make a fine
Miss St. Pete of '39.
Greetings on your natal day,
Watch the boys across the way
Skipping to the park to play.
Don't you worry what they say;
If you'll just be quiet, dear,
They won't even know you're queer;
When you speak be firm and crisp,
Don't be meek, you worm, and lisp;
Stop that quiver on your lip,
Keep your fingers off your hip;
Time that you were settling down,
Moving to the ol' home town;
Taking up the social whirl,
Being Wilkes Barre's "Goody Girl";
Stop the gallivanting stuff.
Goodness knows, you're old enough!
Ah, but really, little one,
After all is said and done.
This is only meant in fun.
You're so really fine to know—
Such a sneaky gigolo.
Vulgar—always on the make—
Such a low, good-humored snake.
Such a trusting, loyal chap—
(Frankly, that's a lot of crap)
What a friend, a pal, the best!
(Steal the lining off your vest)
Ask him over for a bite,
Gobbles everything in sight;
Squeezes every cent he gets;
Smokes up all your cigarettes;
See how nobly now we score you,
See you how we all adore you.
So, in hushed, respectful tones—
Birthday Greetings, Mother Jones!

BOOK NINE

MODERN TIMES, OLD MEMORIES

BOOK NINE

THERE'S A LONG, LONG TRAIL . . .

AS I SIT on that mythical porch of retirement, names in the past flit by and dart about in the evening sky, reminding us how much fun we had along the trail. Each was involved in that whimsical effort to contribute to films that we hoped the world would enjoy.

When Robert first started in pictures, the area that is now prosaically the intersection of Gower and Sunset Boulevard was known as "Gower Gulch." *Real* gunfights took place there because the inhabitants of "The Gulch" were bona fide cowboys, men in transition. Real cowboying was dying out and movies were coming to life as *the* major form of entertainment.

Bob met many of these men before I did, and regaled me with exciting tales. I thrilled whenever I would finally work with one of these obscure stalwarts. We, like those men, grew up in a world that saw the horse and wagon disappear, but still used outhouses and kerosene lamps, a world where radios were a novelty and television sets had not yet been invented.

These were colorful men who gave our world "character."

❄❄❄

"Bear Valley Charley"—what a name. Charley Miller was a hard-riding, hard-drinking cowpoke who worked in hundreds of pictures as a heavy. Raoul Walsh, who directed Bob in the excellent 1947 Warner Brothers psychological Western "Pursued," used Bear Valley many times.

"Raoul invited Bear Valley to a Hollywood party that I also attended," said Bob. "During the first part of the evening, Bear didn't drink a drop; he didn't want Raoul to know that he was a pretty stiff belter. A waiter would come by with a tray of assorted drinks and the cowboy would tensely say, 'No, thank you.' That is, he did until a charming woman came up to Bear, remarking that Raoul had told her that Bear had ridden a bucking horse that no one else ever had or could ride.

"Bear reached out a big paw as the waiter came by and 'Schlurpp'—he downed a straight whiskey in the blink of an eye. 'Yes, ma'am, I did.' ['Schlurpp.' Down went another bourbon.] 'Twas up in Wyoming. That horse was Steamboat. The bronc riders there scoffed, said nobody

Director Raoul Walsh, 1936.

could ride Steamboat. ['Schlurpp— schlurpp'—two more bourbons perished.]

"'He was a mean-lookin' horse, wicked eyes 'n hard mouth. The boys had to put a blanket o'er his head to get a saddle on him. When he was ready, I climbed aboard.' ['Schlurpp—schlurpp'—two more dead soldiers.] 'When they took the blanket offa him, he shot straight up in the air, sunfished 'n came down hard!'"

Breathlessly, the lady interrupted. "'And you rode him?'"

Bear Valley, with a drink poised to disappear, looked solemnly at her. "Bless yore sweet heart, dear lady. You're fuckin' A I rode 'im! Right into the ground!'"

Bob recalled Raoul had his head resting on the bar in riotous dismay, covering his one good eye with his fingers. The black patch on the other helped him blot out the sight of the shocked society woman's gaping.

Brother Robert delights in relating the story of Bear Valley Charley Miller's divorce. "Bear had married a wardrobe girl at 20th Century- Fox Studios," Bob said. "When they finally stood in divorce court before the judge, Bear gasped aloud when it was announced for all to hear that his wife was divorcing him on grounds of cruelty.

"'I've got twelve of the toughest cowpokes who ever sat astride a horse right in this room!' roared the Bear. 'She can whip any one of 'em. I doubt that any of your deputies can whip *her*. Cruelty? Cruelty my ass!'

"'Fifty dollars fine for contempt of court!' The judge banged down his gavel and barked out, 'Divorce granted!'

"Bear Valley Charley sank back in his seat and sighed. It had cost him an extra $50 but he'd let the world know who had the most to fear in the Charley Miller union."

❄ ❄ ❄

And now meet Lennie "Bud" Osborne, who worked in an estimated 215 Western films and serials during his forty-year career. Bud was short but powerfully built for a man of 74 when I met him in 1955. He was considered one of the top "four-up" drivers in the picture business. A "four-up" is any vehicle pulled by four horses and Bud was indeed a master.

We were working on the serial "Perils of the Wilderness" on location at Big Bear Mountain, when Bud told us a story while we played poker. "I was born in the Oklahoma Territory. It wasn't a state then. My folks were Holy Rollers who went to Oklahoma City twice a year to attend conventions.

"Now we had living with us my Cousin Mary, twice removed. She was a divorcee. Folks frowned on divorcees in those days. (She was twenty- six years old and I was fourteen.)

"One night, the folks told us that they were leaving for Oklahoma City early in the morning. They'd be gone a month. It was a ten-day trip by wagon. I was told that my duties were to feed and water the stock, keep the firewood cut and stacked, and to mend fences. Cousin Mary, twice removed, was to keep the house up and do the cooking.

"I worked hard all the next day. I cut firewood, stacked it, fed the stock and watered them, came to the ranchhouse and took a tub bath. Cousin Mary, twice removed, had cooked a nice supper. I helped her with the dishes then commenced to fix a pallet on the floor. 'What are you doing, Bud?' Cousin Mary, twice removed, knew what I was doing but I told her anyway. 'Why, I'm fixin' a pallet on the floor.'

"She looked at me and smiled. 'You'll do no such thing. It's cold on that

Bob and I have a halfsister, Carol Morris, the daughter of Major Hugh Cunningham Morris and our mother Ann. She's done some acting herself but told me "I've never had any movie aspirations—just liked acting and theater work." She's been married twice: first to composer-singer Buddy Worth (a union that gave birth to three daughters and two sons) and then to musician Jimmy Allen. Carol currently works in the personnel department at the Baha'i International Center in Haifa, Israel. Although this photo was taken when she was 18, my sister Julie tells me Carol is still "serenely, exquisitely beautiful."

floor so you're gonna get into bed with me.'"

Bud looked hard at his cards and, with maddening deliberation, raised the ante by five dollars. "I did. And it was the first piece of human ass I'd ever had."

❄ ❄ ❄

Walt Whaley was a casting director at Four Star Studios for years who told me about a bit player named "Sailor" Vincent. He was known to one and all in the picture business because of his rasping voice. Walt related to me of a time when there was absolutely *nothing* happening in the business. No acting or filming, and no paying of money.

"I stared at the phone, day after day, praying for it to ring. Imagine a casting director *hoping* that someone would call. Finally, it did ring. I grabbed for it with trembling hands. 'Hello!' The voice was the Sailor's. He rasped into the phone, 'Walt, how do you cook a wolf?' He hung up before I could answer."

❄ ❄ ❄

Then there was Cap Summers, a physical brute of a man who could have modeled for the Olde English Toby mugs. One Thanksgiving Day he was watching the Army-Navy game on television. His wife repeatedly asked him to leave the set and come to dinner. Finally, in exasperation, she pulled the plug from the wall socket.

In a silent rage, Cap hurled the TV set out of their second-story apartment window. His wife, just as silently, hurled their entire Thanksgiving dinner, turkey and all, onto the bits and pieces of the doomed set scattered in the street. They sat and stared at each other until dark.

❄ ❄ ❄

Gregg Palmer, the actor they groomed at Universal to be a leading man but who never attained stardom, came home very late on a Christmas Eve three sheets to the wind. His usually patient wife, Ruth, met him at the front door with blood in her eyes. "Where've you been?"

"Buying things for the house," he burbled.

Ruth stared at his empty arms. "What things?"

Gregg smiled benignly. "Drinks!"

❄ ❄ ❄

Those of you who saw "Starman" with Jeff Bridges also saw Ted White in action. Ted was the rough cowboy who had killed the deer that the Starman brought back to life. Ted roughed up the hero, then got his comeuppance in return. He also got quite a shock once when he went to visit the stuntman Lenny Geer in Old Topanga Canyon.

One of Lenny's trained horses was standing proudly on the top of a hill behind Lenny's house. Ted got really excited. "Your horse is loose!" he shouted. "I'll go get him!"

Ted sped off on Lenny's dirt bike before Lenny could tell "that damn fool White" that the horse would trot to him at his whistle.

As Lenny later told it, "Ted was racing hellbent toward my horse on my dirt bike, then he disappeared, just plain disappeared. He didn't know it but there was a ravine there about twenty feet deep. The last damn thing I saw of him was that big white hat he wears sinking out of sight."

Lenny wasn't too pleased about the incident. "He did about a hundred dollars worth of damage to my dirt bike to rescue a horse that was a hell of a lot smarter than he was."

❄ ❄ ❄

It was never a big secret that Neville Brand drank heavily. So George Orrison, my stuntman friend, wasn't too surprised when the production manager on "Laredo" (a Western series Brand starred in as a Texas Ranger during the 1966-67 season) offered him an extra hundred bucks a day to keep Neville from drinking on the job.

George never got his hundred. He found out too late that the wily Brand got up very early in the morning (earlier than George, obviously), went to the stables and filled his canteen with straight vodka. That he fell off his horse that day can be attributed to those many times he would scan the horizon, wipe his brow, take a big swig from his canteen, then rasp out, "They went over that ridge."

Brand and James Drury, that gun-happy star of "The Virginian," rebelled against the practice that Universal Studios had of bringing tramloads of tourists to the sets. I agreed—it's difficult enough to portray an authentic Westerner with the noise of the Hollywood/Ventura Freeways droning in your ears, but to be interrupted by a megaphoned tram operator depicting the action was the final indignity.

But money talks, and Universal makes a great deal of it through their tours. Drury would simply walk off the set when the trams rolled by. That caused him numerous trips to The Black Tower. But when Brand *mooned* a tramload of corn-belt sightseers, the Powers That Be had had enough.

An apocryphal (though possibly true) story about Neville Brand goes like this: A group of TV columnists was visiting the studio where "Laredo" was produced and discovered the actor in a private office in a compromising position with a young woman, "firing away" in a manner that well-armed TV Western heroes were usually not seen doing in prime time. Brand is a top-notch actor who has played psychotic villains since 1949 when he debutted in "DOA."

This photo of actor Lenny Geer was taken by Jeffrey Hunter when they worked together on "White Feather" in Durango, Mexico, in 1954. Lenny was always a kidder and when he sent me this picture in 1988 he wrote: "Thirty-four years later and . . . I'm a little better looking now. Your brother is a great guy . . . I wish I could say the same about you, John. I'm only kidding. I don't want you mopping up the set with me."

Their two stars were much too troublesome. "The Virginian" and "Laredo" bit the dust and were no more.

❄ ❄ ❄

Chuck Roberson, John Wayne's double and stuntman, had a falling horse that he was very proud of. Falling horses are trained to go down at a given signal, and Chuck's was one of the best. In the early days of film, a horse would be tripped by a taut wire while at full gallop, and many were killed before the method was outlawed. More than a few riders were killed, too. *Trained* falling horses evolved from such inhumanity and mayhem.

Lenny Geer, a top horseman as well as stuntman, was also attached to his trained mount. One day he and Roberson were drinking beer in a bar in Topanga Canyon, arguing over the merits of their respective horses, when the debate spilled over into a fist fight reminiscent of the battle of David vs. Goliath. Roberson was 6-foot-3 and 220 pounds while Lenny, who weighed 190, stood an even six feet. They were still a match for each other but neither could ward off the minions of the law.

When their trial for disturbing the peace came up, Lenny told Roberson, "Cat, I'll represent us. I've practiced what we've got to say. Got it down pat." Roberson agreed.

Together they stood before the black-robed magistrate, who noticed a black and blue swelling over Chuck's ear. "You boys play pretty rough, don't you?" he remarked.

"Judge, sir, Your Honor!" Lenny stumbled for the right words. "We're the best of friends, Chuck and me. But we got to arguing over who had the best falling horse, so we got into it. *But!*" . . . he paused dramatically . . . "we were not a *public* nuisance, Judge, sir, Your Honor! We *did not* fight in the street. We fought in the *alley*."

The judge laughed, sentenced them to pay twenty-five dollar fines and adjourned the case.

On the steps of the courthouse, Chuck turned to Lenny and snarled, "Don't ever 'represent' me again. You cost me twenty-five bucks!" The fight nearly started all over again.

❄❄❄

Lenny and I did a great many charity shows together. I had the easy job—I emceed the shows and Lenny did horse falls, horse-drags and fight scenes with Ward Bond. Bond, the star of many John Ford Westerns before he commanded "Wagon Train," had a bad leg and would often slip as he aimed his fist. On some unfortunate occasions he would accidentally break Lenny's nose.

Ward Bond in 1952.

Lenny's wife, Dotty, would jump up excitedly during these barroom "brawls." "You watch—he's going to hit Lenny again."

Soon I would announce to the crowd, "And now, ladies and gentlemen, Ward Bond broke Lenny Geer's nose—once more."

❄❄❄

While Bond put Lenny in peril one way, another friend got him caught up in a bizarre situation. Lenny lives in Old Topanga Canyon, a picturesque place that winds through the Santa Monica Mountains at the northern end of the San Fernando Valley. It gets extremely hot there during the summer months and to offset the heat, Lenny drank a goodly amount of cold beer.

He had already downed a large-size six-pack when his old buddy, Von Dutch, came by to see him, riding a new motorcycle. He grandly offered it to Lenny to try out, not paying any attention to Lenny's stash of empty beer cans; Von Dutch had consumed a goodly number of his own.

Lenny drove the cycle up the canyon for a few hundred yards, turned it around and started down the grade toward his house. In the heat of the day the macadam road had turned very soft, and the cycle skidded into a spin. Lenny went sailing into the air and, like the skilled stuntman that he is, tucked and rolled as he hit the center of the roadway. When Von Dutch and some other friends of Lenny got to him, they were horrified to see the body of a large black Pacific rattlesnake twisting violently between his legs. Von Dutch lifted the stunned Lenny and broke out laughing.

The rattler, as it crawled across the gummy macadam, had the misfortune of being directly beneath the catapulted stuntman. Its head was deeply imbedded in the soft tar and its fangs were useless.

Dotty, Lenny's wife, insisted on checking to see if he had been bitten. Passing motorists stared in amazement as they witnessed a weaving, besotted spectacle of a man standing naked from the waist down, being examined by a frantic woman who was checking his private parts, while a small group of men were convulsed with laughter—to the staccato rhythm of an angry, six-foot rattler whose fangs were buried in the road.

GETTING THE BOOT CAN BE REWARDING

A RECENT development is the Golden Boot Award, conceived to pay homage to stuntmen and stuntwomen and actors who have specialized in the Western film genre.

In 1987 I was again invited (with my new wife Bonnie) to that gala by Tom and Marilyn Corrigan, who ramrodded the excellent barbecued steak and beans to 1,400 people in the huge Equestrian Center in Burbank.

Tom is the son of the late Ray "Crash" Corrigan, a famous cowboy stuntman of the '30s and '40s. Tom and Marilyn opened up a restaurant, Corrigan's Bar & Grill, in Thousand Oaks, and due to Tom's charisma (he's 6-foot-3 in his bare feet and 6-foot-9 in his cowboy boots and Stetson), the business has taken command of his life.

Once limousined luxuriously to the Awards, I became reacquainted with an army of actors that I have worked with over the years: Ben Johnson, Harry "Dobe" Carey Jr., Royal Dano, Bill Campbell, Lindsay Crosby, Buddy Ebsen, Robert Fuller, Ty Hardin, Jock Mahoney, Dale Robertson, John Russell, Patrick Wayne, Hank Worden . . .

Bruce Boxleitner, who has contributed his share of Western action in Kenny Rogers' "Gambler" TV movies, emceed the show. Iron Eyes Cody—in full Indian regalia—read the invocation in sign language as well as words. The dress code of the event was Western, all the way from well-washed jeans and plaid shirts to fringe, feathers and gussied-up leather.

Charlton Heston presented an Honoree award to Rhonda Fleming; Gene Autry so honored Robert Livingston; Royal Dano did so for Glenn Ford; Marie Windsor gave an award to John Russell; Jock Mahoney honored Gene Barry; Ben Johnson awarded his old saddle partner "Dobe" Carey, while Robert Blake bestowed an Honoree award to Woody Strode.

Woody was the first Black actor to rise to prominence in Westerns, notably in John Ford's "Sergeant Rutledge" and "Two Rode Together." He and his lovely Indian wife added a dimension of grace to the proceedings.

In the 1986 Golden Boot affair, I had been the presenter for The Sons of the Pioneers' award. This year I sat back to watch the major award presented to Joel McCrea who, because of illness, could not attend. Joel is an amazing man who started out in the extra ranks. He was chosen for a small part, doing it so well that he was selected for bigger roles. He wound up investing in land in Nevada that soared in value to make him a tremendously wealthy man. He never changed from the kind, thoughtful, warm man that he was as an actor. I worked with McCrea on one of his last films.

It was good seeing my old friend Rome Johnson from the Sons of the Pioneers. He could only find me after my name was announced over the public address system as an honored guest. I guess we all need to feel a continuity in life . . .

I was impressed with one autograph seeker with whom I had worked at Lockheed some 43 years ago. That's a long time to remember a face . . .

And it was an evening to remember.

❄❄❄

In 1988, the Corrigans asked me to see if Brother Robert would like to receive the 1988 Golden Boot Award. He's done a great many Westerns and is a helluva horseman.

Bob enthusiastically said he'd be delighted.

Logistics were being planned by us all, but the entertainment industry bolixed up the works unexpectedly with the conclusion of a quicker-than-expected film deal for Bob in New Zealand over an eleven-week period—and the Award was smack dab in the middle. Business is business, even at *his* exalted status in the industry.

Bob regretfully had to decline the Award.

Too bad. Bonnie and I would've loved to have sat at the "ringside" table with Bob and Dorothy Mitchum and with our hosts, Marilyn and Tom Corrigan, to see Bob get a well-deserved honor.

❄ ❄ ❄

No, it's almost impossible to get away from the entertainment business. The past keeps flooding into the present and the future seems always filled with excitement and promise.

Bob's made plenty of Westerns over the years—starting with the Hopalong Cassidy programmers in the 1940s and moving up into class-A productions after World War II. Raoul Walsh's "Pursued" (1947) was one of his best in which he played a young man haunted by nightmares of his childhood. Others have included Robert Wise's "Blood on the Moon" (1948), Lewis Milestone's "The Red Pony" (1949), Otto Preminger's "River of No Return" (1954), and Richard Fleischer's "Bandido" (1956). As this photo from the late 1940s reveals, Bob is well suited to outdoor settings and rugged action.

Boxing great Floyd Patterson made a cameo appearance with James Cagney in the TV-film "Terrible Joe Moran" in 1984.

FIGHTERS CAN BE FUN—SOMETIMES

ON MY 67th birthday, my daughter Cindy, her husband Steve Azbill, my son Jack, and his lady friend, Chalice Hilyard, hosted me (and about 60 dear friends I hadn't seen in ages) to a surprise birthday party with marvelous country fiddling and banjo plucking music, food and fun presents.

Bob and Dorothy were there, as were Sister Julie and our mother, Ann Morris. A dear friend, Bonnie Duff (more about her later), and her mother, Marion Duff, prodded me into going to a "business" appointment. It's a good thing I grudgingly went. All those surprise guests would have waited in vain and I would have missed a helluva party.

Lots of photos were taken but they were stolen, negatives and all, presumably because many of them pictured Bob prominently. It's happened before.

Brother Robert gave me two presents. Aware that I was moving to the Sierra Foothills in Northern California, he bought me a down-filled coat that I would sorely need in that crisp, winter air. The second present was a trip to Las Vegas with him to see the world's championship boxing bout between Michael Spinks and a big Norwegian challenger.

Bob and I have always been associated with fights and fighters. Now we're in $500 front-row seats—part of the public relations' freebie to Bob by the Hilton Hotel in Las Vegas—and I'm sitting next to Ingemar Johansson and shaking hands with Muhammad Ali. It was an unforgettable experience.

Floyd Patterson, who at 21 became the youngest heavyweight champion ever, stretched out his arms to Bob in cat-like fashion. It was obvious that the two had an enormous respect for each other. "How do you do it, Floyd? You're as trim as you ever were."

Patterson smiled at Bob. "Just keep workin' out, Bob. Who knows, I may get another chance at it." He looked over to Johansson who had taken his title in 1959 and they smiled amicably. Floyd had taken the title back in a 1960 ring war and they still were friends.

Bob and I were seated next to fight fan Rodney Dangerfield. When they were introduced, Dangerfield paid my brother a great compliment. "What," the fabulous comedian asked, "do you say when you meet Bob Mitchum?"

* * *

Fighters are a different breed. As a result, laymen have many impressions of them that are often wrong. In Peter Heller's book in which 40 world champions tell their stories, "In This Corner," Tommy Loughran (light-heavyweight champion of the world from October 1927-August 1929) wrote: ". . . this is what I'm meant for, to be a fighter, and I applied myself to it like I would to a profession. . . . There are few people that have had the privileges we've had. We have been blessed by having boxing ability to start with. . . . We have learned to conduct ourselves in our profession in such a way, we can't afford to lose our temper. If we do we get our heads knocked off. We pay for it immediately. We learn to put up with pain, push pain aside, disregard it entirely. . . . We know how it is to carry on in the face of

Robert and Dorothy are shown seated at Yankee Stadium on September 21, 1955, when they attended the Archie Moore-Rocky Marciano heavyweight title bout. Bob's in all his glory at the fights. To find out what happened that night, see the picture on Page 331.

Jimmy McLarnin in a 1933 pose.

pain. I fought seven rounds with a broken rib. . . . four rounds with a sprained ankle . . . fought for years with a broken right hand. I didn't let it affect my ability . . . We are regarded by a great many people with a contemptuous attitude because they figure that we're brutal, . . . we're going to smash through everything. That we don't have brains enough to see how we should conduct ourselves. I try to explain to people how there are always one or two people in every identification that are a little bit screwy, a little bit off base somewhere, and they are the ones that are held up as representing the whole identification. We hurt ourselves by thinking wrong, we help ourselves by thinking right."

The great welterweight champion of the world Jimmy McLarnin (May 1933-May 1934, September 1934-May 1935) explained: "I was in the fight game for 20 years, and very rarely have I run across a fighter I didn't like. . . . it's a hazardous business. I came up as a poor youngster, and I think most of the boys that ever get into the fight game are poor kids. They learn to take and to give. I think a lot of them have learned from experience that it pays to be nice. James J. Corbett used to come out to my [training] camp . . . and advise me: . . . 'Jimmy, remember one thing. A fighter can always afford to be a gentleman.' And I've never forgotten that."

❄ ❄ ❄

Throughout the years, Bob and I have known fighters who are not only warm and genuine people, but colorful and funny.

One such fighter was middleweight Abie Bain, who had a total of 485 fights in his long career.

Abie did extra work in films for many years and was well known to hundreds of picture people.

He used to shuffle around the sound stages crooning to himself. In a raspy baritone, he spoke of his innermost desires.

"You know, Mitch, I coulda been a song-and-dance man. Watch this!" He'd go into a spasmodic dance, complete with left-hand feints, weaving and bobbing to his own singing version of "I Don't Dance, Don't Ask Me," until I couldn't stand it any longer.

"Abie," I said one day, "I heard you fought 'two-ton' Tony Galento."

On the set of "Requiem for a Heavyweight" (1962): Mickey Rooney, Abie Bain, Anthony Quinn and Jackie Gleason.

Bain stopped short. "I went six rounds with the bum." (The record books show that he went four, but who's to quarrel?)

I shook my head. "Abie, how could you, at 158, get into the ring with the 240-pound Galento?"

"Oh," he said loftily, "I had a manager with a lot of courage."

❄ ❄ ❄

In 1961, on the flight back from Bend, Oregon, after my two segments of "Have Gun Will Travel," Richard Boone, once a very good boxer himself, delighted in recounting to me an Archie Moore story.

"Archie was just finishing up his training for a championship bout and was only four pounds over the 175-pound limit. At 179, he was edgy and irritable, barking at his children and snapping at his wife," Dick said.

In order to calm down, Archie took a long drive in the mountains in his Cadillac. In a reverie over the coming bout, he drifted across the road and almost collided head-on with a pickup truck. Its driver, angry at the near accident, roared around Archie, cutting him off. He leaped from his truck and ran over to Archie's car. Archie, who in those days wore dapper suits to avoid the 'fighter' image, was getting out of his car when the rancher, who stood some 6-foot-3, pulled him to his feet by his establishment threads.

"Why you sonofabitch!" he snarled. "You almost got me! I oughta . . ." He stopped for a moment, eyeing the "Old Mongoose" apprehensively. "Don't I know you?"

Archie smiled up at his huge antagonist. "You ain't acting like you do," he whispered.

The now-somber man walked slowly back to his pickup and waved

Here are challenger Archie Moore (left) and heavyweight champion Rocky Marciano posing in Madison Square Garden a day before their fateful match at Yankee Stadium in '55. Both men weighed 188 at weigh-in time. Marciano threw the right punch and Moore went down to lose the fight.

respectfully at the great fighter. It had been the pick-up driver's second near-miss of the day.

Moore was such a great fighter that for seven years he begged for a chance at the light-heavyweight title. He even paid for newspaper ads, declaring his intention to get a title shot and to win it. Eventually he got the chance—and held the title for seven more years. He even fought Rocky Marciano. Few people know that he was over forty-two years of age when he slugged it out with Rocky.

I was on the sound stage of "Bonanza" when Dan Blocker and the great Marciano met for the first time. Hoss, at 6-foot-4, 285 pounds was tongue-tied for almost a minute as he stared down at the 5-foot-9, 190-pound champion. "Rocky" Marciano was equally in awe of the giant Texan: It was a mutual-admiration event.

One of Moore's perennial foes was a fighter named Joe Kahut. Kahut and Moore were so skilled as to be evenly matched and so great that no other fighters wanted to get in the ring with them. So it was that they fought each other nine times. They had to make a living. Moore shaded Joe six of their nine bouts.

Brother Robert sparred one time with Charley Burley, another of Moore's fearful opponents. Seeing an opening, Bob stung Charley with a left to the cheek, then suddenly felt a terrible burning in his side. Burley, in retaliation, had sunk a right hand into Robert. As Bob gasped for breath, Burley whispered in his ear, "That's the name of the game, baby."

❄ ❄ ❄

A very well-known boxer on the West Coast is Art Aragon, famed as the "Golden Boy." In July of 1958, George Fargo met him on the street, marvelling at him. "Art, I read you're gonna mix it up with Carmen Basilio."

The stocky, one hundred and forty-pound Aragon stopped short. "Yeah, pal. We're fightin' next month." (Basilio is one of the toughest fighters to have ever pulled on a pair of gloves.) Fargo clucked sympathetically. "How did you ever get sucked into it?"

Art looked at George intently. "I don't know. I went to my manager and told him, 'You got me booked in with Basilio. He's from the East Coast. Those guys are serious!'"

Sure enough, Basilio mangled him.

❄ ❄ ❄

The classic story belongs to Jack Roper, a studio electrician and journeyman heavyweight fighter. He had a left hand that would move a house. He once enthralled me with the story of his match for the world's championship against the great Joe Louis. Louis was on his famous "bum of the month" campaign, a challenge to anyone who thought he might have a chance to wrest the crown from his head.

"I had a left that could drop a mule." Roper spoke with a whisper. (He died a year after he told me the story; he had throat cancer but didn't know it at that moment.) "I couldn't crush an egg with my right. To psyche me out, my trainer made me throw a ten-pound shot to develop the right. I got so tired of running after the shot, I started throwin' it against an oak tree. Almost cut the tree down. Now, I'm ready! I didn't know it, but I still couldn't hurt an egg with that right."

Roper whispered on. "Now the night of the fight comes around. I'm sittin' in my corner, listenin' to the crowd. Four thousand people there. Most of 'em Hollywood people, watchin' to see one of their own fight for the title. Now, the announcer comes in. 'Ladies and gentlemen, for the heavyweight

Art Aragon was found guilty of bribery and sentenced to prison, but he took the case to the District Court of Appeal. The higher court ruled he hadn't received a fair trial and ordered a new one, but the D.A.'s office decided to drop the case at that point. So on Dec. 4, 1957, Superior Court Judge Herbert V. Walker dismissed the case and Aragon left the courtroom looking like Rocky Balboa, a free man once again.

Here's one that sounds like a movie plot: Jack O'Halloran, in September 1978, was in his home in San Diego when eight men burst through the door armed with pistols. They abducted Jack and his lady friend into a van, and took off for Los Angeles, but when the van slowed at an intersection, O'Halloran and the woman escaped. In 1988 O'Halloran's acting career took a stride forward when he co-starred with Chuck Norris in "Hero and the Terror," portraying a psychotic killer who hides the bodies of his female victims in the attic of a Los Angeles movie theater.

championship of the world, in the black corner, at 205 pounds, our own Jack Roper!' The crowd goes wild."

Jack Roper's eyes held a faraway look. "'In the white corner, at 211 pounds, the heavyweight champion of the world, the great Brown Bomber, Joe Louis!'" Of course, the crowd is screamin'. The bell sounds and I hit Joe with a left hook that had him sittin' on the bottom strand of the ropes. He is dazed and lookin' up at me in pain. I should have hit him with another left, but no. I'm lookin' at my right and sayin' to myself, '*Now* the world's gonna see that Jack Roper has a right hand!'"

Jack looked at me, shaking his head. "That's the last thing I remember."

❄ ❄ ❄

In the 1975 version of "Farewell, My Lovely," it is generally recognized that Bob played Raymond Chandler's private eye Philip Marlowe as well as any actor, although I think he did it better. Purely a personal observation. But the story at hand concerns actor Jack O'Halloran, who played "Moose" Malloy in the picture.

O'Halloran is a huge man who had to quit fighting because doctors found that he was suffering from acromegaly. The doctors arrested the pituitary condition that triggers the affliction, but warned him that punches to the head could do irreparable damage.

O'Halloran came on the set one morning and told Bob that he had gone to a bar in Long Beach the night before. He put a $20 bill on the bar and asked for a Scotch and soda. He then went to the men's room and came back to find there was no drink—neither was there a $20 bill.

"'Barkeep, did you take the twenty I put down on the bar?'" The bartender told him that he hadn't been down at that end of the bar yet. According to Bob, Jack was starting to get a little hot. "I looked down at the guy that was sitting on the next stool to me. 'Did you see my twenty that I put on the bar?' I waited for an answer and he started smirking. 'I saw a twenty but I didn't see no name on it.' The guy had a lot of nerve. Now, I was mad! I looked straight into his face. 'Did *you* take my twenty?' He looked up at me, still smirkin'. 'I took a twenty—wid no name on it!'"

At that point in the story, O'Halloran paused to look at Bob, then said, "I blew up. I slapped him an open-handed shot, pulled his head back and started stuffin' money down his throat! 'You want money? Okay! Here's money!' And I kept crammin' it down his throat."

Bob asked him where he had stopped.

"A hundred and forty-three bucks worth." O'Halloran didn't crack a smile.

❄ ❄ ❄

On a flight from El Paso to Los Angeles, Dan Blocker told me of his experiences as a boxer. "While I was at Sul Ross College in Texas, one of my classmates talked me into entering the Golden Gloves Tournament. Hell! I'm no boxer. I told him so, but he convinced me that I should try it."

"'You're big and strong. There's no tellin' how far you could go.'"

"One of the boys at the school trained me. Before my first fight, I told 'em that at my first loss, I'd quit, that I'd want a case of beer for my troubles. Now, I'm in Dallas and lookin' across the ring at the meanest lookin' man I'd ever seen. Somebody must have beaten him with an ugly stick. Well, the bell sounded so I hit him with a left over the heart. He went down. And out. 'What hath God wrought?' I asked myself.

"The next fight was in Oklahoma City against a big Indian. He was meaner lookin' than the first one. Wham! A right hand on the chin and he is gone. Now that went on for five fights and I began to think I was mighty good.

"The final bout for the regional championship comes up while I'm back in Dallas. I looked across the ring at my opponent but I can't believe my eyes. Sittin' there is the sweetest lookin' boy I've ever seen. Soft, round eyes. He looks like a baby. Not a mark on his face. 'How dare they,' I commented to myself, 'put a lamb like that in with a tiger like me.' I looked at my gloved fists and said to myself, 'Here stands the next heavyweight champion of this-here world!'"

"The bell rang and I never did stop spinnin'. I never saw the boy. Whop! A left and I'd spin around. Whomp! A right, and back I'd go the opposite way. I had blisters on my feet from spinnin' around. He never did knock me out, but I was prayin' he would. When the final bell rang and I could talk, I barely whispered to my manager, 'Where's my beer?' That ended my boxin' career."

❄ ❄ ❄

A cardinal rule in the ring is that every boxer protects himself at all times. Men have died from severe beatings in the "squared circle." One such death resulted from a bizarre set of circumstances that involved Emile Griffin and Benny Paret.

Griffin had an enterprising business outside of the arena as a hat designer. Paret made a huge mistake by taunting Emile about his successful sideline, making questioning allusions to Griffin's manhood.

In the ring, Griffin exploded into total fury. He caught Paret with a solid hook that stunned him and left him standing in the corner with his head against the ring post. Griffin delivered a dozen straight righthand shots full into the head of the now doomed fighter. Too late, the referee pulled away the frenzied Griffin. Paret died ten days later.

The Death of Kid Paret

The full tragedy of the Benny (Kid) Paret-Emile Griffin fight at Madison Square Garden on March 24, 1962, is recaptured in these photos. At right the two contenders weigh in. That's the Kid in the white trunks, looking ironically euphoric, while Griffin looks less pleased at right. Between them is James A. Farley Jr., commissioner of the New York State Athletic Commission. Below left, Paret has already taken a horrific beating in the 12th round and the fight is about to be stopped. But it's already too late. The Kid, shown in a boxing pose at bottom right, would never wake up.

It has recently come to light that many superb athletes are homosexual. Obviously, they are not the limp-wrist stereotyped "gays" that are so subject to scorn and ridicule. A lot of them are tougher than rawhide.

❄❄❄

My friend Abel Fernandez—excellent fighter, drinking buddy, and a fine actor in "The Untouchables" TV series—recently sent me a written memory of an event shared with Brother Robert. Abel called it "A Look Back":

"Year = 1953. Location = Mexico City. Site = Restaurant, Charity Ball. Time = 8:00 p.m. It all began at a charity ball that was attended by the cast of RKO's 'Second Chance,' a film then being made in the faddish 3-D system: Robert Mitchum, Jack Palance, Linda Darnell, Abel Fernandez.

"It was a gala affair. Of course, the attraction was Robert Mitchum. When he and his wife Dorothy entered the hall, the show in progress had to stop because of the fans. We reached our table and were called on stage to say a few words. We did.

"The audience was mixed with many American students living and studying in Mexico. They were becoming belligerent and making bad remarks to us. Came the moment for presentations to the charity. First, the RKO Studio rep went up and gave them a check for $2,000 pesos.

"Bob was introduced to the thrill of the crowd; he gave them a check for $5,000 pesos. The house came down! Anyway, trouble started. Their mistake? To try to pick on Bob! Needless to say the students (American) backed off when Bob and I confronted them. Bob was ready to flatten a big redhead who pulled on his tie and talked right in his face. Bob put a hand on his chest and shoved, and the guy flew into his friends. I stepped in but they just talked and we walked out.

"Later, we went to a restaurant on La Reforma. Something happened as we walked in. There was a general, his aides, his wife and bodyguards. The general knew Bob so he was very happy. Suddenly a table was thrown across the room. The general and his aides pulled *guns*; we were in the line of fire. Bob, Dorothy and I talked to the general in Spanish and we got out—no shooting! We were lucky, right? Ask Bob about that. He should remember that."

Family Portrait: Sister Julie Sater, me, Bob and our mother, Ann Morris.

I've fought a lot and won a lot, but must confess that I want no part of Brother Robert in a free-for-all. I can attest personally to the fact that it ain't much fun to get involved with him. *Nobody* wins when it's just the two of us.

❄ ❄ ❄

Twice in my life I was offered a chance to become a fighter in stables of very good boxers—the first time when I was still stationed in Honolulu and the second after I returned to the States. I most reluctantly passed up the two dream-of-a-lifetime opportunities because I met with so much opposition from my wife (first ex-) and her mother that it became a forbidden subject in my own home. *And a nagging ache in my heart for years.*

Their vehemency didn't spring from any fear that I might be hurt, but rather it was beneath *their* dignity and social status. Their concept was that all fighters were barbarians and that *they* would be tarred and feathered as such if I became one.

I'm confessing now, after all these years, that I should have listened to my own instincts. As Marlon Brando once said in a classic motion picture: *"I coulda been a contender."*

Bob had an interesting character role as Bibic, a wise, Old-World patriarch, in the 1983 Golan-Globus production "Maria's Lovers," which was filmed on location in a Pennsylvania mining town. It starred Nastassia Kinski, John Savage and Keith Carradine. The story takes place shortly after World War II when a young man returns home to his bride, unable to adjust to civilian life and cope with his mental problems.

THE WEAKER SEX — ?

AFTER THE Spinks fight in Las Vegas, Bob and I were asked to come to the VIP room at the top of the Hilton. It was flooded with expensively gowned women and their escorts. Many of the women, behind their escorts' backs, mouthed lascivious, explicit invitations to Robert.

He was not impressed. "Why won't they leave me alone?" he whispered to me.

I left him and went down to the casino to try my hand at the slot machines. I was glumly losing my quarters when a pretty young Black lady sat next to me. She had seen Bob and me walk across the casino earlier and asked me if we had come to see the fights. I told her that we had. She got down to business immediately.

"I'm a professional too, you know." (That possibility had occurred to me.) As in all modern advertising, she used the "only" word casually. "Only five hundred dollars."

I laughed so hard I nearly fell off the stool. Paying for sex to me is an exercise in futility. Without caring for another person, it's about as interesting as a proposition put to me by "Bear" Hudkins when we were filming "Paint Your Wagon" in Baker, Oregon.

I saw the "Bear," the brother of the formidable welterweight fighter, "Ace" Hudkins, rambling down the main street of Baker one night.

"Want to come along?" he asked.

"Where you going?"

"I'm going to the warehouse to watch 'em unload the Safeway trucks."

I excused myself from the enterprising lady and went up to my suite. Within twenty minutes she was at my door (having ascertained my room number through her grapevine, no doubt), asking if she could have a drink. I had a bottle of wine so I poured her a glass. It didn't take her long to ask "Where's your brother?" She eyed me expectantly.

"Up in the VIP room." I looked at her coolly. "With two dozen ladies who'd give their eyeteeth to hop into the kip with him. For nothing."

She borrowed my turtleshell comb from my etui and never gave it back. I guess she figured she'd at least get something from a Mitchum; the evening shouldn't be a total loss.

Bob required an armed escort to his suite, but the women followed him all the way to his front door. Only the presence of security guards kept him from further assault.

❄❄❄

In the spring of '85, my long-time friend Will Hunt played the lead in a musical play with the improbable title of "Back County Crimes" in an Equity-waiver Hollywood theater. He asked me to write new music for it; the artistic director couldn't afford expensive royalties. It was a challenge I couldn't ignore. I composed a complete score—and fell in love.

After three marriages, I had vowed never to try it again. And then I met Bonnie Duff, one of the leads in the play and the group's only trained singer. (I was to find out later that she is also a professional actress, ex-dancer/teacher, published writer of children's stories, and a legal word processor.) She looked at me, I looked at her. I went on point like a bird dog in a

This is Bonnie Duff, the woman I married in 1986 on a sunny afternoon and with a sigh of relief that I'd finally nabbed her for my own after 18 months of passionate courtship. Before I knew her she had been an actress in Hollywood for four years in the 1960s and for four more years in the'80s working in TV commercials—but then she'd had enough. She's a published author of children's stories, poetry and newspaper articles; a singer; a helluva good secretary; a mural painter, and an actress and director of more than 30 stage productions in Seattle, Colorado Springs, Scottsdale and Hollywood (and she's won some acting awards along the way). She's also laid out the blueprints for our dream house. She's a multi-talented lady who remains loyally at my side. I can finally tell my mother I did good.

Photo by John Stanley

meadow of quail. We locked in an energy field of electricity, our eyes riveted on each other. When we touched hands, the years fell magically away from me. I was young again. Life was once more full of rich flavor.

I thought she was married and reluctantly kept my distance. Two months later, at the play's wrap party, I strode up to Bonnie, stood nose to nose with her and bluntly stated, "I just found out that you *aren't* married."

Bonnie looked startled, then said, "Oh, no wonder you didn't come after me. I *wanted* you to."

"Well, what're we going to do about it?"

"Let's get on with it," she boldly declared.

We got on with it, though not without a few handicaps. Several jealous—let's say "neurotic"—females tried to keep us apart, including an ex-girl friend who threw away my address book. (It took me over a year to restore those precious phone numbers.) The same lady went so far as to report to the police that Bonnie had threatened on the phone to kill *her*. A tap was put on Bonnie's phone for about a month, but since it was a lie made by a pathological liar, nothing came of it.

Others tried the divisive means of pitting us against each other with lies and half-lies, gossip and insinuations. There were episodes of aggressive behavior that made *me* want to become aggressively violent, but I contained myself. Bonnie and I fortunately saw through all these possessive machinations. I guess we were meant to be together. Kismet.

October 19, 1986: The day of my wedding to Bonnie, when Father Vaughan said in a perfect mime of John Wayne: "Well, alright Pilgrim, you can kiss the bride now." That's Brother Bob standing off to the right as my Best Man, wearing his first smile of the day.

Right after the marriage ceremony, Bonnie and I posed with actor/good friend William Vaughan, who served as one of my attendants that afternoon. The wedding photos on the opposite page are proof positive that life begins at 67.

A year and a half after that fateful meeting, on October 19, 1986, we were married in a garden ceremony at the Glendale hilltop home of John Staley, who is a business tycoon, an inventor, a racehorse owner and a pool shark. He and his wife Louise wanted us to "go all out" in spite of *our* limited wherewithal.

It was an event to be remembered on a breathtakingly beautiful day; the circling mountain backdrop added a touch of timeless charm as a breeze fluttered the maypole ribbons over our heads and bees hummed among the chrysanthemums on our makeshift altar.

Brother Robert carried the ring as my best man, while my son Jack "fathered" the bride. My 92-year old mother, Ann, and Bonnie's 82-year old mother, Marion, gently cautioned us to behave ourselves. A Scots bagpiper played "Amazing Grace" and had us singing in tears. We floated to the altar with the piper skirling a Scottish lockstep tune, escorted by family members and dear friends, with rose petals scattered at our feet by touchingly ernest

granddaughters Corina and Vanessa Azbill. Friends old and new—one hundred and sixty of them—made it a day of beauty.

Methodist Pastor Tony Yim read from Kalil Gibran's "The Prophet": "But let there be spaces in your togetherness, and let the winds of the heavens dance between you . . ." Bonnie got a lesson in how thorough a knot Father Thomas Vaughan can tie when he puts jazz piano aside and dons white Episcopal robes. Even solemn Brother Robert smiled broadly when Father Vaughan—in a perfect mime of John Wayne—looked at me and intoned, "Well, alright Pilgrim, you can kiss the bride now."

A four-foot cake with icing of Italian amaretto-flavored whipped cream was given by a generous new friend. I made a mental note to get to it before the hordes. Bonnie and I never got to eat any of the gorgeous food Matron of Honor Cindy and Attendant Chalice had made. (Chalice later became Jack II's bride, much to our delight.)

Afterward, Bonnie and I danced. It was a timeless time.

Brother Robert, as taciturn as ever, decided to split for his home in Montecito, despite the lamentations of his wife Dorothy, our sister Julie and our mother who were all enjoying themselves. He had the car, so they left. (They didn't speak to him for two days.)

Bonnie and I revelled in a luxurious honeymoon at a Pasadena hotel, a generous gift from Bob and Dorothy, getting our new lives off to a fine start.

Y'ALL COME! (BUT DON'T STAY)

BONNIE AND I moved to the Mother Lode country from Los Angeles one week after the wedding and immediately plunged into the busiest schedule we had ever known. Grass Valley and Nevada City—approximately sixty miles northeast of Sacramento—are loaded with antiquity and charm. They are deep wells of talent; the activities of The Music in the Mountains, the Nevada Theatre, the tours of the historial Empire Mines and the cities themselves attract visitors from all over the world.

Millions of dollars in gold were taken from the mines in the days of the Forty-Niners. There is much more down there when one considers that the shafts, although aditing at the 2,500 foot level, sink down to over 4,000 feet. Much of the mine is below the ocean and it's been estimated that it would take nine years just to pump the water out to get the millions in gold still waiting there.

Grass Valley and Nevada City are studded with buildings that go back into those times. Churches, stores, hotels and bars hosted miners from all parts of the globe and their influences still are boldly implanted into the lifestyle of the community. We never tire of coasting through like tourists, showing off to our out-of-town friends.

While searching the area for a permanent place to live, we saw our first stage production in Nevada City, "Blithe Spirit." Halfway through the play we looked at each other and spontaneously agreed that we had found our theater "home." This area was no backward place in which to retire into dust. It *is* a place to come and live it up, with all the verve one can muster.

Nevada City hosts a musical group called Music in the Mountains and it works hand-in-glove with the Foothill Theatre Company. It didn't surprise me that when they did "Pirates of Penzance," Mabel was performed by Lucy Becker, who had won the regional auditions for the Metropolitan Opera tryouts in San Francisco; she opted to stay in her beloved foothill country

Michael Joseph of Nevada City snapped this portrait of me while I was in the cast of "Noises Off," presented in the spring of '88 at the Nevada Theatre in downtown Nevada City. The play won four Elly awards for Northern California-area excellence.

A New Life in Nevada City

Here I'm with one of Bob's thoroughbreds stabled at the Tackitt Stock Farm outside Grass Valley, California. It's beautiful grazing land--one of the reasons Bob decided to keep his horses permanently stabled there. Below left, I'm squatting next to one of the gravestones in the old section of the Nevada City Cemetery, just one of many sites that makes our town a picturesque place to live, and which attracts tourists year-round.

Photos by John Stanley

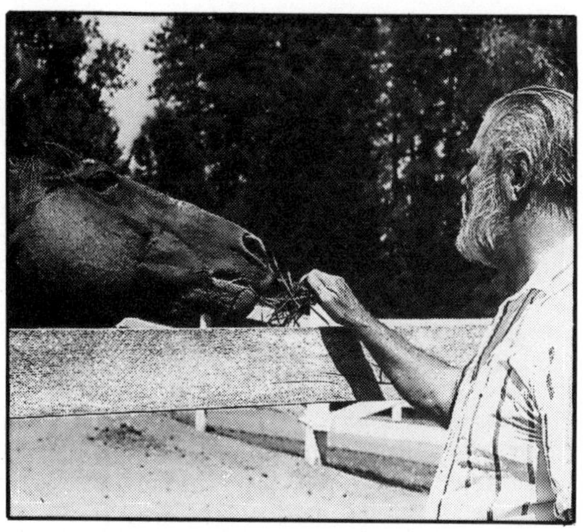

I've always loved the outdoors and find the Tackitt Ranch a place where I enjoy hanging out with Bob's horses. But if there's any one place where Bonnie and I spend most of our time, it's at the Nevada Theatre (below) in downtown Nevada City. The site was made an historical landmark in 1974. We've been in several Foothill Theater Company productions there, and Bob was in the audience when I did "Noises Off" in the spring of '88.

rather than move to New York.

In rapid order Bonnie auditioned for and got lead roles in "Harvey," "I Remember Mama," an original Easter season play, "The Two Fools," and "The Foreigner." She still belongs to three stage companies. I played two roles in "Mama" and ran around madly in the British farce "Noises Off." We feel that the talent in the Foothill Theatre Company, particularly, could hold its own with professional groups in Hollywood.

Theater, music, fine restaurants, history and historical monuments to a vital past keep this area bustling with activity. And it all takes place in an atmosphere graced by pristine mountains burgeoning with deer, fast-running streams filled with trout, heavily forested glades and lush meadows that host some of the most beautiful horses in the world.

The Loma Rica Ranch, run by Henry Frietas, produced champion thoroughbreds for over thirty years. Penn Valley's Polly and Jay Parsons (formerly of Rough and Ready, that secessionist town of the Civil War located only a few miles from Grass Valley) had five mares who foaled quarter horses whose earnings topped the $100,000 mark. Parsons, a famous millionaire in our area, now has a ranch near the Tackitt Stock Farm.

Don Guerro, Brother Robert's magnificent stallion, the running champion of 1974, is back "home" to the 6-B Ranch (aka the Tackitt Stock Farm) in Grass Valley, leased and operated by Dale and Annie Tackitt.

As I watched Dale work out a yearling in a manure-dotted field, I couldn't help but reminisce about my riding in that 1956 movie serial "Perils of the Wilderness." Until then my horsebacking was practically nil and I rode my steed with the ill-advised notion that I should emulate the jockies who rode Gallant Fox or Secretariat. I thought I looked classical leaning over the horse's neck and slipping the wind. That is, until the head wrangler took me aside.

"Johnny," he said, "I like you. Otherwise I wouldn't be talking to you like this. But for God's sake, sit up straight and tall in that saddle. Look like you own that horse. Cripes!" He looked furtively around and then whispered, "You look like a monkey fuckin' a watermelon."

❄❄❄

The governor of Oregon endorsed a slogan for tourists to his state: "Y'all come—but don't stay!" I thought that it sprang from a smug complacency about that beautiful state and I vaguely resented it. Now in the environs of the foothills, I see more and more traffic, more and more people. And I turn to Bonnie and growl, "We're bein' crowded out."

I have begun to have an uncomfortable alliance with the philosophy of the governor of Oregon.

THIS IS RETIREMENT?

THE DICTIONARY STATES: "Retire—to withdraw oneself from business, public life or active service." When we moved to the Mother Lode country that's what we thought we were doing. But with five or six plays under our belts, singing engagements at service clubs, books to write and fund raising activites for four motion picture scripts, I've taken a long look at the word and its meaning. We are meeting new friends by the score and are in close touch with old acquaintances.

Among the new friends are John and Erica Stanley of Pacifica, near San Francisco. John is a journalist who has covered movies and television for *The San Francisco Chronicle* for several decades, the author of several books and a publisher (it is the latter activity that explains why you are reading this book). Although John had first interviewed me on the set of "The Enforcer" in the summer of 1976, we had remained out of touch until we were re-introduced by Mick Martin of *The Sacramento Union.* Mick is a bear of a man whose real love is music. He is an accomplished writer and journalist but loves to wail out the blues on a harmonica. We met the Stanleys at Lake Tahoe during their mini-vacation at the High Sierra Resort at Stateline, Nevada.

Lake Tahoe, one of the most scenic spots on earth, is over 30 miles long. It is a veritable jewel nestling amidst fir-clad mountains—and yet most visitors in this paradise spend their waking hours in the casinos that dot its northern and southern shores. We fell into the casino trap too. John took us to see his good friend, the comedian Ronnie Schell. Ronnie's show is clean and exhilerating; we laughed so hard our sides ached. Some of his patter and visual effects centers around outtakes from his witty television commercials. Those dealing with "contented cows" have hilarious—uh, utterances.

❄ ❄ ❄

Sandwiched into our hectic activities have been meetings with Bonnie's delightful sons and their lovely wives: Michael Stipek and his bride Peggy from Denver, Colorado; Danny Stipek and Marcy with long-awaited daughter Ashlee Dana (Bonnie's first grandchild) from Fortuna, California; none of whom were able to come to our quickly planned wedding. And Jack II and Chalice gave me my sixth grandchild—Sarah Anne—in the summer of '88. In my hearts of hearts I've always wanted a big family—now I've got one.

❄ ❄ ❄

New life. And death. All part of Life.

❄ ❄ ❄

The San Francisco Chronicle ran these lines: "John Huston died after a long, lingering illness on August 28, 1987." Three days later Bob, running on a hectic schedule, called me to say he had just finished a role in "Mr. North," a picture that John's son, Tony Huston, directed. John, originally scheduled to play the role, had to pull out because of failing health. He called Bob, the only one he would accept, to replace him. Bob agreed.

Prior to Huston's death, Bob had flown to Fall River, Massachusetts, to see the ailing film maker in the hospital. "I found John sitting up in a wheel chair with an oxygen tank attached," Bob told me. "I told him that he didn't look so ill that he couldn't have finished the picture himself."

Bob said that John had laughed quietly. "Biggest hoax I ever pulled, kid."

The nurses told Bob that Huston wasn't eating enough, so Bob confronted the 81-year-old miscreant. "I'm eating enough," Huston grumbled.

Bob persisted. "If I prove to you that you're not, will you at least confess it?" Huston allowed that he would.

Bob brought in a very pretty young nurse. He had her lift up her skirt to

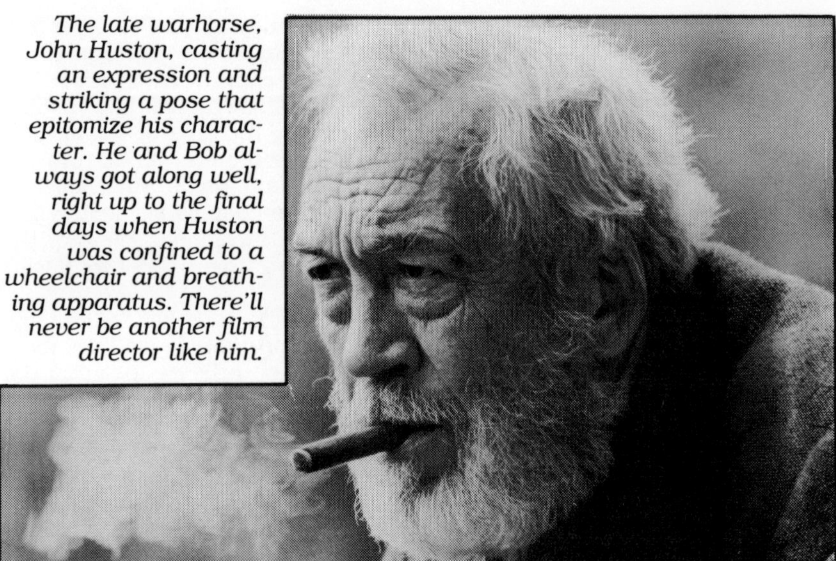

The late warhorse, John Huston, casting an expression and striking a pose that epitomize his character. He and Bob always got along well, right up to the final days when Huston was confined to a wheelchair and breathing apparatus. There'll never be another film director like him.

the waist, slowly turn around and "moon" Huston. Bob eyed him the while, delighted to see a slow grin lighting up the emaciated face. "You're right, kid," the old man chortled. "I'm not eating enough."

Robert loved John Huston. He bridled when "Entertainment Tonight" asked him to appear to comment on John's passing. Bob felt that Huston's death was hardly entertaining.

"I should have told them that if they were so hot to make his death a part of their 'entertainment,' they should drive an oak stake through his heart. It would've been the only way to make sure that great soul was gone."

❄ ❄ ❄

Brother Robert had just finished working on "Mr. North" when he had two frantic visitations from the staff of Edward Woodward's TV show, "The Equalizer." Woodward had suffered a temporary heart problem; would Bob do two guest segments? Bob reluctantly agreed.

At the ripe old age of 70 (but definitely not looking it), he worked for nearly a year on "War and Remembrance" (about 30 hours of air time), the sequel to "Winds of War," did "Mr. North," filmed two strenuous television segments and romped through an impertinent "Saturday Night Live" in New York for his writer-daughter, Trina. On reflection, it seems to refute the prevalent opinion that after thirty you're finished in the business.

❄ ❄ ❄

Of course Father Time finishes us all eventually—as it stilled the once indomitable Lee Marvin. Near midnight in August, 1987, Father Thomas Vaughan telephoned me. John Huston's passing and Marvin's dying so soon after had given him pause to look back over the years. His reason for needing to talk is my belief in our all-seeing, eternal God. My faith is serenely sure, so sure that I can match the often ribald Father story for story.

He told me once that he is uncomfortable when surrounded by what he

Bob in one of his biggest roles of the 1980s: Captain Victor "Pug" Henry, the American naval officer who is the catalyst in the TV version of Herman Wouk's "The Winds of War."

calls "the penguins," those groups of priests waddling around in their black suits and white collars.

To that end he asked me if I knew Dick Contino, the accordionist. I told him that I didn't know him personally but admired his ability. Father Vaughan told me that he had suggested to Contino that they open a new parish music school to be named "Lady of Spain." Contino, puzzled, had asked why. Tom Vaughan said, "Because without that tune to fall back on, accordionists would die."

I told him of my raunchy Monty Woolley story when I first hit California and he retaliated.

"I was a student at Yale University when Woolley taught there. He would go out into the ocean at low tide and put himself into a trance while the cold sea water crept up his legs to slowly engulf his private parts. When his

In the 1980s Bob moved further into the TV-movie genre. At right he's with Wilford Brimley in "Thompson's Last Run," in which he portrays a tired old convict who breaks out of the slammer. Wilford plays a one-time friend-now-lawman determined to bring him in.

At left, Bob is with Virginia Madsen in "The Hearst and Davies Affair," which depicted the scandalous romance of newspaper magnate William Randolph Hearst and actress Marion Davies, the couple who ran Hearst Castle. Orson Welles had loosely based his great motion picture "Citizen Kane" on their unusual relationship.

balls were fully immersed, he would heave a great spasmodic sigh of relief and, totally spent, clamber back to the strand and to reality."

By the late 1980s, Robert and I should have been taking our shoes off and watching sunsets. No way. Bob threaded his way halfway around the world finishing up "War and Remembrance" and he continues to be deluged with offers to work and, although he protests that he doesn't want to, he's constantly accepting. In no way does this mean that he hasn't occasionally found the time to have fun.

On July 5, 1987, Bob and Dorothy threw a lulu of a wingding at their home with live music, a sketch artist and a houseful of people. I looked over and saw Stuart Whitman kissing Bonnie's hand with an air of old-world gallantry.

I was distracted by Jonathan Winters, who stopped to tell me a bit of his family history—I *think* it was history. When Jonathan relates a tale, he does it with all the suggestive intrigue of a KGB agent. His eyes half-closed, he whispers furtively three inches from your ear, and he looks around as if half-expecting a bomb to be thrown.

"When I got out of the service, my father grabbed me by my jacket," Jonathan muttered. "He pointed at my two stripes, sneering in disdain. 'Is this the best you could do?' I said, 'Dad, it's better than you being caught playing with yourself in a C.C.C. camp in Montana!' 'Who told you that?' he cried, then he rapidly changed the subject. 'You're a faggot!' daddy screamed. 'I saw you wearing a dress on the TV!' 'That's my role as Maudie Fricket!' I defended myself. 'Wouldn't you wear a dress for ten thousand dollars?' He glared at me. 'I wouldn't wear a dress for a million dollars.'"

Jonathan looked swiftly around us to spot any would-be assassins. Those shifty eyes finally centered on mine. "I looked Dad full in the face and told him what for. 'Mother always said you were an asshole!'"

John Ireland stopped to tell me that he was in the throes of writing his tell-all autobio. Shelley Winters is prominently featured in it.

I didn't have the heart to tell him that in the early 1950s, Bob, Shelley and I were seated together in a booth at a bar called The Black Watch. Shelley was impatiently staring at her watch, waiting for Ireland to appear for a date. She suddenly had her fill of waiting. "Well, it looks like the son of a bitch isn't going to make it," she snarled. She swivelled around and stared at me. "How about you?"

I passed. I'm old-fashioned enough to enjoy being able to do my own picking and choosing.

On January 25, 1984, Brother Bob received the 1775th star to be implanted in the Hollywood Walk of Fame that runs along Hollywood Boulevard. It's located between the stars belonging to Cecil B. De Mille and John Carradine. Celebrating this historic occasion with him were his daughter Trina and his wife Dorothy. He only had to work in pictures for forty-two years to earn his own star. I sometimes wonder what it takes to prove yourself in this crazy acting business.

Fess Parker greeted us warmly. Fess is at least 6-foot-5 but is so gentle and warm, his great height seems modified. We talked of cameraman Jack Swain, who photographed his "Daniel Boone" TV series. Jack, who had once been my neighbor in Van Nuys, was gone now, another cancer victim. He was a good camerman, but a poor pugilist. I was forced to knock the hell out of him one night when he got overly belligerent during a political argument. The police came and only their threat of the pokey over a long weekend saved me from cooling off via courtesy of the city.

I introduced Bonnie to Jane Russell, a sultry beauty whom Brother Robert had long dubbed (for some obscure reason) "Hard John." The last time I had seen Jane was in Kanab, Utah, where she starred in a segment of "Death Valley Days" and I was one of her cowhands.

One day she had suggested that I go for a swim in the hotel pool. Since I hadn't brought a swim suit, she had promptly reached into her wardrobe mistress' bag, got a pair of scissors and cut my blue jeans down to almost bikini size. I hadn't explained that the jeans were the only pants I'd brought with me to the location. It wouldn't have phased her.

"Hard John" is quite a gal.

And it was quite an evening.

OF "WAR AND REMEMBRANCE"

IN NEARLY A HALF-CENTURY of being one of the most enduring stars in the film business, Bob has been the subject of reams of print attempting to capture his elusive character. Fittingly enough, as he draws to the end of that magnificent career, he has been dubbed by Rick Du Brow, TV editor of the *Los Angeles Herald Examiner*, as a "solid anchor" in the most prestigious and far-reaching miniseries ever produced for television.

In search of a better perspective than mine alone, I talked with Dan Curtis, the executive producer, director and co-writer (with Earl Wallace) of the epic novel-for-television, "War and Remembrance," based on the best seller by Herman Wouk. As we talked the very week that the show was being aired on ABC in November, 1988, Curtis strengthened my belief that "Winds of War" (the first half of the story, aired in late 1983) and "War and Remembrance" could do more to mirror man's inhumanity to man than has ever been done before on film, or will probably be done for many years to come.

How Curtis was able to make his enormous tour de force—the longest (30 hours) and most expensive ($110 million) series ever made for television—can be better understood with the help of two thumbnail sketches about his character. Barbara Steele, a one-time actress who helped Curtis produce the series, remarked, "He has this absolutely knockout, drop-dead energy. His strength is in sticking to his vision, even when horrible calamities are going on. He just is like a rabid wolf. He'll get his teeth into an idea and get it through at all costs!"

Bob has his own opinion of Curtis, which he expressed to *TV Guide* writer Lawrence Eisenberg: "I would much prefer working with Dan than with those sort of quasi-, self-styled cerebral directors who tell you what the character is thinking. Dan doesn't give a [expletive] what [the character's] thinking as long as [the actor] gets the job done."

As for my brother, Curtis said: "I love him. We're old friends. He felt both of us had gotten too old on this. But I couldn't find someone to replace him.

Bob returned as "Pug" Henry in November, 1988, when ABC-TV aired part of "War and Remembrance," the most expensive, and longest, TV mini-series in history. It didn't do great in the ratings but it had the guts to depict the tragedies of World War II as never before, and I thought Bob did a great job in portraying a naval commander who has to watch his war-ship sinking beneath the waves after a sea battle with the Japanese.

I called him up and said, 'Look, there *is* no other Pug Henry.' We had lunch and I said, 'Hell, you look better than you did four years ago.' He said, 'If you think I should do it, I will.' We stood up and hugged each other."

❄ ❄ ❄

How well I remember December 7, 1941, the day the Japanese attacked Pearl Harbor. First on radio, then in newsreel footage, the graphic horrors of war were plainly laid out for the American people—and yet they barely hinted at what lay ahead. The Japanese swiftly overran a large portion of the globe and the Germans destroyed the cities and towns and the wills of most of the people of Europe.

"War and Remembrance" (ironically its initials spell WAR) dug deeply into the hearts and minds of the people who were a part of that dreadful time. A friend called and commented on the "slow pace" of scenes set in Singapore while the languid Britishers (symbolized by Robert Morley's radio commentator) extolled their "impregnable fortress," when indeed there was no line of defense at all. I listened to my friend in disbelief until I remembered that he was much too young to recall that at the very moment depicted, a huge army of Japanese was marching almost unopposed toward that complacent city, for which there was no protection at all except for an imaginary line of defense created solely by the propaganda ministers.

The attitude of the British has its counterpart in the millions of young people today whose eyes were graphically opened by the scenes that recreated the unbelievable atrocities committed by the Nazis at the notorious death camps, Auschwitz and Birkenau. Curtis had the courage to photograph these war crimes as they have never been photographed before, and insisted that ABC not cut away at the guts of his film.

"The chilling effect of it is so important," said Curtis. ""People have seen . . . films, thousands of films . . . endless footage of bulldozers pushing mountains of corpses and emaciated bodies, but what has never really been shown is what it was like while it was happening. That's the true horror."

To the everlasting credit of Brandon Stoddard, ABC's Entertainment President, those uncompromised scenes became chillingly alive on millions of screens throughout the world.

Brother Bob said to me recently, "A number of young people spoke to me the other day in hushed tones about seeing the awful truths of the death camps depicted in the film."

Curtis related a moving story about young Germans coming to him with tears in their eyes and saying, "When I think that my parents were involved in this, it makes me want to cry."

Curtis was questioned by a reporter who asked: "Do you feel that shooting the segments on the Holocaust changed you? Are you haunted by the scenes?"

Dan's answer summed it up: "No more. No. It was terrible while we were there. I have gotten it out of my system, I think, by doing it. The people that will be haunted by it, even more so than we were, were the German crews. Those young guys are the ones who really suffered. As bad as it was for us, for them it was terrifying."

Curtis said that on the first day of shooting at Auschwitz "I felt such a presence of evil that I gathered the whole group around me and I said a

"Scrooged," a Bill Murray comedy, was a take-off on Charles Dickens' "A Christmas Carol" and starred Bob as Preston Rhinelander, the chairman of the IBC television network. This kind of role, though small, is indicative of Bob's continued popularity into the late 1980s. While most of his contemporaries are dead or retired, Bob keeps plugging away. For example, shortly after he returned from a year of off-and-on work making "War and Remembrance," he was offered two episodes of TV's "The Equalizer" to replace ailing series star Edward Woodward. The monetary offer was considerable. Bob said yes!

prayer because I felt we needed protection."

The *Los Angeles Herald Examiner* TV critic David Gritten wrote of my brother: "His craggy grace is seen to terrific advantage in a moving scene when the ship he commands is destroyed in battle. Watching it sink beneath the waves, Mitchum stares impassively, shaking his head almost imperceptibly, and evoking profound sadness."

One of the film's most dramatic scenes is one in which Hart Bochner, as Byron Henry, Pug's son, is aboard a submarine in a running battle with Japanese destroyers. It is as graphic and compelling a submarine depth-charge attack sequence as those in "Run Silent, Run Deep" and the German film "Das Boot." Bochner's portrayal while under attack is as telling as Bob's while he participates in the Battle of Midway.

A question posed to Curtis centered on our attitudes toward the Japanese during the war and our attitudes now. The film used such terms as "Japs," "Nips," "slavering Orientals," "rapists" and other demeaning terminology. "Do you anticipate any problems with the Japanese from using those terms as many times as they do?"

Curtis replied, "I don't know. They may kick me out of the Riviera [a Japanese-owned country club]. No, I don't."

I am reminded of a grim happening on Peleliu, a Pacific island which was invaded by the U.S. Marines in 1944. My friend Will Hunt, then a combat marine, told me about a Japanese soldier's corpse that lay athwart a path that led to his company's command post. The body had been sprawled there for several weeks and the hundreds of men who used that path blithely stepped over the rapidly decomposing remains until one day its head rolled away from the trunk. By then the dried remains didn't even warrant avoidance and it soon took on the appearance of a piece of ragged overalls. I remarked to Will that it must have been a terrible revelation to see how a human being could be so reviled.

"No," reflected Will, who today is a kind, warm and rational man. "We were so brainwashed by our training and by the violent actions we'd been

Dan Curtis got his start with a TV soap opera, "Dark Shadows," and went on to produce and direct several classic TV horror films, among them "Dracula" with Jack Palance. When he was casting the role of "Pug" Henry for "Winds of War" in 1982, he had placed Bob low on his priority list, thinking him too old for the role. Reluctantly, he agreed to have lunch with Bob—and immediately changed his mind when Bob walked into the restaurant. "I did a double take. Mitchum looked young. There was no question in my mind when I left that table—this man was 'Pug' Henry. I was so happy I couldn't see straight. Mitchum is flawless. You just smile when he's doing it."

in that we'd sit around and thank God we weren't in the European Theater. There, we reasoned, we would have had to kill human beings. We were made to actually believe we were fighting subhumans."

It is frightening to see what real-life "Winds of War" can do to human beings, for at that moment a wraith-like vision of Auschwitz hovered in the back roads of my mind.

Considering that "Winds of War" and "War and Remembrance" are a combination of three years of research by Herman Wouk and four years of off-and-on filming by Curtis and a cross section of the greatest acting talent in the world, it should be an honor to have played even a remote part in it. There are some scenes so brilliantly acted (especially those of John Gielgud's), directed, photographed and musically scored, I'm sorry that I can't pay homage to them all individually here.

"Bellwether" Mitchum asked Wouk what he wanted of him in playing Pug Henry. "The sense of control," Wouk told Bob. And Bob told me: "Except for family foibles, the character was in explicit control of himself and his life at all times. And he [Wouk] said I was ideal. He called it loyalty, basically—patriotism."

Bob then related a story to Wouk about Slade Cutter—whom I had known well in the late 1930s in Long Beach when I dated his sister Honey. Slade was All-American at Navy, and Navy's undefeated heavyweight boxer from 1932-35. He turned down a lucrative offer to turn professional, choosing instead to remain in the service. He became a naval hero in the submarine fleet during World War II.

"When I told Wouk about Cutter," Bob said, "he looked at me for a long moment and then ended the discussion by saying, 'Yes, Robert, men like Slade Cutter. That's what I meant.'"

In a world where names like Churchill, Eisenhower, MacArthur, Halsey and Bradley blazed their way like comets in a wartorn sky, the word "patriotism" was a revered thing. "Winds of War" and "War and Remembrance" have kept its light very much alive.

This is the blurb that accompanied Slade Cutter's photo in the Navy Yearbook: "Slade was a pure farm lad . . . His only vice was flute-playing, and his favorite pastime corn-husking. But evil companions, Navy Juniors, led him astray and taught him to chew tobacco and swear. Plebe Summer, Spike Webb thought he'd make a good punching bag for the varsity heavyweights, but [Slade] turned out to be so fast that he practically realized his ambition of getting through every fight without having his hair mused . . . Slade has always been an ardent exponent of the "strenuous life." . . . His strongest characteristic is volatility." That volatility certainly served him well during World War II.

James McHenry Bosworth is the role Bob played in the 1988 Samuel Goldwyn Company release "Mr. North," a film based on Thorton Wilder's semi-autobiographical novel "Theophilus North." John Huston was originally slotted to play the Bosworth role, but died during production. Bob agreed to step in for his late friend. Bosworth is a wealthy, retired diplomat who is kept prisoner in his own home by his daughter. He dreams of one day using his money to open an Academy of Philosophy by the sea. Huston co-wrote the script, which was finally directed by his son Danny Huston.

THE LATE, GREAT John Huston said of Bob, "I'd been told that Bob was difficult. Nothing could have been further from the truth. He was a delight to work with [on "Heaven Knows, Mr. Allison"] and he gave a beautiful performance. When I say he's a fine actor, I mean an actor of the caliber of Olivier, Burton and Brando. In other words, the best in the field."

***

I met Charles Laughton while Bob was working on "The Night of the Hunter." We were sitting by a small lake out in West San Fernando Valley when Laughton said to me, "Your brother is not only a magnificent talent, but a remarkable man. He has an innate toughness, but the real Bob Mitchum shines through as a tender and a very great gentleman."

***

My oldest daughter, Victoria, needed to see a specialist at a San Francisco hospital and I drove her there, leaving her husband Jim and sons Tuffy, Andrew and Matthew to fend for themselves. Her Uncle Robert gave me a large sum of money to make her trip more pleasant. Months later, she drove to Bob's home and handed him a check to reimburse him. He took the check, sighed, then tore it up. "Why do you have to make me be physical?" He raised his eyes heavenward . . .

***

Dale and Annie Tackitt run the Tackitt Stock Farm on what is still known as the 6-B Ranch in Grass Valley. They are superb horse people, which is why they have Bob's stable of twenty-four quarter horses and two thoroughbreds—including several babies—in their care.

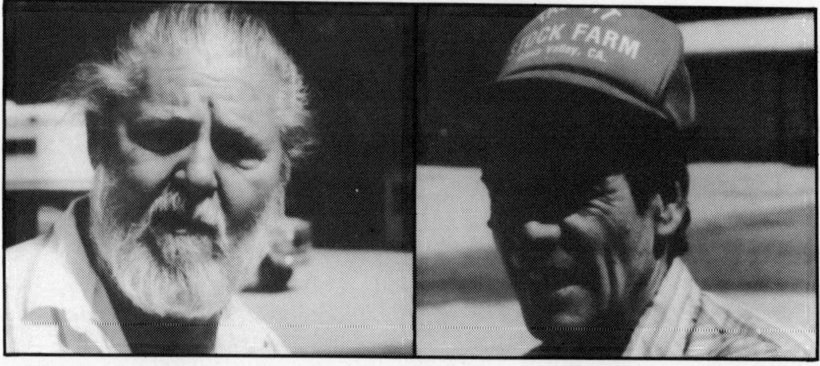

That's me with my good friend Dale Tackitt, on his 6-B ranch outside Grass Valley, California. He was under great duress the afternoon this photo was taken by John Stanley because a fire that had broken out the day before was raging only a few miles away, and he was in the process of transferring the valuable horses he has stabled and pastured there. Fortunately the fire never reached the ranch.

"Dorothy keeps one great set of accounts and records in that family," Annie said of Bob's wife.

"He's one of us," said Dale of Bob. "He's a walking encyclopedia on horse pedigree, going back five or six generations off the top of his head. He's bred a World's Champion, Don Guerro, and might have three more in his latest batch of young ones."

Dale looked straight at me. "Hell, he's a Mitchum!"

***

Segueing from the Tackitt Stock Farm, Bob, Dorothy, Bonnie and I lunched at Wang's Chinese Restaurant at the top of Bitney Springs Road. It was amusing to watch the cooks, waiters, hostess and busboys excitedly peering at Robert from every angle in the place. Our waitress finally gathered up enough courage to whisper, "Are you *the* Robert Mitchum?"

Tom Drummond, fall of 1988.

Bob graciously wrote out an autograph for her and she brought it back to her co-workers to hover over in adulation.

We then drove down Bitney Springs' green-arched and winding road to visit Tom and Julie Drummond, who are among our dearest friends. The afternoon turned out to be a revelation. I had always thought that much of what Bob had told me about his Vietnam trips was rather exaggerated. I learned otherwise. We sat open-mouthed as those two compared notes, though their paths had never crossed in that torn land.

Drummond, at that time a master segeant in the USAF, had been a top B-52 mechanic. From 1965-67 he had taken many flights to Guam, Okinawa and Utaphau, Thailand, for maintenance purposes. On Guam he had marveled at the fact that as many as seventy of the huge bombers were sent aloft in a single day. "In the States," Tom mused, "getting two or three off the ground was quite a feat."

Drummond had been transferred from Beale Air Force Base in California to Westover, Mass., to join the 99th Bombardment Group for B-52 maintenance. Every one of the planes was painted black and flown to Guam to undergo maintenance check-up, loaded with bombs and flown to Vietnam. "Imagine," he said, "flying in a formation of seventy planes, all of them with no running lights and coal black. Six of them were lost in mid-air collisions during turns!"

Occasionally Tom would get caught in a "hard hat" run when he was aboard one of the high-altitude bombers. On several small plane hops between bases, he was often elected "door gunner," getting shot at and returning fire; an adventure for a master mechanic.

He and Bob laughed about visiting the Cave, a rowdy bar dug into the rocky hillside outside of Cameron Bay, complete with movie theater. The area was slyly called "Vacationland." They talked of the Montenards, who sat around the airports with burlap sacks stuffed with their treasured dead rats and balls of rice. (I had never believed it; Tom vowed it was true.) "My rat is bigger than your rat" seemed to be a sign of superiority. And Bob still wryly gags at the thought of eating some mysterious meat concoction that was finally identifed as one of those highly-priced and prized rats.

Bob had told me of being in towns where it was tacitly agreed that the Americans controlled its bistros until eight o'clock at night and then the Viet Cong controlled them until daylight. GIs were under strict orders to get back to their bases by eight. Anyone found on the streets after that hour faced the danger of being shot. "No exceptions."

Bob and Tom agreed that "Vacationland" had been a very strange war.

❄ ❄ ❄

Lest one think that Brother Robert has become all sweetness and light in his mellow years, I'll let you in on a few snide sides of him that border on being ornery—and one story that is definitely ornery.

I've played second fiddle to Clint Eastwood, Robert Taylor, John Wayne and a host of other film actors and actresses. But none of those worthies ever made me feel as humbled as when Brother Robert recently came to Nevada City—not so much to visit us and see me in "Noises Off," a smash hit, but so that he might view firsthand his newly foaled thoroughbed filly out of a mare named Dancing Spirit. When I demurred at being placed down the line on his list of importance, he said: " . . . Dancing Spirit was eighteen years old and hadn't foaled for five years. The filly's sire is Pied a Terre out

That's Bob at left as an Irish doctor in the TV miniseries "The Blue and the Gray"—and that's him at right in "The Ambassador," an interesting study of a U.S. Ambassador in Israel who is trying to find a peaceful solution to war and who must put up with an unfaithful wife.

of Liloy and Ticarissima, while Dancing Spirit is out of Viking Spirit and Ravella from Requested by Bolero."

I got the picture. The frisky young filly prancing out in the pasture was class.

However, he did enjoy watching the sold-out Foothill Theatre production, even letting his guard down far enough to outright belly laugh a couple of times in between chuckles. While I was prancing in and out of stage doors and windows, Bob was protectively flanked by Dorothy and Bonnie—an unspoken agreement between the ladies—to slow down the courteous but determined autograph hunters.

❄ ❄ ❄

Bob's never been one to voice a true opinion when thanked for an act of kindness or consideration. One of Bob's and Dorothy's Christmas presents to us comes on a monthly basis from a fruit-of-the-month club in Oregon. Bonnie called to thank them for the box of magnificent plums we had just received. Bob's reply: "Don't flush 'em down the terlet or they'll plug up the drain."

I called to congratulate Bob on becoming a grandfather for the sixth time, Jimmie's and Vivian's baby. His answer: "Another mouth to feed." It's a rare event when he doesn't turn away a heartfelt interest with the foil of disinterest. He's still almost impossible to get to.

❄ ❄ ❄

Before my last birthday and in a spirit of warmth, Brother Robert called and told me to go to the local Grass Valley Western Union office. I did and was startled to find two checks there, one for $500 and the other for $1,000. The operator gave them to me and I deposited them in my bank. A few hours later I found that an embarrassing error had occurred: Bob had sent me the five big ones alright, but the larger check belonged to his son James. The operator saw the "J. Mitchum" on the computer screen and assumed both were mine.

In the morning Robert discreetly called the matter to my attention. I told him I'd go to the bank, draw out the $1,000 and give it to the Western Union girl to send on to Jimmy. When I reached the telegraph office I found the poor girl with a large paper sack over her head labeled, "The Unknown Operator." I sent the bag on to Robert but called him to let him know the transaction had been made. I heard a very audible sigh of relief on the phone. Then his hidden fear surfaced. "I thought you'd be in Reno by now."

❄ ❄ ❄

Once in awhile Brother Robert can make a mistake and he made a doozy in Hong Kong while making "The Amsterdam Kill" with American-Chinese actor Keye Luke, perhaps best remembered for his role as Master Po on TV's "Kung Fu."

Everyone could feel the Chinese crew's contempt of Americans, though it was masked by extreme politeness. Robert Clouse, who directed the film, related in his book "The Making of 'Enter the Dragon'" that Brother Bob—normally considerate to his crews—for some insane reason followed the other Americans' ignorant example. He would call the Chinese technicians "assholes" and other epithets, and smile at them, certain they didn't understand a word of English.

They understood all right. At the wrap party the Chinese went through a ritual called Yam Sing, which means "drink to the finish." The underlying reason for the ritual is revenge. Luke warned Clouse of this and explained that a man would come up to your table with two twelve-ounce glasses, one empty and one filled with Mao Tai, a colorless liquor best described as a bomb. While the Chinese man holds up the full glass as if to toast your health, he pours the deadly drink into the empty glass for you.

Clouse said he drank his half-glass in one gulp. "Oh my God!" he wrote. "It was a thunderbolt! My lips were dead."

Clouse saw Brother Robert surrounded by a half-dozen Chinese systematically trying to destroy him by offering him fearful (perhaps lethal?) quantities of Mao Tai, which he downed in answer to their challenge. Bob's wife, Dorothy, with the help of other Americans, struggled desperately to get him down the stairs and into a cab. Back at their hotel, Bob fell in the bathroom and broke two ribs.

In the morning he demanded that he be put on a plane for the States, stating flatly that the Chinese were trying to kill him.

According to Clouse, that was probably true. When Bob related the story to me, he made no mention of the names he had called the Chinese. He did say that he thought they wanted to kill him to collect the insurance that was placed on his life for the duration of the filming. Either way, my advice is to talk nicely to people, whether they understand you or not. Especially if they are Chinese.

❄ ❄ ❄

Brother Bob shows, on rare occasions, a temper as volatile and devastating as sheet lightning. That temper came to the fore at a party given by the famous pianist, Freddie Slack, back in the late '30s. Still a bachelor, Bob was talking to a very pretty young lady when he was rudely accosted by a burly bull dyke who told him in no uncertain terms that she had *her* eye on the damsel.

"Would you fight me for her?" inquired Bob.

When the dyke bellowed out an obscene challenge, Bob gave her a straight right hand to the chin, knocking her ass over tea kettle. Then he slipped away from the party before she regained what little sense she had left.

❄ ❄ ❄

It is my strict belief that the ability to be an actor must have a basis of talent. The Reader's Digest Great Encyclopedic Dictionary defines talent as a "particular and uncommon aptitude for some special work or activity." I further believe that you can beat an untalented person all day long with a 4-by-4 and he or she still won't be able to act. In my own case you could point a shotgun at my head and tell me to paint a picture and my only answer would be "Go ahead and pull the trigger." I drew a horse for my granddaughter Vanessa once and she couldn't suppress her laughter.

My advice to any neophyte performer, be it on stage or screen, is to read and reread the script until the entire picture is firmly in your mind. Only then can you relate to your part as a whole; the path becomes very clear. This has been my method of associating the contents of the entire story with those people and events that inevitably find some connection that I can draw on. I guess I'm what the experts would call an instinctive

I was a cute kid in the crib in 1919 . . . and I haven't changed a bit in seventy years . . . or have I?

actor—that is *my* talent.

As the underlying thread of this book points out, each of us is touched by the people and events around us. The true actor absorbs everything he sees, feels and senses to such a degree that a smile, a gesture, an intonation, an emotion can be unearthed—usually subconsciously—and used adroitly in whatever scene is being portrayed. Thus an actor hones his skills constantly and that honing, with an innate talent, makes for an actor who can always be counted on for a good performance.

❄ ❄ ❄

In 1946, astrologer Carroll Righter had done a complete astrological chart on me, coming up with two pertinent observations. The first was a fatal flaw in my psyche. "You are the most intolerant man I've ever met." His declaration astounded me and I blurted out an objection. "No," he said, "you're the most intolerant man against intolerant people I've ever come in contact with." On that point I must ruefully agree, then and now.

"Late in life," Carroll continued, "you're going to be a famous and wealthy person."

Carroll, I'm still waiting for that one . . .

POSTMITCHUM-SCRIPT

By Bonnie Duff Mitchum

YOU MAY HAVE noticed that John Mitchum doesn't have any "holier-than-thou" friends—or attitudes. And he has chosen to bypass mentioning the innumerable charities to which he has given a part of himself.

In the early 1950s, he was deeply touched by the courage and devotion of Sister Margarita Terrasita, a Carmelite nun from Old Mexico. His eyes were opened to the needy in the world when he found that she and her Sisters had arrived in Duarte, California, penniless and with only a devotion to God to sustain them. They had come to establish a tubercular hospital for young girls. Their original hospice was, as was their Lord Jesus' birthplace, a barn. They were deeded the barn and the land it stood on by an incredulous rancher who saw them scrubbing the place on their hands and knees until the ancient wood shone clean.

Today, a shining hospital stands there.

The City of Hope sprang up close by.

In their clinic's infant stages, the Sisters needed help. Just before their first Christmas, John collected a hundred dolls from relatives, friends and even strangers so the hospital's patients would have new dolls.

One benefactor wanted something in return for his donation. "I've got two old maid aunts visiting me from New Hampshire," he told John. "Could you get them in to see a movie set?"

Robert was filming "His Kind of Woman" with Jane Russell at RKO so John called and asked if he might bring the ladies around. "Sure, bring 'em along," Bob answered.

When they came on the set, Robert was on a studio soundstage bare-chested and lying on sand that simulated a beach in Acapulco. He strode over to greet John, zipping up his trousers. After the introductions, one old lady quavered, "Oh, Mr. Mitchum, we're so thrilled. We have never seen anything like this before. We're from the Far, Far East."

Robert stared at his brother for a long moment before he quipped, "What in the hell did you bring me, John? A couple of Mongolians?"

❄ ❄ ❄

John's daughter, Cindy, recalls the many Christmases that were highlighted by a posada in their neighborhood, which John put together by collecting monies, clothing, toys and food stuffs from the surrounding areas. With the assistance of his old friend, Natividad Vacio, they took the bounty to families in the poorer sections of Los Angeles. Cindy and her pre-teen peers still remember hand-delivering presents to people who had nothing.

"And Dad, sly fox that he was," recalls Cindy, grinning, "would always include a bottle of good red wine for the astonished man of the house. My father has no idea how many lives he has touched."

❄ ❄ ❄

In January, 1988, John and I spent several days at Bob's and Dorothy's home, visiting Mom Mitchum Morris and Sister Julie Sater from Arizona. We all gathered to discuss family plans, play Canasta with Mom, sing around the piano to Julie's playing; and we all ate too much. Bob gave us a couple pounds of newly dressed wild pork sausage which he spiced himself, and told us he was thinking of retiring. That was hard to imagine.

It all seemed very ordinary. But as Dorothy Spence Mitchum and I agreed on over a hot cup, one must be a very strong person and know oneself thoroughly in order to survive and thrive in the Mitchum clan, especially as an in-law. No snivelers need apply.

Robert, my brother-in-law, is a worldwide public figure but an intensely private soul; one of the greatest broad-ranged actors of the world but not lauded nearly enough by America's award-givers; Leo the Lion for showmanship but remarkably modest; verbally unpredictable—ornery as hell when he wants to be—but the most dependable actor in the entertainment business; fist-*tough* (I'd surely want him on *my* side in any kind of a battle) but secretly heart-sensitive.

That same weekend—in a rare moment of revealing his true feelings—Bob was filled with anguish when he told me that when he or John fought any other man, it was survive or die. Period. His voice was rough, his eyes were glittering with angry, held-back tears. I don't think anyone but Bob and John can know the traumatic terrors of all the years of survival they have shared, together or apart. It must have been like watching the atavistic ferocity of a Neanderthal battle for life when they fought.

I can't speak for Bob, but from what I've seen occasionally in John I vaguely sense that the brothers are alike in the same bitter disillusionment when their trust has been violated. Exit the Christian ethic, the humor and tolerance. Enter a terrifying violence of spirit that fears no judgment; there is no forgiving, no forgetting. A stalking vengeance remains for all time even after the maniacal fury has raged. And then, thank God, sanity once more seeps in; the cool heads return to control the hulking predators within. Those of us around them can once more breathe deeply, no longer in fear of having to either visit a caged beast with a file in a cake, or lay pretty flowers on a watery Neptune funeral.

When Robert smiles his rare smile, he could melt butter. He's a darlin' singer with a magnificent ear for melody and harmony; a skillful but largely unsung poet; a fantastic horseman; a prodigious reader of many subjects; highly complex; staunchly loyal; most generous and kind but pretends he's cranky and ungracious; independent as a hog on ice—and utterly charming, when he wants to be. A world-class, blue-ribbon enigma.

❄ ❄ ❄

John my husband—Jack of the Norwegian, Scots, Irish, Blackfoot heritages—is also a man of many contrasts and layers: Joyful child/vital man; street fighter/wide-eyed wanderer of museums; naive hobo/universal traveller; superb character actor with diamond facets/serious truth seeker; prolific writer of many moods, whether fiction or documentary; sensitive poet capable of touching the planets; a deeply emotional but thoroughly technical composer-musician-director. He's a Virgo-fussy perfectionist about his acting craft and music, but shows his originally planned Scorpio birth traits (he was born two months too soon, remember) in his passionate, devil-may-care, enthusiastic approach to life.

His wacky sense of humor and mimicry can make one *believe* that he really sees a herd of elk on the eighth fairway at dawn, or a polar bear in the oak trees when the frost is heavy. And try to imagine 220 pounds of elfin dancer as he trips merrily to some lisping ditty, pointing his undainty feet and waving his powerfully muscled arms. I don't think anyone enjoys a raunchy joke more than John, a lusty laugher and jokester.

John's singing voice—whether stomping through a lively country Western song, plucking heartstrings with a tender ballad, or wafting an aria in operatic Italian or German—would charm a frozen bird out of a tree. He's so sweet-tempered and long-suffering that people are often foolishly tempted to push him too far with their demands—then the Neanderthal comes roaring up through the Paleolithic crust; I strongly recommend that the implacable caveman be left to slumber.

He is awesomely competitive and ornery (as he must have been in the streets or in the boxing ring); a fierce fighter with the same ferocious power as his brother to simply—dispose—of his opponent. And he is an instant defender of the put-upon in "civilian" life.

He's not always as aware of what's going on around him as I'd like him to be for he's got what I call a "laser-brain," beaming sharply in on one thing at a time—memorizing a script, reading an article, thinking through an idea—to the exclusion of most else: Stop signs, or "Turn right here," or a question such as "Did you hear me?" But he possesses the tenderest of hearts; he is a delicate soul.

John Mitchum: Earth-earthy man/child of God; a lover of women, children, men (*some* of them), his family, loyal friends, food—oh yes; a good Scotch, an inexpensive wine, all music, our crazy Siamese cat, any kind of weather, beautiful scenery, solitaire (single or double), penny ante poker, Scrabble and dominoes, fine artwork—and me. A wonderfully loveable man. A rare man. One of a kind.

❄❄❄

As John's and Robert's mother so succinctly wrote to John on his 17th birthday:

" . . . For always, whatever the environment, the circumstances, or the inducement, you will be you and neither veneer nor buffering can eliminate the You."

Mother
Sept. 6, 1936

INDEX

— A —

— B —

— C —

— D —

— E —

— F —

— G —

— H —

— I —

— J —

— K —

— L —

— N —

— O —

— P —

— Q —

— R —

— S —

— T —

— U —